JAMES L. CLIFFORD

Young
Sam Johnson

A HESPERIDES BOOK

New York   Oxford University Press

1961

TO PERCY LAITHWAITE AND THE
MEMORY OF ALEYN LYELL READE

Printed in the United States of America

Preface

EVERYONE thinks of Dr. Johnson as an old man. At the first mention of his name the vision rises of the familiar massive, wrinkled face, the bushy bob wig, and the dull-brown coat with metal buttons. It is as the Great Cham of literature, lumbering on an uncertain course down Fleet Street, or talking to his friends at the Mitre, that he lives. He has become almost a symbol of the wise old moralist, and many readers have the impression that he sprang to life full-grown. So fixed is the image that it requires a violent wrench of the imagination to think of him as young.

Boswell, Mrs. Thrale, Fanny Burney — all those who described him best — knew him only during his later years. Their accounts are so vivid and entertaining that they overshadow the remote, and often uncertain, recollections of his boyhood. The well-known portraits by Sir Joshua Reynolds, Opie, and Barry, and the bust by Nollekens, show him as an older man. Used over and over again as illustrations, they have established the picture.

Yet many readers must have wondered what he was like as a boy. How did he grow into the colorful figure Boswell so marvelously described? What were the causes of Johnson's neurotic eccentricities, his strong prejudices, his morbid fears of insanity? How explain his somber Christian pessimism, and the fact that he was a Tory with a deep compassion for the common man? Why was his temper apt to flare, his caustic wit to sear? In brief, what fashioned the personality and character of the great Moralist? The present book tries to answer some of these questions.

Boswell provided clues, but he was of necessity vague concerning long periods of his subject's youth. Johnson was not the kind to volunteer intimate confessions. He "did not delight in talking much of his family," Mrs. Piozzi recorded. "One has (says he) *so* little pleasure in reciting the anecdotes of beggary." [1] And since all of the contemporary biographers were denied the sight of Johnson's only revealing fragment of autobiography, they often had difficulty with even the most essential facts.

Boswell knew little specifically about the family relationships and tensions in the Johnson household, or about the tempers and tastes of the parents. He did not have the twentieth century's interest in rivalries between brothers, thwarted early desires, and emotional crises. Having a wealth of information about the period he knew best, he skimmed lightly over the years for which the meager details came through others. And it is well that he did so, for the vivid scenes from his journals are the high points of the *Life*.

Because Boswell had relatively little to say about the Lichfield years, most readers have assumed that there was not much that could ever be known. Yet for over a century and a half scholars have been at work patiently filling in the gaps, and their discoveries have been embedded in expanding footnotes and appendixes to the *Life*. In our day the process has moved at an even swifter pace. Mr. Percy Laithwaite in Lichfield has dug deep into the local records with amazing success. The great Oxford editors, Professor D. Nichol Smith, Dr. R. W. Chapman, and Dr. L. F. Powell, have made many discoveries as they carefully annotated the texts. Lt. Col. Ralph H. Isham has gradually gathered together the fabulous collection of Boswell's private papers, and the able staff at Yale University is now bringing order to that chaotic mass. In their remarkable collection Mr. and Mrs. Donald F. Hyde have accumulated much unpublished material. Most indefatigable of all, the late Aleyn Lyell Reade, of Blundellsands, devoted over fifty years of his life to assembling every available fact concerning Johnson, his relatives, and his friends, for the period before 1740, and published his findings in a long succession of notes and in many privately printed volumes of *Johnsonian Gleanings*.

Without the work of these men and women the present biography would have been impossible. Indeed, what I have chiefly attempted to do is to put into a straightforward narrative what they have made available in footnotes, in brilliant articles, and in scholarly volumes. If I have been able to add new details to the picture, I can claim no such startling discoveries as those of my predecessors. My debt to them is greater than can be expressed.

Something should be said of the general plan of the book. In contrast to "old" Dr. Johnson, I consider him "young" up to his fortieth year. The biography covers the period in Johnson's life from his birth to the publication of *The Vanity of Human Wishes*, the first published work to bear his name on the title page. As a summing up of his attitude toward life, this greatest of his poems is an ideal stopping place. By 1749 his convictions and tastes were well formed. He had become the Johnson of tradition. Although it would still be fourteen years before he would meet his destined biographer, he was essentially the man so graphically described in the *Life*.

For a biographer of Johnson, one constant problem is that of authenticity. What is trustworthy and what is not? So many of the stories necessarily come second or third hand. For some of the more famous episodes there are often four or five different versions. Which one is to be chosen? Much of what has survived is merely hearsay or casual gossip.

To evaluate each scrap of evidence thoroughly would require volumes. Moreover, if every detail were weighed and assayed, the patience of the reader would be sorely tried. I have avoided such discussions as much as I could, and have tried to choose only what appeared to me to be close to the truth; and where conclusions are doubtful, I have said so. In general, I have used the first recorded account of each incident. Thus I have quoted, when feasible, from Mrs. Thrale-Piozzi's journal *Thraliana* instead of her published *Anecdotes*, and from Boswell's original notes instead of the more polished versions in the *Life*.

From Sir John Hawkins, author of the official life; from William Shaw, who secured important information from the daughter of Johnson's godfather; from Thomas Tyers and the other early biographers, I have accepted stories when they appeared credible and have discarded others. Fortunately much of the careful weighing of evidence had already been done for me by A. L. Reade, and, with rare exceptions, I agree with his conclusions. For those readers who wish to check the original documents, I have indicated in the notes the places in Reade's volumes where the material may be found.

The annotations, for the most part, list sources rather than give additional facts. Not intended for the casual reader, they are for those skeptical of my authority or for scholars wishing to go further in specific research. Not all statements are documented. Had they been, the book would have turned into a weighty reference work. But every new discovery is noted, as well as the source of all important anecdotes. Often, however, miscellaneous material in a long passage is explained by a single composite note.

Prose quotations, either from manuscripts or from printed sources, have been normalized to modern practice in spelling and capitalization. Where eccentric spellings might possibly provide useful information they have been retained.

Those who expect a modern psychological interpretation of Johnson's complexes may be disappointed. I have consciously avoided the use of the technical language of psychiatry, though occasionally, where the conclusions appear obvious, I have suggested interpretations of motives and tensions. No significant fact has been suppressed. The reader who so desires can make his own analysis.

In brief, I have tried to put together an account of Johnson's development as a child, adolescent, and young man. Wherever possible, I have let him tell his own story. I have described his early surroundings and attempted to make his intimate friends something more than mere names. It is my hope that by the end of the book readers will have a better comprehension of how young Sam Johnson, the handicapped bookseller's boy from the Midlands, became "Dictionary" Johnson, the most celebrated professional writer of his age.

JAMES L. CLIFFORD

Acknowledgments

MUCH as I should like to do so, it is impossible to list all those who have helped in the preparation of this book, or to be specific about the nature of their contributions. But I am anxious to make public acknowledgment, even if only to list some of their names. Scholars, public officials, and collectors everywhere have given unfailing and generous assistance. Of those outside the United States, I wish to thank H. J. Callender and other local authorities in Lichfield who allowed me to search through masses of uncatalogued documents, George Birch and the firm of Hinckley, Birch and Crarer, the Rev. Harold Cresswell, F. W. C. Long, and Agnes Bertha Mear. My debt is great to the Oxford scholars R. W. Chapman and D. Nichol Smith, and to G. W. Bond and G. R. F. Bredin of Pembroke College. I wish to express sincere thanks to Geoffrey W. Beard, G. H. C. Burley, David Erskine, Marguerite Gollancz, S. Hopewell, S. C. Roberts, Lord Rothschild, Phyllis Rowell, M. R. H. Sadler, Sir Harold Williams, and David Woolley. The particular assistance of others is indicated in the notes.

Thanks are due in my own country to scores of scholars who have unselfishly given time and energy to my perplexing problems: to Donald L. Clark, Bertram H. Davis, Gilbert Highet, F. W. Hilles, Benjamin B. Hoover, Gwin J. Kolb, E. L. McAdam, Jr., Robert Metzdorf, James M. Osborn, Frederick A. Pottle, Marion Pottle, Edward Ruhe, Arthur Sherbo, George Sherburn, James H. Sledd, Clarence R. Tracy, W. K. Wimsatt, Jr., and Marshall Waingrow, who has also kindly read the proofs.

Officials of the Birmingham Reference Library, the British Museum, the Bodleian Library, the William Salt Library, and the Yale University Library have been very kind in giving me permission to use manuscript material. My gratitude to courteous librarians on both sides of the Atlantic is unlimited. The search for evidence was largely made possible by a fellowship from the John Simon Guggenheim Foundation.

My greatest obligation is to a number of long-suffering friends who have read my manuscript at various stages, in whole or in part, and have offered valuable criticism: to Edward C. Aswell, Donald J. Greene, Allen T. Hazen, Donald and Mary Hyde, Joseph H. Iglehart, Joseph Wood Krutch, Edward Kuhn, Jr., Percy Laithwaite, Herman W. Liebert, Maurice Quinlan, and, most of all, to L. F. Powell and Richard and Frances Hanson. Like Samuel Johnson, I have been "fond of consulting" my wife in all my "literary pursuits."

Contents

List of Illustrations

LICHFIELD
AND THE MIDLANDS

Prologue

The centuries have brought little alteration to Lichfield. The place where Sam Johnson spent his youth has spread outward, but otherwise is much the same as it was in the eighteenth century. To this day it is an episcopal seat, a market center, and an army garrison town. Though thundering trucks and streams of motorcars make the narrow streets more noisy and hazardous, and the ever-present groups of soldiers in battle dress are less colorful than Captain Garrick or Cornet Harry Hervey, the ladies of the Close still keep very much to themselves, and the country folk sell their wares on market day according to an unchanging pattern.

Most of the old landmarks remain, though some are changed. Those three graceful spires on the cathedral — affectionately called "The Ladies of the Vale" — are still reflected in the smooth surface of the Minster Pool. The untidy margins of Stowe Pool have disappeared, and it has become a well-tended reservoir. Instead of Michael Johnson's factory and the racks of drying skins on its banks, there are cottages fittingly called "The Parchments." If the actual building where Hunter used to flog unhappy pupils has been rebuilt and is used for other purposes, the Grammar School now at the edge of town continues to educate the sons of Lichfield tradesmen. It is not difficult to find Dame Oliver's cottage, where Johnson learned to read, the home of his friend Edmund Hector, St. Mary's Church, the George. The rather grim-looking house where Johnson was born even now dominates the market place. The selfsame cobblestones of the square are a trial to pedestrians' feet.

While the traditions are revered, the manner of observance

3

might startle a visitor from the eighteenth century. On September 8 the sheriff still rides about the city's boundaries — what used to be called the "sixteen jolliest miles in Staffordshire," but now are more often described as eighteen. Yet a recent sheriff made what he could of the trip by jeep. Mace-bearers and sword-bearer in colorful costume continue to precede the local dignitaries on their way to formal meetings, but it is not hard to imagine what the bailiffs of Michael Johnson's time would have thought of a mayor who was a retired schoolmistress. Least changed of all, the Cathedral Close retains its quiet charm. And tourists today, as they stroll down the Dean's Walk absorbing eighteenth-century atmosphere, might never suspect that in the very room of the palace where David Garrick made his first stage appearance the late bishop used to broadcast over the B.B.C.

Everywhere there are reminders of Dr. Johnson. He is Lichfield's "first citizen." There is a massive seated statue of him in the market place; his birthplace is a museum; his furrowed countenance peers out from postcards and guidebooks. But what would have pleased him most is the stone statue on the outside of the cathedral. High up on one of the southern buttresses of the choir stands the gowned effigy of the bookseller's son holding his Dictionary. *Along with the saints of the church and the noble lords and warriors of the past, Samuel Johnson looks down soberly with complacent pride.*

"Here is a Brave Boy"

Sept. 7, 1709, I was born at Lichfield." Samuel Johnson's pen scratched across the paper. In the drab quarters just above the ground floor of No. 1 Inner Temple Lane he was beginning an account of his own early years.[1] At intervals he made half-whistling sounds and soft clucking noises with his tongue, or talked to himself in a low voice. As his head shook tremulously, his body moved backward and forward. He rubbed his knee rhythmically with the palm of his hand.

In January, 1765, at the age of fifty-five, he was one of the best-known professional writers in London, regarded by many as an oracle. A royal pension had released him from financial worries. Yet he was deeply depressed. The black fit of melancholy was back again, and he found it almost impossible to force himself to complete his edition of Shakespeare. Often all he could do was to wander restlessly from room to room, sighing and groaning in his misery.[2]

There was a kind of morbid pleasure in brooding over his early handicaps. Of course, he was used to such musings. But at this time a stray remark, perhaps, or a question dragged him out of his usual lassitude. If sometimes his mind appeared to be wavering, it might be well to set down what he could remember before it was too late. The mere act of writing might help to clear his thoughts.

So he tried to recall his childhood — not only what he himself had seen but what others had told him. Slowly the pen moved on: "My mother had a very difficult and dangerous labor, and was assisted by George Hector, a man-midwife of great reputation." With sober exactness, he added a note concerning the day of the month, "18, of the present style."[3] Yet he saw no reason

5

to describe the place of his birth, the new four-story house which his father, the local bookseller, had built overlooking the market place. His account would be concerned with persons rather than places, with events rather than their settings.

At the start he was sparing of detail. But one can easily imagine the bustle and apprehension inside the house that day in September, 1709. The expectant mother was over forty, and though she had been married for more than three years this was her first child. Her husband was fifty-two. As the hour of delivery approached, Sarah Johnson lay in the long bedroom just over her husband's shop. Through the side windows came the sound of traffic in Sadler Street, the most important thoroughfare of the town. Through the front windows she could see St. Mary's Church across the way and the cobblestone pavement of the square. Since it was Wednesday, there was little activity in the market place — few stalls and cattle pens, no milling crowd of countrymen or carts filled with produce.

Neighbors and relatives were anxiously waiting, among them doubtless her elder sister Phoebe, wife of John Harrison, the saddler. Phoebe had lived in Lichfield for over a decade, and it was probably through her that Sarah Ford had met the tall, industrious bookseller, Michael Johnson.

George Hector, the "man-midwife," whose house was not over a hundred yards away, was nothing if not versatile, as ready to set broken bones, cure tumors, or treat scalded legs and dog bites as to deliver babies.[4] On this day he worked harder than usual for his fee, for the slender Sarah had trouble in bringing her firstborn into the world. It was not until four in the afternoon that the long, exhausting labor was over. "I was born almost dead," Johnson wrote, "and could not cry for some time." As a bit of bravado, and probably masking his own anxiety, Hector called out, as soon as he had the child in his arms, "Here is a brave boy." But life for the newborn infant appeared so precarious that arrangements were made to have him christened that very night in his mother's bedroom.

Presumably, the vicar of nearby St. Mary's, the Rev. William Baker, performed the ceremony. The two godfathers were Richard Wakefield, a prominent citizen of bookish tastes, who had been coroner and town clerk since 1688, and Dr. Samuel Swinfen, a young man of good family and education, who chanced at the time to be living with the Johnsons. Although Swinfen's ancestral home was only a few miles outside Lichfield, he had taken lodgings in Michael Johnson's capacious new house in order to be near his medical practice. The fact that Samuel started life with two such godfathers suggests not only Michael's local standing, but also his ambitions for his son. No ordinary shopkeepers would do.

While the name Samuel may have been intended partly as a compliment to Dr. Swinfen, more likely it came from the boy's uncle, Sarah's elder brother, Samuel Ford. It certainly had nothing to do with the Johnsons. Always scornful of her husband's background, Sarah was inordinately proud of her own. Probably she insisted on a name from her family for her first-born. If Michael objected, there is no record of it. No doubt he was too happy at the birth of a son, even one so sickly, to worry about such minor matters. "Samuel" he was christened, though for his mother and boyish companions the name was early shortened to "Sam."

The very day after Sam's arrival Michael had an important official task to perform. The previous July he had been elected sheriff, and it was customary on September 8 for this officer to ride some sixteen miles around the city's boundaries. The ceremony of the "Riding" was one of the customs most cherished by Lichfield citizens. Ever since the charter of Queen Mary had separated the town from the County of Stafford and given its inhabitants the right to choose their own sheriff, the annual ride had been enacted. In those days, before accurate surveys or maps, the boundary line of each parish and township had to be perambulated regularly by as many citizens as possible, so as to perpetuate from generation to generation the remembrance of landmarks and legal boundaries. According to an order of the Lichfield Court Leet, one member of every household was required to accompany the sheriff on his ride, or to provide an acceptable deputy. Gradually it became a social event, with much drinking and gaiety along the way, and a collation at the Guildhall at the end.

This year Michael was in an expansive mood. When Sarah weakly asked him from her bed whom he would especially invite, he proudly answered, "All the town now." According to his son, Michael "feasted the citizens with uncommon magnificence," almost the last of the sheriffs to maintain the true splendor of the "Riding."

At Michael's insistence, the child was placed in the care of a wet nurse — "one Marclew, commonly called Bellison" — the second wife of John Marklew, bricklayer, who lived in George Lane in the parish of St. Chad's. Before her marriage, as Joan Winckley, she had been a servant in the household of William Robinson in Sadler Street, and possibly in Michael's. Her own first child, John, was a year and a half old, so that the Johnson baby could have taken his place just as hers was being weaned.

Since George Lane was only five minutes' walk from the square, Sarah made frequent trips to see that all went well. But such was her fear of ridicule by her unsentimental neighbors that she "used to go different ways" — through Lombard or Tamworth Street, around by the Moggs and Stowe Pool, or by a little path which led from Dam Street straight across the back fields. Pathetically, she manufactured excuses for her visits, "and often left her fan or glove behind her, that she might have a pretense to come back unexpected; but she never discovered any token of neglect."

On the forty-year-old mother with her first child, every unusual circumstance made an indelible impression. These she repeated so often to her son that later they seemed to become part of his own memories. A few weeks after his birth, "an inflammation was discovered on my buttock, which was at first, I think, taken for a burn; but soon appeared to be a natural disorder. It swelled, broke, and healed." So he was told, and remembering long afterward soberly set it down in his account. The business of the biographer, he once insisted, was "to lead the thoughts into domestic privacies, and display the minute details of daily life." [5]

It was early discovered that the baby's eyes were in some way infected, and while he was in George Lane an incision designed

to drain the infection was cut in his left arm, which he thought
was not allowed to heal until his sixth year. Of this painful operation he took "no great notice," since he had his "little hand
in a custard." Yet recalling the details so long afterward, Johnson was forced to add: "It is observable, that, having been told
of this operation, I always imagined that I remembered it, but I
laid the scene in the wrong house. Such confusions of memory
I suspect to be common."

Another malady soon appeared, a tubercular infection of the
lymphatic glands of the neck, variously called scrofula or "the
king's evil." Since Sam's foster brother was similarly afflicted, it is
likely that Dr. Swinfen was correct in his diagnosis that the disease was derived through his nurse's milk. Sarah, for once not
bragging about her own relations, thought the disease inherited
from her family. Subsequently the affected glands of his neck
were operated on, leaving large scars. An attack of smallpox left
further marks, and it is difficult to tell how much of Johnson's facial disfigurement was the result of scrofula and how much from
other causes.[6]

In the latter part of November Sam was taken back to the
house in the market place, "a poor, diseased infant, almost blind."
One of his aunts, the wife of Nathaniel Ford, later told the boy,
with a brutal frankness which is a bit startling, that "she would
not have picked such a poor creature up in the street." Dr. Swinfen used to say that he had never known a child reared with so
much difficulty. With inverted pride, Johnson appears to have
taken a fierce delight in stressing his own early troubles. Deaf in
his left ear, almost blind in the left eye, afflicted with tubercular
glands, he had much to overcome.

One of Sarah Johnson's well-to-do relatives was Mrs. Harriotts,
who lived in the comfortable brick and stone manor house at
Trysull near Wolverhampton. A childless widow, some eight
years older than Sarah, she took an interest in the difficulties of
her first cousin's sickly baby. Despite her open disapproval of
Michael, who envied her superior position, she was willing to
help. As a result of her intervention, sometime during his second
year Sam was carried about twenty miles to Trysull, there to be

seen by a well-known young Roman Catholic physician, Dr.
Thomas Attwood of Worcester, who specialized as an oculist.

A more important, longer trip came when he was two and a
half years old, a journey to London to be touched by the Queen
herself.[7] In the twentieth century it is difficult to appreciate how
universally accepted was the belief in the efficacy of the royal
touch in the cure of the so-called "king's evil." Many enlightened
physicians believed implicitly in the cure, and the fact that
scrofula sometimes was actually arrested naturally added proof
apparent to all. In the register of a country parish five miles from
Lichfield is the record of a man who had been "touched and
cured" of the king's evil by Charles II.

In 1687 Michael had probably been in Lichfield for the visit
of James II when, in the middle of the choir of the cathedral,
"divers persons" were touched by the King. Remembrance of that
ceremony may have been in Michael's mind when he arranged
to have his son taken all the way to the capital to see Queen
Anne. But it was Sir John Floyer, the celebrated Lichfield doctor
— proponent of cold baths and first to use a "pulse watch" —
who was chiefly responsible. As a former physician to Charles II,
he had unbounded faith in the royal power.

While William III was on the throne the ceremony had been
allowed to lapse, but Anne was induced to resume "touching" as
a means of asserting her hereditary right to the throne, in contrast
to the parliamentary authority of William and the Hanoverians.
Formal announcements were read in all the parish churches and
appeared in the newspapers. A specific incitement for the Johnsons in the spring of 1712 was a statement in the *London Gazette*
of March 1 that the Queen intended to "touch" on March 19
and weekly thereafter throughout Lent.

To be included among the privileged few to receive the royal
favor, however, was not always easy. There were many formalities
to be attended to — rigorous restrictions made necessary by the
numbers of unscrupulous "invalids" who were lured by the gold
token which accompanied the "cure." In addition to a physician's
order, one had to have a certificate from the minister and churchwardens of the local parish stating that the patient had never be-

fore received the royal touch. And some influence was obviously required. But with the backing of the Reverend Mr. Baker and of Sir John Floyer the Johnsons felt certain of success, and arrangements were speedily made. Because of her intense desire to make the journey, Sarah concealed from everyone the fact that she was again in the early stages of pregnancy.

Sometime in March, 1712, with two guineas safely sewed in her petticoat lest she be robbed, with other cash for expenses, and no doubt with a long list of business errands for her husband, Sarah and her son set out for London by stagecoach. In those days the trip from nearby Birmingham to the capital took almost three days. "I always retained," Johnson wrote, "some memory of this journey, though I was then but thirty months old. . . . We were troublesome to the passengers; but to suffer such inconveniences in the stagecoach was common in these days to persons in much higher rank. . . . I was sick; one woman fondled me, the other was disgusted."

In London Sarah stayed with one of her husband's friends, the bookseller John Nicholson, in Little Britain off Aldersgate Street. Little Britain was the heart of the London book trade, as well as a favorite spot where old volumes and old clothes were sold. It was also conveniently near the home of her cousin, Cornelius Jesson, ironmonger and steward of Christ's Hospital. Sam had a hazy recollection of Nicholson's shop, the King's Arms, with the counter "on the left from the entrance," and of a "little dark room behind the kitchen, where the jack weight fell through a hole in the floor," into which he once slipped his leg. Vaguely, too, he remembered that he "played with a string and a bell," which his cousin, Isaac Johnson, gave him, "and that there was a cat with a white collar, and a dog, called Chops, that leaped over a stick." With his usual honesty, however, he added, "I know not whether I remember the thing, or the talk of it."

The day before the ceremony Sarah had to go to the office in Whitehall to show her credentials and to pick up her ticket. Then on March 30, with all the preliminaries attended to, she carried Sam to St. James's Palace for the expected cure. Since some two hundred people were to be "touched" that day, there

was much noise and activity outside the old turreted gatehouse —
a stream of sedan chairs and coaches, hurrying pedestrians, and
the inevitable knots of curious onlookers. In the very atmosphere
of anticipation there was something tense and exciting.

Although it was customary to scoff at St. James's as unsuitable
to the grandeur of a British monarch (it was used only because
the palace at Whitehall had been destroyed by fire), there was
more than enough pomp and finery to impress a housewife from
the country. Just inside the entrance there were the stiff guards
in the "Colour Court," then the grand staircase leading to the
state apartments where such a large group would most likely have
been received. As she and her small boy were shepherded along
by officials, Sarah would have glimpsed damask-covered walls,
pier glasses which stretched to the ceiling, shining candelabra and
chandeliers, stately portraits of royalty. There was magnificence
in the furnishings, if not in the irregular old brick building itself.

During the audience Queen Anne sat in state, surrounded by
court officials and chaplains. The ceremony was much shorter
and more businesslike than the lengthy one in vogue during
former reigns. It opened with a familiar collect from the communion service, and there followed readings from the Gospel of
St. Mark, versicles, responses, and prayers. All was done strictly
according to the form printed in the contemporary prayer books.

At a particular point in the service one of the chaplains knelt
by the Queen's side, holding on his arm hundreds of white rib-
bons hung with thin pieces of pure gold. The sick were presented
one by one, upon their knees, and the Queen laid her hands upon
them and then put around their necks or upon their arms the
special gold piece. Queen Anne's "touchpiece" was considerably
larger than that of James II and had the impress of St. Michael
the archangel on one side and a ship in full sail on the other.
That Sam cherished his is certain, for he wore it around his neck
for the rest of his life.

When asked if he could remember anything of the actual ceremony, he told Mrs. Thrale that "he thought he had some confused remembrance of a lady in a black hood." Also there was a

vivid recollection of another boy crying at the palace. But that was all.

While in London, Sarah made a few purchases. "She bought me a small silver cup and spoon, marked SAM. J. lest if they had been marked S.J. which was her name, they should, upon her death, have been taken from me. She bought me a speckled linen frock, which I knew afterwards by the name of my London frock. . . . She bought at the same time two teaspoons, and till my manhood she had no more."

The long journey home was made in the stage wagon, the poor man's coach. These great lumbering vehicles, carrying heavy goods as well as up to twenty or thirty passengers, were not designed for speed or comfort. Drawn by four or five horses, with the driver often walking by the side, they jolted noisily along. They started early in the morning and reached inns late at night. In contrast to the ordinary conveniences available to people who went by coach, those who traveled by the stage wagon often had difficulty finding accommodations on the way and were subject to snubs and insults from drivers and innkeepers alike. Sarah justified the change to this rougher vehicle because of her child's violent cough, which would have been troublesome to the other passengers in a stagecoach, but her son suspected that the motive was the hope of saving a few shillings. "Not having been accustomed to money," she "was afraid of such expenses as now seem very small."

In retrospect, and with vivid memories of later poverty, Johnson probably gave a false impression of the financial condition of his family during his early years. It was naturally humiliating for him to think that his mother had been stinted in anything, or had even considered suffering indignities to save a few shillings. But the truth is that in 1712 the Johnsons were far from poor. The fact that Michael could send his wife and child on such an errand is proof enough.

To most observers the bookseller would have appeared a man of substance and dependability. He had come a long way from his humble beginnings. From the very time in 1681 when he set up business in Lichfield, after completing his apprenticeship in London, he had taken a prominent part in local affairs. His shop was on the main business street of the city, with the most prosperous citizens, the Talbots, Minors, Dyotts, as his near neighbors. Within four years he had been elected one of the joint wardens of the Conduit Trust, through whose charity he had himself been educated. In 1687 he became an overseer of the poor. Two years later he was a churchwarden and in 1693 one of the town constables. At various times he filled most of the important posts in the Lichfield local government.[8]

In the summer of 1712, a few months after Sam's return from London, Michael was elected a magistrate and Brother of the Corporation. According to the charter, the twenty-one Brethren, together with the two bailiffs, made up the body which managed town affairs. Usually they were respected citizens of some wealth, or prosperous tradesmen. After election to Brotherhood, a man's name in the local records was invariably prefixed by a "Mr." or followed by "Gent." Once elected, a magistrate held office for life and could be removed only if he committed some crime punishable in the courts, or was reduced to poverty. Since the bailiffs were always chosen from among the Brethren, and since vacancies in the Corporation were replaced not by a vote of all the citizens but merely by the acting senior bailiff, the civic authority was in reality an oligarchy. To have become one of this closely knit group was a decided step up in the world, and shows how highly Michael was regarded by his fellow merchants.

The Brethren were required to wear gowns at church and on official occasions. According to the statute, the members of the Corporation were to meet in their official regalia at the Guildhall every Sunday morning and afternoon, when the bells of St. Mary's Church began to chime, and to attend the bailiffs from the hall to the church nearby. Only in summer weather was there a special dispensation to leave off their hot gowns in church. It must have been a constant source of pride for little Sam to see his father don his gown and march to the church with the other dignitaries.

True, the various civic positions brought no ready money into

Michael's pockets. The posts, indeed, were not much sought after. They give more evidence of his responsibility and pride than of his financial condition. Undoubtedly he had been pleased in the year of his son's birth to have been chosen sheriff. But the office carried with it no remuneration, and involved much expense. Sometimes the bailiffs had trouble in getting anyone to accept the honor, even though refusal entailed a large fine. In later years they actually raised money by electing various people sheriff who, they knew, would rather pay than serve. Once they fined ten men before finding a willing victim. Perhaps it was the desire to impress his wife's family that led Michael to make the sacrifice.

A similar motive may have been behind the rather ostentatious new house he had built in 1707 and 1708 at the corner of Sadler and Breadmarket Streets.[9] With over fifteen rooms, it was larger than he needed, and probably cost more than he could well afford. Obviously he was eager to give the impression of solid success. Unfortunately the prosperity was more apparent than real, for early in his career he had contracted heavy debts which he was never able to pay off. As the years went by, they grew rather than diminished. He could make enough to live comfortably, but not enough to be wholly free from the haunting specter of insolvency. He was never able to relax. Financial worries thus represented a continuing source of tension in the Johnson family. But there were other, more serious tensions, the result of general incompatibility between husband and wife.

Little is known about Michael's relations with women before he met Sarah. The sensational story of a serving maid named Elizabeth Blaney who pined away and died of unrequited love for the bookseller is, in the light of recent discoveries, highly improbable.[10] Only once, so far as can be told, did he come close to marriage, and then it was to Mary Neild, the twenty-three-year-old daughter of a prominent Derby tradesman. On December 30, 1686, a license was issued in Derby for her marriage to Michael Johnson, of Lichfield, "bachelor," then twenty-nine years old.[11] But something intervened, and almost two years later she was wed to James Warner instead.

So Michael continued to live soberly as a bachelor in his house in Sadler Street, devoted to his church and active in civic affairs. A man of eminent respectability, he was chaste in conversation, steady, reserved, devout — not the kind to have casual love affairs. He was known to have a morbid fear of mental trouble and kept himself constantly traveling about on business matters.[12]

He was almost fifty before he finally married Sarah Ford, a spinster of thirty-seven. What were Sarah's attractions? What was it about her that overbalanced the charms of all the other ladies he had known? It is impossible to tell. Edmund Hector later called her "a very remarkable woman for good understanding." [13] But she was no lover of books, she had no skill at business, she had no wit or social graces, she was not beautiful, and her dowry was only moderate. Perhaps the answer lies, as it does so often, in timing and propinquity. Though keeping house for her father at Packwood in Warwickshire, Sarah may have made long visits to her elder sister Phoebe in Lichfield. It would have been tempting for Phoebe and her husband to turn matchmakers — to bring together the spinster and the aging bachelor.

Michael needed a wife to take care of his home and to help with the shop while he was away; he undoubtedly desired a son to carry on the business after he was gone. He wanted a woman of good family and blameless character, and Sarah seemed a sensible choice. For her part, marriage to an intelligent tradesman with excellent prospects must have appeared more attractive than becoming an old maid. In some such prosaic fashion the two began their married life.

In the years that followed, Sarah devoted herself to domestic concerns. Never having had any intellectual interests, she was not mentally stimulating. Her husband, on the other hand, was something of a scholar, at the least a serious, inquiring man. He was "no careless observer of the passages of those times." With such different tastes, they had little to draw them together. "My father and mother," Johnson commented, "had not much happiness from each other. They seldom conversed; for my father could not bear to talk of his affairs; and my mother, being unacquainted with books, cared not to talk of anything else. Had my mother been more literate, they had been better companions. She might have sometimes introduced her unwelcome topic with more success, if she could have diversified her conversation." If theirs had been a love match, the lack of common interests might possibly have been overcome. But it was a union of simple practicality, without ardent affection, which offered scant chance of a happy home.

Evidently there was continual friction, with one minor irritation after another. No one can say who was to blame. They were both good, sober, well-meaning people. But domestic discord, as Johnson had Nekayah point out in *Rasselas,* is not easily avoided. "Even the virtuous fall sometimes to variance, when their virtues are of different kinds and tending to extremes."

Although steady and punctual in his business concerns, Michael was never very methodical, and his wife kept nagging him about it.[14] She was always afraid of spending more than they could afford. "Of business she had no distinct conception; and therefore her discourse was composed only of complaint, fear, and suspicion. Neither of them ever tried to calculate the profits of trade, or the expenses of living. My mother concluded that we were poor, because we lost by some of our trades."

There was friction, too, over various attempts at saving money. One of Michael's petty economies was in discouraging his wife from "keeping company with the neighbors, and from paying visits or receiving them." This was in order to avoid buying tea, which in those days was very expensive. Sarah grudgingly obeyed, though many years later she confided to her son that "if the time were to pass again, she would not comply with such unsocial injunctions."

One of the most deep-seated causes of irritation came from Sarah's inclination "to think higher of herself than of her husband." She was constantly harping on the superiority of her own family. "My mother had no value for his relations; those indeed whom we knew of were much lower than hers. This contempt began, I know not on which side, very early." The worst of it was that Michael could not contradict her claims.[15] He could never boast that the Johnsons had ever been so successful or eminent as the Fords. As a result, Michael kept as quiet as possible about his own ancestry, and many years later Dr. Johnson admitted to Boswell that he could scarcely tell who was his grandfather.[16] The humble beginnings of his grandfather, William Johnson of Cubley in Derbyshire, were undeniable.

According to one account he was only a day laborer, though his sons in later official documents variously described him as a "yeoman" or "gentleman." Probably he was a small tenant farmer and not a mere cottager. About the year 1664 William Johnson moved to a house in Tamworth Street in Lichfield, with his wife Catherine and four children — Michael, Benjamin, Andrew, and Margaret. Michael, the eldest, was seven at the time. The family cannot have been well off, for when William is first mentioned in the churchwarden's accounts of St. Mary's Church, in 1666, he was rated next to lowest in the list of 246 householders. Until his death in February, 1672, he continued to pay levies at the same figure. The fact that the Johnsons were continually moving about from house to house may represent more evidence of their poverty.

After his death his widow's levy in the church accounts continued low, and she became the recipient of several gifts of "wast coats" from the parish. The appearance of her name in the records of the Smith Charity bears mute evidence not only to her need, but also to the fact that she was considered a respectable person. The churchwardens and overseers of the poor dispensed their gifts only to those of good repute and undeniable industry. Her three boys were all educated through another local charity, the Conduit Lands Trust, which provided the money needed to send Michael to London to be apprenticed to a stationer.[17]

Sarah's family, the Fords, were in a different class. An old, respected family, somewhat above the run of yeoman farmers, they were by marriage connected with well-to-do gentry. Among her immediate relatives Sarah could point to a number who had entered the professions, one a successful London barrister, another a popular physician. Her own father, Cornelius Ford, was a small landowner, who was not without intellectual interests. Though Dr. Johnson once remarked that in the rural surroundings where his mother grew up most of the older people "had seldom learned to read," her father's private library gives proof of his own bookish tastes.[18]

Sarah's constant bragging about her family undoubtedly created resentment which might flare up at any time. There was Sarah's rich cousin, Mrs. Harriotts of Trysull, who had been so concerned over Sam's bad eyes. As much as possible, Michael kept out of her way, but when she came for a visit he showed his independence "by sending his horses from home on Sunday," which she considered "a breach of duty." As a High-Churchman, he was quite willing to flout such Puritanical scruples of his wife's relative.

Nevertheless, despite these tensions, Michael and Sarah did not "live ill together on the whole," for the simple reason that the husband learned how to avoid trouble. "My father could always take his horse and ride away for orders when things went badly." [19] But a father who was "little at home" did not provide much companionship for his son.

Because of his physical disabilities, Sam needed special encouragement. Even more than most children he required devoted care and understanding from both of his parents, and above all the feeling of security which grows out of being part of a happy family group. Unfortunately there was not much warmth and security in the Johnson household. There was little appreciation of the child's emotional needs, and the approach to disciplinary problems was faulty. Neither Michael nor Sarah had any conception of the best ways to offset his deficiencies or to strengthen his self-confidence. It was natural that he should be thrown most with his mother, who alternately spoiled and punished him. She would "gratify his appetite" by giving him coffee which she could ill afford, and indulge many of his childish whims. At the same time she was always trying to teach him rigid ideas of morality and behavior, but her admonitions rarely went beyond empty formulas. "My mother," said he, "was always telling me that I did not *behave* myself properly; that I should endeavor to learn *behavior*, and such cant: but when I replied, that she ought to tell me what to do, and what to avoid, her admonitions were commonly, for that time at least, at an end." From his own experience Johnson looked on older people as "very unfit to manage children; for being most commonly idle themselves" they occupied themselves "by tormenting the young folks with prohibitions not meant to be obeyed and questions not intended to be answered." [20]

Since Johnson later remarked that "no attention can be obtained from children without the infliction of pain, and pain is never remembered without resentment," it is probable that he had some unhappy memories of early physical punishments. If so, they did not alienate him from his mother. There can be no doubt of his love for her. In later life he wrote of his "dear mother" with obvious feeling. On the other hand, his was not a blind, unreasoning devotion. "Poor people's children," he commented, "never respect them: I did not respect my own mother, though I loved her: and one day, when in anger she called me a puppy, I asked her if she knew what they called a puppy's mother." As he grew older and saw more plainly her lack of intellectual interests, his divided attitude became even more pronounced.

When Sam was a little over three years old his emotional attitude toward his mother was further complicated by the appearance of a younger brother, Nathaniel. Now there were two to share her love and attention, and Sarah does not appear to have been very clever at minimizing jealousies. As Johnson told Mrs. Thrale, the two boys early became "rivals for the mother's fondness." Yet, strangely enough, there are very few references in all of Sam's later recollections to his only brother.

If he loved but could not respect his mother, his feeling toward his father was the exact reverse. Sam was intellectually drawn to him, but emotionally repelled. Although Michael was a general favorite of the other boys of the town, so much so that he "never received any injury from their petulance and mischief," [21] he was unable to gain the affection of his older son. Perhaps the great difference in age made it hard for the father to unbend; or it may have been merely Michael's reserved, melancholy manner, as well as his many absences from home. In any event, there was no real companionship between them. Johnson confessed to Boswell: "I never believed what my father said. I always thought that he spoke *ex officio,* as a priest does." Sadly he was of the opinion that "there must always be a struggle between a father and son." [22]

The chief cause of friction during Sam's early years arose from Michael's desire to show off his precocious child. At every opportunity he forced him to perform before admiring neighbors and relatives, and bragged constantly about the boy's literary talents. Well known is the awkward doggerel quatrain which Sam was supposed to have composed at an early age after stepping on a duckling.[23] Boswell first heard the story from Johnson's stepdaughter in Lichfield in 1776. She related, on the authority of his mother, that when he was "in petticoats he was walking by his father's side and carelessly trod upon a duck one of thirteen and killed it." So then it had to be buried, "upon which he made these lines

> Under this stone lyes Mr Duck
> Whom Samuel Johnson trode on
> He might have liv'd if he had luck;
> But then he'd been an odd one."

Stoutly refusing to admit the story, Johnson first said that his father had been responsible for half the epitaph; then later, when pressed by Boswell for the whole truth, he insisted that Michael had done almost all of it. Johnson even claimed that he remembered his father making the verses. "He was a foolish old man, that is to say was foolish in talking of his children."

Sarah, too, was exceedingly proud of her son. At the christening of Nathaniel on October 14, 1712, she taught Sam to "spell and pronounce the words *little Natty,* syllable by syllable, making him say it over in the evening to her husband and his guests." Again and again he was subjected to this same kind of torment. His parents so teased him "to exhibit his knowledge etc. to the few friends they had, that he used to run up a tree when company was expected, that he might escape the plague of being showed off to them." [24]

Ultimately he came to dread his father's caresses because he suspected they were merely the prelude to some attempt to make him perform. Because of these experiences, the certainty grew on him that a child of a late marriage was doomed to be miserable. An old man's offspring, he said, "leads much the same sort of life as a child's dog; teased like that with fondness through folly, and exhibited like that to every company, through idle and empty vanity." [25] So strongly convinced was he, that he later hurt the feelings of various friends and acquaintances by refusing to hear their children recite or sing. Once, indeed, when his host suggested that his two sons repeat Gray's *Elegy* alternately so that Johnson might judge which had the happiest cadence, Johnson replied, "No, pray Sir, let the dears both speak it at once; more noise will by that means be made, and the noise will be sooner over."

Another well-known anecdote which shows Michael's pride in his son has to do with the famous Tory preacher Henry Sacheverell. According to Miss Mary Adey, who sent the story to Boswell,

> When Dr. Sacheverell was at Lichfield, Johnson was not quite three years old. My grandfather Hammond observed him at the cathedral perched upon his father's shoulders, listening and gaping at the much-celebrated preacher. Mr. Hammond asked Mr. Johnson how he could possibly think of bringing such an infant to church, and in the midst of so great a crowd. He answered, because it was impossible to keep him at home; for, young as he was, he believed he had caught the public spirit and zeal for Sacheverell, and would have stayed forever in the church, satisfied with beholding him. [26]

It is an amusing story, but doubtful. When Sacheverell made his triumphal tour of the Midlands and was greeted in Lichfield in June, 1710, by the ringing of the church bells and by a present from the Corporation of three dozen bottles of wine, Sam was only nine months old and incapable of showing much interest in the famous preacher. Moreover, this particular year Michael would have been expected to appear formally at the cathedral in his official capacity of sheriff, not carrying an infant on his shoulders.

Sam's earliest instruction, religious and secular, came from his mother. Sometime shortly after the eventful trip to London he was first informed about "a future state." "I remember, that being in bed with my mother one morning, I was told by her of

the two places to which the inhabitants of this world were received after death; one a fine place filled with happiness, called
heaven; the other a *sad* place, called hell. That this account much
affected my imagination, I do not remember." ²⁷ In order that it
might be better fixed in his memory, however, she sent him to
repeat it to Thomas Jackson, their manservant.

If he was too young at this time to grasp the full significance
of what his mother was saying, she must subsequently have made
the dangers of future punishment clear enough. Sarah's approach to the Bible was literal and devout. Since her own father's taste in reading had run to evangelical sermons, it may be
that she had absorbed some of his Calvinism. Hell was real, and
damnation no mere symbolic device. So well did her son learn
the lesson that he was never rid of the terrors of the other world.
In the very year of his death, when Dr. Adams mildly asked him
what he meant by being damned, Johnson passionately burst
out, "Sent to hell, Sir, and punished everlastingly." ²⁸

As have so many mothers in the past, Sarah combined religious
precepts with practice in memorizing. One morning after he had
learned to read she put the prayer book into his hands, pointed
to the collect for the day, and said, "Sam, you must get this by
heart." She started up the stairs, but on reaching the second
landing she heard him following her. "What's the matter?" she
called down. "I can say it," said Sam, who then repeated it distinctly, though he could not have read the passage over more
than twice.²⁹

The instruction was not all religious. There were fairy stories
and tales of adventures to stir his imagination. One in particular
he never forgot, St. George and the Dragon, which he first heard
while sitting in the lap of his mother's maid.³⁰ Johnson always
maintained that tales of adventure were fitter for children than
were utilitarian stories written for their edification. "Babies," he
insisted to Mrs. Thrale, "do not want to hear about babies; they
like to be told of giants and castles, and of somewhat which can
stretch and stimulate their little minds." When Mrs. Thrale urged
that the opposite was proved by the great sale of such books as
Tommy Prudent and *Goody Two-Shoes,* he retorted, "Remem-

ber always that the parents *buy* the books, and that the children never read them."

While Sam possibly learned his letters at home, he was first taught to read by Dame Oliver, a shoemaker's widow, who kept a school for very young children in Dam Street, only about 135 yards from Michael Johnson's house.[31] Since the charity records of St. Mary's Church list many gifts to "wid. Oliver," and since she was not a house owner, it is evident she had very slender means. In addition to the school she later carried on a small confectionery business. As proof of her considerable mental equipment, Johnson once pointed out that she could read the "black letter," and had borrowed from his father a Bible printed in this old Gothic type.

The only surviving anecdote concerning Dame Oliver's school tells nothing about her teaching but something about Sam's early emotional instability. Because he was so young, and because of his bad eyesight, it was customary for a servant to escort him home from Dam Street each day. Even for such a short distance there were hazards along the way, including an open cesspool in the market place and the channels, or "soughs," as the drains in the roadway were called. One day no one came, and the small boy insisted on finding his way back alone. He felt his way down the street with care, and when he came to the deep channel he stooped down on his hands and knees before he ventured to step across. Meanwhile, afraid for her charge, yet realizing his fierce pride and independence, Dame Oliver followed at a discreet distance. As he turned the corner he saw that he was being followed and hysterically rushed back to attack her with kicks and flying fists.[32]

There is no sign that at this early date any of Johnson's well-known nervous complaints had begun to show. Edmund Hector told Boswell, after mentioning the episode of the trip to London to be touched by Queen Anne, that "he was very well when he came to school, and had only the scars." [33] It is certainly possible that the convulsive starts and bizarre movements which later kept Johnson's body in almost constant motion did not appear until adolescence or even later. Nevertheless, if signs of a tic had not yet appeared, the predisposition was there.

There is no agreement as to the cause — whether it was purely physical, arising from a cerebral injury at birth, or a compulsion neurosis, produced by early emotional tensions. There is even less agreement as to the source of the tensions. Freudians, when they sift the evidence, find an Oedipus complex, with an unhealthy attachment for his mother and an unconscious hatred of his father. One recent writer has hazarded the guess that because of his mother's early treatment of him, Sam consciously or unconsciously "rejected her whom he most wished to love" and as a result developed a "torturing sense of guilt and sin." Identifying himself with his father, he fell heir to his father's own fear of madness.[34] Others have suggested an inferiority complex which had its origin in his physical and social handicaps. Still others find in him an unresolved conflict between an uncompromising rationalism and his strong emotional drives. Each describes the disorder according to the terminology of his own school of thought.[35]

But historical-literary psychoanalysis is always hazardous. Especially in Johnson's complex case, no single explanation is sufficient. His later troubles came from a multitude of causes, including heredity, illness, and early emotional conflicts. But whatever the intricate combination of factors, by the time he was six years old a pattern had been formed. He knew he was different from his companions. While he was handicapped physically by the "issue" in his arm, the facial disfigurements, and the faulty vision, he was superior in intellect.[36] That had been dinned into him by the constant bragging of his parents. Life was to be a never-ending struggle to offset one and establish the other.

CHAPTER II

Lichfield

From the windows of his father's house Sam had an excellent view of life in Lichfield. Even with his weak eyes, he probably missed little of what was going on in the cobblestoned square, the center of town activity.

Tuesdays and Fridays were market days, when the place was packed with farmers bringing in their produce, temporary pens for animals, stalls for itinerant traders, housewives with baskets on their arms, peddlers, tinkers, horse traders, careless apprentices. As a responsible merchant, Michael Johnson was expected to take his turn in seeing that the market was honestly run, that the weights and measures were correct, and that the scales were above suspicion. In April, 1713, he was one of four who were elected clerks of the market for the ensuing year. Sometimes he must have been diligent in fulfilling his duties, at others possibly remiss. At least it is known that he and the other clerks were fined 2/6 each the following March at the Hilary Court for not appearing to make their reports.[1]

Since the shop was so conveniently located, there was no need to set up a stall. Instead, there was doubtless a stream of country customers trailing in and out of the house — an occasional clergyman or a gentleman interested in the latest sermon or political pamphlet from London, a farmer wanting an almanac, a lady in need of stationery. Michael had many other things to sell besides books. Letter paper and parchment, writing materials, "paperhangings," "fine French prints, for staircases and large chimney pieces; maps, large and small" — these were all part of his stock in trade. And from advertisements in the London newspapers it is evident that he also dealt in patent medicines. At Mr. Johnson's in Lichfield one could buy such items as "Tinctura cathartica or a tincture of the salt of Epsom, or the purging water," or "Mr. Phillip Bowcher's famous spirits of scurvygrass both golden, purging and plain." His shop was sometimes listed as a place where information could be obtained concerning sales of property in the neighborhood. Whatever offered a source of possible profit or a service to his customers, this energetic merchant attempted to supply.[2]

On special holidays such as Shrove Tuesday the market place was the scene of more robust entertainments. In the center of the square, until late in the nineteenth century, there was a heavy iron ring, fastened by a staple to a huge stone sunk to the level of the cobbles. This was used for bull baiting. The surly animal was first chained to the ring and then set upon by dogs, while the spectators crowded around. A particular breed of dog had been developed for this sport, and no force could unlock their jaws once they were clamped to the sensitive nose of the angry bull. Many a dog was tossed and bitten in his attempt to sink his teeth into a tender spot. It was not uncommon to see the poor bulls, lying exhausted on the ground after having been baited for hours, forced to rise for more sport by having blazing straw pushed under them. Sometimes, too, the infuriated animal broke loose, and then from his window the excited little boy would see the onlookers scatter in fright.

The iron ring exercised a kind of fascination on Sam, who hated every kind of cruelty, and in later years he developed the habit of pulling at it violently every time he passed, as if trying to find out whether he could move it from its place.[3] It was almost as if he had an inner compulsion to compare his own huge bulk and strength with that of the tortured animals.

A memorable event occurred in Lichfield in late May, 1713, with the celebration of the Peace of Utrecht. The long war with France was over, and although ardent Whigs were disgruntled at this betrayal of their hero, the great Duke of Marlborough, the majority of the Staffordshire citizens were happy over the end of hostilities. In the London *Post Boy* for June 4 a letter from Lichfield was published describing how the news had been proclaimed there with great solemnity. The sheriff, bailiffs, and magistrates, dressed in their formal robes and preceded by the mace-bearers, were accompanied around the town by a large number of country gentlemen, "the populace in great crowds followed them with three laurel leaves stuck in their hats with these inscriptions (A.R.) on the middle one, and *Peace* and *Plenty* on each side. Her Majesty's health and long life, was drank at the market place, and in all the streets in the city; and the night concluded with bonfires, illuminations, and all other demonstrations of joy."

It is inconceivable that the three-and-a-half-year-old son of a Tory magistrate was not one of the throng, with laurel leaves and the royal initials on his cap.

The good people of Lichfield loved a celebration, as we can see from the frequent charges in the town expense accounts for ringing the bells. From ancient time, the city had been empowered to hold four annual fairs, the most festive occurring on Whitmonday, when there was a saturnalia of feasting and fun, known for miles about as the "Greenhill Bower." Great crowds of people came in from the country, and the day was spent in ale drinking, processions with garlands, sarabands and Moorish dances, and all manner of frolics. Most of the customs were traditional — the morris dancers, the decorated wagons, the grotesque figures and tableaux — survivals of the ancient "Court of Arraye."

Before Puritan times the simple "Bower" had been erected in St. Michael's churchyard at the edge of town; in Johnson's day it was put up nearby on an open space on Greenhill. Here at noon the worshipful dignitaries, together with the Rector of St. Michael's, partook of a feast and drank time-honored toasts, while the inhabitants were regaled with cold meat, cake, and wine at the expense of the Corporation. The ancient festival of the "Bower" is believed to have originated in heathen times and was perpetuated only because of the sage recommendation of Pope Gregory that old pagan customs be adapted to Christian uses.

Like every other Lichfield boy, Sam must have looked forward eagerly to the Whitmonday celebrations, though with such sober, pious parents he would not have been allowed to participate in all of the riotous amusements. The memory was still strong in

1779, when on one of his annual visits to his birthplace Johnson wrote to Mrs. Thrale: "We went with Mrs. Cobb to Greenhill Bower. I had not seen it perhaps for fifty years. It is much degenerated. Everything grows old." [4] But it was his tastes that had changed, not the traditional merrymaking on Whitmonday, for that was, and still is, filled with the same robust vulgarity which had delighted him in his youth.

Although for his earliest years life would have centered in the market square, there were other parts of the town where he loved to be taken. A favorite spot was the house of his foster mother, Joan Marklew, in George Lane. He later remembered the trees in the shaded street, and the orchard garden where he could gorge himself on apples, pears, and plums. Perhaps with this in mind, he commented in his life of Swift, "Almost every boy eats as much fruit as he can get, without any great inconvenience." [5]

There was much to interest a boy at Michael's parchment factory, situated on the northwest edge of the Moggs, the marshy waste ground made by the gradual shrinkage of Stowe Pool. Michael had sold parchment as early as 1695, and by 1699 he had evidently built up an extensive and prosperous business as a tanner. By 1705 his factory was so well established that the Corporation forced him to take a lease on the land. According to the unreliable Anna Seward, Michael later lost heavily by his parchment manufacture, but during Sam's youth it was undoubtedly a thriving business. The actual work was done by various employees, John Rutter and after him John Barton and their helpers, whom Sam often watched as they cleaned, washed, and tanned the hides and then stretched the skins on the large wooden racks called "tenters." Over a half century afterward he could astonish Boswell and the company at Ullinish on the Isle of Skye by giving "an account of the whole process of tanning." [6]

He would have been familiar, too, with various bathing pools at the edge of town. Under the inspiration of Sir John Floyer, Lichfield aspired to being known as a "spa." Floyer's chief fetish was cold-water immersion. Having acquired an international reputation because of his books on the subject, he set up at Abnalls a bathing place, with a special keeper, and a charge of not more than twopence for any resident of the city or Close. Poor persons were accepted free. On the other side of the town, near St. Chad's Well, he developed a second bathing site, and for years people came great distances to try the chalybeate "waters of Stowe." As always happens, numerous cures were reported. It may even be that Sam had been brought there as a child to test the effect of the medicinal properties of the water on his skin diseases. While the intense cold of the water from the "Unites Well" at Abnalls kept it from any lasting popularity, the Stowe bath was maintained for many years.

It was at another place that Sam learned to swim. At the east end of Stowe Pool there were in those days two outlets which united on the north side of St. Chad's Church to form a good-sized stream emptying into the Trent. Bordered by trees overhanging the deep pools, it was the constant resort of Lichfield boys in summer. Coming back as an older man, Johnson was distressed to find the spot sadly altered, and he expressed his nostalgic feeling in some Latin verses. Perhaps the most personal of all his poems, it embodies one of his few happy recollections of Michael.

> The glassy stream still flows through green meadows, where time and again in boyhood I bathed my tender limbs. Here my arms were tricked and puzzled by the rough current, while my father with mild voice taught me how to swim. Branches used to form a hiding place there, and a leaning tree concealed a secret stretch of water in daytime darkness. Now the old shadows have perished under hard axes, and the watery fields open to eyes far off. The untired stream, however, keeps perennially to its course. . . .[7]

Michael's teaching was effective, for his son became such a strong swimmer that he made one of the professional "dippers" (the forerunners of modern lifeguards) at Brighton exclaim, "Why Sir, you must have been a stouthearted gentleman forty years ago." [8]

The boy's speech was typical of the Midlands. He said "woonce" instead of "once"; and "shuperior" and "shupreme." "There" was pronounced like "fear." Nor would he ever get rid of the Staffordshire mannerisms. Garrick used to take him off "squeezing a lemon into a punch bowl, with uncouth gesticulations, looking round the company, and calling out, 'Who's for *poonsh?*' " Yet Johnson insisted that the people of his native town were "the most sober, decent people in England, the genteelest in proportion to their wealth, and spoke the purest English." [9]

In using the word "sober" to characterize his fellow citizens, he probably forgot an earlier remark to Boswell. "I remember when all the *decent* people in Lichfield got drunk every night, and were not the worse thought of." In the excitement of argument Johnson was unmindful of inconsistencies. Once when confronted with another extreme statement he readily admitted, "I may perhaps have said this, for nobody talks more laxly than I do." [10]

Nor should his old schoolmate, "Tom" Newton, later Bishop of Bristol, be held too strictly to account for the claim that Lichfield in his time had so many pretty women that his friend Hawkins Browne "used to call it the Paphos of England." [11] With some three thousand inhabitants, the place undoubtedly had its share of pretty girls, of "decent drunkards," of proud gentry and humble artisans. It had its own race meeting in the late summer, when hundreds of fashionable people filled all available quarters. It was notable for balls and parties. Indeed, Daniel Defoe found Lichfield "a place of good company, above all the towns in this or the neighboring counties of Warwickshire or Derbyshire."

Gradually Sam would have become aware of the pageantry associated with the administration of local affairs. The bailiffs in their "formalities," with the mace-bearers and the sword-bearer, who made their appearance on every special occasion, were not the only relics of the past. There was the pompous beadle, with his splendid gown, cocked hat, staff of office, and bell, whose duty it was to act as town crier and on Sunday to shepherd reluctant worshipers to church. There was the town watchman, still carrying "bills" as in Shakespeare's time, who kept the peace and speedily assisted vagrants beyond the city limits.

In those days almost every householder owned cattle which were allowed to graze on the extensive common lands within the city's boundaries. On summer mornings Sam may often have been awakened at six o'clock by the horn of the common herdsman, or "bubulcus," as he was called in the old records, whose duty it was to collect the cattle in the morning, remain with them all day, and bring them back at five o'clock in the evening. So many of the citizens farmed portions of the common lands and kept their cattle at pasture that stray animals were a usual sight. As a result, the office of "pinner," or keeper of the pound, was no easy post. There were two pounds, one at the north and one at the south side of the town, just outside the gates. The pinners were continually impounding cows or swine which had broken into the cultivated areas or had escaped to roam about the streets. Furthermore, the pinner had to face the occupational hazard of occasional assault by angry citizens attempting to rescue their livestock from his clutches, and his pound was often broken into at night. Helping or obstructing the pinner as he drove stray beasts out of the streets was a frequent source of delight to Lichfield boys.

The town was fortunate in having an excellent water supply, under the control of what was known as the Conduit Lands Trust. Stemming from the sixteenth century, it had as its chief purpose the conservation and development of the local water supply, but excess revenues were wisely invested in the support of the Grammar School and in gifts to "decayed tradesmen," "poor widows," and deserving boys and girls. The Trust was responsible for the care of the wells, the reservoirs, and the mains which brought the clear, sparkling water to the various sections. No ordinary householder had a private pipe into his home. He might have his own cistern filled by the rains, but for general use he had to carry jugs and pails of water from the nearest public tap. For the Johnsons, the Market Cross Conduit was conveniently located a stone's throw away. The Trust employed a full-time plumber, at six pounds a year, to repair the pipes; and on cold winter mornings he and the wardens were kept busy "thawing cocks" and removing ice from the gutters.

The lighting of the streets was largely a matter of individual responsibility. The householder was urged by the authorities to show a lamp or lighted window during certain hours, except when there was a moon; and anyone who wandered about after dark was expected to carry his own "lanthorn," or be regarded by the watch as a suspicious character. Some responsibility to provide illumination at other places was assumed by the Conduit Trust, which put up lamp standards at the cattle pounds and causeways.

At a time when most houses were timbered and thatched with straw, fire was an ever-present danger, and constant precautions were taken. The universal method of fire fighting was to pull down the roofs, and sometimes even the houses themselves, by means of long poles fitted with iron hooks, while buckets of water were thrown on the blazing embers. The Court Leet ordered the inhabitants of each ward of the city to have ready a ladder of twenty-four rungs, sufficient to reach the higher roofs, as well as poles and leather buckets.

Of more interest to the small boys were a number of hand-operated fire engines, which the Trust also provided. Variously called "ingens" or "Indians," they were well taken care of, with semiannual paintings and puttyings. They were stationed at strategic points about the city, one of the engine houses being close to Sam's home, by St. Mary's steeple in Breadmarket Street, where he must sometimes have gone to admire the contraption.

Each of the machines had a pet designation, such as the "great engon," the "force engon," the "traddle engin," the "squirt ingen." Moreover, there were the "bachelor's" and the "virgin's" engines, though their separate properties were not set down for posterity. It usually cost sixpence paid out in ale or beer to each volunteer worker to have an engine filled with water, and a similar amount to have it taken to and from the scene of a fire. The wells, cisterns, and conduit openings were so numerous in every street that there was never any scarcity of water. Happy were the days when the "Indians" were taken out on parade and "played" for all to see. Doubtless to impress visitors from less fortunate communities, there was a standing order that the engines should be displayed on Guy Fawkes Day, Holy Thursday, and Whitmonday.

The most serious problem for the local authorities was the disposal of rubbish and "dung muck or manure." Rigid rules were adopted by the manorial courts for its disposal, but the records show that there were frequent violations. With no sewage system available, citizens were ordered to deposit their waste in what appeared to be a ready-made dumping ground, the great ditch that Roger de Clinton had constructed in the twelfth century around the old city. But for lazy householders it was much easier to throw their "muck" into the open "soughs" or channels in the roadways, hoping that the next rain would carry it away into the larger cesspools. There was a temptation, also, to stow it away in small nearby alleys, such as Chapel Lane, which ran around two sides of St. Mary's Church. A special ruling required that this passage be cleared once a week by those who lived in the neighborhood.

"Muck" which was shoveled into the street had to be moved in two days' time, and could on no account remain over Sunday. Anyone who violated this law might be fined as much as two shillings. And if the "muckhill" caused "annoyance or hindrance of any persons whatsoever passing that way," the fine might rise to three shillings and fourpence. Like many of his neighbors, Sam's father at times failed to keep these rules, and the records contain such entries as "Mich. Johnson fined 2d for a muckheap in Bakers Lane." In every family the disposal of what was so succinctly called "muck" was a constant problem.

The number of minor rules which had to be obeyed is astonishing — laws forbade the dumping of hot ashes in the streets; leaving any "manner of carrion" even on the common dunghill instead of having it buried; carrying away any of the surface of the roadway; allowing hogs or swine to lie in the streets; sending more than two cows to pasture under the common herdsman. The regulations were explicit and the fines numerous. On and on go the entries — people punished for not "scouring" their ditch, for not sweeping the street, for "a nuisance in Cocke Lane," for "laying rubbage betwixt market cross and the church," for washing "any clothes or filthy foul or nasty thing at the conduits," or for "keeping a mastiff dog unmuzzled." In such a closely knit community every little misdemeanor was at once known to all. With its system of "doceners," who represented each ward of the city, every citizen had a part in making local government work; perhaps this is one reason for the fact that while there were many picayune violations to be punished, there is little evidence of bloodshed or theft.[12] A man's life was fairly well protected, his property respected. Although hygienically Lichfield left much to be desired, it was a reasonably safe, pleasant place to grow up in.

Everywhere that Sam wandered there were still traces of the disastrous Civil War of the mid-seventeenth century, for in the struggle between Charles I and his rebellious Parliament Lichfield had suffered more than most towns. The Cathedral Close, on high ground and surrounded by stout walls and water, actually sustained three sieges and was finally left in ruins.[13] Fortified by the Royalists, it was taken in 1643 by the Parliamentarians after a bitter fight, only to be retaken about a month and a half later by the King's forces, who drained the moat and sprung two mines. In 1646, a few years before Charles was beheaded, it was surrendered again to the Puritan Roundheads, and it remained in their hands until the Restoration.

As a result of the desperate fighting the place was left a shambles. The minster survived with no roof or floor, with battered spires, wrecked windows, and shattered walls. The battlements and towers surrounding the Close were razed to the ground and the debris sold to anyone who cared to buy and carry it away. There are still garden walls, fences, and rockeries in Lichfield built from the ruins. Nor did the town itself escape. The beautiful market cross was gone. Many a house was left a rubbish heap, and scores were burned; some belonging to well-known supporters of the King were demolished by order of the parliamentary authorities.

Of course, by the early eighteenth century much had been repaired. There were new houses, new walls. The minster had a rebuilt roof. Years of hard work had done wonders. But the memories did not die. Every time a Lichfield citizen looked up at the spires of the cathedral he was reminded of the Civil War, for the great central steeple had been rebuilt with stone of a different color. The mutilated statues stood as a constant reminder of wanton destruction.

Of all this Sam must have been keenly aware. From his earliest years he would have sensed the horror in the accounts of sacrilege during those terrible days — how during the first occupation by the Parliamentarians relics had been smashed and old records burned; how every day the Roundhead forces were reputed to have hunted a cat with hounds through the shattered cathedral. There was even a story that, in their desire to show hatred of all religious forms and ceremonies, they once brought up to the wrecked font a calf wrapped in linen, sprinkled it with water, and burlesqued the sacrament of baptism.

One romantic tale connected with the first siege made an indelible impression. This was of the dramatic death of Lord Brooke, the fanatic leader of the parliamentary forces. Having planted a gun against the southeast gate of the Close, he directed fire from a small house in Dam Street. Far up on the battlements of the middle steeple a loyal sharpshooter named "Dumb" Dyott, a mute, was trying to harass the cannoneers. When Lord Brooke in full armor stepped to the door to see what was going on, a stray bullet, glancing from a piece of timber, entered the opened visor of his helmet and pierced his brain. The fact that it was March 2, St. Chad's Day, sacred to the founder of the earliest local church and patron saint of the cathedral, and that as he was coming to the siege Lord Brooke had prayed to God for some token of approbation of his design, naturally led pious Cavaliers to believe his death an act of Providence.

The revered spot where Lord Brooke had fallen was only a short way from where Dame Oliver later had her little school and directly on Sam's shortest route to his father's parchment factory. Passing it frequently as he grew older, he must have recalled the remarkable event. The actual part of the wood porch where the bullet struck was treasured in a Lichfield museum, and as an older man Johnson used to see it there, often expressing his desire "that a monument be erected to celebrate the killing of Lord Brooke by Mr. Dyott." [14]

Such stories of the Civil War were enough to color Sam's feeling about the Commonwealth for the rest of his life. With vivid recollections of what had happened to his own town, he could never be completely objective in his attitude toward Cromwell, Milton, or any of the Puritans. He could never overcome his fear of revolution, or his doubt of the value of any sudden change.

But it would be a mistake to assume, as some have done, that all the early environmental influences on Sam came from the Tory side. Lichfield was by no means a predominantly Tory community, despite the old families that had suffered so much as a result of their loyalty to the Stuarts and the inevitable High-Church clique about the cathedral. In the Close there were some, like the Walmesleys, who were stanchly Whig. And in the town, especially among the merchants, Parliamentarian sentiment was strong.

The fact is that Sam grew up in an evenly balanced political constituency — one which sensitively reflected shifts of opinion throughout the country. Having an unusually large number of eligible voters, Lichfield was not a pocket borough, to be controlled by the whims of one family or group. It was a genuine sounding board of public opinion. In the late seventeenth century, during the reign of William and Mary, it time after time returned to Parliament one Tory and one Whig; for most of Anne's rule, two Tories; and then with the coming in of the Hanoverians, two Whigs.[15] From 1715 until 1734, through almost all of Sam's youth in Lichfield, his town regularly elected Whig representatives. Any attempt to explain his later conservative opinions as a result of the prevailing political climate of his home community would be a mistake.

Nor is it certain that he heard only the Tory side even in his family circle. His mother's relatives, the Fords, were mostly Whigs, and there is no contemporary evidence that Michael's reputed love of the Stuarts was really so strong as some of his son's biographers would have us believe.[16] His loyalties, like those of so many others of the day, were divided.

In order to sense his political environment, one needs to understand the tensions of that particular time, for modern attempts at simplification tend to give a false picture. Political divisions were more than usually complex. Because of the twentieth century's sharp distinctions between labor and capital, between radical and conservative, there is a temptation to transfer this same dichotomy to earlier periods. This is particularly true of Ameri-

cans, who, recalling their own Revolution, instinctively characterize Whigs as liberal and progressive, and Tories as callously
reactionary. But such a division did not hold true for the England of Johnson's youth.

For one thing, there were no well-developed party organizations. Political divisions were based either on the rivalries of
small groups or on deep temperamental and social oppositions.
In those days the chief disruptive forces were the new mercan-
tilism and religion. The large moneyed class, the extensive landowners and wealthy merchants, tended to be Whigs. Opposing
royal prerogative, they wanted additional power for Parliament,
partly because the latter was much more responsive to financial
considerations. Generally speaking, they were the "ins," the
Treasury party, the followers of the court oligarchy. On the other
hand, the lesser squirearchy, the small landowners and county
families — the so-called country party — were largely Tory. They
were the "outs," suspicious of the new science, the tricky experiments in finance, and the rising power of business, which they
associated with Whiggery. They were quite willing to jog along
as they were, rather than take chances of destroying society altogether. While they worshiped the throne in principle, they dis-
trusted government in practice. And for the earlier part of the
century the smaller businessmen were basically of the same opinion.[17] The poor, who could not vote, were scattered in both
camps. A beggar could see little difference in his lot between a
government run by the great Whig lords and one run by their
Tory rivals. As a class, the proletariat was not yet on the Whig
side. Indeed, in the early eighteenth century the "mob" was more
often roused by the Tories.

Religion was also a vital factor. Roman Catholics and High-
Churchmen, who stressed conformity, were apt to be Tories; English Low-Churchmen and dissenters, Whigs. There was a curious
split within the Church of England itself: the rank and file of
curates and poor parsons were Tories, and the bishops, who were
largely political appointees sitting in the House of Lords, were
active Whigs.

The question of the succession to the throne provided further cross currents. Thus a Scottish Presbyterian, against his normal religious convictions, might support the Catholic Stuarts by reason of national pride. In England a small country landowner, against his general belief in the legitimate succession, might be just as violent a partisan of the Hanoverians. Many who were economically conservative were as unalterably opposed to a Catholic monarch as they were to the new policies of the Whigs. Each man had to make up his mind as to which consideration carried the most weight.

The Tories insisted that Whigs were dangerous experimenters who were tinkering with accepted political and religious traditions, corrupt place-hunters lacking in reverence for God or king, so obsessed with commercial concerns that they forgot all the old decencies, foolish optimists who failed to understand the basic depravity of man. For their part, the Whigs thought their opponents hopeless reactionaries, Jacobites who were ready to plunge the nation into civil war merely to put on the throne another arbitrary Catholic monarch, old-fashioned die-hards who were jealous of the rise of the new industrialism and blind to the possibilities of the new science.

Both sides exaggerated. Neither was so black as the other painted it. Nor were the differences as wide as the modern split between left and right. A prominent Whig and a prominent Tory would have agreed on most fundamental problems of society. Such a sober Whig as Joseph Addison could scarcely be called a reckless innovator or a devotee of a new social order. And there were Tories, like Jonathan Swift, who desired a Protestant ruler as ardently as did their opponents. Only a small percentage of the Tories were active supporters of the Pretender, though the majority might regret the personalities of the Hanoverian rulers and deprecate the necessity of deviating an iota from the normal line of succession. A Tory in power might act in most instances just as would his rival. Except for the sharp split on religion, which determined the matter of the succession, there were few basic cleavages.

While Queen Anne was alive many were able to avoid taking a stand. After all, she was a Stuart, in the direct line of descent.

But at her death in 1714 and during the turbulent days following the accession of her second cousin, George of Hanover, rebellion was in the air. At last the supporters of James's son, the Pretender — those who had been sentimentally toasting "The King over the Water" — were forced to make a choice. It was a time of soul searching for Jacobites everywhere. There must have been wild-eyed excitement in the Johnson household when what the London newspapers called a "French and Popish mob" rioted and attacked nonconformist meetinghouses all over Staffordshire. The *Flying Post* of July 19, 1715, carried the news that "one just now come from Lichfield says he saw the meetinghouse there in a flame yesterday morning at three o'clock." Actually there was less trouble in Lichfield than in other neighboring towns, but danger was always present.

At a meeting of the Corporation on August 20 a humble address to the King was drawn up "upon the occasion of the late tumults occasioned by the invasion of the Pretender." As often happened, business kept Michael away from this midweek gathering of the Brethren. Subsequently, however, he supported the address and signed the oaths of fidelity and allegiance to King George.

Boswell says of Michael that he "retained his attachment to the unfortunate house of Stuart, though he reconciled himself, by casuistical arguments of expediency and necessity, to take the oaths imposed by the prevailing power." [18] But there is not a shred of contemporary evidence that he disagreed in any way with the actions of the town's governing body. If, as his son remarked, in making the decision "he was to settle with himself," there is no proof of any protracted struggle. He took the oaths over and over again. Every time he was elected to office there was the same procedure. On the surface he conformed without a quibble.

During these years there was a continual bother over taking the oaths. On page after page of the Hall Books of the Corporation appear the signed statements, each man who assumed office swearing solemnly to abjure the Pretender and give allegiance to Queen Anne and afterward to King George. "Without any equivocation, mental evasion or secret reservation whatsoever," the signer agreed that the son of James II had "not any right or title whatsoever to the crown," and that "no foreign prince person prelate state or potentate hath or ought to have any jurisdiction power superiority preeminence of authority ecclesiastical or spiritual within this realm."

With plentiful "so help me Gods" Michael had to reiterate his abhorrence and detestation of the impious and damnable doctrines of the followers of James. At other times he subscribed to the statement that "I do believe that there is not any transubstantiation in the Sacrament of the Lord's Supper or in the elements of bread and wine at or after the consecration thereof by any person whatsoever."

The line between passive obedience to the Protestant succession and active plotting to bring back the Catholic Pretender sometimes seemed dangerously thin. In the back of everyone's mind was the possibility of foreign intervention — from Rome or Paris. Friends could not be sure of friends, relatives of their kinfolk. And so the insistence on oaths, not once, but again and again. Everyone must be made to show his true colors. Yet the many signatures and the countless pledges tell very little about inner convictions. They indicate what a group of practical citizens decided on. As loyal tradesmen and public servants they did what the law told them to do. If some of them, like Michael, may have yearned for the old dispensation, they were too sensible to mix sentiment with sober common sense.

All this is not to say that they were hypocrites. One can vaguely wish for one thing and see that another is necessary and proper for maintaining peace and order. A man could quite honestly swear loyalty to George and abjure the Stuart Pretender at the same time that he wished the necessity for such a choice had never arisen. He could talk in the privacy of his home as a Jacobite, and still realize that, as with other romantic dreams, there was nothing he really wanted to do about it. In just this way Michael probably talked Jacobitism, but in practice grudgingly accepted the turn of history as inevitable. Such was to be his son's position later in the century.

Michael's willingness to abjure any belief in transubstantiation in the communion service, moreover, did not mean that he took

his religion any less seriously. Though High Church by conviction, he was always a loyal Protestant. He was actively involved
in all parish affairs and was pious and regular in church attendance. As far back as 1690 the records show him paying for
a seat in St. Mary's Church, and as soon as he was married there
was a further payment for Sarah. When his two boys grew old
enough, he undoubtedly expected them to accompany their parents to Sunday service.

One may assume that on the morning of Easter Sunday, 1716,
Sam was sitting in the family pew when a few pieces of stone
and mortar fell from the spire onto the roof of the church. Because it was well known that the steeple was in bad condition,
there was immediate panic in the congregation. A humorous eye-
witness account of what then ensued was sent by a local journalist to the London newspapers, and was printed in the *Weekly
Journal or British Gazetteer* for Saturday, April 14, 1716.

> Lichfield April 2. Yesterday the Reverend Mr. Baker read divine
> service, and Mr. Stevenson, schoolmaster of the Free School, preached
> in the chapel church: and as he was going to make application, some
> part of the south side of the battlements of the upper roof moldered
> down with a rumbling noise, upon the lower leads of the south aisle;
> which so affrighted the young minister, that he made but one leap
> down the pulpit: the women cried out, some murder; others, Lord
> have mercy on us; Oh the Presbyterians! The parson who made but
> one step from the top of the pulpit stairs to the bottom, was the first
> that got out of the church, ready to faint away. The people (being a
> numerous congregation) crowded so fast, that they tumbled upon
> one another, and lay crawling in heaps; some cried out they were
> killed; others hastened out at the windows, and strained their knees
> and ankles; some bruised their legs and arms; others made very
> strong smells, though more afraid than hurt. Capt. Dy—— was very
> nimble, and so was Mr. Wake, who got out at a window. Parson
> Baker could not move for fear, and so put his head under the pulpit
> cloth, that he might not be an eyewitness of his death, which he
> fancied was at hand. Hats, books, hoods, scarfs, cover-sluts, or long
> riding hoods, headdresses, spectacles, gloves, clogs, snuffboxes, fans,

etc., were left in abundance; so that this morning the bellman made
proclamation for all persons to come to the town, to own the things
they lost.

With his tongue still in his cheek, the reporter added, "But some
persons, who had got better hats and other things than their own,
did not appear." If he was present, Sam never divulged whether
he remained cool during all the commotion, or whether he followed the example of his distinguished godfather Richard Wakefield, and crawled out of one of the side windows.[19]

At a meeting of the parishioners held three or four weeks afterward the decision was made that for safety's sake the whole spire
should be taken down to the level of the battlements and the stone
used to repair the rest of the church. This meant closing for a
long time. The seats and pews were carried to the chapel of St.
John's Hospital, over a quarter of a mile away, where worship
was continued for the following five years.

Without much inclination to go to services anyway, Sam used
the disturbed conditions as an excuse to avoid attendance altogether. Always sensitive about his bad eyesight, he dreaded the
thought of new surroundings, with strangers commenting on his
infirmities.[20] And his parents were sensible enough not to force
him. Instead, he developed the habit on Sunday of walking and
reading in the nearby fields.

"Rod, I Will Honor Thee for This Thy Duty"

NOT to name the school or the masters of men illustrious for literature, is a kind of historical fraud, by which honest fame is injuriously diminished: I would therefore trace him through the whole process of his education." [1] Thus wrote Samuel Johnson about Joseph Addison. No doubt he would have approved the use of the same procedure for himself.

By the year 1716 Sam had left Dame Oliver's little school and was being instructed by Thomas Browne, whose house was close by in Dam Street. Like Peter Oliver, "Tom" Browne had been a shoemaker, and it is possible that the families were closely associated. [2] There may have been a friendly arrangement by which he took over the Dame's pupils once they reached a certain age. Browne's chief claim to remembrance has been that he once produced a spelling book, which he dedicated — with a flourish — to the Universe. However, no copy of this book, from which Sam may have learned the mysteries of spelling, has ever been discovered. In Browne's sparsely furnished schoolroom Sam absorbed the elements of English syntax. Then, at the beginning of 1717, when he was almost seven and a half, he entered the Lichfield Grammar School.

He could scarcely have found a better place, for among the smaller institutions in England it was deservedly famous. A succession of remarkably able masters had given it an enviable reputation. Few schools with similar resources could boast of having produced so many scholars, bishops, judges, scientists, and literary men of the front rank. At one time in the eighteenth century there were sitting in the Westminster Courts seven famous judges who had been educated in the Lichfield Grammar School.[3]

It is probable that Michael Johnson had also attended the Free Grammar School. Where else during the late 1660s and early 70s could he have acquired his knowledge of Latin and the classics? The headmaster in his time was Thomas Bevans, during whose administration Hebrew and Greek were added to the curriculum. Michael's genuine interest in the school is shown by the fact that while he was one of the wardens of the Conduit Trust steps were taken to build a house for the headmaster.

The Grammar School, an unpretentious brick building with four gables, was in St. John Street on the side opposite the ancient Hospital of St. John. Except for a little chamber over the entrance, there was only a single large oak-paneled room, furnished with massive oak desks for the pupils, and with raised ones near each end for the master and usher. A prominent object in the room, which must have sent shivers down the spine of each entering pupil, was a rough three-legged stool, used as a flogging horse. At recreation time the boys amused themselves in a small enclosed playground or, if they chose, in a nearby open field owned by Theophilus Levett.

The distance from Sam's home in the market place to the school was about a quarter of a mile, whether one kept safely to Bore and St. John Streets, or instead took Wade Street or Frog Lane, or circled back through the pasture. The latter was the most pleasant way on good days, across an old stile at Castle Ditch at the north end of Levett's Field, and by footpaths to the back of the school. Jumping over this stile became one of Sam's favorite pastimes.

Sam's first and best-liked teacher at the Grammar School was Humphrey Hawkins, a perfect example of the kindly, self-effacing, poverty-ridden pedagogue. Appointed underschoolmaster about 1685, he remained as usher until his death in 1741. For some fifty-six years he ruled the lower school, teaching the rudiments of Latin to some who were to be among the greatest men of the country. Yet because he had no university degree and had not taken orders, he never rose above this humble post.

With a salary of only five pounds a year, in 1705 he asked per-

mission of the feoffees of the Conduit Lands Trust to be allowed
to use the school buildings during vacant periods for private instruction. After a moving petition, which still survives, he was
given as a "gratuity" an additional five pounds.[4] When he married and became the father of a rapidly increasing family, he
sought other ways of making money. From 1712 he handled the
St. Mary's churchwarden accounts, at an annual salary of five
pounds, and his unmistakable copybook handwriting can be found
today in the records of many other local organizations. He and
his wife did all sorts of chores. In the churchwarden's accounts
there are entries such as this: "paid Mr. Hawkins for washing the
surplice and other linen — o.11.6." The man who helped mold
the minds of Johnson and Garrick, of several bishops and chief
justices, was forced to such menial tasks to earn a living.

If not an outstanding scholar, Hawkins was considered by Sam
to be an excellent and discerning teacher. He must at once have
recognized the abilities of the bookseller's boy, for Sam remembered that he was "indulged and caressed" by his master.[5] In
consequence, the two years and four months spent in the lower
forms were probably the happiest of his school career.

Although there is a great gap of thirty-eight pages in the manuscript of Johnson's account of his early years, enough remains to
give some details of his studies under Hawkins.[6] The basic curriculum for the grammar schools had not varied for hundreds of
years. What Sam absorbed in the early eighteenth century was substantially what the early humanists Erasmus and Colet had
recommended two centuries earlier. His daily routine was similar
to that of a boy in Stratford in the sixteenth century, or to that of
young Milton somewhat later at St. Paul's. His days were given
over almost exclusively to the study of Latin — Latin grammar,
readings from the easier Roman authors, the writing of simple
themes and exercises in Latin. There were no courses in French,
modern history, economics, or science. Such frills a boy was expected to pick up for himself. An educated man must have the
ability to read and write Latin, and some knowledge of the more
important Greek authors. By the slow process of memorizing,
translating, composing in the ancient tongues, with constant

Johnson's birthplace (1), St. Mary's Church (3), and the market place, Lichfield. Engraving from a drawing by Stringer (1785), in the William Salt Library, Stafford.

View from Stowe to the cathedral. A favorite walk of Samuel Johnson. Sepia drawing (1841) by John Buckler, in the William Salt Library, Stafford.

Supposed to be Michael Johnson. Engraved in 1835 by E. Finden from a drawing then in the possession of the publisher John Murray. See note 1, Illustrations.

recourse to the "rod" as a means of stimulating attention, the English schools turned out a long succession of scholars and dolts. The capabilities of the individual student made the difference. For his part Sam Johnson thrived under the system.

As the generations came and went, only the textbooks changed. There were new ways of teaching the same old grammar, new devices to help pupils through the age-old knotty problems. The "black letter" introductions disappeared, to be replaced by more modern explanations. There were better exercises, more attractive selections of readings. But that was all.

The entering student, even before he had any knowledge of the language, was forced to memorize the rules in Latin. Then he was gradually taught to parse and construe. He was brought to read the simplest ancient authors — fables and childish stories. Through classroom drill and prolonged examinations the precepts were slowly beaten into his head.

The chief text which Sam and the others used was a later version of William Lily's famous *Grammar*. By the eighteenth century the current editions had more of the commentary in English, but the regimen of memorizing the rules as stated in Lily's Latin verses still persisted. Lily believed that a boy would remember a rule better if it were put in jingling verse. And so generations of pupils learned about nouns and verbs and participles in this way, and the various sections became known colloquially by their first phrases. The section on nouns was referred to simply as "Propria quae Maribus," and that on verbs as "As in Praesenti."

"Propria quae Maribus," Johnson recalled, he could repeat very easily. "I used to repeat it to my mother and Tom Johnson; and remember, that I once went as far as the middle of the paragraph, 'Mascula dicuntur monosyllaba,' in a dream." Tom was Andrew Johnson's son, a young lad of about fifteen or sixteen, who at this time lived with his uncle Michael and apparently served as an apprentice at the parchment factory. Doubtless Sam was happy to impress his older but less erudite cousin by mouthing the newly acquired Latin phrases. Even at this early stage Johnson had pronounced likes and dislikes. "To learn *Quae*

Genus was to me always pleasing; and *As in Praesenti* was, I know not why, always disgusting."

Once the rules had been learned by rote, the process was reversed, and the boys were required to parse and construe, using simple examples given in the textbooks. Much of the parsing was done out of Charles Hoole's *Terminationes,* first published in 1650. Sometimes, Sam remembered, the class proceeded "in order of the rules, and sometimes, particularly in *As in Praesenti,* taking words as they occurred in the index."

Many years later, through curiosity, Johnson looked over some of the texts he had used as a boy. To his surprise he found very few sentences which he would have recognized had he run across them in other books. "That which is read without pleasure is not often recollected nor infixed by conversation, and therefore in a great measure drops from the memory. Thus it happens that those who are taken early from school, commonly lose all that they had learned."

Under Hawkins the first part of the week was given over to memory work and constant drill; then on Thursday the pupils were examined on what they had learned. Because there were no new assignments for that day, and because the questions were usually ones which had been asked over and over again, the boys eagerly looked forward to Thursday. Saturday, too, was a day of examination, at which time they might also be expected to recite the Catechism. Having been brought up strictly in a devout household, Sam was startled to find that his schoolmate George Hector, the younger son of the "man-midwife" who had brought him into the world, had never been taught his Catechism.

When being examined, the boys were required to give the paradigms of verbs, going through the same person in all moods and tenses. At the start Sam found this particularly difficult. "I was once very anxious about the next day, when this exercise was to be performed, in which I had failed till I was discouraged. My mother encouraged me, and I proceeded better. When I told her of my good escape, 'We often,' said she, dear mother! 'come off best, when we are most afraid.'" He further recalled that when his mother asked him about making paradigms, he answered that he "did not form them in an ugly shape." "You could not," said she, "speak plain; and I was proud that I had a boy who was forming verbs."

Other assignments included the memorizing of passages from the Latin version of Aesop's Fables, or from some of the colloquies of Mathurin Cordier, the sixteenth-century French pedagogue. These last were standard fare for English schoolboys. A character in Fielding's *Tom Jones* once exploded, "And there's Corderius, another d——d son of a whore that hath got me many a flogging." [7] Yet, like the rest of his early instruction, Sam could remember few of the actual details of what he had memorized of Corderius or Aesop, except "a passage in one of the Morals, where it is said of some man, that, when he hated another, he made him rich." This he repeated emphatically in his mother's hearing, "who could never conceive that riches could bring any evil. She remarked it, as I expected." Perhaps Sarah's failure to understand the paradox of how wealth could be a curse was more the result of bitter personal experience than of too little mental acuteness. [8] In any event, the only thing Johnson recalled from his early memorizing was his reaction to what he considered his mother's narrow intellectual outlook.

For clever students the constant repetitions and review and the periods of waiting while other groups in the different forms recited naturally proved tedious. John Milton complained of the long hours spent in learning rules, time which would have been passed much better in reading books filled with solid information and true wisdom. He thought it a mistake to spend seven or eight years "in scraping together so much miserable Latin and Greek, as might be learned otherwise easily and delightfully in one year." [9] There is no direct evidence that Johnson similarly rebelled at the slow pace. Apparently he accepted the fact that acquiring the rudiments must be a dull process. No doubt he shuffled his feet, whispered to his neighbors, and daydreamed along with the rest of the boys. But it was not for him to question the established order, and years later when he was setting up his own school he introduced no revolutionary changes.

Unlike many schoolboys, Sam looked forward with pleasure to

the week or ten days of examinations at the end of term. With his keen mind and photographic memory, there was nothing in tests to frighten him. Anything which removed the drudgery of homework was to be eagerly welcomed.

During these years Sam's closest friend was Edmund Hector, nephew of the doctor, who lived nearby in Sadler Street. Although Edmund was more than a year older, they were for many terms in the same class. In and out of school they were inseparable, and from Hector come the most intimate and revealing accounts of Johnson's boyhood.[10] Together the two boys bought tarts from Dame Reid; together they roamed about the streets and neighboring fields.

Because of his bad eyesight, Sam refused to join in many of the popular sports (he could never have caught a ball). Yet he remarked to Boswell "how wonderfully well he had contrived to be idle without them." [11] Actually he had inherited the large, rugged frame of an athlete, and on both sides of his family there was a tradition of manly strength. Michael Johnson was tall and rawboned. His brother Andrew, Sam's uncle, as a bookseller's apprentice in London had been celebrated as a boxer and wrestler. One year he successfully held the ring at Smithfield against all comers. According to one account, Andrew taught his nephew to box, so that Sam was always well able to take care of himself in a fight.[12]

There was athletic prowess on his mother's side also. Her brother, Cornelius Ford, while taking a journey once stopped along the wayside to read an inscription which had been set up in honor of a man who had made a certain leap near that spot. As Johnson told the story to Mrs. Thrale, "Why says my uncle I can leap it in my boots — and he did accordingly leap it in his boots." [13]

Sam himself took great delight in jumping. It was one thing he could do well. He loved to vault over the stile leading into Levett's Field and to sail over other fence posts. Even when he was over seventy years old, the memory of that boyish pleasure was still strong. The story is told that in Lichfield in 1781, when returning from a walk, he was accosted by a friend who asked him how far he had been. "The Doctor replied, he had gone round Mr. Levett's field (the place where the scholars play) in search of a rail that he used to jump over when a boy; 'and,' says the Doctor in a transport of joy, 'I have been so fortunate as to find it. I stood,' said he, 'gazing upon it some time with a degree of rapture, for it brought to my mind all my juvenile sports and pastimes, and at length I determined to try my skill and dexterity; I laid aside my hat and wig, pulled off my coat, and leapt over it twice.' " [14]

Tree climbing was another diversion which did not depend on good eyes, and when he was in his fifties he astonished Frances Reynolds and some other ladies and gentlemen by the ease with which he was able to swarm up a large tree in the grounds of Gunnersbury House. He would have gone right up into the high branches, Miss Reynolds records, "had he not been very earnestly entreated to descend; and down he came with a triumphant air, seeming *to make nothing of it.*" [15]

Though he could not surpass his comrades at most of their sports, he was able to dominate them by the force of his personality, just as later he did the members of the club at the Turk's Head. He had early learned that if he was to excel it must be intellectually. Denied physical attractions and skill at games, with no inherited wealth or social position, he knew he could be looked up to only because of the superiority of his mind and pen.

As so often happens to children who feel insecurity at home, it became more and more natural for him to rule elsewhere. He never let his companions see him studying, but, with his keen memory, took pride in astonishing them by the ease with which he could do his work. Hector, indeed, was impressed by the way in which he seemed to learn by intuition the contents of a book.[16] On every possible occasion he showed off his mental powers. As a result, the boys openly respected him, and he was able to lure them into all sorts of menial services in return for his help. Hector later described what happened: "As his uncommon abilities for learning far exceeded us, we endeavored by every boyish piece of flattery to gain his assistance, and three of us, by turns, used to call on him in a morning, on one of whose backs, supported by the other two, he rode triumphantly to school." And in winter when Stowe Pool was frozen over, he delighted in making one of the boys pull off stockings and shoes and fasten a garter around him and draw him along the ice.

In the late spring of 1719, at Whitsuntide, the happy days under Hawkins came to an end, and Sam's class was moved into the upper school. The promotion, which was unexpected, came about in this way. The sons of Lichfield citizens had the right to free education at the school. But there were others who did pay. The masters had long ago learned that they could scarcely subsist on their salaries and on allowances from the local Conduit Trust, and consequently accepted day students from outside the city limits, who were charged fees. By the seventeenth century they had also begun the practice of taking in as boarders the sons of substantial gentlemen from some distance away. Since these last often paid at the rate of fifty pounds a year, it was inevitable that the needs of the town boys should be sacrificed in order that the master could devote most of his energies to the boarders. By the time Sam entered the school this practice had become notorious. John Hunter, who was then headmaster, had built up a large clientele from county families from all over the Midlands. According to one possibly exaggerated report, Hunter once had nearly a hundred boarders living with him and under his tuition.[17] In order to accommodate them all he took over several neighboring houses and used them as dormitories.

In concentrating on the needs of his well-to-do students, Hunter had developed the scheme of keeping the town boys in the lower school as long as he could. Naturally, this rankled in the hearts of the city fathers, and finally Richard Wakefield, the town clerk, registered a strong protest. It proved successful, and in the spring of 1719, "sooner than had been the custom," Sam and ten others were transferred to the upper school. Of all those involved in the change only two seriously showed any regret: Hawkins, the poor usher, for whom it meant some reduction in fees, and Sam, who wept at leaving his beloved teacher.

All this would have been excitement enough, but coinciding with the change came another memorable event — his first long trip away from both parents.[18] It was time, Sarah felt, that her two boys should have new experiences, and during the holidays in late May, Sam, aged nine and a half, and Natty, aged six and a half, were sent to Birmingham to visit her relatives. There they stayed for something over a fortnight, dividing their time between the homes of her brother Nathaniel Ford, the clothier, and brother-in-law John Harrison, the saddler, who had left Lichfield some years before.

Most of the visit was spent at the Fords', where they were much "caressed" by their aunt, "a good-natured, coarse woman, easy of converse, but willing to find something to censure in the absent." Here occurred the earliest recorded example of Sam's gluttony, an incident which evidently became a byword in the family. "At my aunt Ford's I eat so much of a boiled leg of mutton, that she used to talk of it. My mother, who had lived in a narrow sphere, and was then affected by little things, told me seriously that it would hardly ever be forgotten. Her mind, I think, was afterward much enlarged, or greater evils wore out the care of less."

His uncle John Harrison was a widower, whose house was kept by his niece, Sally Ford, "a young woman of such sweetness of temper, that I used to say she had no fault." A pleasant playmate in the household was Harrison's daughter Phoebe, who was within a few months of Sam's age. Yet, despite the attractions of Sally and Phoebe, the boys were not completely happy there. "My uncle Harrison did not much like us, nor did we like him. He was a very mean and vulgar man, drunk every night, but drunk with little drink, very peevish, very proud, very ostentatious, but, luckily, not rich."

Harrison's shop was in the High Street, next door to the Castle Inn and directly opposite the bookseller's shop of Andrew Johnson. Although visiting his mother's relatives, Sam undoubtedly saw something of his father's brother, the erstwhile boxer. Andrew had fallen on evil days. With an ailing third wife, who had run up large doctor's bills, he was chiefly preoccupied with staying out of debtor's prison.

Only a short distance away in the High Street was a mercer's shop, where lived Harry Porter, with his wife Elizabeth and their two children.[19] Sam and Mrs. Porter may have passed each other often on the street, or even met in a neighbor's house. How incredulous they would have been had someone jokingly suggested that someday there might be a closer relationship — that this boy of nine and the matron of thirty would actually become man and wife! Perhaps it is just as well that such a vision sixteen years into the future was denied them.

Sam always retained vivid memories of this trip to Birmingham. Although he later wondered "why such boys were sent to trouble other houses," it was exhilarating to be away from parental authority. He showed his independence by insisting on staying for a few days even after the school vacation was over, and writing home in a peremptory fashion that he "desired the horses to come on Thursday of the first school week; and then, and not till then, they should be welcome to go." In the end, however, came the inevitable humiliation. "When my father came to fetch us home, he told the ostler that he had twelve miles home, and two boys under his care. This offended me." Michael had a fatal facility for irritating his son.

As so often happens, strange isolated details connected with this trip stuck in Sam's memory — the rattle on his whip, with which he was so pleased that he wrote home about it to his mother, the fact that his father was carrying a watch which he had merely on approval, and which he had to give back when the day came to pay for it. And there was the recollection of the first time he was ever aware of the power of concentration. Even during holidays there were school exercises to be done as homework. Since he knew he would be returning late for the beginning of term, Sam evidently did one while visiting at the Harrisons'. "I was writing at the kitchen windows, as I thought, alone, and turning my head saw Sally dancing. I went on without notice, and had finished almost without perceiving that any time had elapsed." But such close attention, he was forced to confess, he was seldom able to approach again.

On his return from Birmingham, Sam began work under a new teacher, a young usher of twenty-four, the Rev. Edward Holbrooke, whom he found to be a "peevish and ill-tempered man" and a sad contrast to Hawkins. To be sure, Sam's friend John Taylor long afterward called Holbrooke "one of the most ingenious men, best scholars, and best preachers of his age," but Taylor may have been thinking of his later career.[20] Only three years out of Cambridge, Holbrooke failed to impress his pupils with any wide knowledge. On one occasion the boys perceived that the usher did not know the meaning of a Latin phrase; and on another, when sent up to the upper master to be punished, they complained that when they had tried to get assistance from the usher he had refused to help them. Once suspected of ignorance and lack of interest, Holbrooke must have found it difficult to keep the respect of his pupils.

At the time of their removal to the upper school, Sam's class appears to have been somewhat behind common practice elsewhere, for they were still reading Aesop and doing exercises in Garretson. As a help with the latter, a friend gave Sam a collection of Latin words and phrases designed for putting English into Latin. Although it was soon lost or stolen at school, the little book did leave one vivid memory. With typical intellectual honesty Sam remembered that from it he had taken the word *inliciturus,* which he did not understand but used anyway.

Sam heartily disliked doing the assignments, even though once started he could do them easily. He worked by fits and starts — one exercise done quickly, then after a long delay, the rest completed in a burst of speed — all of which kept his mother puzzled and worried. Sometimes in a perverse fashion he refused to show the master all that he had done. Once, having completed twenty-five exercises, while others in the class had done only sixteen, he kept five of them hidden for a long time in a drawer in his father's shop.

His recollection of the system of teaching in the upper school was not as distinct as of the lower. Gone was the pleasant freedom from grammatical exercises on Thursdays and Saturdays. Now they began writing Latin prose following the syntax, and at midday learned how to punctuate their exercises. They continued translating the artificially constructed dialogues of the German philologist, Christopher Helvicus, in order to learn vocabulary, but Sam remembered that they worked at them with little progress.

The class soon left Aesop behind and began to read in Phaedrus, which was the only book they memorized to the end. He recalled the fable of the wolf and the lamb, *"to my draught — that I may drink,"* and the length of the assignments. "In the latter part thirty lines were expected for a lesson. What reconciles masters to long lessons is the pleasure of tasking." It was Phaedrus that brought Sam under the eye of John Hunter, the dreaded headmaster, and twice the class was sent up to him to be punished. Later it became the practice every Friday afternoon for them to recite to Hunter what they had learned.

All readers of Boswell are familiar with the methods of this stern disciplinarian.[21] "Very severe, and wrongheadedly severe," Johnson called him, and the memory of his brutality was never forgotten. He "used to beat us unmercifully," Johnson commented, and in retrospect came to the conclusion that the master's chief error was "in not making a distinction between mistake and negligence; for he would beat a boy equally for not knowing a thing, as for neglecting to know it." Hunter would ask a boy a question "and, if he did not answer it, he beat him, without considering whether he had an opportunity of knowing how to answer it." What need was there for a teacher if the pupils could answer every question?

While he wielded the rod, Hunter used to say, "And this I do to save you from the gallows," a sardonic joke which may be a little more comprehensible if we remember that according to the penal code of the day there were a hundred and sixty separate offenses which could be punished by hanging. The standard procedure was for the boy to lean over the three-legged "flogging horse," with his stomach on the top of the horse. Other boys held down his arms while the master whipped his posterior. If the punishment was also intended as a disgrace, the boy's trousers were taken down, for exposing the bare skin was considered a shameful humiliation.

Johnson's dislike of Hunter did not stem from any conviction that the method was wrong. Once when a schoolmaster in his presence bragged of the abolition of flogging, Johnson commented, "Sir, I am afraid that what they gain at one end, they will lose at the other." [22] Hunter, he felt, exceeded what was necessary. "He was not severe, Sir. A master ought to be severe. Sir, he was cruel." Yet Johnson well knew what he owed to his master. When asked one day by Bennet Langton how he had acquired such an accurate knowledge of Latin, he replied, "My master whipped me very well. Without that, Sir, I should have done nothing." And he himself always preferred physical punishment to other, less direct methods. To Boswell he insisted that he would rather "have the rod to be the general terror to all, to make them learn, than tell a child, if you do thus, or thus, you will be more esteemed than your brothers and sisters. The rod produces an effect which terminates in itself. A child is afraid of being whipped, and gets his task, and there's an end on't; whereas, by exciting emulation and comparisons of superiority, you lay the foundation of lasting mischief; you make brothers and sisters hate each other."

Johnson's punishments at school were seldom the result of faulty scholarship or lack of understanding. He had such a tenacious memory that with very little work he could keep well ahead of his fellow students. His troubles were matters of deportment. As Hector remembered, "I never knew him corrected at school, unless it was for talking and diverting other boys from their business, by which, perhaps, he might hope to keep his ascendancy." And another pupil long afterward described Sam as "a long, lank, lounging boy, whom he distinctly remembered to have been punished by Hunter for idleness." [23]

The boys soon found ways of placating the wrath of the headmaster. Hunter was a sportsman as well as a scholar, and if a culprit could slyly inform his offended master where a covey of partridges was to be found, he might be sure of a speedy pardon. [24]

Hunter was much more than a boorish wielder of the birch. He was a cultivated man. He had a taste for music, and in the evenings kept his right arm limber by playing the bass viol. At least one of his pupils remembered him as "an excellent master," and his reputation for scholarship was widespread. Moreover, he continued to have an active interest in his pupils, even after their schooldays were over, and his house and table were freely open to "old boys" who might drop in.

Among the younger boys, however, his stern look, his pompous formality — he never appeared in the schoolroom "without his gown and cassock, and his wig full dressed" — and his ready recourse to the rod, kept him from being popular. Even the fact that Hunter was an ardent High-Churchman did not render his memory less terrifying to Johnson, and he later confessed that he could tremble at the mere sight of Hunter's granddaughter, Anna Seward, because she looked so like her grandfather.[25]

Just as he comes to his schooling under Hunter, Johnson's account of his early years breaks off. For the next six years there is nothing to draw on except random references, and only by guessing is it possible to tell anything about the subsequent curriculum. Doubtless, as in similar schools in England, the Lichfield boys proceeded through Ovid, Cato, and Cicero, with Terence and Erasmus thrown in as examples of more colloquial Latin. In time there would have been an introduction, at least, to Greek grammar, and readings from the Greek testament. There might even have been some translation of the Greek poets Hesiod, Pindar, and Theocritus. In the later forms, certainly Virgil and Horace, and perhaps some Persius and Juvenal, would have been used to inspire poetic fire.

Like others in every century, the Lichfield boys devised various means of getting out of work and were particularly proud of their way of hiding the forbidden "cribs" and "ponies." As an old man, Johnson visited the Grammar School and delighted to show Mr. Price, the headmaster, "a nook in the schoolroom, where it was usual for the boys to secrete the translations of the books they were reading." [26]

In order to lessen the labor of translation, the boys also had other schemes. It was the practice for one boy to get the lesson and then teach the rest. Sam, however, would not join in, preferring, despite his constitutional laziness, to do all his own work. It was not, we are told, that he had any moral scruples at the time, but rather that his feelings had been hurt by another boy's having once refused to assist him. As a result, Sam resolved to be independent, a decision he rigorously held to until near the end of his school career.[27] This did not mean that he refused to help others with their lessons. "Verses or themes he would dictate to his favorites, but he would never be at the trouble of writing them."

Since no old records for the Grammar School exist, it is impossible to name Johnson's school companions with certainty. But from other evidence a considerable list can be put together of boys who were under Hunter at the same time.[28] In a one-room school Sam would have been well acquainted with pupils much older than himself. Among these were Isaac Hawkins Browne, the elder, a minor poet whose conversation Johnson later much admired; Robert James, the inventor of the celebrated fever powders; and, for a short time, "Tom" Newton, ultimately Bishop of Bristol. More nearly his own age were John Eardley Wilmot, who was knighted and became Chief Justice of the Common Pleas; Charles Congreve, the future Archdeacon of Armagh, whose final almost comatose state of mind under the influence of a daily bottle of port disgusted Johnson; William Bailye, apothecary; Andrew Corbet, son of a well-to-do country gentleman; and Theophilus Lowe, a rival "town boy," son of a local plumber, who showed early scholarly promise but eventually settled down as a respected and amiable clergyman.

All these were eminently respectable in later life, and thus easily traced. Others, less successful, are more shadowy. Yet Johnson retained just as affectionate a regard for them. There was Harry Jackson, a "low man, dull and untaught," red-faced and unkempt, with whom Johnson and Boswell dined at Lichfield in 1776.[29] Never a snob, Johnson was still fond of this sad failure, because of their old associations.

Of Hunter's "boarders" the one whose friendship was the strongest and most enduring was John Taylor, son of an Ashbourne attorney. Although he was several years younger, he and Sam became fast friends, and even their widely divergent tastes and points of view never drove them apart.

From Taylor comes corroboration of Sam's idleness at school, of his rivalry with Theophilus Lowe, of Charles Congreve's continued dislike, of the eminence of Hunter and his ushers. Boswell was a trifle suspicious of some of his anecdotes and ignored, perhaps rightly, one account of a quarrel between Taylor and Johnson over some silly verses.[30] According to the story, at breakfast at the school one day, Taylor repeated before Mrs. Hunter and some of the boys a jingling epigram:

> Here lies honest Sam as quiet's a lamb
> Who in his life ne'er did much evil
> His bones are here laid but his soul I'm afraid
> Is gone to the highroad of the devil.

Because he was a day student and had his breakfast at home, Sam was not present, but when one of the boys told him what had happened he was very angry. He hated to be talked about behind his back, or to have the future of his soul jested about, even in so absurd a manner. In telling the story long afterward to Boswell, Taylor insisted that he had not known the authorship of the verses, but the suspicion remains that the clumsy piece was his.

Despite a negligent pose and lounging manner, Sam was always eager to excel. He was never willing to have other students best him in intellectual concerns, and he saw to it that boys and masters alike knew his worth. Yet the only record of his winning a prize is the statement by Hawkins that as a reward for some Latin verses Johnson was once given a guinea by the Earl of Berkshire, one of the patrons of the school.[31] Nevertheless, Johnson made it clear to Boswell that he had been distinguished above the others. "They never thought to raise me by comparing me to anyone; they never said, Johnson is as good a scholar as such a one; but such a one is as good a scholar as Johnson." It was only the other "town boy," Lowe, who was ever so compared, and Johnson quickly added, "I do not think he was as good a scholar." [32]

Despite his superiority in school, he much preferred the long vacations, when he and Hector would idle away the hours sauntering in the fields.[33] As they rambled, Sam talked, more often to himself than to his companion. Talking to himself became a habit which stayed with him to the end of his days.

Rarely during the holidays could he bring himself to do anything about assigned schoolwork. Hector vividly described his attitude: "His dislike to business was so great, that he would procrastinate his exercises to the last hour. I have known him after a long vacation, in which we were rather severely tasked, return to school an hour earlier in the morning, and begin one of his exercises, in which he purposely left some faults, in order to gain time to finish the rest." Johnson always had an aversion to the practice of setting tasks to be done out of school term. He told Mrs. Thrale that "he had never ceased representing to all the eminent schoolmasters in England, the absurd tyranny of poisoning the hour of permitted pleasure, by keeping future misery before the children's eyes, and tempting them by bribery or falsehood to evade it." [34]

Everywhere through the records of Johnson's early years runs the theme of procrastination. The hardest thing he ever had to do was to force himself to get down to work. As he often confessed, repeated resolutions were useless. So he wrote on his birthday in 1764, allowing himself rather remarkable precocity, "I have now spent fifty-five years in resolving, having from the earliest time almost that I can remember been forming schemes of a better life." [35] And to Boswell he admitted, "I have been trying to cure laziness all my life, and could not do it." The trouble was too deep-seated to be eradicated by mere wishing.

One way his sluggishness showed itself, he thought, was in his inability to get up at a reasonable hour in the morning. His later prayers are filled with resolutions for early rising and with shamefaced admissions of failure. He was still keeping up the struggle when at the age of sixty-five he wrote, "As my life has from my earliest years been wasted in a morning bed my purpose is from Easter day to rise early, not later than eight." [36] Yet the more he resolved, the more fixed the difficulty became. Sometimes his inner struggle became so intense that he sank almost into a state of inertia. He once told his friend John Paradise that occasionally he had been "so languid and inefficient, that he could not distinguish the hour upon the town clock." [37]

Without more evidence it is difficult to tell whether the original cause was glandular or neurotic. Every time he reproached himself for what he thought was a moral weakness, he nourished a sense of guilt. Yet this same sense of guilt was at least partly responsible for his condition. Thus there was a never-ending circle of tormenting cause and effect. Happily the inherent toughness of his mental and physical fabric was so great that he was never wholly destroyed by this condition. If he sometimes felt near the edge of breakdown, he was always able to drag himself back.

Genealogists like the late Aleyn Lyell Reade find a ready explanation in the intricate strands of his family inheritance.[38] On his father's side there was a record of morbidity and instability. Sam's grandfather, his father, and his uncles were ultimately all failures, with deficiencies of character that frustrated whatever natural ability they possessed. On his mother's side there was solidity and balance and a tradition of sanity and competent success. It is likely that Sam's sturdy residual strength, which saw him through those later dark days, came from the Fords. In his teens there was no immediate danger of a breakdown, and it is doubtful if much of his trouble was apparent to his companions. They probably thought him a rather queer sort — brilliant, but moody and eccentric. He was all right if handled cautiously and given his head.

Unfortunately, the few surviving records of the attitude of his contemporaries were perhaps too much colored by later events. At one extreme there is the story that Johnson in his school days "had the appearance of idiocy, and the sons of a gentleman in the town were reprimanded for bringing home with them that disagreeable driveler." [39] At the other, there is the reputed prediction made by William Butt, another Lichfield citizen who had several sons about Sam's age. Overhearing his children scornfully speaking of Sam as "the great boy," Butt supposedly remarked, "You call him the great boy, but take my word for it, he will one day prove a great man." [40] More likely at this time there were few in Lichfield who took much interest in the ungainly and strong-willed Grammar School boy.

CHAPTER IV

The Bookseller's Boy

S AM learned to read and write Latin and was introduced to the principal Greek and Roman classics at the Grammar School. But there was much more to be absorbed at home. As the child of a bookseller, he had unique opportunities. Whenever he wanted to he could rummage about in his father's shop, pick out any volume which caught his eye, and casually turn its pages. If he wished, he could take it up to his bedroom on the floor above or, in cold weather, down to the basement kitchen, where there was a fire. This warm spot was the center of family life. Thrifty tradesmen did not have fires in the parlor except on Sunday.[1]

Although there is no detailed record of his early reading, we do in a general way know something of his tastes. After the childish tales of giants and ogres had begun to pall, he speedily moved on to stories on a slightly higher level. According to Bishop Percy, Johnson as a boy was immoderately fond of romances of chivalry, a preference which he retained throughout life.[2] By his ninth year he had fallen under the spell of Shakespeare. One day when he was reading *Hamlet* in the kitchen, he was so powerfully moved by the ghost scene that he suddenly rushed upstairs to the street door in order to see people about him.[3] His imaginative involvement in what he read was so great that Cordelia's death in *King Lear* came as a terrific shock. Horrified by this apparent violation of poetic justice, he could not force himself to reread the last scenes of the play until many years afterward, when the dull duties of an editor made it necessary.

From all accounts he had no settled plan, being content to nibble whatever came his way by chance. The manner in which he came to read Petrarch was characteristic.[4] In a preface to another work he had seen this author referred to as the "restorer of poetry," a phrase which aroused his curiosity. Sometime later, as he was searching the upper shelves of the shop for apples which he suspected his brother had hidden behind the books, he came upon a copy of Petrarch's works. His search forgotten, he was at once absorbed in the new-found treasure.

Another time he found a little notebook containing an account of Lichfield Cathedral, the death of Lord Brooke, and various ecclesiastical matters. In order to check the date and the source of this anonymous manuscript, Sam compared the names given to Lichfield streets with those in two earlier printed histories and jotted down his findings on the inside of the cover.[5]

Though he browsed widely, he never studied conscientiously. Seldom did he read a book through. He dipped, he sampled, he skimmed, as the impulse led him. He read for pleasure, not as a task, and because he chose only what he liked he always felt that he received more profit. Imposed assignments might be speedily forgotten; a boy's own discoveries remained fresh and happy memories. His inability to do sustained work was part and parcel of his emotional difficulties. He could never concentrate on anything for long periods. As he once confessed to Boswell, he had from his earliest days "loved to read poetry but hardly ever read any poem to an end." [6] And his scorn of others who tediously insisted on completing what they had started is proverbial.

In later life he used to advise young people "never to be without a little book in their pocket to read at by times when they had nothing else to do." It was by this means, he added, that most of his own knowledge had been acquired. Obviously he did not delight in lengthy volumes. He remarked that there were only three books that readers ever wished longer than they were: *Don Quixote, Robinson Crusoe,* and *Pilgrim's Progress.*[7]

Gradually he learned to read with amazing rapidity, appearing to take in an entire page from top to bottom almost at a glance. And when questioned he could repeat the gist of what he had skimmed. He developed, says Boswell, "a peculiar facility in seizing at once what was valuable in any book, without submitting to the labor of perusing it from beginning to end." [8] It might almost be said that the rapacity with which he dug into a book was only equaled by the speed with which he put it down.

As he read he kept himself in constant motion. According to William Shaw, who obtained his information from Dr. Swinfen's daughter, Johnson "never thought, recollected, or studied, whether in his closet, or in the street, alone, or in company, without putting his huge unwieldy body, in the same rolling, awkward posture, in which he was in use, while conning his grammar, or construing his lesson, to sit on the form at school." [9] Another witness described his convulsive movements when reading by saying that his head "swung seconds." With a book close before his eyes, and swaying with his peculiar rhythm, he moved from one cramped position to another in the crowded shop.

How much literary guidance Sam received from his father it is impossible to tell. Michael was too busy to do much reading himself, and when at home, he was harassed by numerous business problems. Once he put into his son's hands a copy of Martin Martin's *Description of the Western Islands of Scotland,* an act for which he deserves our gratitude, since it first roused the boy's curiosity about the Hebrides.[10] Michael may also have been responsible for furthering in his son other interests in geography. Still in existence is a copy of *Visscher's Atlas* in which Sam numbered the pages and laboriously wrote out a table of contents at the back.[11]

About the shop he would have picked up all sorts of literary gossip — from chance remarks of his father or from arguments with the customers. For the future author of the *Lives of the Poets* this was invaluable training. Indeed, it is impossible to estimate how much of his intimate knowledge of seventeenth-century authors came merely from keeping his ears open during his early years. One remark which made a deep impression was Michael's vivid recollection of the enormous sale of Dryden's *Absalom and Achitophel.*[12]

Michael probably kept no records of what passed through his shop, and the turnover at times may have been fairly rapid. A constant stream of new and old books arrived from the London printers and publishers, many of them to be passed on immediately to customers in Lichfield and in neighboring towns. There would have been packages of secondhand volumes, or small private libraries brought in to be appraised, broken up, and sold — the collections of country clergymen or literate tradesmen.

Michael's most extensive investment, so far as is known, was made in September, 1706, some years before Sam's birth. It was then that he purchased the complete library of the ninth Earl of Derby, at least 2,900 volumes, mainly huge folios of church fathers and French history.[13] In order to offer this "great and noble" library for general sale, Michael prepared a catalogue — of which, however, no copy has survived.

Although Michael's main shop was in his home, he is known to have had branches, or at least to have set up his stall, in neighboring towns on market days. On the title page of one of his publishing ventures there is the statement that the work was to be had at his "shops at Lichfield and Uttoxeter, in Staffordshire, and Ashby-de-la-Zouch, in Leicestershire." [14] On occasion he may also have had temporary establishments at Birmingham, Burton, Abbots Bromley, and other places. Further details about his customary procedure come from a series of letters from Sir William Boothby of Ashbourne.[15] Though they were written long before Sam's birth, they undoubtedly describe conditions and methods which persisted in later years. While Sam was growing up there would have been other customers like Sir William, whose problems and complaints would have been much the same.

An avid reader and collector, the baronet kept the young Lichfield bookseller busy with orders and queries. Each week Michael dispatched a parcel of books to Sir William, some twenty-five miles away. They were evidently "on approval," for he was permitted to send back any he did not want. The usual plan was for the parcels to be picked up by one of Sir William's servants at Uttoxeter, only ten miles from Ashbourne, where Michael set up his stall every Wednesday. This saved time and expense. Delivery, however, was ever a problem, and Sir William asked that his parcels be made up before Michael left Lichfield, "for you are in that hurry at Uttoxeter as not to be able to do it there — and so he

I appoint to bring them doth not, but you send them by some other hand which is a great uncertainty and charge."

Always waiting impatiently for the next parcel, Sir William could not restrain his disappointment when none arrived. "Not hearing from you last Wednesday," he once wrote, "I thought you had neglected me and I have chid Tho. Levett and I have marked in your catalogue some few with the letter B——." Two months later he again complained: "I am afraid you grow weary of my custom, for I never have received any books from you since you was here. . . . I would not have you fail of sending something new every week."

Sir William begrudged every interruption. "My company is gone so that now I hope to enjoy my self and books again which are the true pleasures of my life all else is but vanity and noise." He was not narrow in his tastes. During the years covered by the surviving correspondence, hundreds of titles are mentioned specifically — history, biography, theology, and some poetry and drama.

There were always troubles of one sort or another. Sir William kept protesting about the imperfections of Michael's bookbinding: "Your books do open very ill so that it is troublesome reading pray mend this great fault." The workmanship was often slipshod, with weak boards, small lettering, and narrow margins, even cutting into the print. There were occasional grumbles, too, about the prices: " I find you exceed in the prices and must abate or else we shall fall out," and "I take notice you rise much in your rates. . . . I find you use me best at first." Nevertheless, relations between seller and purchaser were evidently cordial, since Sir William signs himself, not formally, but "your friend."

A provincial bookseller had to be a jack-of-all-trades. He not only sold books and stationery, patent medicines, and house furnishings, but also served as a traveling "question and answer man." He was expected to give his customers help on all manner of problems. Thus Michael was consulted by the baronet about the selection of a private secretary who knew Latin and had a good writing hand; and on the subject of a schoolmaster for Sir

William's son. Moreover, there were scores of others who expected the same kind of aid. Everywhere he rode Michael brought advice, as well as books in his saddlebags.

Over thirty years later he was still keeping his customers supplied with instruction. On St. Peter's Day in 1716 the Rev. George Plaxton, chaplain to Lord Gower, wrote from Trentham: "Johnson, the Lichfield librarian, is now here; he propagates learning all over this diocese, and advanceth knowledge to its just height; all the clergy here are his pupils, and suck all they have from him; Allen cannot make a warrant without his precedent, nor our quondam John Evans draw a recognizance *sine directione Michaelis."* [16] Yet too much must not be read into this tribute to Michael's scholarly ability, for Plaxton was an inveterate joker and sardonic wit. While the reference does bear witness to the bookseller's general knowledge of Latin, the point of the ironic remark is the ignorance of the clergy in the neighborhood.

Michael himself was not much given to levity. His tastes were serious. The books he published — for on occasion he acted as a kind of publisher, arranging for the printing and marketing of the manuscripts of friends and customers — were sober works of instruction and piety. Merely the titles of a few will be enough to show their character: Sir John Floyer's *Touchstone of Medicines* and *The Preternatural State of Animal Humors Described,* Samuel Shaw's *Syncritical Grammar,* and John Bradley's *An Impartial View of the Truth of Christianity, with the History of the Life and Miracles of Apollonius Tyanaeus.* [17]

How Michael transported his stock in trade to exhibit in the provincial towns is not known. There were various means he could have used — horseback, special wagon, or public carriers. The records of the local turnpike trust, of which Michael served his turn as trustee, show that there was a continual traffic between Lichfield and nearby places of wagons, carts, and pack horses. He would never have had to wait long for transport in any direction.

There is a tradition at Uttoxeter that he reserved a room at the Red Lion Inn, just opposite the location of his stall, where he stayed when in town, and where he kept his supplies between the

Wednesday markets. The actual place, known as "Mr. Johnson's room," fitted out with shelves and cabinets suitable for storing books, was for many years pointed out at the inn as being of historical interest.[18] And it is likely that Michael did follow some such procedure in each of the towns where he had a regular stall. It would have been too difficult a task to carry all his stock with him over the miserable country roads, either by horseback or by wagon.

With Wednesdays at Uttoxeter, Mondays or Saturdays (or both) at Ashby-de-la-Zouch, with numerous country gentlemen to visit on the way, Michael spent a large part of his time in the saddle. Sometimes, too, there were longer trips — as far as Scotland and Ireland in search of skins for his parchment business. Sam always thought that this hard exercise in the open air preserved his father's mental and physical health. At least he never had gout.[19]

On occasion the son must have accompanied his father to the nearby towns, to the public auctions, to the fairs, and to country houses. Somewhere in his youth Sam acquired a good "seat," so that in later life he could follow the hounds with his friend Thrale for fifty miles on end and "never own himself either tired or amused." [20] No praise was ever quite so welcome as the remark of William Gerard Hamilton, who called out one day on the Sussex Downs, "Why Johnson rides as well, for aught I see, as the most illiterate fellow in England." Yet he never delighted in riding merely as a pastime, and confessed to Hawkins that he had once gone to sleep in the saddle.

As part of Michael's multifarious activities, he conducted auction sales all over the Midlands — at Gloucester, Tewkesbury, and Evesham, among other places. Happily there is an actual record of one such sale, since a copy of the sale catalogue survived at least into the nineteenth century.[21] Chatty and informal, it tells much about what Michael had to sell and his auctioneering methods. The place was the Talbot in Sidbury, Worcester. "The sale to begin on Friday the 21st of this instant, March [1717–18], exactly at six o'clock in the afternoon, and to continue till all be sold."

Included were specific rules covering disputes between would-be purchasers, the handling of books later found faulty, and the size of the bids. On the back of the title page of the catalogue Michael ingenuously explained his sales approach.

> You must not wonder, that I begin every day's sale with small and common books, the reason is, a room is some time a-filling, and persons of address and business, seldom coming first, they are entertained till we are full: they are never the last books of the best kind of that sort, for ordinary families and young persons, etc. But in the body of the catalogue, you will find law, mathematics, history; and for the learned in divinity, there are Drs. South, Taylor, Tillotson, Beveridge, and Flavel, etc., the best of that kind: And to please the ladies, I have added store of fine pictures and paper hangings, and by the way I would desire them to take notice, that the pictures shall always be put up by the noon of that day they are to be sold, that they may be viewed by daylight.
>
> I have no more, but to wish you pleased, and myself a good sale, who am your humble servant, M. Johnson.

It is obvious that Sam did not acquire his prose style from his father.

Because some of the actual receipted bills exist, it is possible to tell something about Michael's charges for books and for binding them.[22] It cost the "Honored Mrs. Holt," for example, in July, 1718, 2/6 for a copy of Sallust, and 12/ for a three-volume English version of Tacitus. Sermons might be had for as little as threepence, and "Haversham's Speech" was once sold to "Dr. Fowke" for twopence. Important books, of course, came higher. Gilbert Walmesley was willing to pay 13/6 for a lexicon and £1/4/0 for a law book. The cost of binding varied considerably. Magazines or pamphlets might be bound for a shilling, though books were apt to be over twice that amount. Current publications, such as Michael de la Roche's *Memoirs of Literature*, were supplied to customers at a shilling a volume. Michael's bills, scribbled on chance pieces of paper, covered various periods of time, from six months to over a year, and it is evident that they were never very systematically handled.

Michael was forced to do his share of haggling over prices. One customer who insisted on having a book for much less than it was worth, when his other attempts at persuasion failed, "had recourse to one argument, which, he thought, would infallibly prevail: — 'You know, Mr. Johnson, that I buy an almanac of you, every year.' " [23]

A source of increasing irritation and worry was the parchment factory. As part of his stationery business Michael was continually buying hides and skins, the poorer ones being merely tanned and sold as leather. Not having served the usual seven-year apprenticeship, however, Michael was not legally allowed to practice the trade of a tanner, and on October 10, 1717, he was indicted at the Lichfield Quarter Sessions for violating the law.[24] A true bill was returned, and he was ordered to appear at the next court session in January. Through a long series of delaying actions, the case dragged on, probably not being decided until October, 1718.

Michael defended himself by claiming that he had never done any actual tanning, having always turned the skins over to someone properly trained, who was not a hired hand, but had a financial interest in the business. Moreover, he insinuated that the present prosecution was merely one of spite, instigated by a former employee who had recently been passed over in favor of a new man. Because the court records are lost we cannot tell how well the bookseller convinced the jury, but presumably Michael was cleared.

For us the chief importance of the trial lies in the fact that by chance a manuscript copy of Michael's defense, in his own handwriting, has survived. Evidently he was well instructed in legal matters, for he uses the proper forms, with the clauses duly numbered. The draft was originally written in the first person and then changed to the legal third person. The spelling is no more wayward or individual than might be found in informal first drafts by most intelligent people of the day. It is a shrewd presentation of the facts, hurriedly set down.

Some seven years later Michael was again in trouble with the authorities, this time over taxes. In the records of the commis-

sioners of excise there is a letter dated July 27, 1725, written to
the supervisor in Lichfield, complaining of the difficulty of convicting Michael in the local courts.[25] "Since the justices would
not give judgment against Mr. Michael Johnson, *the tanner,* notwithstanding the facts were fairly against him, the Board direct
that the next time he offends, you do not lay an information
against him, but send an affidavit of the fact, that he may be
prosecuted in the Exchequer." It requires little stretch of the
imagination to see in these punitive threats the source of Sam's
later violent feeling about the excise. Besides being generally regarded as a Whig tax, it was one which was a constant nuisance
to a merchant somewhat lax in his business methods. When Johnson came to define "excise" in the *Dictionary* it was possibly the
vivid memory of his father's troubles that made him describe the
collectors as "wretches hired by those to whom excise is paid."

Michael's difficulties did not affect his local reputation. Sympathy appears to have been all on his side. While his suit over
the tanning business was pending, he was elected junior bailiff,
and in 1725, when being investigated by the excisemen, senior
bailiff. It was almost as if he were rewarded with high office
each time he had to defend himself against the law.

With his election as senior bailiff Michael reached the peak
of his career as a public servant. The office, corresponding to our
modern mayor, might be characterized as that of "first citizen" of
Lichfield. According to the charter, the senior bailiff was chosen
each year by the bishop from two or more names submitted by
the Corporation. In 1722 Michael's name had been suggested,
and again in 1724, but each time another candidate was selected.
His colleagues continued to submit his name, and on July 25,
1725, Michael was finally successful.[26]

In the thirteen years since he had first been made a magistrate,
Michael had not been very regular in attending meetings of the
Brethren of the Corporation. The Hall Books show him absent
about half the time. He was rarely present on Wednesday, when he
had to attend market at Uttoxeter. Yet there is no record of his ever
having incurred the usual fine of half a crown for missing a
meeting. The nature of his business evidently brought him a

special dispensation. In July, 1718, when he was first elected junior bailiff, the entry reads: "Mr. Johnson being now at Bristol Fair, day is given him to take the oaths of his office until Friday the first of August next." Yet when he occupied the chief post he conscientiously attended all the official gatherings, being careful to see that none were set for the middle of the week. Indeed, during Michael's term as senior bailiff there was more activity on the part of the Corporation than for many years, though there is no certainty that the new vigor all stemmed from him. There were an unusual number of meetings, or "Common Halls," as they were called, and more new projects, including a better way of handling vagabonds and a new master of the house of correction. The Corporation's very first move during Michael's term was one of economy. A statute was passed forbidding the expenditure from the town funds of any amount ("except on the usual rejoicing days and then the expenses not to exceed forty shillings upon any one day") without the express order of the Corporation. Actually, the Brethren had very little money in the treasury, and the senior bailiff was himself responsible for any spending in excess of income. Thus the new ordinance may have had a double purpose — to curb the zeal of Lichfield citizens who delighted in extra celebrations, and to protect the chief magistrate from any drain on his own pocket.

Michael needed such protection. His election as "first citizen" came at a time when he was beginning to feel the pinch of poverty. Never methodical about money matters, he had now brought his affairs to a difficult position. In 1725 he was four years in arrears with his taxes. Although the confidence of his colleagues helped to bolster his waning pride, he could not risk going further into debt. He might wholeheartedly throw himself into working for the good of the community, but he could no longer spend lavishly on entertainment, as he had done in 1709 when sheriff.

In the summer of 1725 Sam was almost sixteen. Undoubtedly he was proud of the elevation of his father. Any boy would have delighted in the colorful ceremonies, the shining regalia, and the extra respect paid to the head of his family. He could maintain his position among his schoolmates with a little more assurance. Even the constant necessity for strict economy at home was made temporarily less galling. But he can scarcely have taken much further interest in the administrative problems of the Corporation; his attention was doubtless centered on himself.

There are few records of his years of adolescence. Nothing survives to tell us of his relations with his only brother Nathaniel — of their possible jealous quarrels and the constant rivalry for their mother's attention. There is no mention of everyday household tensions. But the fact that Sam never liked to talk about his early family life is a sign that these years had left scars.

A few stray anecdotes provide glimpses of what was going on. He took little interest in the church: "He said that he was early inattentive to or indifferent about religion." [27] According to Mrs. Thrale, he had some occasional doubts. "At the age of ten years his mind was disturbed by scruples of infidelity, which preyed upon his spirits and made him very uneasy: the more so perhaps as he revealed his uneasiness to no one, being naturally of a sullen temper and reserved disposition." Searching diligently for evidences of the Christian faith, he finally recollected a book he had once picked up in his father's shop, *De Veritate Religionis* by Hugo Grotius, and blamed himself for not consulting that. At the first opportunity he examined it, but finding his knowledge of Latin insufficient to understand the work perfectly, he laid it aside, with his conscience temporarily at rest. It never entered his head to ask about books in English on the same topic. At least he knew that someone more learned than himself had wrestled with similar doubts and conquered them. "From the pain which guilt had given him, he now began to deduce the soul's immortality."

In revealing this to Mrs. Thrale, Johnson knew that sensible people might find it a strange account. "I cannot imagine says he on a sudden what makes me talk of myself to you so, unless it is that confidence begets confidence, for I never did relate this foolish story to any one but to Dr. Taylor and my wife." But a boy of ten is not always logical or rational. It is quite possible that by some such vague reasoning his skepticism was quieted for a few years.

After St. Mary's Church was reopened late in 1721 and he was forced to resume attendance at Sunday services, Sam continued his equivocal attitude. He told Boswell that he "came to be a sort of lax talker, rather against religion in his conversation though he did not much think against it." It was fun to shock his mother with skeptical remarks. "This now," he remarked another time to Boswell in reference to some arguments that a poor Turk must of necessity be a Mohammedan, "is just such stuff as I used to talk to my mother, when I first began to think myself a clever fellow; and she ought to have whipped me for it."

Even when not required to attend church regularly, Sam was still involved in some religious instruction. There were family readings from the Bible, including some from the Apocrypha. He remembered having read or heard "Bel and the dragon, Susannah, some of Tobit, perhaps all. Some at least of Judith, and some of Ecclesiasticus." [28] And there were other less interesting assignments. "Sunday was a heavy day to him when he was young. His mother made him read *The Whole Duty of Man* on that day; and when he read for instance the chapter on theft he was no more convinced that theft was wrong than before; so there was no accession of ideas." The method, he later remarked, was all wrong. "A boy should be introduced to such books by being directed to the arrangement, to the style, to other excellencies; and he would of course attend to the doctrine — that the mind would not weary, if directed thus to various subjects."

With adolescence inevitably came an awareness of sex. Mrs. Thrale recalled that once as he watched her son set off for school, Johnson said to her suddenly, "Make your boy tell you his dreams: the first corruption that entered into my heart was communicated in a dream." When she tried to draw out of him what it was, he replied with much violence, "*Do* not ask me," and walked away in apparent agitation.[29] It was every boy's normal discovery of erotic desires in open conflict with accepted morality, but for Sam, already neurotically disturbed, it was more than usually upsetting. As his later prayers would show, he continued to be torn by this basic struggle for the rest of his life.

He began to write poetry. Yet except for the dubious "duck" quatrain, there is no definite record of anything until he was about fifteen. If, like Pope, he "lisped in numbers," he was even more rigorous in destroying the early productions. The chances are that his natural indolence kept him from writing down what he composed. Hector reported only his willingness to dictate verses to his school favorites.

In the classroom he learned how to translate and to imitate the Roman poets. The earliest verse translation that he kept, and later printed in a revised form, was his version of Horace's *Integer Vitae* (Book I, Ode 22). His first attempt at a Latin poem of his own had as its subject the glowworm, but no copy has survived.[30] The odes of Horace, he later confided to Boswell, were the compositions in which he took most delight, at the same time admitting that only the odes caught his imagination, for it was a long time before he liked to read the epistles and satires.[31] In this first stage his inspiration was definitely lyric.

The same partiality is apparent in his own verses in English. In desultory reading in his father's shop he had sampled most of the popular seventeenth-century poets, and it is not surprising to find his earliest existing piece largely a pastiche of moods and phrases echoing Herrick, Marvell, Herbert, and the rest. The title may astonish those who think of Johnson only as a sturdy city satirist. He called it "On a Daffodil, the First Flower the Author Had Seen That Year." Hector, who gave a copy to Boswell, believed it to have been written between Sam's fifteenth and sixteenth years.[32]

The fact that Boswell failed to print this early poem may puzzle many readers. But why should he? It was obviously not one of Johnson's better efforts. There were a number of other juvenile experiments which were closer to his later style. And how could Boswell know that Wordsworth was going to write a more celebrated poem on the same topic? He could not anticipate what for us is an irresistible comparison.

In four-line stanzas, it is in mood and phraseology close to Herrick's verses in the *Hesperides,* "To Daffodils" or "The Primrose." Yet it is not strictly an imitation of any one writer or poem. It is more like a boy's unconscious reassembling of poetic ideas and expressions which had delighted him in his reading.

> Hail lovely Flower first honour of the year!
> Hail beautious earnest of approaching Spring!
> Whose early Buds unusual Glories wear,
> And of a fruitful year fair omens bring.
>
> Be thou the favorite of the indulgent Sky,
> Nor feel the inclemencies of Wintry Air,
> May no rude blasts thy sacred bloom destroy,
> May Storms howl gently o'er and learn to spare.

In succeeding stanzas there is the usual amount of personification: "lambent Zephyrs" gently wave; "balmy Spirits" play; and the morn sheds early tears. Herrick's primrose "thus bepearl'd with dew" becomes "And thou impearl'd with dew"; and there are "throngs of beautious Virgins" to crowd around the flower. Divine Cleora's smiles dispense "a genial warmth." It is all very much in the early seventeenth-century tradition. The closing stanzas, too, re-echo Herrick's mood.

> But while I sing, the nimble moments fly,
> See! Sol's bright chariot seeks the Western Main,
> And ah! behold the shriveling blossoms die,
> So late admir'd and prais'd Alas! in vain!
>
> With grief this Emblem of Mankind I see,
> Like one awaken'd from a pleasing Dream,
> Cleora's self fair Flower shall fade like thee;
> Alike must fall the Poet and his Theme.

For Johnson, as for Herrick, the daffodil was a symbol of the fleeting joys of man. Yet there are obvious differences. The earlier poet wrote pure lyrics; Johnson's is a moralized song. There is more stress on the truism that man must die. On the other hand, the ever-present thought of death does not make Johnson highly subjective or personal in the manner of the romantics. The flower is no source of transcendental joy. He may have delighted in the sight as much as Wordsworth, but if he remembered the experience when lying on his couch, his heart did not fill with rapture and dance with the waving blossoms. External nature for a poet in 1725 was useful for what it showed him about mankind. The short life and fading splendor of the flower furnished an obvious parallel to human life. It would have been a waste of time to meditate and write merely about the aesthetic pleasure of the moment. Even as a boy of fifteen Sam was well adjusted to the prevailing climate of opinion.

Here, too, are the first stirrings of Johnson's sound critical sense. According to Hector, Johnson never much liked this poem; and, "as he thought it not characteristic of the flower," did not willingly pass it around. He realized that what he had written might just as well have been said about any other flower, but it never entered his mind to write another poem on the subject which would have been more "characteristic." He was not interested in blossoms except as symbols. "No, Sir," he once replied to a gentleman in the country, "I am not a botanist," and added, alluding to his nearsightedness, "Should I wish to become a botanist, I must first turn myself into a reptile." [33]

While instinctively recognizing the futility of writing poems to external nature and filling them with general terms about mankind, Johnson could not bring himself to revolt entirely against the tradition. Instead, like so many others of his time, he merely avoided the whole genre. His period of delight in the lush verses of Herrick quickly came to an end, and in the voluminous records of Johnson's later life there is no significant comment about the poet who had obviously been an inspiration to him at sixteen. Sam never again addressed a serious poem to a flower. He moved, as did Pope, away from the pastoral tradition and the maze of fancy to the proper study of mankind.

Sam's next poem which has survived, and which Hector thought was written the following year, was entitled "Friendship, an Ode." [34]

Above: Lichfield Grammar School. Drawn after Johnson's time by John Buckler, engraved by Charles J. Smith. *Below:* Hogarth's *A Midnight Modern Conversation.* Parson Ford is at the punch bowl, ladle in hand. Courtesy of the Metropolitan Museum of Art, New York City.

The bishop's palace in the Close. Sepia drawing (1833) by John Buckler, in the William Salt Library, Stafford.

Gilbert Walmesley. Artist unknown. Formerly in the library at Stowe Hill.

Friendship peculiar boon of Heav'n,
The Noble mind's delight and Pride,
To Men and Angels only giv'n,
To all the lower World deny'd.

With the favorite classical topic *De Amicitia* he found his proper theme. Even at sixteen Johnson was able to harmonize a conviction of life's basic melancholy with an eager desire for affection, to combine an awareness of the vanity of human wishes with hope for some happiness through human relationships.

Sam never revealed who inspired the ode to friendship, but about this time he did meet someone who was to become a major influence on his mind and character. This was his sparkling but erratic cousin, Cornelius Ford — parson, gentleman of fashion, and urbane scholar. He was a new kind of friend for the bookseller's boy, and at the moment just the catalyst he needed.

Stourbridge

THROUGHOUT his life Johnson had a weakness for dissipated men of wit; he delighted in their conversation and overlooked their moral lapses. He was never a prig. So long as he was not affronted by profanity or obscenity, he made no effort to pry into the private lives of his companions. It was not that he condoned vice. It was merely that for Johnson there were two kinds of crimes — one which he could never tolerate, the other which he was forced to accept as a part of human frailty. Always he made a real distinction between errors which struck at the roots of society, and those which destroyed only the individuals who committed them. No person who scoffed at religion or who attacked the basic stability of government could ever be his friend; but drunkards and rakes, if they did not parade their weaknesses before his eyes, were acceptable. The first of a long succession of brilliant but dissipated companions was his first cousin, Cornelius Ford.

Apparently the two first met in September, 1725, when Cornelius became involved in legal matters connected with Sarah Johnson's marriage settlement. Harassed by debts and always lacking ready money, Michael Johnson had never been able to comply fully with all of the stipulations.¹ In June, 1706, when the document had been signed, it had been agreed that £200 of Sarah's total dowry of £430, together with an additional £100 to be provided by the bridegroom, should be placed in the hands of two trustees — her brother, Dr. Joseph Ford of Stourbridge, and Richard Pyott, who lived two miles outside Lichfield — the whole to be held in trust for Michael, his wife, and future children. But Michael did not complete his part of the bargain. As the years passed by, he found it impossible to raise £100 in cash. Then, too, for some reason Pyott refused to act as trustee, so that Sarah's money merely remained in the hands of Joseph Ford.

In March, 1721, Dr. Ford died, and the responsibility for the dowry devolved on his son and Sarah's nephew, Cornelius Ford. Still matters dragged on. At last in the late summer of 1725 Michael and Cornelius worked out a compromise settlement. Michael conveyed his Lichfield house to a new set of trustees, and in return he received £100 in cash for his own use out of the £200 still held by the Fords. For the moment the arrangement helped the bookseller's financial position, but it left his estate further entangled.

The legal document was signed on September 16, 1725, and presumably Cornelius came to Lichfield to see the house and make the necessary arrangements. He met Michael's elder son, and there was an immediate rapport between them. Cornelius was a scholar and a man of the world; his talk of books and literary men must have fascinated the eager boy. Moreover, the visitor was shrewd enough to sense something unusual under Sam's unprepossessing exterior. Some spark of intellectual affinity was ignited, and Cornelius invited the youth to come back to Pedmore with him. The invitation was at once accepted, and Sam set off for what was originally intended to be a visit of a few days.[2] He remained for more than six months.

Physically the two cousins made a dramatic contrast: Sam, a large, rawboned youth of sixteen, restless and always in motion, with short neck, broad shoulders, and coarse, fleshy features; Cornelius, a plump, well-fed man of thirty-one, with bright eyes in a dimpled childish face, yet with an air of complacent worldliness.[3] They were even farther apart in experience and sophistication, for "Neely" Ford, as his friends called him, had already been a Cambridge don, a gay London spark, a wit and man of fashion. He moved in the best circles and was an intimate associate of such men as Philip Stanhope, later Lord Chesterfield, and the Hon. Charles Cornwallis. He was acquainted with Alexander Pope and haunted the London theaters with the lesser poets, William Broome and Elijah Fenton. To the provincial bookseller's son he must have appeared the kind of man one wistfully read about but never knew personally.

In the autumn of 1725 Ford was temporarily rusticating in retirement from the vices and expenses of London society. Having spent most of his patrimony and accumulated the usual harassing debts, he had only a little over a year before followed the time-honored method of release from his difficulties — he had married a spinster of forty-three, the daughter of a successful Quaker ironmaster, Ambrose Crowley, with whose small fortune he had paid off some of the mortgages and settled affairs with Michael Johnson. As part of his determined reformation, Cornelius had gone even further and had decided to enter the Church. The preceding January he had been ordained a deacon, though he had not as yet secured a permanent benefice. He was living at Pedmore, about a mile and a half south of Stourbridge in Worcestershire, on property which he had inherited from his father.[4]

It was at this turning point in his host's career that Sam came for a visit. By chance the two were thrown together just when Ford was feeling the need for intellectual stimulation. Judith Crowley, the woman thirteen years his elder who had become his wife, was probably an admirable and industrious housekeeper. She may even have adored her attractive husband with virtuous passion; at least she was willing to give up her Quaker faith to join his church, and to allow her fortune to be spent in settling his debts. But the two can scarcely have had much in common intellectually. After a year and a half of such a marriage, Ford would have been bored by his existence and ready to welcome into the household someone with whom he could talk about literature.

Ford's worldly wisdom, his broad scholarship and excellent taste, his personal knowledge of London literary life — all this opened new doors into strange and fascinating worlds for young Sam Johnson. For a time he could forget the narrow concerns of the Lichfield household, the bickerings and jealousies, his father's financial worries. For a while he was removed from Hunter's insensitive bludgeonings at the Grammar School. And so, as the autumn days went by and his host urged him to stay, he found it difficult to tear himself away. The opening of school passed, and he was still at Pedmore. Finally it was too late to go, and he stayed on month after month. Instead of sitting in the schoolroom in Lichfield learning his lessons by rote, he studied the classics with an attractive and sympathetic tutor. Together he and "Neely" read and translated, but chiefly they talked.

How much actual instruction Ford gave to his younger cousin it is impossible to guess. Hawkins says that in order to make up for Sam's absence from school, the older man actually "became his instructor in the classics, and farther assisted him in his studies." [5] As a means of enlivening the tedium of country life, Ford may have played at being a schoolmaster for a time, but it is more likely that the two merely discussed what Sam was reading. Ford's library, which provided the texts, would have been well stocked with classical authors not normally read by school-boys of sixteen. It may be that Johnson's fondness for the epi-grams of Martial, a taste which later shocked more staid observers, was acquired at Pedmore. And perhaps it was Ford who introduced him to Anacreon's *Dove,* the first Greek verses to make a deep and lasting impression. He later told Mrs. Thrale that he had planned a translation at sixteen, though the lines were not completed until he was sixty-eight.[6]

Ford was an accomplished scholar, as well as a wit and a raconteur. He had been well trained as a Latinist, first by one of the best-known grammarians of the day, Richard Johnson of Nottingham, and later at this master's old college, St. John's at Cambridge. When at school, we are told, Ford "made so quick a proficiency, that he no sooner learned a *rule,* but he made an *exception* serve for an *example.*" [7] And at college "his mastery of the classics, and elegant *Latin* and *English* style was conspicuous."

At Cambridge Ford had been eminently successful. After taking his B.A. in 1713, he had migrated from St. John's to Peter-house, where he later was elected to a fellowship. If he had wished, or perhaps if he had been more prudent, he might have had a brilliant university career. But to him, as to Christopher Smart some years later, the fleshpots proved too enticing. He could not settle down to the quiet life of a don; besides, he had never been a thorough scholar. It was literature he loved. It was literature he read and talked about with Sam. He had never had any taste for philosophy, thinking "the flower and fruit of sense in witty writers better than the stalk, leaves, and bitter roots of it, among the pedantic thrashers of logic, ethics, physics, and metaphysics." In college he had succeeded best in verses and declamations, where his taste and lively imagination could have full scope.

He loved company too much ever to become a pedant or a bookworm. As one of his friends later commented, "I doubt, some of his acquaintance are to answer for his falling a little short in his character of a student; he could not resist the attractives of pleasing conversation, and perhaps, *that is study,* and some men must *study hard* to be disenchanted from it." It was talk that he loved most, a preference easily appreciated by his young cousin. Ford not only rejected pedantry for himself but disdained it in others. At St. John's College he had for some time shared a chamber with William Broome, who was to aid Pope with the translation of the *Odyssey,* and he scornfully described his roommate as "a contracted scholar and a mere versifier, unacquainted with life, and unskillful in conversation." [8]

At Pedmore the literary talk cannot all have been about the classics. There would have been anecdotes about Pope and other living writers whom Ford had known personally. His favorite modern authors were Garth and Prior, Congreve and Addison. Their works he knew thoroughly, and he was ever "desirous to transfuse the quintessence of them" into his conversation, which he could do "as smoothly as you rack off a bottle into a decanter." The urbane wit of the coffeehouse, the light social satire and bright epigrams of the gentlemen-authors — these were what he admired most. If Johnson in later life did not retain a similar enthusiasm for the amorous poems of Prior or the satires of Garth, he undoubtedly learned much about them during the happy months at Pedmore.

In the long hours of talk, Ford gave Sam many useful bits of advice. Two in particular he remembered. The first was an ad-

monition to seek general knowledge — not to be a man able
to talk on only one subject. He advised him "to study the principles of everything, that a general acquaintance with life might
be the consequence of his inquiries." "Learn," said he, "the leading precognita of all things — no need perhaps to turn over
leaf by leaf; but grasp the trunk hard only, and you will shake
all the branches." [9] Sam learned this lesson well. The other ad-
monition proved not so congenial. "You will make your way the
more easily in the world, I see, as you are contented to dispute
no man's claim to conversation excellence; they will, therefore,
more willingly allow your pretensions as a writer." [10] Perhaps
Ford had already seen evidence of his younger companion's eagerness to win an argument at all costs, to knock down an opponent
with the butt end of his pistol if it missed fire.[11]

Pedmore was no lonely spot, cut off from all social life. A
mile or so away was Hagley Park, home of the Lytteltons, who, it
is likely, had been patients of Cornelius's father. The families
were on friendly terms. George Lyttelton, who was Sam's age,
was away at Eton much of the time, but he would have been
home during vacations. Then may have begun those "colloquial
disputes" which, according to tradition, were to prejudice Johnson unfairly against the future Lord Lyttelton and to make the
grudging account of the nobleman in the *Lives of the Poets* a
storm center of acrimonious argument among the bluestockings.[12]

In Stourbridge, moreover, there were numerous well-to-do Ford
relatives, and Judith, Sam's hostess, was well connected. Her
half brother, Sir Ambrose Crowley, the butt of Addison's satire
as Jack Anvil, had acquired a large fortune which helped other
members of his family to make alliances with the aristocracy.[13]
At Pedmore Sam was thrust into higher society than he had yet
known.

Some modern readers, well aware of Ford's later reputation
for licentiousness, have been puzzled by the affectionate regard
in which Johnson always held him. But Sam knew his cousin
only in the country, at a time when he was living decorously
with a sober wife. There would have been no profligacy here or

bacchanalian orgies to shock a serious-minded boy. Ford may have drunk heavily, but that was all, and, according to one account, the parson's capacity was so great that no liquor could ever fluster him.[14] Even at his worst Ford's conversation was never profane. He would allow no irreligious talk in his company, and when anything of that nature was begun, he would say, "So you are resolved, I see, to send the poor parson to bed."

Ford's unsavory reputation developed later, when Lord Chesterfield presented him with the rectory of South Luffenham in Rutland, and when, "finding nonresidence, nonpreaching, and pluralities something in fashion," he spent most of his time in the piazzas in London, drinking with his gay companions. This was the Parson Ford immortalized by Hogarth as the punch-loving clergyman in "A Midnight Modern Conversation." [15] Johnson never saw him during these days. And doubtless Ford's licentiousness has been exaggerated. According to various accounts, even with his riotous companions he "was remarkable for defending the honor and cause of the clergy against the cavils of some freethinking associates." He was endowed "with better qualities, than some have been pleased to allow him." He had a weakness for witty conversation and for the bottle; he found a tavern chair more attractive than one in a study. Certainly he was a misfit as a clergyman, but he was not a vicious man.

One thing further may be said in Ford's favor; he did not try to hide his frailties. The story is told that he once wished to accompany Lord Chesterfield as his chaplain on an embassy to The Hague. "You should go," said the peer, "if to your many vices you would add one more." "Pray, my Lord," asked Ford, "what is that?" "Hypocrisy, my dear doctor," was the unexpected reply.[16]

Ford's influence on the young Johnson cannot be overemphasized. Sam was at an impressionable age, and the long talks about life and literature with his cousin had a lasting effect on his character. Some intimation of the value he placed on this friendship is seen in the brief manuscript *Annales* in which Johnson at the age of twenty-five set down in Latin the most important events of his life.[17] References to Ford stand out among the meager entries as memorable landmarks.

Sam remained happily at Pedmore all through the winter and spring of 1726, but finally returned home in early June at Whitsuntide.[18] There he found that Hunter, resentful of his pupil's truancy, refused to take him back at the Grammar School. The Johnsons were faced with the difficult problem of how to continue the education of their precocious son. Possibly with the help of Skrymsher relatives, application was made to have Sam admitted as a scholar and assistant to the Rev. Samuel Lea, headmaster of the Newport School in Shropshire. But nothing came of this proposal, and matters became desperate. In the emergency Cornelius Ford came to the rescue and was able to get Sam admitted to the Stourbridge School. So back he went to Worcestershire, presumably after the Whitsuntide holidays.

In Johnson's day the King Edward VI School at Stourbridge was a long, low brick building set far back from the High Street. Hidden by the headmaster's and usher's houses, it was approached by a narrow entry from the street. Sandwiched in between the Vine Inn and the Old Horse Inn, the school property was not extensive, and the boys had little space for playground. Probably Sam lived in the headmaster's house, along with the other boarders, an arrangement which may explain his later remark that at Lichfield he had learned "nothing from the master but a good deal in his school" and at Stourbridge, "a great deal from the master but nothing in his school." [19] Eating at the same table and living in the same house, Sam would have become more intimate with this new teacher than he had ever been as a day boy with Hunter at Lichfield.

In charge of the school was the Rev. John Wentworth, a bachelor, who had been headmaster for over twenty years. He was an Oxford graduate and an excellent scholar, but he was indolent, more interested in vacations than in his professional duties. In the classroom he did little for Johnson, although he was severe in discipline. Looking back, Johnson thought he could see why. He had been "idle, mischievous, and stole." [20] He had shown little reverence for authority. And there was another reason. As he commented to Boswell, "I was too good a scholar. He could get no honor by me. Saw I would ascribe all to my own labor or former master." Yet if Wentworth was lax in his supervision, he was appreciative of his pupil's abilities. The fact that so many of Sam's school exercises were saved is proof of that. No master goes to the trouble of preserving a stack of old assignments unless he thinks them unusual or suspects that the boy will someday make his mark.

The usher at the time was Seth Shepperd, from Balliol College, who had been at Stourbridge for about ten years.[21] A few years later he gave up his post to become vicar of Shifnal. There is no evidence that he left any impression on the young Johnson, but it is interesting to find that both masters at Stourbridge were ·Oxford men.

It is not certain just what Sam's position was at the Stourbridge School. According to Bishop Percy, he was an assistant to the master, receiving his own instruction gratis for teaching the younger boys.[22] If so, it must have been a very loose, informal arrangement, for he could not have had any official post.

Officially the school day began at six in the morning and lasted until five in the afternoon; but not all of that time could have been devoted to study. Evidently a strict formality held sway, for in the streets the boys were required to address each other in Latin, and if they violated this rule they were subject to a whipping. As in all schools of the day, punishments were apt to be severe, varying from the usual flogging to being tied by the leg in the coal hole. Attendance at church, especially during Holy Week, was mandatory. The curriculum was similar to that at Lichfield, concentrating on Latin and the classics, and there was a specific rule of the school that "no boy was to be admitted only to learn writing and accounts." [23] The governors did not wish theirs to become a vocational school fitting boys merely for a useful trade.

Sam was not confined to the school grounds all the time. Just on the other side of the Old Horse Inn, and across the entry which served as an approach to the back of the school, was Gregory Hickman's handsome home, known as "Green Close," with its severe classic front and extensive gardens at the rear.

Hickman, a half brother of Cornelius Ford, was one of the leading men of the town, and it was probably through his intervention that Sam, despite the fact that he came from outside the Stourbridge–Old Swinford area, was accepted at the school. His home proved a convenient spot for relaxation and sociability; his daughter, twelve years old and not yet the source of poetic inspiration for Johnson she would become at seventeen, was probably a pleasant, garrulous companion.

The Hickman family was not alone in offering hospitality to the boy from Lichfield. Stourbridge was filled with his relatives. There was his uncle Nathaniel Ford, who had married Gregory Hickman's sister; there was Daniel Scott, clothier and governor of the school, who had married another sister. There were the Moseleys, Actons, Crowleys, and other prominent families connected by various ties. Naturally Sam would have continued to see much of "Neely" Ford at Pedmore, and he may at times have visited the formally regulated household of his mother's rich cousin, Mrs. Harriotts, at the Manor House at Trysull, only about seven miles away. For once in his life he was surrounded by well-to-do relatives who evidently were anxious to be kind to the gifted, if ungainly, youth. Indeed, Bishop Percy, himself a native of that part of the Midlands, gives evidence that Johnson's "genius was so distinguished, that, although little better than a schoolboy, he was admitted into the best company of the place, and had no common attention paid to his conversation; of which remarkable instances were long remembered there." [24]

One adjunct of the school which he must have found particularly attractive was the library. As far back as 1665 the celebrated controversialist and public orator at Oxford, the Rev. Henry Hickman, Gregory's great-uncle, had presented the school with numerous valuable volumes, most of them great folios, and to this original gift others were later added. In 1718 the governors furnished the library with eight chairs, a table, fireside furniture, and steps. At the same time there was further outlay for binding the books. One can imagine Sam spending much of his time sprawled on these chairs, skimming through the massive old volumes.[25]

Some suggestion of the nature of his studies comes from his surviving school exercises. He translated passages from the first and fifth pastorals of Virgil. He attempted some Greek and put into English heroic couplets part of the dialogue between Hector and Andromache in the *Iliad,* showing his independence of the popular version by Pope. He also turned Addison's Latin poem, "The Battle of the Cranes and Pygmies," into couplets. Years later he could laugh about one ludicrous mistake he made in the verses, pleading guilty to the lines:

> Down from the guardian boughs the nests they flung,
> And kill'd the yet unanimated young.

Then he added, "And yet I trust I am no blockhead. I afterward changed the word *kill'd* into *crush'd.*" [26]

Chiefly he concentrated on his favorite Horace. He turned at least three of the odes into English quatrains, and tried his hand at two of the epodes.[27] The renderings are accurate enough, though there are some youthful mistakes in translation. He catches the smooth style of Horace, though by making everything clear and simple in meaning he misses much of the complexity of the original. If he sensed the compression of Horace and the highly complicated word order, he did not try to reproduce these qualities in the translations.

Keeping generally to the strict order of prose, Johnson avoided many of Horace's strange inversions; and following a simple stanzaic form, he had little chance for variety. Already in evidence is his well-known device of repetition and expansion. For Horace's single word "piety" is substituted "vows and prayers," and where Horace says "the fugitive . . . years slip away" the translation has "the fleeting years in everlasting Circles run, . . ./They roll, and ever will roll on."

In the two epodes, neither of which Boswell included in his sampling of the juvenilia, Sam apparently felt more at home, enjoying their rather bitter, more down-to-earth tone. And in one of them he tried to represent the uneven movement of the original by using a more complicated rhyming scheme. If the translations missed a good deal of the subtle art of Horace, at

least they were unusual school exercises for a boy of sixteen. So
Wentworth thought, and so probably did others in Stourbridge.

Sam did not confine himself to renderings of Latin classics.
During the Stourbridge period at least three original poems are
known to have been written, and probably there were scores
more. When Mrs. Cornelius Ford's niece, Olivia Lloyd, came to
visit, he addressed verses to the attractive Quaker maid, two years
his senior.[28] Perhaps as a composition on a theme set by his master,
he wrote *Festina Lente,* filled with typical neoclassical doctrine,
as well as self-admonition: [29]

> Whatever course of Life great Jove allots,
> Whether you sit on thrones, or dwell in cots,
> Observe your steps; be carefull to command
> Your passions; guide the reins with steady hand,
> Nor down steep cliffs precipitately move
> Urg'd headlong on by hatred or by love:
> Let Reason with superiour force controul
> The floods of rage, and calm thy rufled soul.

The most unusual of all his early verses is what appears to be a
kind of "office" hymn for the feast of St. Simon and St. Jude. If so,
it was written for October 28, 1726. As has recently been pointed
out, "It stands by itself not merely among Johnson's early poems
but among all his poems, both in its metrical form and in the
scope allowed to 'extatick fury.' " [30] Written in the stanzaic form
usually associated with Christopher Smart's *A Song to David,*
which appeared over thirty years later, it has a romantic ardor
which Johnson later rigidly curbed.

"Let vulgar Poets sing" of battles and victorious kings, he
wrote,

> While I to nobler themes aspire,
> To nobler subjects tune my lyre;
>   Those Saints my numbers grace
> Who to their Lord were ever dear,
> To whom the church each rolling year
>   Her solemn honours pays.

In vain proud tyrants strove to shake
Their faith, or force them to forsake
  The Steps their Saviour trod;
With breasts resolv'd, they follow'd still
Obsequious to his heav'nly will
  Their master and their God.

After six more stanzas concerned with the careers of Jude and of
Simon, who traveled from the Lybian sands to Britain, the poem
ends with the outburst:

Thrice happy Saints — where do I rove?
Where doth extatick fury move
  My rude unpolish'd song;
Mine unharmonious verse profanes
Those names which in immortal strains
  Angelick choirs have sung.

Astonishing in many ways, the poem is most valuable in showing Johnson's deep religious capacity at seventeen. Though he
might still on occasion speak slightingly of the church and was
"lax" in his thinking, there was within him a passionate depth
of submerged religious feeling.

Apparently during these early years Sam was experimenting
widely with verse forms. Because Boswell in his selection in the
Life printed only poems in heroic couplets and simple quatrains,
the impression was given that from his youth Johnson had been
devoted to regular meters. Now that more of the juvenilia have
come to light, it is evident that though his adventurous period
may have been short, he at least tried other forms. In the pieces
there is proof, too, of his growing command of language and
rhythms. He was feeling his way toward a surer grasp of poetic art.

Another incidental value of the poem on St. Simon and St.
Jude is that it indicates Johnson to have been still at Stourbridge toward the end of October, 1726. Very soon afterward,
however, he returned to Lichfield, after a residence at the school
of less than six months. The reason why he left is not clear. Hector
told Boswell that it was the result of an argument with Went-

worth over the "purity of a phrase" in an exercise.[31] Since such a trifling reason appeared dubious to Boswell, he chose to ignore it. But it is possible that the quarrel over style was merely the last straw, following a long succession of imagined slights. Perhaps the master had sarcastically pointed out what Sam himself realized was only too true, that his work in helping the younger boys had not been a success. In any event, sometime in the late autumn of 1726 Sam packed his few belongings and said good-by to his friends at Stourbridge. It had been an invaluable year away from home, one in which his whole intellectual and social outlook had broadened.

Gilbert Walmesley

S AM found conditions at home unchanged. His father had completed his year as senior bailiff, and in due time his official accounts for the year were accepted. But his personal finances were so straitened that he was forced to the occasional expedient of borrowing from friends.[1] All thought of continuing his son's education had to be abandoned. Instead, it appears likely that the decision was made to turn him into a bookseller.

It must have been galling for the seventeen-year-old boy to see others with less ability preparing for the professions, while he had to become a shopkeeper. Yet he did not rebel against the general scheme of things which made such injustice possible. For Sam the pattern was inner conflict rather than open insubordination. Grudgingly, he tried to adapt himself to the new plan.

Among other duties he learned to bind books. Once, many years later, coming into the Lichfield shop of the successor to his father's business and taking up one of the volumes, he "recollected the binding to be the work of his own hands." [2] He took his turn at tending the shop, though he could never be a successful salesman. Often he was so engrossed in a book that he lost track of what was going on about him. The story is told that "being often chid for disobliging some of the best of his father's customers and friends, in this manner, he replied with great shrewdness, *that to supersede the pleasures of reading, by the attentions of traffic, was a task he never could master.*" [3]

It could scarcely have taken long to convince Michael that his eldest son was not fitted for a business career, if indeed he had ever had any illusions on that score. But what else could he do with the boy? With so many disabilities, he was not particularly suited for any steady position. It was a difficult problem, for

94

which at the time there appeared no solution, and so Sam lived merely from day to day.

He thought he was being completely idle, and constant worry increased his inability to focus his powers.[4] But he was not really wasting his time, for during the next two years he continued his wide reading. He told Boswell that the books he had read during this period were not works of mere amusement, "not voyages and travels, but all literature, Sir, all ancient writers, all manly: though but little Greek, only some of Anacreon and Hesiod." Yet he added that in this irregular manner he had "looked into a great many books, which were not commonly known at the universities, where they seldom read any books but what are put into their hands by their tutors."[5] By the time he was nineteen he could read Latin as easily as when he was an old man, and once he even went so far as to claim that at this age he knew almost as much as he ever did. Although the volumes were largely from his father's stock, occasionally he acquired a favorite for himself. Still in existence is a copy of Petronius, inscribed on the inner cover, "Sam: Johnson 1727." The year before, he had secured an excellent Latin dictionary and a two-volume edition of Sophocles, with texts in Greek and Latin.

Month followed month through 1727 and most of 1728, while Sam continued his uncertain existence in his father's shop. Yet he was no recluse. It was probably during these years that he developed a sentimental passion for the sixteen-year-old sister of Edmund Hector. As Sam made repeated trips up Sadler Street, ostensibly to see his closest friend, it was also to be in the same room with the attractive Ann. His was a typical adolescent infatuation. Almost fifty years afterward, Johnson remarked to Boswell, as the two were passing through Birmingham, "You will see, Sir, at Mr. Hector's, his sister, Mrs. Careless, a clergyman's widow. She was the first woman with whom I was in love. It dropped out of my head imperceptibly; but she and I shall always have a kindness for each other."[6] Later that same day he talked again of his first sweetheart, and added laconically, "If I had married her, it might have been as happy for me."

Life at Stourbridge had shown him the delights of polite society. In Lichfield, too, there were a number of well-bred, intellectual people, who bought their books from Michael and were ready to receive his son into their homes. Sam was a welcome guest in the households of Theophilus Levett, successor as town clerk to Richard Wakefield; Stephen Simpson, the lawyer; John Marten, the apothecary; William Butt, and others. There was the family of the impecunious but genteel Captain Peter Garrick, who lived just outside the entrance to the Cathedral Close. And although Dr. Swinfen moved to Birmingham in 1727, he continued his fatherly interest in his godson.

If the boy at times may have appeared clumsy and boorish, the local people had grown used to that, and he well knew how to conduct himself in formal gatherings. He had no lack of self-confidence in any surroundings. Although he later told Henry Thrale that "he had never sought to please till past thirty years old, considering the matter as hopeless," he nevertheless always tried to avoid "apparent preference of himself." [7] He was gradually developing that "complaisance" of manner in the company of ladies of good breeding which as an old man he exhibited in the bluestocking assemblies.

Besides, he had many qualities which make an agreeable companion. Too great stress on his morbid, gloomy disposition is apt to obscure another side of his character. When the melancholic fit was off there was a hearty gusto about everything he did. He could be infectiously merry. He was capable of enjoying life just as vigorously as he brooded about it. As Mrs. Thrale commented, "No man loved laughing better, and his vein of humor was rich, and apparently inexhaustible." He was always willing to join even in childish amusements, and he was "incomparable at buffoonery." With better eyesight, "and a form less inflexible, he would have made an admirable mimic." [8]

Of all those who were kind to him and influential in his development, one man in Lichfield stands out above the rest. It was Gilbert Walmesley, perhaps even more than Parson Ford at Pedmore, who put his stamp on Sam Johnson's mind. One of the most moving passages in all Johnson's works is his well-known tribute to Walmesley: [9]

I knew him very early; he was one of the first friends that literature procured me, and I hope that at least my gratitude made me worthy of his notice.

He was of an advanced age, and I was only not a boy; yet he never received my notions with contempt. He was a Whig, with all the virulence and malevolence of his party; yet difference of opinion did not keep us apart. I honored him, and he endured me.

He had mingled with the gay world without exemption from its vices or its follies, but had never neglected the cultivation of his mind; his belief of revelation was unshaken; his learning preserved his principles; he grew first regular, and then pious.

His studies had been so various that I am not able to name a man of equal knowledge. His acquaintance with books was great; and what he did not immediately know he could at least tell where to find. Such was his amplitude of learning and such his copiousness of communication that it may be doubted whether a day now passes in which I have not some advantage from his friendship.

In 1727 Gilbert Walmesley was forty-seven, a well-to-do bachelor, living comfortably in the Cathedral Close, where he leased the bishop's palace. For almost twenty years he had held the lucrative post of register of the ecclesiastical court of Lichfield.[10] In addition he had other sinecures, one of them picked up in 1718 "to inspect, examine, and control all the accounts and moneys for a £1,500,000 lottery," with a yearly stipend of £250. Walmesley was never forced to work hard for a living.

The only surviving portrait, evidently made in later life, shows him as a man of rather stern visage, with shrewd eyes and a firm mouth. His wig is admirably curled, his clothes of conservative cut. He has an air of quiet confidence and authority.

There was no doubt in anybody's mind that Walmesley merited respect. Anna Seward called him "the most able scholar and the finest gentleman in Lichfield or its environs" and stressed his taste and learning, his dignity and polished manners.[11] She emphasized, too, his open liberality and generous willingness "to waive every restraint of superiority" in stooping to be kind to "the huge, overgrown, misshapen, and probably dirty stripling," Sam

Johnson. But Anna, who was not born until twenty years after the events she was describing and was only four years old when Walmesley died, was only relaying stories heard from others.

More revealing are the few scattered letters written many years earlier between Walmesley and his youthful friends.[12] Here he appears as a serious-minded young rake, with a warm heart and determined political opinions — just the character one might have inferred from Johnson's tribute. This image of Walmesley which evolves so clearly from his letters deserves elaboration, if only for what it shows of the human qualities behind the formal façade of the later portrait.

Although he was a native of Lichfield — his father was for fifteen years chancellor of the diocese and briefly a member of Parliament — there was nothing provincial about Gilbert Walmesley. As a young man he had moved in the best of society. First at Trinity College, Oxford, and then when he was preparing for the law at the Inner Temple in London, his associates were wits and men of fashion. When he returned home to assume the post with the ecclesiastical court, he kept up with his exuberant companions through long visits to the capital. His closest friend was George Duckett, of Hartham in Wiltshire, who had means and ability, but no reputation for temperance. Another older Oxford crony was Edmund, or "Rag," Smith, enough of a poet to be included in *The Lives of the Poets,* whose "pranks and vices" and "riotous misbehavior" kept him constantly in trouble with the authorities and did not cease when he was forced to leave the university and settle in London. With Duckett and Smith, and later with a gay blade, Tom Burnet, the youngest son of the Bishop of Salisbury, Walmesley was a member of a wild set of Whigs, who were as violent in their antipathies toward the Tories as they were toward sobriety.

In 1711 Duckett deserted the town to marry and live quietly in the country. Belatedly, late in December, Walmesley wrote to congratulate his friend on his marriage, adding that he himself was such a cripple with gout that he could only move about on crutches. His very congratulations have a rakish air. "For let the libertines say what they will, one must have more true satisfac-

tion (even in the voluptuous sense of the word) from one mistress
(for so my Lord Bacon calls a young man's wife) than from a
thousand. For, hang it, she loves you, and takes a delight in giving you pleasure; when they —— and do everything besides for
pay, and as it were, like a pack horse, by rote." He added the political news that the "Protestant cause has still a majority in the
House of Lords, who 'tis to be hoped will stand betwixt the House
of Hanover and danger."

In his next letter Walmesley ironically commented on the marriage of another friend not remarkable for his understanding, yet
a general favorite of the ladies. "The noisy empty impertinent
shallow fellows ever have the greatest share of their esteem. . . .
P's God d——m me, madam will gain more in a quarter of an
hour than all the other's dying looks and ogles and elaborate lines
in twelve and twelve long months." Even by the following May,
Walmesley's letters show that he was still crippled with gout,
hobbling about with the help of a stick.

In the autumn of 1712 he was in London, and one hears of him
through Tom Burnet, his new acquaintance. Burnet, who in an
earlier letter wrote to Duckett that he was sober for the first time
in a month, and that drinking and whoring were injuring his
constitution (and he not yet twenty), wrote to Duckett in the
middle of November, "You must know before this that Walmesley
is in town, because he told me he had writ to you. We are pretty
well acquainted, and I like him much, for he is a fellow of sober
good sense, and very good parts, and though he is not a wit himself, yet he is as good a judge of it as anybody." Shortly after,
Burnet commented again, "Gill Walmesley and I drink your
health thrice a week at least. . . . Gill is too sober a man for me,
I never can get him to drink above one bottle, which is below my
dose a great deal."

Then in a satire "writ at Tom's in Covent Garden," taking off
all his acquaintances, Burnet characterized his new friend in the
lines:

> Shall Walmesley too, with such a Saintlike Face
> Talk Bawdy with the Lewdest of the Place?

Tho' the best natur'd man the World ere saw,
Yet Satyr could not spare this only flaw.

And in the same letter he added: "I showed your letter to honest Gill, who promises that he'll write to you, but when he cannot fix; for he is a man who hates epistolizing mortally." In later letters there are numerous references to drinking Duckett's health with "honest Gill W," once with the additional comment "and remain till I am fuddled."

Walmesley's own letters give even clearer insight into the basic combination of violent prejudices, worldly wisdom, and soft sentimentalism which made up his character. In the tense last years of Queen Anne's reign, Burnet and Duckett threw themselves into the political controversy, writing scathing attacks on the Tory writers. In Lichfield, Walmesley eagerly kept track of what was going on, and commented on February 11, 1713: "I do not see that they pretend to write on the other side: except the Conduct of the Allies [a pamphlet by Jonathan Swift], I haven't seen one of 'em that has attempted to write seriously; and I am sure whatever the author of that pamphlet might pretend, in his heart and in his conscience he did no such thing." As to the rest of the crew of Tory writers, "I look upon 'em to be such a pack of abandoned scoundrels, as no honest man of any party or denomination would read; otherwise than to give him a just idea of how low human nature is sometimes capable of sinking."

Duckett's happiness in his retirement, with choice books, a good wife, and children, made Walmesley envious.

O that my good stars had placed us somewhere near to one another! I have pleas'd myself ten thousand times with the beautiful images that such a position of life would have afforded me. Methinks I'd have a wife, such a one as you have, and two or three prating little rogues, first to divert me in my retirements from study and thought; and afterward to take up most of my time in forming 'em to just and noble sentiments. I fancy sure it will be a great pleasure to you when your little boy begins to prattle, to be teaching him those true principles of virtue and knowledge that all his lifetime afterward will ward him off from being either knave or fool. I am sure, considering the present character our country bears, we cannot be too careful in endeavoring to mend posterity.

Walmesley never had any "little rogues" of his own to educate, but his passion for mending the present sad state of the world through bettering posterity found release years later in his kindly interest in a number of talented Lichfield boys. He was much sobered by the death of his father in the summer of 1713 and commented to Duckett in September: "Hitherto my life has been pretty much upon the pin of pleasure, without much care or vexatious concern. But I begin now to think I shall soon shake off my old ways, and become a man of absolute gravity." He never went so far as that, yet in the years that followed, his continued gout and a natural distaste for letter writing weakened the ties with his rakish London companions. Gradually he settled down to his existence as a gentleman bachelor in Lichfield, with his beautiful home, his comforts, and his beloved books.

As a collector, Walmesley was, of course, a regular visitor to the shop at the market square. Possibly he spent long hours browsing among the books, snorting with contempt at some piece of arrant Jacobitism, or openly approving another of sound Whiggish sense. A Tory bookseller needed powers of restraint to keep from being drawn into an argument and losing a customer. No open break ever occurred, and Michael retained Walmesley's patronage for many years. To the library at the bishop's palace he sent a constant stream of old books and tracts, monthly journals full of foreign news, expensive treatises on the law, and the popular works of belles lettres. Some of the actual bills are still in existence.[13]

From these come corroboration of Walmesley's avidity for keeping up with the newest London best sellers. Though he hated the Tories, he was ready to read their works as soon as they appeared. In the autumn of 1726 he secured an early copy of *Gulliver's Travels,* and he must have exploded over Swift's covert gibes at the Hanoverian court. He read *Cadenus and Vanessa;* he bought the *Dunciad Variorum* and Pope's *Letters.* After he had read them, we may be sure he talked about them to his guests. Conversation at the bishop's palace was literary and up to date.

Of the local young people in whom Walmesley took a special interest, three became well known. To have been the early patron of such men is claim enough to remembrance. The eldest was Robert James, who in 1727 was twenty-two, a graduate of Oxford, and engaged in medical studies at Cambridge. Though he became a clever and able doctor, he was never noted for delicate manners or for his morals, and is reputed to have been drunk for twenty years without a break.[14] Yet he was an inveterate worker and his *Medicinal Dictionary*, to which Johnson later contributed, is a huge compilation. Considering himself an excellent scholar, James once bragged to Beauclerk that he knew more Greek than did his early mentor, Walmesley. When Johnson heard of the boast, he was shocked. "Sir," said he, "Dr. James did not know enough of Greek to be sensible of his ignorance of the language. Walmesley did."

Next in order of age was Sam Johnson, who was not yet eighteen. Youngest of all was ten-year-old David Garrick, destined to be the most famous actor of the century. Of the three he became the greatest personal favorite of the middle-aged bachelor. Living close by, young "Davy" was constantly in and out of the palace.[15] Blithe, effervescent, and full of gaiety, he charmed all about him. He had a natural taste for mimicry and a passion for the theater. Just about this time the young people of Lichfield became active in amateur theatricals, and when some ladies proposed to act in Ambrose Philips' *The Distressed Mother*, Sam Johnson wrote a special epilogue, giving it to Edmund Hector to convey to them privately.[16] Stage gossip was in the air.

When the youthful Garrick saw the great pillars and huge beam across the ceiling of the north withdrawing room of the bishop's palace, he may well have been reminded of a proscenium arch. Here was obviously a perfect spot in which to act a play. Curtains could easily be hung; separation of stage from audience could be effectively managed. No sooner planned than executed! He organized a company of young actors to play Farquhar's *Recruiting Officer*. Parts were apportioned; one of his sisters played

a chambermaid, and he himself took the role of Sergeant Kite. De-
siring a new prologue, he applied to young Johnson, already known
to be clever at that sort of thing. But something intervened, or Sam
was slow in getting the piece done, for the play appeared without
it.[17]

Though he failed to provide the requested prologue, one can
imagine Sam in the audience that night for this first dramatic appearance of David Garrick. Whether or not he applauded as
vociferously as the others are reputed to have done, he, too, must
have marveled at the "ease, vivacity, and humor" of the ten-year-
old boy playing Kite. Not that Johnson would ever think very
highly of the acting profession. His later scorn became proverbial.
Actors were "no better than creatures set upon tables and joint-
stools to make faces and produce laughter, like dancing dogs." [18]
One performer was superior to another only "as some dogs dance
better than others." Yet from the start he recognized that young
Davy Garrick was unusually gifted, even in this lesser sort of skill.
And he admired him for it. At the time the difference in ages kept
Sam and Davy from being close friends, but they were often to-
gether at the bishop's palace.

At Walmesley's hospitable table, just as at Pedmore, Sam sharpened his wits and learned more about the art of conversation. He
heard sensible literary talk from a man who was not a professional
writer himself but an excellent critic and a judge of wit in others.
As the guest of a trained lawyer, Johnson was introduced to the
study of law,[19] and he gained admirable practice in political argument.

Sam and his host thought themselves fundamentally poles apart.
Yet years later Johnson could remark on the importance of personal opposition in emphasizing and increasing differences of political opinion. "There was a violent Whig," he added, "with
whom I used to contend with great eagerness. After his death I
felt my Toryism much abated." [20] It was undoubtedly Gilbert
Walmesley he was referring to.

Some people have assumed that Johnson's references to the
violence, even malevolence, of Walmesley's Whig opinions were
really only a reflection of his own vehement Tory prejudices. But

all the evidence shows that Walmesley was fanatical in his hatred of the High-Church Jacobites and was passionately devoted to the Protestant succession. In 1713, when the Tory Peace of Utrecht was jubilantly proclaimed in Lichfield, he left the city in dudgeon, the newspapers ironically reported, "as 'tis supposed, disturbed with the music of the bells." [21] Long afterward, to celebrate the nuptials of one of the Hanoverian princesses, Walmesley illuminated his house from top to bottom, treated everyone who came to see the sight to rack punch, and gave them cockades for their hats.[22] There was never any doubt as to where he stood. In his letters there are continual gibes at what he thought was a local Jacobite cabal and "their old cursed anti-Revolution opinions."

It was partly to bait him that Sam developed his own rabid counterarguments. All his life he enjoyed taking the other side of a controversy. Sometimes, indeed, he consciously took a perverse position, just for fun. "When I was a boy," he once remarked, "I used always to choose the wrong side of a debate, because most ingenious things (that is to say, most new things) could be advanced upon it." [23] He was inordinately proud of his intellectual dexterity, his agility in fashioning arguments on either side. But even more important was an exaggerated sense of competition. His whole habit of mind was aggressive. Because the turbulent mind dwelt in a sick body, he felt a continuous compulsion to thrust himself forward.

Courage, physical and mental, thus became his most characteristic trait. He was recklessly brave in the face of open danger. Ferocious dogs or treacherous currents in a bathing pool only stirred him up to dramatic trials of strength.[24] In conversation, the more eminent the opponent, the more Sam strove for mastery. "When I was beginning the world," he once confessed to Fanny Burney, "and was nothing and nobody, the joy of my life was to fire at all the established wits! and then everybody loved to halloo me on." [25] Passionately needing the praise of others, he felt that the only way to secure it was by fighting.

Besides, in the Walmesley circle he never quite belonged. He was an outsider, tolerated and even pampered, but not one of the inner group. Even while he grasped eagerly at the social warmth, he knew instinctively that he could never be more than a spectator. These Whig intellectuals, with their money and position, their physical comforts, their feeling of certainty, their easy assumptions about life in general, exerted an irresistible fascination at the same time that they stirred up his opposition. He admired them; he loved them; but he sensed somehow that he could never succumb wholly to their blandishments. Had he been willing, life would certainly have been much easier. A little more flattery, a bit more open compliance, a few experiments at being a sycophant, and he might have wormed his way into the entrenched Whig hierarchy and become a lesser cog in this comfortable society. But something held him back. Call it integrity, or a sense of realism. He could never quite stifle the feeling that he was different. Always at the back of his mind was the realization of his own awkward appearance, his shabby poverty, his melancholy, his awareness of the tragic depths of life. Just as at Pedmore and at Hagley, where he had been first taken up by Whig society, he was intensely stimulated but never wholly absorbed.

Even at this age Sam had seen too much of the real miseries of the world to accept romantic illusions. The toughness of his mind kept him from adopting any graceful compromise. While he passionately longed to be accepted by these pleasant people, his honesty made him argue with them about their unrealistic theorizing. This was the reason why he developed the habit of taking the other side. It was his sign of independence, his way of showing that he could not be bought. Whatever was fashionable, he seemed to be saying, was to be challenged.

As one critic has recently pointed out, Johnson was temperamentally always in revolt.[26] He had all the surface qualities one usually associates with a young radical. He was violent, bitter, poor, conscious of intellectual superiority not yet recognized. To any casual observer he was a natural rebel. But one important quality kept him from ever becoming a revolutionary firebrand. This was a basic skepticism which pervaded all his thought. He had inherited too much of the Pyrrhonist tradition of the seventeenth century to accept untried solutions. His willingness to argue on either side of a question was one part of the tradition; another was his questioning of easy answers. It was this spirit of doubt, perhaps even more than his perverse delight in opposition, that made him an opponent of fashionable Whiggery. There were firm convictions underlying all the show of petulance. In the long political discussions with Walmesley at the bishop's palace he was deadly serious. Here was a ready-made opponent whom he loved and respected, yet whom he thought fundamentally wrong. Sam could muster all his powers of debate on a side to which he was deeply drawn.

Whiggery to Johnson meant an easy optimism, a bland acceptance of fashion, a willingness to experiment and tamper without absolute certainty of improvement, a sophistical use of theory instead of a realistic approach to the ills of mankind. Whiggery to him meant a negation of principle, where ends justified means. This spirit showed itself in many ways — the callous adoption of any policy if it brought large increase of wealth to the nation. Wars of conquest or stealing lands from savages might be excused if England prospered financially. Expansion of overseas business had become the *sine qua non*. Yet, as Johnson later wrote, "Trade may make us rich; but riches, without goodness, cannot make us happy." [27] And for him there appeared no great merit in the rise of great fortunes if the lot of the poor was not also bettered.

Poverty was the one unmitigated ill. When the Whigs talked vaguely of benevolence and of ways to improve mankind in the mass, he thought of the individual. Unsupported theory always left him cold. How could a particular human being be made happier? How could charity be made to help specific cases? While he found the Whigs full of liberal sentiments and broad plans for the betterment of the world, he was not convinced that they were also actively at work alleviating the sufferings of this unfortunate person or that. As an old man, Johnson once commented that the character of Sir Andrew Freeport in *The Spectator* was "a true Whig, arguing against giving charity to beggars, and throwing out other such ungracious sentiments." [28]

The Whigs, as Johnson saw them, put too much faith in the theory of natural goodness, naïvely confident that changing systems and eliminating political and social inequalities would make everything all right. For Johnson the problem centered on man himself. He was skeptical of any experiments that were not based on the moral betterment of particular men and women. Like Jonathan Swift, he was unconvinced that the lot of the average person could be improved by innovations or by experiments of politicians and economists. The new schemes might appear to make a splendid country, but the individual became more and more restricted.

Moreover, Whig innovations were dangerous. They cut at the very heart of whatever stability man had achieved. Whiggery meant too sharp a break with the past. It implied the assumption that man by his own decisions could casually break age-old laws. It was not liberal aspirations that Johnson feared, but reckless gambling with what had already been accomplished. When he later said that the first Whig was the devil, he was referring to the rebellion of Satan, the earliest recorded defiance of authority.[29] These new ideas were apparently leading to open insubordination against long-tested truths. Once a breach was made at any point, there was no telling how far revolution might go.

When he was eighteen it is doubtful that all this was clear in his mind, but in the long arguments with Walmesley he was probing for the truth and ordering his thoughts. In the heated exchanges with his admired Whig patron his convictions were gradually being fixed.

It is always difficult to point out the exact qualities which draw two people together. What was it in Gilbert Walmesley that so appealed to the young Johnson? The older man had breadth of learning, eloquence in argument, kindliness — but so had others who made no lasting impression. There must have been something more. Perhaps it was Walmesley's vigorous honesty of expression — his insistence on saying exactly what he thought, regardless of the consequences, yet with a willingness to hear the other side — his delight in calling a man a rascal whether he was in high or low estate. On occasion he might have been "irritable and violent," but the explosions were quickly over.[30] These qualities one recognizes at once as typically Johnsonian, part and parcel of the hero of Boswell. If such traits could ever be learned or absorbed, Sam had a perfect model before him in Gilbert Walmesley.

In speaking and writing, Walmesley expressed himself with tough mental vigor. Years after this period, when the bishop made a half-hearted effort to get back possession of the palace in the Close, Walmesley wrote a number of scorching letters which would have pleased the future author of the celebrated epistle to Lord Chesterfield.[31] To the bishop's son he commented angrily on the malice and ill-will of the bishop's advisers and of the "Jacobite faction," who were "using all their arts in pushing him to extremities with me, in order to drive me from Lichfield." At the same time he warned that he was provided with every defensive weapon. "I thank God, I am not more afraid of him than I am of the lowest curate in the diocese. The bishop has indeed heaped up great riches, and may better afford to throw away his money in litigious pursuits than I am. But I should rather advise him to go off the stage in a better temper of mind than with needless oppressive lawsuits upon his hands, which can be calculated for no rational good end." With perfect candor Walmesley suggested that his correspondent show the letter to his father.

A few weeks later he drafted another letter to be sent direct to his lordship. "Is it not a vain and an idle thing my Lord to talk of God, or his Providence, or to expect his favor of protection, when we cease to do by others, as in the like case we would they should do by us. Though you have had the good luck of disposing of all the best preferments, in your diocese, to your own family, and of being, as your brother of Durham observ'd very truly the father of your church, there may yet be some terrible judgment in reserve for you: and I shall expect to live to see it." A man who could think of writing to his bishop in such terms had obviously a forceful mind and a fearless pen.

Walmesley's vigor and forthrightness inspired deep respect. His breadth of spirit was infectious. The explosive violence, his young protégés knew, was only on the surface, for they had so often sampled the genuine kindness underneath. Endowed with the rare quality of instinctive sympathy for rising genius, he was liberal and impartial in giving praise. In Sam Johnson he found a boy who merited all his patience, understanding, and encouragement.

CHAPTER VII

Oxford

IT WAS natural for a boy with Sam's abilities to dream of going to the university. For him the distant towers of Oxford symbolized release — escape from the dismal future of counters and workbenches, of market stalls and saddlebags stuffed with packages. Even more, Oxford meant opportunity; it represented the sure way into the world of the professions. He was obviously unsuited to business. He was too moody and unsystematic to settle down as a humdrum clerk. He had neither the money nor the inclination for a successful career as a soldier. Yet for any occupation that appealed to him — lawyer, physician, parson, or teacher — he would have to have special advanced training, either at one of the London Inns of Court or at Cambridge or Oxford. There were no lesser provincial universities, no special professional schools, where a poor boy might work toward a degree.

There was also a social distinction in having a university connection. Even an impecunious member of an Oxford college could mix with men of any rank and not feel inferior. For one not endowed with wealth or position, such a background brought with it an aura of respectability. How well Johnson realized this is clear from the tone of his later references to Oxford.

In the years following his return from Stourbridge, however, the possibility of any further education seemed remote. Meanwhile he watched his old companions from the Grammar School, many of whom he knew to be foolish and stupid, go up to the universities. He heard their stories of college life. He listened hungrily to their accounts of pranks and follies and talked with them about their studies and the vagaries of their tutors. With ill-repressed longing he must often have imagined himself in such surroundings.

Then in the early autumn of 1728 the boy's whole future suddenly brightened. Instead of continuing unhappily in the bookshop, Sam found himself preparing to go to Oxford, his mind filled with new problems — the perplexing matters of clothes, proper shirts and shoes, of hose and possibly a wig — the selection of the books he wanted to take from his father's ample stock. As Sarah supervised one department and Michael the other, there was excited activity in the house by the market square.

Many have wondered what was responsible for this sudden decision, since there is no sign that Michael's affairs were any more prosperous. The answer doubtless lies in two unrelated events. The most important was a legacy of forty pounds which Sarah Johnson received at the death of her well-to-do cousin, Mrs. Harriotts of Trysull, the one who had been so solicitous about Sam's poor eyesight and who had disapproved of the boy's father.[1] The inheritance could not be used to bolster up the bookseller's failing finances. The will made it very clear that the money was for Sarah's "own separate use," and was to be withheld until Michael had given his bond not to touch it himself. But for Sarah, the needs of her elder son took first place. What better way of spending the windfall than to send Sam to the university? Though not a large sum, forty pounds would have been enough to give him a start.

Then came another offer of help. One of the boarders at the Lichfield Grammar School had been Andrew Corbet from Shropshire. About the same age, he and Sam had become fast friends. By this time Corbet was a gentleman commoner at Pembroke College, Oxford. Knowing his friend's eagerness to go to the university and also his lack of funds, Corbet spontaneously undertook to pay part of the expenses in order to have him as a companion. Moreover, as a beginning, he offered to let Sam occupy his rooms at Pembroke while he was away.[2] Since both of Corbet's parents were dead and he was master of his own fortune, he could easily afford to be generous. He could make an impetuous gesture, but, as it turned out, he could as quickly forget it.

For the Johnsons the offer was too tempting to reject. Besides, they had many other ties with Pembroke. This had been Dr. Swinfen's college, and his name was listed in the buttery books all the time his godson was in residence, though there are no charges to indicate even a short visit. Sarah's cousin, Henry Jesson, had been at Pembroke, as had Michael's good friend Richard Pyott.³ There were many reasons for the choice, apparently none of them based on the scholarly reputation of the institution or its fellows.

As Sam was packing and making last-minute preparations, something happened which touched him deeply. His first teacher, Dame Oliver, came to make him a present of some gingerbread, and to tell him that he was the best scholar she had ever had.⁴ It was a tribute he never forgot.

Late in October the great day arrived. Michael and his nineteen-year-old son proudly said good-by and started off for Oxford. Presumably they rode horseback — through Birmingham and Stratford, a journey of some seventy-eight miles — while Sam's books and clothes went by wagon.⁵ On the thirty-first Sam entered Pembroke College as a commoner, and paid his seven pounds caution money, as a guarantee of payment of future charges.

On the very first evening his father took him to meet the Vicegerent, his future tutor.⁶ He might have known what would happen — the same old embarrassing experience of being shown off to strangers as a prize prodigy. This time Michael bragged to the fellows and tutors of what a good scholar his son was, how he was a poet and wrote Latin verses. The youth with the massive shoulders and fierce gray eyes brooded gloomily in the background while his father did the talking. The company thought him strange-looking indeed, yet were favorably impressed by his modest silence. Then something was said which drew him into the conversation, and he astonished all in the room by quoting Macrobius, an author whom a schoolboy would not have been expected to know. Michael's point was made. The new student was marked as out of the ordinary.

William Jorden, his tutor — "a very worthy man but a heavy man" — did not at the start make a favorable impression. On the day after he arrived, Sam attended Jorden's lecture on logic, then stayed away for four. On the sixth day, when tutor and pupil met casually, Jorden inquired in a friendly manner why he had not been to his lecture and what he had been doing. "I have been sliding upon the ice in Christ Church meadow," was the nonchalant reply. When telling the story to Boswell, Johnson commented: "I had no notion that I was wrong or irreverent to my tutor." BOSWELL. "Why that was great fortitude of mind." JOHNSON. "No Sir stark insensibility." [7]

After dinner Jorden sent for him to come to his room. "I expected a sharp rebuke for my idleness," Johnson told Thomas Warton, "and went with a beating heart. When we were seated, he told me he had sent for me to drink a glass of wine with him, and to tell me, he was *not* angry with me for missing his lecture. This was, in fact, a most severe reprimand. Some more of the boys were then sent for, and we spent a very pleasant afternoon."

Jorden's tact in handling the affair was characteristic of the man and shows why he soon enlisted his pupil's affectionate regard, if not his wholehearted admiration. "Whenever a young man becomes Jorden's pupil, he becomes his son." Johnson loved him at the same time that he despised his want of learning. He told Mrs. Thrale that Jorden would "defend his pupils to the last; no young lad under his care should suffer for committing slight improprieties, while he had breath to defend, or power to protect them." Johnson even went so far as to say, perhaps in a rush of sentiment, that if he had had sons to send to college, they would have been placed under Jorden as their tutor.

One question has bothered some readers of the *Life* — the presence of ice in Christ Church meadow in early November. It would have been the sixth of the month, or the seventeenth according to new-style dating. Yet happily for doubters, an old weather diary lists the earlier part of November, 1728, as "cold" and the latter half unusually so.[8] On the twenty-fourth (old style) there began a "great snow" which lasted two or three days.

Sam's first college exercise was probably due on November 5, the anniversary of the Gunpowder Plot, less than a week after he had entered. On that day it was the tradition at Pembroke to

have a celebration. In the evening there was a special "Gaudy" —
when the Master dined in public and the juniors were obliged
to observe an ancient custom of "going round the fire in the hall,"
accompanied by various bits of hazing. It was customary for
undergraduates to make verses, preparing two copies — one to
present to the master, the other to post in the hall. Johnson failed
to produce the required lines, but to apologize for his neglect
handed in a short copy of verses entitled *Somnium*. Briefly they
explained "that the Muse had come to him in his sleep, and
whispered, that it did not become him to write on such subjects
as politics; he should confine himself to humbler themes." As
Boswell added, though the idea was common enough, "the versi-
fication was truly Virgilian." [9]

Sam was similarly dilatory in preparing his initial prose decla-
mation. As he told both Mrs. Thrale and William Windham, he
had neglected to write it until the very morning it was due, and
then had time to make only one copy.[10] This he was forced to put
into the hands of the tutor, who stood at the bottom of the hall
to receive it. Part of the piece he had got by heart while walking
from his room, but the rest he had to deliver extempore. Nevertheless, he finished with ease, to the astonishment and applause
of those of his companions who knew what had happened. In later
years he would never admit that he had taken any great risk, at
this or other times: "No man leaps into deep water, unless he
knows he can swim."

In 1728 Pembroke College was much smaller than today. There
was only a single quadrangle. During Johnson's first week fewer
than forty men were living in college, including the fellows and
students. Seldom were there many more in residence, though numerous others appeared officially on the books. It was a small,
closely knit group, where men of all classes knew each other well —
rich gentlemen commoners, who in return for paying double fees
had the privileges of dining at high table with the fellows and of
presenting a piece of silver plate to the college on departure; commoners, who paid their way entirely; scholars, the recipients of
special grants to help them meet their expenses; battelers, who
paid lower fees and in return were expected to fetch their own

meals and generally look after themselves; and servitors, also expected to look after themselves and in addition to do certain menial tasks for the commoners and scholars. There was but one common room, where they played games and whiled away their spare time. The hall, where they ate, had a large fireplace in the middle, about which they gathered on cold days.[11]

There was no chapel, though construction of one had begun the previous spring. While Johnson was in Oxford, work proceeded slowly on the new building. For daily prayers he had to go across the narrow lane to St. Aldate's Church, where for more than a century the college had had the south aisle set aside for its use.

His own quarters were over the gateway, in what was then the top of the tower. At nineteen, he would have thought nothing of the forty-odd steps — up the two winding flights from the entrance, in the square staircase flanked with heavy oak beams. But on his last visit to Pembroke, as a man of seventy-five, he had to be pushed up the narrow stairs by a porter. From one end of his rooms a double window overlooked the quadrangle, and from the other he could see St. Aldate's and the towers of Oxford. With his own fireplace, heavy wooden bedstead, and furniture, Johnson was probably as comfortable as the average commoner of the day.

For dramatic effect some writers have overstressed Johnson's poverty at Oxford. Yet during most of his residence — certainly for the early part — he was not especially pinched. He never served in any menial capacity. He worked for neither his board nor his tuition. He was a commoner whose way was being entirely paid by his family. His rooms were cared for by servants. Apparently there was no stinting on food and drink. Except that they show no extra expenses for entertaining, such as are found in the accounts of the gentlemen commoners, his battels, or weekly bills, are normal for a student in his position.

Anyone examining the buttery books at Pembroke is certain to be struck by the detail in which the records were kept in the eighteenth century. There is a series of minor charges following Johnson's name for every day that he was in residence. Sometimes as many as sixteen individual items appear for one day. The totals can easily be computed, but the key is lost which would explain what each charge was for.[12] Could the sequence be determined, one might be able to tell how many meat pies and how much bread Sam ate; how many pints of ale he consumed; how much he was charged for having his bed made; what were his common-room and incidental expenses. It could even be known how many letters he received, at least those on which postage was charged. It is tantalizing that the records are there, yet cannot be deciphered. But they do show that for over thirteen months Johnson never left Pembroke College for more than a day or so, that he was regular at commons, and that his physical wants were well provided for.

The college day began fairly early with chapel. Attendance, nominally obligatory, was not rigidly enforced. From Johnson's later remark that except on a few special occasions he did not remember ever rising early "by mere choice" since he had left Oxford, it can be assumed he did not waste all forenoon lying in bed. Breakfast was hardly a full meal — normally not much more than "a glass of ale and a crust." [13] During the mornings there were occasional lectures, which might include recitations and translations by the student and some individual tutoring. The dinner hour was getting progressively later at Oxford. In the early 1700s it had been eleven; by Johnson's day it was probably noon; by mid-century it reached one o'clock. Social life began after dinner, with long drowsy séances over pipes and wine for the fellows, and ale, talk, and sports for the undergraduates. Supper came about six in the evening. It was an easygoing, pleasant existence, with no one overexerting himself.

Long afterward Johnson expatiated to Boswell on the advantages of Oxford for learning: "There is here, Sir, (said he,) such a progressive emulation. The students are anxious to appear well to their tutors; the tutors are anxious to have their pupils appear well in the college; the colleges are anxious to have their students appear well in the university; and there are excellent rules of discipline in every college." [14] On another occasion he sentimentally referred to Pembroke as a "nest of singing birds." In retrospect life at the university was seen in a nostalgic glow. In reality conditions were not quite so ideal. An intelligent boy could learn much, but there were few incentives for the laggards.

In March, 1729, almost five months after Sam's arrival, John Taylor of Ashbourne came to Oxford, accompanied by his father.[15] The moment he alighted at the Crown Inn, young Taylor hurried off to find his friend, bursting with excitement over obtaining his father's consent that he too enter Pembroke. This was the happy conclusion of a plan long nurtured by the two boys. But now Taylor met objections from a surprising source. With typical conscientiousness, Sam insisted that Taylor go elsewhere. The tutor under whom he would have to work at Pembroke had turned out to be such a "blockhead" that studying under him would be a complete waste of time. Despite a longing to have his old schoolmate close by, Sam knew that Taylor would fare better elsewhere.

Sam went all about the university making inquiries and finally found that Edmund Bateman of Christ Church was reputed to be the best tutor. Accordingly Taylor was entered in that college. Fortunately it was just across the street, and Johnson went over every day in order to hear at second hand what Bateman had to say on the classics, logic, ethics, and mathematics.

Another topic that the two often discussed was the law. Taylor, whose father was an attorney at Ashbourne, was intended for the bar, of all professions the one which most attracted Johnson. More than once he confessed his "inclination to the practice of the civil or the common law." But other matters besides inclination may determine a man's profession. When in Edinburgh with Boswell, Johnson put the case succinctly. JOHNSON. "I could as easily apply to law as to tragic poetry." BOSWELL. "Yet, Sir, you *did* apply to tragic poetry, not to law." JOHNSON. "Because, Sir, I had not money to study law." [16]

How much Johnson participated in the everyday life of the town, how often he wandered through its noisy streets, it is impossible to tell. He and Taylor undoubtedly shared the general excitement on March 30, when a small boy was found dead in the fountain in the quadrangle at Christ Church, quite obviously murdered.[17] Later in the summer of 1729 they may well have gone to gaze on the young man forced to stand in the pillory for sodomy, to see the famous horse thief, "Black Bess," hanged at the castle prison, and to examine with morbid reflections the very spot where the young Brasenose student was drowned in the river.

The diary of a Pembroke undergraduate of a few years previous tells of horse races at Portmeadow, about a mile outside the town, once with the added attraction of a "foot race between several tailors for geese"; of formal parties in the evening at the Angel in the High Street, at a guinea a "touch"; of fishing up the river, or riding out to Shotover for the view; of witnessing a cockfight in Holywell, fought between the "town cocks" and those of a nobleman; or attending the Poetical Club at the Tuns, drinking wine and listening to verse fables.[18] But the writer was a well-to-do gentleman commoner, and the bookseller's son could not have afforded many of these amusements. The diarist wrote: "I was made free of the Bodleian Library, and took the usual oath not to embezzle the books, etc." — one action which Johnson probably duplicated.

Because he kept largely to the orbit of Pembroke and neighboring Christ Church, it is doubtful that Johnson met many undergraduates of other colleges, such as William Pitt, who was at Trinity. He may not even have seen his former schoolmate Charles Congreve, who was at Magdalen Hall.[19] Nevertheless, it would be incorrect to assume that he was a recluse, a sober scholar avoiding other students. In his small group at Pembroke he had a number of intimate friends with whom he ate and talked and wasted time.

There were Phil Jones and John Fludger, both "scholars," with whom he used to play at draughts in the common room. When visiting Pembroke with Boswell in 1776, Johnson remembered those games and made some caustic remarks on the later careers of his two old college mates: "Jones loved beer and did not get much forward in the Church. Fludger turned out a scoundrel, a Whig, and said he was ashamed of having been bred at Oxford.

He had a living at Putney and got under the eye of some retainers to the Court at that time; and so was a violent Whig. But he had been a scoundrel all along to be sure." Boswell asked if he had been a scoundrel in other ways: "Did he cheat at draughts?" JOHNSON. "We never played for money." [20]

Phil Jones was evidently the college character. In the buttery books the servitors, or whoever made the entries, were constantly scribbling insults and sharp comments about him. "Jones is an ass and a foolish long guts etc. — Milly Jones," or "O yes O yes come forth Phil Jones and answer to your charge for exceeding the battails last — ubi Jones — Philip Jones is an affected fellow, foppish dog, alias Coxcomb — O yes O yes come forth Phil: Jones alias Vinegar hold up your hand at the bar — ubi Jones ibi Philip et ubi Philip ibi Jones, et ubi Jones ibi vinegar ergo ubi vinegar ibi Jones." In one place there are scrawled some rough caricatures showing him with a very long nose and a stubbled, unshaven chin, and wearing a freakish hat. He was a jovial drinking companion and an entertaining clown, whose inability to rise in the Church is not surprising.

John Fludger, son of a mayor of Abingdon, who entered shortly after Johnson, had a special scholarship on the Wightwick Foundation. His Whiggish inclinations, which may have stirred up arguments even when he was in college, would have seemed out of place in the predominantly Tory atmosphere of Oxford. Coming directly from long arguments with Walmesley, Johnson was more than ready for Fludger, who, it would seem, did not have the saving grace of broad knowledge and humanity to off-set his Low-Church opinions. Yet Johnson kept track of his later career at least enough to disapprove of his connections and perhaps even of his published works.

Johnson's chief rival for excellence was "honest Jack Meek," another "scholar," who finally became a fellow of the college, where he remained for the rest of his uneventful life. When in 1754 Johnson called on him in Oxford along with Thomas Warton, there was great cordiality on both sides. On leaving, Johnson remarked to Warton: "I used to think Meeke had excellent parts, when we were boys together at the college: but, alas! 'Lost in a convent's solitary gloom!' I remember, at the classical lecture in the hall, I could not bear Meeke's superiority, and I tried to sit as far from him as I could, that I might not hear him construe." Yet comparing their achievements, Johnson could not forbear exulting: "About the same time of life, Meeke was left behind at Oxford to feed on a fellowship, and I went to London to get my living: now, Sir, see the difference of our literary characters!" [21]

Among the other commoners, whom he must have known well, but whose names never crop up again in later reminiscences, there was John Carew from Cornwall ("Tall Boy Carew — Carew alias Longguts Shanks") who was in residence every week of Johnson's time, even through the long vacations; and Samuel Keynton, noted as a "dunce" in the buttery books. There was the wealthy gentleman commoner, George Overman, who presented the college with a great silver tankard which would hold half a gallon, an indication, perhaps, of his convivial tastes. And there were the fellows, who would have kept somewhat to themselves, among them John Ratcliff, who eventually became Master and disgusted Johnson years later, in 1754, by receiving him coldly and not inviting him to dinner.

Johnson never mentioned the battelers Richard Laurence or William Toye ("Toye got drunk the twenty-fifth of July last — Toye was drunk 19th of June — Toy the Tailor") or the lowly servitors, Josias Packwood or Edward Moy, with whom a commoner would not normally associate. Yet observing their lot may have strengthened Johnson's distaste for the whole system which set up social barriers between students. According to Hawkins, Johnson was later very severe in his censures of the universities for making poor students wait on the more wealthy at meals. "He thought that the scholar's, like the Christian life, leveled all distinctions of rank and worldly preeminence." [22]

Something is known about everyone who was at Pembroke with Johnson.[23] They were an average lot, no more brilliant or dull than those at other colleges. Their names are remembered only because they ate and drank and talked with the large, awkward student with the acid tongue and nervous manner, whom they probably set down as a queer dog, too ill-balanced ever to make his mark in the world.

Sam evidently threw himself wholeheartedly into the undergraduate activities. Even with his poor eyesight he tried his hand at cricket — possibly of a kind now called stump cricket — in the limited space inside the Pembroke grounds or in the neighboring fields. He went sliding on the ice and wandered in Christ Church meadows. He played games in the common room and made Latin verses on the badness of the ale.[24] Small wonder, he maintained, that Virgil sang so worthily of arms and the man and that the students' muse sounded so affected. It was good Falernian wine that gave Virgil his force; the sly Pembroke steward supplied but a muddy draught. If better lyrics were to be created a clearer drink was needed.

He also haunted the nearby taverns, where he spouted poetry. The memory of a day so spent was forcibly brought back nearly fifty years afterward, in 1778, when he met one of his old college mates by chance in a London street. This was Oliver Edwards, endeared to all readers of Boswell as the solicitor who tried hard to be a philosopher, only to be defeated because "cheerfulness was always breaking in." Since Edwards had entered Pembroke as a commoner only shortly before Johnson left, and they had never been intimate, Johnson at first did not recognize him. But gradually the old memories came back, and in amazing detail. As they walked along, Johnson suddenly exclaimed, "O! Mr. Edwards! I'll convince you that I recollect you. Do you remember our drinking together at an alehouse near Pembroke gate. At that time, you told me of the Eton boy, who, when verses on our SAVIOUR's turning water into wine were prescribed as an exercise, brought up a single line, which was highly admired: 'Vidit et erubuit lympha pudica DEUM,' and I told you of another fine line in 'Camden's Remains,' an eulogy upon one of our kings, who was succeeded by his son, a prince of equal merit: 'Mira cano, Sol occubuit, nox nulla secuta est.' "[25]

Sam was generally to be seen lounging at the gate directly under his rooms with a circle of companions, whom he entertained with witty sallies and kept from their studies, "if not spiriting them up to rebellion against the college discipline." So thoroughly did he give the impression of complete happiness in his new surroundings that William Adams, then a junior fellow, later told Boswell that Johnson at this time was "caressed and loved by all about him, was a gay and frolicsome fellow, and passed there the happiest part of his life." But all his boisterous gaiety only masked the distress underneath. When he heard what Adams had said, Johnson burst out: "Ah, Sir, I was rude and violent. It was bitterness which they mistook for frolic. I was miserably poor, and I thought to fight my way by my literature and my wit; so I disregarded all power and all authority." [26]

In such a mood he was resentful of rules and regulations and took pleasure "in vexing the tutors and fellows." [27] He refused to do imposed punishments when caught idling by the Master. Hawkins described another way his natural dislike of discipline showed itself. When a servitor, by order of the Master, checked each room to see that the men were studying, Johnson willfully refused to answer the knock, preferring to be censured rather than to bow to the hated system. Then for revenge he would join the others in the noisy game of "hunting" the unfortunate snooper, who was only doing his duty, with a bedlam of noise from pots and candlesticks, while they all chanted to the tune of the ballad *Chevy Chase* the line "To drive the deer with hound and horn." [28] At times the poor servitor's very life was endangered by the rebellious students.

Reputedly Johnson displayed at Oxford an overbearing disposition that would not brook control and was negligent of college rules and hours. He stayed away from some of the lectures, "for which when he was reprimanded and interrogated, he replied with great rudeness and contempt of the lecturer." [29] Hawkins even tells the story that once when Johnson had been fined for such absences he said to his tutor, Jorden, "Sir, you have sconced me twopence for nonattendance at a lecture not worth a penny." While these anecdotes may be dramatic exaggerations, there can be little doubt that Johnson was independent and occasionally defiant. On the other hand, he was not an uncompromising rebel. Adams, indeed, insisted that Johnson had been regular in his attendance at lectures. The occasional mild expostulations of this worthy and scholarly junior fellow, so Johnson confessed later, made him feel ashamed of himself at times, though he was too proud to show it.

Just as among his comrades in Lichfield, Johnson dominated many of his Oxford companions by the sheer force of his personality. Already discriminating in his choice of words, he would tolerate no inaccuracy from those about him. That characteristic was one of the things Oliver Edwards most clearly recalled. "Sir," he said, "I remember you would not let us say *prodigious* at college. For even then, Sir, [turning to Boswell] he was delicate in language, and we all feared him." [30]

If on the surface he was brazenly self-confident, there were moments of homesickness and romantic reveries. Once as he was turning the key of his chamber at Pembroke he distinctly heard his mother call, "Sam." [31] Yet he knew she was far off in Lichfield. Although Johnson told the story as an example of the supernatural, more likely it was simply his subconscious longing for home.

He daydreamed of what he would do after college. The outside windows of his chambers were only a few feet from the walls of the Master's house. One day, while he was sitting in his room quite alone, Dr. Panting, the Master ("a fine Jacobite fellow" Johnson called him), "overheard him making this soliloquy with his strong voice. 'Well I have a mind to see how they go on in other places of learning. I'll go see the universities abroad. I'll go to France and Italy. I'll go to Padua and I'll mind my business — for an Athenian blockhead is the worst of all blockheads.' " [32]

Despite his dilatory handling of assignments, Johnson soon acquired something of a reputation as a poet. At the suggestion of Jorden — not as a punishment, as was sometimes reported — and to give tangible evidence of what he was capable of doing, Johnson turned Alexander Pope's *Messiah* into Latin verse. It was to be a Christmas exercise, and once started, if we may believe Hector, the 119 lines were completed at breakneck speed — about half one afternoon and the rest the next morning. It was much admired, and copies were passed around, one evidently being sent home to Lichfield. According to Taylor, Michael Johnson proudly had the verses printed without the knowledge or consent of his son, and may even have sent a copy to Pope. When he heard what had been done, Sam was very angry and in the heat of passion said violently that "if it had not been his father he would have cut his throat." [33] The whole business was particularly annoying since he had all along been planning to have some common friend present the translation to Pope with the proper acknowledgments. Later someone did give him a copy — reputedly Charles Arbuthnot, a gentleman commoner of Christ Church, whose father was the celebrated physician and member of the Scriblerus Club. Pope is said to have commented merely that it was well done but that he had seen it before.

To be sure, it is not very clear what happened, for Hawkins gives another version. According to him, when the younger Arbuthnot did show Johnson's translation to Pope, the latter returned the encomium: "The writer of this poem will leave it a question for posterity, whether his or mine be the original." [34]

Whether or not Michael printed it, the Latin translation of *Messiah* was to be the first of Johnson's compositions to be published, for it was included in 1731 in *A Miscellany of Poems* edited by a young Fellow of Pembroke, John Husbands. Perhaps this was the version ultimately presented to Pope. Merely one of a collection of college verses, it naturally caused little stir.

At another time Johnson turned lines of Dryden into Latin, a practice in which he had acquired considerable skill. [35] Though he probably did not write much English poetry while at the university, it is likely that sometime during this year he described in "The Young Author" the pitfalls of a literary career. [36] There were sufficient models at Oxford from which to draw his moral. The poem begins with a description of the peasant who forsakes his peaceful fields only to sicken with fear in an ocean tempest. Then follows the comparison:

> So the young author panting for a name,
> And fir'd with pleasing hope of endless fame,
> Intrusts his happiness to human kind,

More false, more cruel than the seas and wind,
"Toil on, dull croud, in extacy, he cries,
"For wealth or title, perishable prize;
"While I these transitory blessings scorn,
"Secure of praise from nations yet unborn."
This thought once form'd, all counsel comes too late,
He plies the press, and hurries on his fate;
Swiftly he sees the imagin'd laurels spread,
He feels th'unfading wreath surround his head;
Warn'd by another's fate, vain youth, be wise,
These dreams were *Settle's* once and Ogilby's.
   The pamphlet spreads, incessant hisses rise,
To some retreat the baffled writer flies,
Where no sour criticks damn, nor sneers molest,
Safe from the keen lampoon and stinging jest;
There begs of heav'n a less distinguish'd lot;
Glad to be hid, and proud to be forgot.

Twenty years later in *The Vanity of Human Wishes* he could picture the scholar's ills more effectively, through personal experience.

In general his college period was one of absorption, not production. He was not yet ready to create. His time could be more profitably spent in conversation and with books. "The particular course of his reading while at Oxford," says Boswell, "cannot be traced." Yet Johnson told his biographer that "what he read *solidly* at Oxford was Greek; not the Grecian historians, but Homer and Euripides, and now and then a little epigram." [37] Hawkins adds that his favorite subjects were classical literature, ethics, and theology, "in the latter whereof he laid the foundation by studying the Fathers."

At some stage he had prepared a huge "adversaria," a great plan of study, to cover all branches of knowledge, but as always his reading was spotty and not sustained.[38] He once told Windham that he had never gone through the *Odyssey* completely in the original. Nevertheless, Boswell was wise in pointing out that one must be careful of judging Johnson by his own exaggerated standards. Looking back, he could say that he had been "very idle and neglectful," that he had never studied hard. But he was forced to add that he had never known anyone who had. In many ways Johnson had come to the university better prepared than most students, and at Pembroke he certainly added to his stock of knowledge. Adam Smith, years later, remarked, "Johnson knew more books than any man alive."

He evidently thought a good deal about the merely mechanical problems of wide reading. While at Oxford he set down some calculations of "the number of lines in each of two of Euripides's tragedies, of the Georgics of Virgil, of the first six books of the Aeneid, of Horace's Art of Poetry, of three of the books of Ovid's Metamorphosis, of some parts of Theocritus, and of the tenth satire of Juvenal." Then he carefully made out a table, as Boswell describes it, "showing at the rate of various numbers a day, (I suppose verses to be read), what would be, in each case, the total amount in a week, month, and year." [39] He jotted down, too, the names of a number of old Latin authors that he most desired to have — among them Velleius Paterculus, "Justinus," and Graevius's edition of Cicero's letters.

He had brought to Oxford what would have been an extensive personal library for an undergraduate of those days — well over a hundred volumes. Though troublesome and expensive to transport, they represented one item which Michael could supply with ease. From a complete list which Sam himself wrote out it is possible to tell much about his preferences at that time.[40]

In his library were the usual classics: Homer's *Iliad*, Sophocles, Theocritus, Anacreon, Virgil, Horace, Ovid, Lucretius, Longinus, Cicero, and Quintilian. Livy, Tacitus, Suetonius, Seneca, Lucan and Catullus were represented, along with numerous later writers, among them the two Scaligers and Vida. Nearer his own time there were poets who wrote in Latin, such as George Buchanan, Jean Le Clerc, Claudius Quillet, John Barclay, to mention only a few. He had copies of More's *Utopia* and of Erasmus's *Colloquies*.

But the collection was not solely given over to Latin writers. There were a few prose works such as Locke *On Education* and Sherlock *On Death*, but chiefly his taste ran to poetry. Included were volumes of Spenser, Milton, Butler, Waller, and Pope. He had three of the great favorites of his cousin Parson Ford — Garth, Prior, and Addison, the last in four volumes. He owned five volumes of Dryden's translations and all of Pope's *Homer* in eleven volumes.

There were odd volumes of such minor poets as Ambrose Philips, Blackmore, Young, Rowe, and even "Rag" Smith, Gilbert Walmesley's old friend. Nor was religion neglected. He had a Bible, a Prayer Book, and Robert Nelson's *The Great Duty of Frequenting the Christian Sacrifice*. One hortatory work, perhaps a parting present from some solicitous friend or relative, was the Rev. J. Barecroft's *Advice to a Son in the University*.

The books demonstrated the wide interests of an inquiring mind. Though for modern readers there are glaring omissions — Dante, Chaucer, Shakespeare, Swift — that is not to say that he was unfamiliar with their works. He had read Shakespeare avidly as a child. He would have had other volumes in Lichfield, not carried to the university, and his reading was not confined to his own collection.

At Pembroke, as at home, there were chance discoveries. Once he found a book by Jonathan Richardson, presumably his *Essay on the Theory of Painting*, lying on the stairs. He took it to his room and read it through with astonishment. "I did not," he later told Sir Joshua Reynolds, "think it possible to say so much upon the art." [41]

His eyes were being opened, too, in other ways. He happened on a copy of Joachim Le Grand's French translation of Father Jerome Lobo's travels in Abyssinia and was fascinated by the picture of life in this little-known country. About this time he first read the works of Mandeville, but unlike so many others, he did not find the paradox of the *Fable of the Bees* — that private vices produced public benefits — either shocking or puzzling. From the start he was impressed by Mandeville's crude realism and shrewd insight into character, so that ever afterward he was "very watchful for the stains of original corruption both in himself and others." [42]

One new book which he took up, expecting to find it dull and something merely to laugh at, was William Law's *Serious Call to a Devout and Holy Life*. But it proved "an overmatch" for him.[43] As Gibbon once remarked, "if Law finds a spark of piety in his reader's mind he will kindle it into flame." Johnson had that spark. His lax talk against religion, indulged in intermittently since his fourteenth year, had been only an external sign of independence. Such sneers were not tolerated at Oxford, he found, nor was he allowed to stay away from regular formal worship. Gradually his mind had been prepared for the proper stimulus, and the strange combination in William Law of practical common sense and mystical intensity provided what was needed. From this time on he never deviated from his sturdy, if sometimes gloomy, acceptance of the truths of Christian faith.

With the inspiration of his rediscovered faith, he made new efforts to reform. In October, 1729, he made a memorandum: "Desidiae valedixi; syrenis istius cantibus surdam posthac aurem obversurus" — "I bid farewell to Sloth, being resolved henceforth not to listen to her siren strains." [44]

But resolving and carrying out a resolution are two different things. It was still as difficult to work, as hard to get up early in the mornings. And there is no evidence that his new religious zeal brought him increased happiness or freedom from care. Indeed, for a while quite the reverse proved true. The more convinced he became of his own sinful nature, of his own weaknesses, the more pronounced became his depression.[45] During the last months of 1729 he sank into a mood of deep dejection.

One of his chief worries concerned money. His limited supply was rapidly running out, and he could see little possibility of getting more from home. Moreover, none of the fine promises of Andrew Corbet had ever materialized. Having left college the very week that Johnson entered, he had never returned, nor had he advanced one shilling toward his friend's support.

At last, according to Taylor, Johnson was so shabby that his toes showed through gaping holes in his shoes. For a man of his fierce pride, this condition was humiliating. When he saw that some of the Christ Church men were aware of his plight, and possibly sniggering behind his back, he refused to set foot again in that college. There was nothing any of his friends could do, for such was his independence that he disdained offers of help. When William Vyse, a gentleman commoner from Staffordshire, in pity directed a servitor to place a new pair of shoes outside Johnson's door, Sam indignantly threw them away.[46]

Not letting his friend see that he had noticed any change, Taylor thoughtfully volunteered to come over to Pembroke to repeat the substance of Bateman's .lectures, and this he did for the remainder of Sam's stay in Oxford. Hearing lectures second-hand, however, had its disadvantages. Once, in December, Taylor tried to report the solution of a problem in algebra, but found he had lost the answer. He went around and asked two or three of his fellow students, only to find that they too had forgotten it. Determined not to be balked, he went to the rooms of a gentleman commoner named Whitehorne, where it chanced his tutor was visiting. When Taylor admitted his difficulty, Bateman very kindly went over the problem again. At once Taylor rushed back to Johnson, but still was unable to explain the solution clearly enough to make his friend understand.

As it turned out, this was the last time that Taylor brought his reports to Pembroke. The crisis had been reached. Miserably poor, Johnson could remain no longer without money, for he was already a full quarter behind in the payment of his fees.[47] The approach of the Christmas vacation offered an excuse for going home to see what conditions really were and to explore possibilities of further financial assistance. So after something over thirteen months of continuous residence, he prepared to leave Oxford.

Obviously intending this as no final departure, he left his extensive library with Taylor for safekeeping. As Sam said good-by to his friends, he could have had no intimation that it would be almost twenty-five years before he would again see his beloved college.

About the twelfth of December, early in the morning, he set out for Lichfield, "having hid his toes in a pair of large boots." [48] His faithful friend Taylor accompanied him as far as Banbury, then sadly returned to Oxford that same night.

Dejection and Indolence

O N HIS return to Lichfield in December, 1729, Johnson was in the grip of a severe attack of melancholia. He had reason to be discouraged — his own real or imagined physical ills, the increasing difficulties of his father, and the fading prospect of a career in any of the professions or as a cloistered scholar. Boswell says that "he felt himself overwhelmed with an horrible hypochondria, with perpetual irritation, fretfulness, and impatience; and with a dejection, gloom, and despair, which made existence misery." [1] His state of mind was a constant source of worry to his friends, and Edmund Hector was afraid that there might be something radically wrong with his constitution, which might endanger his sanity, or even his life. In one depressed moment Sam even "strongly entertained thoughts of suicide" and actually talked to Taylor about the possibility.[2]

Feeling himself on the verge of a breakdown, Johnson tried to avoid it by bodily exertion. He frequently walked to Birmingham and back, a distance of over thirty miles, "and tried many other expedients, but all in vain." [3] In Birmingham he consulted Dr. Swinfen, then living in the Old Square, and even went to the trouble of writing out in Latin a complete statement of his symptoms and fears of insanity, which the doctor, struck with its "extraordinary acuteness, research, and eloquence," proceeded to show to several people. No doubt Swinfen's motives were excellent, but Johnson's anger is easily understood, when he heard that his most intimate confessions had been passed around for others to see. According to Elizabeth, the doctor's fourteen-year-old daughter, Johnson was never afterward completely reconciled to his godfather. Such a breach of confidence he thought inexcusable.

This attack of melancholia was the beginning of a lifetime dread of the disease. Although there would be long periods of comparative calm, he would become oppressed, again and again, by the morbid obsession that he was losing his mind. What appeared paradoxical to Boswell was that these terrifying fancies came at the same time that he was giving remarkable proofs of the vigor and soundness of his judgment.[4] But other people had social position, family, money to rely on. All Johnson's hopes were dependent on his wits. Any threat to them was a threat to life itself.

In the Johnson household in 1730 there was not much to revive his depressed spirits. These were the days of "beggary" which he long afterward described to Mrs. Thrale. But the word must be considered an exaggeration. Michael kept on with his business in the usual way, and although the parchment factory was reputed to have been the cause of his reverses, when the lease of his waste lands on the edge of Stowe Pool came up in 1730 he was careful to see that it was renewed. He still "preserved himself," wrote Shaw, "by his industry and attention in a state of honesty and independence," and "whatever disappointments and crosses occurred in his intercourse with the world, he discovered the same innate fund of satisfaction and cheerfulness which marked the most prosperous circumstances of his life." [5] Regularity and punctuality had always been two of his distinguishing traits. Now, even when the parchment factory building had "fallen half down for want of money to repair it," Michael "was not less diligent to lock the door every night, though he saw that anybody might walk in at the back part." [6]

Although never actually destitute, he may have been close to insolvency, and perhaps it was about this time that William Innys, the bookseller in St. Paul's Yard, London, assisted him with money or credit so that he could continue in business. Long afterward, as he was dying, Michael's son remembered this act of kindness and arranged to repay the debt to Innys's heirs.[7]

Throughout these years Michael continued to be active in civic affairs. In the summer of 1729, when steps were taken by the Turnpike Trust Commissioners to borrow a large sum for the improvement of neighboring roads and the installation of toll gates, he was present at two of the most important meetings. He was conscientious, too, in attending meetings of the Lichfield Corporation. In 1730 he missed only one, and the next year, the last of his life, he was present at more than half of them. The fact that he remained a magistrate up to the end proves that he could not have died bankrupt.

Despite his straitened circumstances Michael was still highly regarded in the community. In 1731 the Conduit Lands Trust, of which he had once been a warden, granted him ten guineas as "a decayed tradesman." [8] It was one of the highest disbursements, except for the schoolmasters' salaries, ever made by the Trust, and represented a tribute from his colleagues to a man who had served the city long and well. Nevertheless, it must have been distressing for the Johnson family to be even partially supported by charity.

With the sudden interruption of his education, Sam was faced with the immediate problem of what to do next. Between the long walks to Birmingham and other strenuous attempts to throw off his melancholia, he moodily considered the various possibilities. Undoubtedly what he wanted most was to return to Oxford. His books were still there, waiting for him. But where could he find the necessary money? No one appeared willing or able to help him on that score. He could continue in his father's bookshop, become a halfhearted salesman and binder of books. Not an attractive prospect, though logical. On the other hand, he might strike out for himself as a writer, poet, translator, or journalist. Or he could teach school, provided there was one which would take him without a degree. But if he chose either of the latter alternatives, some effort, some forceful decision was required. In his present frame of mind that was impossible. It was easier to sink back into the old indolence and postpone any choice from week to week.

But he did not withdraw into himself completely. There was still the stimulus of the long arguments with Gilbert Walmesley at the bishop's palace. And he was quite ready to make new friends. One such was a young army officer, Cornet Henry Hervey, who was quartered with his regiment in Lichfield in 1730.[9] Attractive, wayward, reckless, he was to become another of that group of men of fashion with literary tastes — like Ford and Walmesley — who took a kindly, if patronizing, interest in the bookseller's son.

As the fourth son of the Earl of Bristol, and brother of Lord Hervey, the powerful court politician whom Pope pilloried as "Sporus," "Harry" Hervey was socially above most of Sam's other early friends. During the preceding twenty-nine years he had caused his noble father many a headache. "Wildest of the wild" he had been called; most careless of the careless he certainly was. Yet he had inherited also the Hervey intelligence and charm. He spent a short time at Christ Church, Oxford, long enough to begin amassing the inevitable pile of debts, and to break two bones in his left leg jumping over a hedge and ditch. Then his father bought him a commission in the 11th Dragoons, and he cut something of a figure as a gay officer in Gloucester and London. But even with his court connections, his constant absence from quarters and other lapses kept him from speedy army promotion. He much preferred the company of ladies, to whom he wrote verses, to the dull routine of an army post.

Shortly after coming to Lichfield, he married a potential heiress, Catherine Aston, eldest of eight daughters from Aston Hall in Cheshire. Though she had relatives near Lichfield, it is evident from the content of his love verses that much of the wooing was done at her home. It is tempting to say more about Harry's verses to "Kitty" — still preserved in a manuscript volume of his poems — "To Mrs. Kitty Aston on Her Being Silent in Company for an Hour," "To Mrs. Kitty Aston on Her Being Indisposed," "On a Fly That Killed Itself in Mrs. Kitty Aston's Eye," "To Mrs. Kitty Aston on Her Having No Trumps for Three Deals Together when Hearts Was the Suite." In the light, graceful style of Prior, they are affectionate and amusing. Though never outstanding, they help to explain why Hervey became a welcome member of the Walmesley circle in Lichfield, and why he could gain and hold the friendly loyalty of Johnson.

Not in a mood for much serious composition, Sam, too, wrote a few occasional poems. Almost impromptu he tossed off an "Ode on a Lady Leaving Her Place of Abode." [10] Another time he scribbled "On a Lady's Presenting a Sprig of Myrtle to a Gentle-man," at the insistence of his friend Hector, who about the year 1731 had settled in Birmingham as a surgeon. The verses were not for Hector himself but for a friend, Morgan Graves, elder brother of the author of *The Spiritual Quixote*.[11] Having been presented with a branch of myrtle by a young lady he was court-ing, Graves asked Hector for help in writing some verses upon the occasion. Hector turned to Johnson, who was visiting him in Birmingham. As usual, Johnson forgot or delayed. When re-minded a week or so later he ran upstairs as if to fetch the com-pleted verses, and in a few minutes brought down the fourteen lines which he had speedily written.

These were only temporary diversions. As time passed, it be-came evident that Sam must really bestir himself. Only by find-ing a position elsewhere would he be able to get out of the stulti-fying atmosphere of the shop. During the late summer of 1731, upon hearing that changes were in prospect at the Stourbridge Grammar School, he went over to see what the influence of rela-tives could do for him. The usher, who had been in residence less than a year, was leaving, and after years of quarreling, the gov-ernors of the school were finally considering the dismissal of Wentworth, the headmaster, a prospect which may have made the post of usher even more attractive to Sam.[12]

In all probability he was in Stourbridge late in August and early September, doing what he could to win the selection, and incidentally renewing old friendships. George Lyttelton was back from the grand tour and may well have been at Hagley Park, ready for more colloquial disputes.[13] At "Green Close," or at Wollaston Hall, Sam found Dorothy Hickman grown into an at-tractive and accomplished young lady of seventeen. Never un-moved by feminine charms, he was captivated when she played on the spinet, and wrote a set of complimentary verses about her.

But there was one who was missing from the Stourbridge circle; Parson Ford had died suddenly in London on August 22. The newspapers on the twenty-fourth included among the deaths the simple announcement: "On Sunday morning at the Hummums [a hotel and bagnio] in Covent Garden, the Rev. Mr. Ford, well known to the world for his great wit and abilities." A few weeks later some of the papers carried less restrained comments, including a supposed tribute tossed off by Ford's notorious crony, the Rev. John Henley:

> Ford is not dead, but sleepeth; spare his fame, I charge ye,
> One ounce of Mother-wit is worth a pound of Clergy.[14]

Which only occasioned further ribald remarks.

The news must have come as a great shock to Sam. Although he and his cousin had not seen each other for a number of years, there had always been the possibility of renewing those long talks which had made the visit to Pedmore in 1725–1726 so pleasant. Probably Sam had not heard much about Ford's financial troubles, his frantic borrowings, and his imprisonment in the Fleet early in 1731, although rumors of his extravagance, his writ-dodging, and his unsavory companions may have found their way to Lichfield, certainly to Stourbridge. But it was Ford's good points, not his failings, that Sam was to remember.

Mourning for his half-brother did not keep Gregory Hickman from pushing Sam's application at the Grammar School, unfortunately without success. Johnson's lack of a degree definitely stood in the way, and Wentworth may have been instrumental in blocking the appointment. In any event, on September 6 John Hughes, listed as holding a B.A. from Trinity College, Oxford, was chosen for the post, and Johnson returned to Lichfield empty-handed.[15]

Hickman was so pleased by the verses on his daughter that he suggested the school affair as a possible topic for some satiric, or perhaps rueful, lines, a proposal which struck no spark of fire in the young poet. After long delay, Sam finally drove himself to reply to his sponsor. Dated October 30, it is the earliest of his letters which have survived.

> I have so long neglected to return you thanks for the favors and assistance I received from you at Stourbridge that I am afraid you have now done expecting it. I can indeed make no apology but by assuring you that this delay, whatever was the cause of it, proceeded

neither from forgetfulness, disrespect, nor ingratitude; time has not made the sense of the obligation less warm, nor the thanks I return less sincere. But while I am acknowledging one favor I must beg another, that you would excuse the omission of the verses you desired. Be pleased to consider that versifying against one's inclination is the most disagreeable thing in the world, and that one's own disappointment is no inviting subject, and that though the desire of gratifying you might have prevailed over my dislike of it, yet it proves upon reflection so barren that to attempt to write upon it is to undertake to build without materials.

As I am yet unemployed I hope you will, if anything should offer, remember and recommend . . .[16]

About this time occurred one of the best-known events in Johnson's early life. One day, when Michael was confined to his bed with illness, he asked his eldest son to go to Uttoxeter to visit the market and attend the stall in his place. Because of pride, Sam refused. To sell wares in the open market place seemed below the dignity of an Oxford man. He stubbornly remained deaf to his father's request, and the incident was closed. But his rigorous conscience never allowed him to forget; the refusal remained at the back of his mind as a constant goad to his sense of guilt. Finally, fifty years afterward, he felt an overpowering desire to expiate this act of filial disobedience, and one day slipped away from his friends in Lichfield, drove to Uttoxeter, and stood bareheaded in the market place at the spot where his father's stall had been, "exposed to the sneers of the standers-by, and the inclemency of the weather." [17]

There is a possibility that the original insubordination was fixed more firmly in Johnson's mind by the fact that, if this dating is correct, his father died less than six weeks later of an inflammatory fever. This sequence of events would explain much about Johnson's later feeling of guilt and his celebrated penance. All that is actually known is that in his seventy-fifth year, early in December, 1731, Michael's stubborn struggle was ended. He was buried on the seventh at St. Michael's Church. It was Catherine Chambers, Sarah's companion and maid, who, as the only clear-headed member of the household, shouldered the responsibilities of arranging for the funeral.[18]

The death of Michael, though a serious emotional shock, did nothing to change Sam's condition. With so little to leave, Michael had made no will, and there is no record of any formal administration of the estate.[19] Legally his personal property should have been divided one-third to the widow and two-thirds to the boys. But according to the marriage settlement, all the household furnishings and the stock in trade of the shop were Sarah's for her lifetime. Michael's fine plan for leaving five hundred pounds to be divided among his children had long since faded completely away.

Since Sarah intended to carry on the business with the help of Nathaniel, who was now nineteen, it was more and more desirable that Sam should find a job, so that he would not be a further drain on the family income. Happily (or as the event turned out, unhappily) within three months he secured a post at the Grammar School at Market Bosworth in Leicestershire. The terse entry in his manuscript "Annales" gives us the important date: "1731–32 Mar¹ 9no S. J. Bosvorthiam petivit." [20]

Undoubtedly he was able to get the appointment through various friends who were connections of Sir Wolstan Dixie, the chief patron of the Bosworth School.[21] Actually the statutes required that the usher must have a B.A. degree, as well as be free from infectious and contagious diseases and be honest, virtuous, and learned. In addition to an annual salary of twenty pounds a year, it was stipulated that he be provided with a house. But Sir Wolstan cared little for rules or, indeed, for much besides his own pleasure. He was probably uninterested in the applicant's personal or scholarly qualifications, so long as he was recommended by a relative. Casually overlooking Johnson's lack of a degree, Sir Wolstan also forgot about the house, and forced the new underschoolmaster to live at Bosworth Hall, his own large and splendid mansion set in a fine park, close by the church and only a few minutes' walk from the school. Here Johnson was supposed to act as a kind of lay chaplain in the household.[22]

Such an arrangement might have been tolerable had Sir Wolstan been a reasonable man. Instead he was an ignorant bully. A bachelor of about thirty, he was the kind of boorish, egotistical sportsman who finds delight in poking fun at those more sensitive and intellectual than himself. Because of his violent temper he was constantly in trouble, becoming involved in lawsuits with former servants whom he had tyrannized, and in squabbles with neighbors.

Sir Wolstan's ignorance was proverbial. The story is told that once his attempt to stop the public use of a path through his park resulted in a fist fight with a neighbor, whom he beat into insensibility (or was himself beaten, as another version has it). Later when the baronet was presented to the German-bred King George II as "Sir Wolstan Dixie of Bosworth Park," His Majesty, wishing to show some knowledge of English history, said "Bosworth — Bosworth! Big battle at Bosworth, wasn't it?" "Yes, Sire. But I thrashed him," replied Sir Wolstan, oblivious of any other fight than his own.[23]

The stories of his autocratic behavior are just as numerous. If only half are true, Taylor's characterization of the man to Boswell as an "abandoned brutal rascal" may well be accepted as accurate. According to one account, only a few years before Johnson came to Market Bosworth, Sir Wolstan was dining one day with some boon companions, and while bragging about his absolute control of the local school, claimed that he could appoint as headmaster anyone he chose. When challenged by one of his guests to appoint the handsome butler at Bosworth Hall, the baronet immediately told the man to pack his box and be ready to take over the post. Surprisingly enough, the records of the school give some substantiation to this bizarre anecdote.[24]

The months spent under Sir Wolstan's roof were among the unhappiest of Johnson's life. Nor did he find his teaching duties pleasant. In the past the school had had able headmasters — among them Richard Smith and Anthony Blackwall — but the present incumbent was an elderly parson named John Kilby, who would hardly have inspired his undermaster.

The routine of the school must have been much like that at Lichfield or Stourbridge. Before Johnson's time, the school hours were from six to eleven in the morning and from one to five in the afternoon with half holidays on Thursdays, Saturdays, and holy evens. Greek and Latin were the only languages spoken during school hours, English being specifically forbidden. Indeed, speaking English, along with swearing and unseemly talk, was a punishable offense. There were also rules for the protection of students. If a master should strike a scholar about the head or face, he was subject to a fine of one shilling, though, of course, nothing was said about thrashings of other portions of the body. Commenting on his own particular duties, Johnson wrote to Hector that he had "to teach Lillie's Grammar to a few boys, and it was hard to say whose difficulty was greatest, he to explain nonsense, or they to understand it." [25]

He further described to his friend the "dull sameness of his existence" with the quotation "Vitam continet una dies (one day contains the whole of my life)." It was as "unvaried as the note of the cuckoo." [26] Disgusted by the humiliating treatment he received at the Hall, and bored by his routine teaching of grammar, he spent his leisure time, according to Shaw, "assiduously in the pursuit of intellectual acquisition and amusement." Only in this way could he temporarily forget his dismal position.

There was one bit of light in all this gloom. Sir Wolstan Dixie's younger brother, the Rev. Beaumont Dixie, who was the rector of Market Bosworth, had married the sister of Andrew Corbet, whose rooms at Pembroke Johnson had been supposed to share. John Corbet, an agreeable younger brother, described by Johnson as "a youth once very delightful to me, and not because, if I am right, he then loved me most," was sometimes in the neighborhood.[27] When dining at the rectory Sam was apt to find more agreeable companionship than at the Hall or the school.

Meanwhile at home some efforts were being made to settle Michael's affairs. About the middle of June, Sam made a hurried trip to Lichfield to see what was going on. A few scattered diary entries, made later in a little memorandum book first begun at Oxford, tell the meager details (the original entries are in Latin). "June 15 — I laid by eleven guineas; on which day I received all of my father's effects which I can hope for till the death of my mother (which I pray may be late), that is to say, nineteen pounds; so that I have my fortune to make, and care must be taken that in the meantime the powers of my mind may not grow languid through poverty, nor want drive me into wickedness." [28] Actually the entire amount of his inheritance was twenty pounds, but apparently at an earlier time he had borrowed one pound, which necessitated the deduction.

The next day he walked the twenty-five miles back to Market Bosworth — through Tamworth, Polesworth, Orton on the Hill, and Sheepy Magna — back to the old drudgery. But with a few pounds in his pocket, at least he could be more independent in his attitude toward the bullying Sir Wolstan Dixie, and sometime early in July the two quarreled for the last time. Johnson quit his job and returned to Lichfield a free' man. He was probably back in the bookshop by the second week of the month, when he corrected the Latin and typographical errors in a book he chanced to pick up. The volume — *Manuductio ad Coelum,* by Giovanni Bona, published at Cologne in 1671 — still bears the inscription "Sam: Johnson," the date July 13, 1732, and a list of Latin words and phrases which he thought wrong.[29]

Leaving one position did not blind him to the necessity of securing another speedily, and when on the night of July 26 he heard from Corbet of the sudden death of the usher of the school at Ashbourne, he tried at once to get the post. The next day he dashed off letters to Corbet, to George Venables Vernon of Sudbury, then M.P. for Lichfield and a possible influential backer, and to his intimate friend John Taylor, now practicing as an attorney at Ashbourne. Assuming that Taylor would do all in his power to help his application, Johnson asked his opinion "of the means most proper to be used in this matter." [30] He added, "If there be any occasion for my coming to Ashbourne, I shall readily do it. Mr. Corbett has, I suppose, given you an account of my leaving Sir Wolstan's. It was really e carcere exire [coming out of prison]."

When the governors of the school met on August 1, however, Johnson was not chosen; indeed, it does not appear that he was even formally considered.[31] His Ashbourne friends had evidently

not been very assiduous on his behalf, or were not very powerful.
The fact that the winning candidate was not a university graduate shows that this time the lack of a degree was not the only
thing which stood in Johnson's way.

There followed more unprofitable months at home, with nothing to do but read and help his mother and brother in the shop.
It is doubtful if even such exciting events as the winning of a
wager by a gentleman who rode all the way from London to
Rugeley in Staffordshire in fourteen hours, or the robbing of the
Lichfield stagecoach by a single highwayman, roused him from
his depressed state.[32] Then finally, in the autumn, his friend
Edmund Hector came to the rescue with an invitation to visit him
in Birmingham.

Only a few years later another visitor to Birmingham, William
Hutton, was impressed by its handsome outskirts, the elegance
of the new buildings, and the absence of old-fashioned thatched
roofs, as compared with the wretched dwellings seen in nearby
towns. He was astonished, too, by the alertness and vivacity of
the people. He had been living, he thought, among dreamers;
now he saw men awake. In this happy and prosperous place
progress was in the air.[33] As a much older man, Johnson could
afford to be scornful of the rising industrial city, and when Boswell pointed out the idleness of Lichfield citizens, Johnson retorted: "Sir, we are a city of philosophers: we work with our heads,
and make the boobies of Birmingham work for us with their
hands." But in 1732 he, too, must have found something exhilarating in the bustle of the rapidly developing "seat of the mechanic
arts."

There was nothing to indicate that this would be any different
from other casual visits to old schoolmates. Hector asked him to
come, and Sam accepted, not knowing whether he would stay a
week, a month, or even longer.[34] In his state of mind any diversion was welcome. He could have had no intimation that the
trip would prove momentous, that it would ultimately provide
him with a wife.

On Sam's arrival, it was natural for Hector to introduce his
guest to his own intimate circle — to another John Taylor whose

genius in the gilding and japanning trade later brought him a
fortune, and to a Huguenot refugee, M. Desmoulins, a writing
master at the Birmingham Free Grammar School who married
Dr. Swinfen's daughter Elizabeth. Nearby there was the family
of a mercer and woolen draper named Harry Porter, from whom
Hector bought his clothes. Possibly Sam knew something of the
Porters already, since Harry's sister was married to the dreaded
headmaster of the Lichfield Grammar School, John Hunter.[35]
But it was only through Hector that Sam met Mrs. Porter, the
woman who would one day become his own adored "Tetty."

At the time she can have appeared little different from other
middle-aged ladies whom he knew. Whether he remembered
vaguely having seen her on other trips to Birmingham, whether
he was at once attracted by her charm or stirred by her conversation, Johnson never told. The only account of their meeting
comes from someone else who was present, Lucy Porter, the eldest
of the children. Long afterward she described for Boswell what
happened.

At first their guest's appearance seemed particularly forbidding.
"He was then lean and lank, so that his immense structure of
bones was hideously striking to the eye, and the scars of the
scrofula were deeply visible. He also wore his hair, which was
straight and stiff, and separated behind; and he often had, seem-
ingly, convulsive starts and odd gesticulations, which tended to
excite at once surprise and ridicule." [36] Yet Mrs. Porter was so
delighted by his conversation that she overlooked these faults,
and said to her daughter when he had departed: "This is the most
sensible man that I ever saw in my life." He must also have impressed the head of the household, for in succeeding months
Johnson was often at the mercer's house.

The forty-one-year-old Harry Porter is a shadowy figure. No
one — his wife, children, or friends — thought it worth while
to describe him for posterity. Why should they? He was an ordinary merchant, better born, to be sure, than many, but not pre-
eminent either in business ability or intellectual attainments. He
came of an old Warwickshire family, of which many had been
well-to-do mercers. His father had been a governor of King Ed-

ward's School in Birmingham. Brought up in the trade, Harry had had no time for a university education. Yet he seems to have been a pleasant and hospitable companion.

His wife, two years his elder, had been Elizabeth Jervis, daughter of a Warwickshire squire, who brought with her a dowry of over six hundred pounds. A plump matron in her early forties, she had ripe full lips and expressive eyes. Her hair was "eminently beautiful, quite blond like that of a baby," so Johnson later told Mrs. Thrale.[37] There was a rounded fullness in her face, with an expression wholly feminine. Her manner was sometimes a bit affected, with the coy archness of one who knows her own charms and refuses to be taken for granted. Yet behind the flashes of pretended roguishness there was a fund of sound common sense. There was nothing silly or foolish about her intelligence. Doubtless it was this combination of full-blown femininity and keen wit that appealed to Sam Johnson. Yet there could have been no thought of falling in love. Mrs. Porter was merely an attractive lady old enough to have been his mother, the wife of a new-found acquaintance, with whom he found it pleasant to while away dreary hours. At the Porters' he could be sure of good talk and convivial hospitality.

As a young man Johnson was not the total abstainer and hardened tea drinker of the Boswellian years. His favorite beverage when in Birmingham was "Bishop," a concoction of port wine with sugar and a roasted orange. This he took freely, and by his own confession sometimes misjudged his capacity. "I used to slink home, when I had drunk too much," he admitted, adding that a man accustomed to self-examination would be conscious when he had gone too far, though a habitual drunkard would not.[38] Such occasions, however, were rare, and he once boasted to Boswell that no man alive had ever seen him drunk. When Hector chanced to hear of the claim he told Boswell an amusing story, not included in the *Life*, about one occasion when Johnson had at least approached that state.[39]

It was during 1733 or 1734, when one of the Fords from Stourbridge — possibly one of Sam's cousins, Gregory or Joseph — came to Birmingham on a trip and asked Johnson and Hector to spend the evening with him at the Swan Inn. Knowing the man's reputation as a hard drinker, Sam was afraid of what might happen, but because of past obligations the invitation had to be accepted. A plan was devised whereby he and Hector would divide the evening, one taking the earlier part and the other the later. Sam drew the second shift, but by the time he arrived three bottles of port had been consumed and Hector, being in no condition to go home, went to bed at the inn. Sam, who had been injudiciously drinking at the Porters' instead of "saving himself," wound up in the same bed with his friend. Strictly speaking, Hector had not seen Johnson drunk, but from his condition the next morning was sure of the fact.

Though he occasionally drank too much, Johnson was not lax in his sexual behavior. There was no doubt in Hector's mind on that score. "Johnson never was given to women," he insisted, "yet he then did not appear to have much religion." [40] Hector took pains also to refute one particularly scandalous tale which was later spread by Benjamin Victor, a theatrical manager, that Johnson, along with Dr. James and Victor himself, had been a lover of the dissolute wife of the inventor Lewis Paul. But James had left Birmingham before Johnson arrived, and there are so many other chronological difficulties that it is obvious the tale was preposterous. Hector's definite assertion is surely worth a hundred such wild rumors.

Hector's apartments, when Sam visited him, were in the house of Thomas Warren, the first established bookseller of the city, in the High Street by the Swan Inn. The two young men also had their meals at Warren's table, with Hector footing the bill. The neighborhood was familiar to Johnson, since the homes of his two uncles, Andrew Johnson and John Harrison, whom he had first visited when he was nine years old, had been nearby. The disagreeable "Uncle Harrison" was probably still there.

In November, 1732, the enterprising Warren started a local newspaper, with the title *The Birmingham Journal* — a folded sheet of four pages which appeared every Thursday. For the most part the contents were lifted verbatim from the London papers, and there was a minimum of local news, together with a few advertisements. In order to have some original material he tried including a new periodical essay in each issue. Living and boarding in the same house with the publisher, Johnson agreed to contribute some pieces.[41] But not a single copy of *The Birmingham Journal* for the autumn of 1732 and the winter of 1733 is known to have survived. His first printed essays, the goal of all Johnsonian detectives, remain undiscovered.

After some six months, on the first of June, 1733, Johnson left Hector and Warren's house and took lodgings with F. Jervis, who lived in the lower part of the city.[42] The immediate cause of the move is not indicated, but after such a long dependence on his friend's hospitality, Sam may have had twinges of conscience. Shortly afterward, Hector took a house of his own in the New Street section.

Life in busy, cheerful Birmingham did not alter Johnson's habits. Apparently he still was idle most of the time, lounging about with his few friends, doing little work. As Hector remembered, he would occasionally steal away to read, but proudly tried to hide the fact that he ever studied. He liked to give the impression that his talk was all original. Nor had his melancholia been more than temporarily arrested by his host's kind ministrations. Once he moved into a room by himself, he again grew depressed and moody. He was absent-minded and distraught; he talked to himself and peevishly picked quarrels with his best friend. Then when Hector kept aloof for a while, Sam would come and coax him back.

His condition became so desperate that Hector really worried about his sanity, and Johnson was afraid to ask his friend's opinion lest it corroborate his own worst fears. It was a critical moment in his life, for he might well have broken down completely. But some inner drive kept him going. Despite the pose of indifference he affected, underneath he was fiercely ambitious. Though apparently indolent and supine, he was constantly goaded on by some inner compulsion to show the world that he was superior. He was far from content to sink back into passive mediocrity.

Perhaps one reason was the memory of his father. Here was an ever-present object lesson. From infancy Sam had identified himself in many ways with Michael at the same time that he was unable to love him. The two had many of the same qualities. Both were creatures of sharp contrasts, with huge physiques and active but unstable minds. Only by hard exercise had Michael been able to ward off the black fits of melancholy which constantly threatened his sanity. A man of great gifts and personal attraction, he missed success because of some hidden flaw of character. With fascination Sam had watched his father's debacle, seeing the inevitable results of personality traits which he recognized only too clearly in himself. He must somehow steer a different course. The way was not yet clear in his mind, but this settled ambition, combined with a tenacious courage, gave him an ultimate resiliency to failure and depression.

Obviously what he most needed was something to take his mind off himself. The wise Hector pressed him to set to work on a project which had earlier been suggested. One day at Warren's table Johnson had mentioned that at Oxford he had read a French translation by Joachim Le Grand of the travels to Abyssinia by Father Jerome Lobo, a Portuguese Jesuit, and suggested that an abridgment and translation into English might prove a profitable undertaking. Much of the story, with its descriptions of an exotic unknown land, had romantic appeal. Also there was possibly a political aspect which might affect the sale. The alliance with Portugal was considered one of the keystones of Whig diplomacy. Yet here was a book which gave a rather unfavorable view of Portuguese colonial activity. Although Johnson did not see the account as a piece of Tory propaganda, the political implications did not render it any less attractive to him or to a publisher.

The trouble was that no copy of Le Grand's volume could be found in Birmingham, so that the project had to be postponed. It was not until late in 1733 that Hector was able to borrow from Oxford a copy of the one-volume Paris edition of 1728, and Johnson could begin his translation.[43] Even then the work moved slowly. With his customary procrastination, Sam was incapable of sustained effort.

Finally Hector decided to use another approach, this time to work on his friend's humanitarian sympathies. He told Johnson that while the translation was hanging fire Warren's printer was unable to get other work done, and in consequence he and his family suffered. Moved by such an appeal, Johnson struggled on, though even then the job was completed only through Hector's active cooperation. Johnson lay in bed, with the French volume propped up before him, and dictated his English version. Hector wrote it down, recopied most of the manuscript, carried it to the printer, and even corrected most of the proofs.

For this labor Johnson received five guineas and Hector the happiness of being helpful to his friend. But since the busy young surgeon could not devote all his time to goading his companion to work, Sam's future remained as bleak as ever. Consequently, in February, 1734, Johnson returned to Lichfield in practically the same state of mind as when he had left it.[44]

Not until early in 1735 did the *Voyage to Abyssinia* finally appear, and it must be admitted that Johnson was never particularly proud of it.[45] He knew very well that his first published volume was largely a routine translation (in parts an exact rendering and elsewhere an epitome) of the work of another man. He recognized that much of the body of the text was pedestrian writing. On the other hand, historically it has some importance. Even in an abridgment there is evidence of a writer's own tastes and convictions, and in the preface he reveals a great deal of himself.

Throughout, Johnson tried to be eminently fair to the Jesuits. To be sure, at the beginning he makes it clear that he himself is not a Papist, and he condemns with some passion the sanguinary zeal of rabid missionaries who "preach the gospel with swords in their hands, and propagate by desolation and slaughter the true worship of the God of Peace." Nor does he mince words in castigating "those who are continually grasping for domination over souls as well as bodies . . . studying methods of destroying their fellow creatures, not for their crimes but for their errors," particularly as part of the spread of Portuguese commerce.[46] But Johnson never explicitly attacks basic Catholic doctrine. He was always sympathetic to high ideals and courage wherever he found them.

Elsewhere in the preface there are signs of the real Johnson.

By 1734 his basic concepts, as well as his style, were well formed. His beliefs were not unusual for the time — the skeptical common sense, the Lockian insistence on acquisition of knowledge through sense impressions, the refusal to believe that mankind was much different anywhere throughout the world, the distrust of romantic fiction unless labeled as fiction. But he was not merely paying lip service to these ideas; he had come to them through his own unhappy experiences and as a result of his own deep thought. By temperament and training he was even at this early date prepared to be a spokesman for his age. It might as well have been the sage of seventy as the youth of twenty-four who wrote:

> The Portuguese traveler, contrary to the general vein of his countrymen, has amused his reader with no romantic absurdities, or incredible fictions; whatever he relates, whether true or not, is at least probable; and he who tells nothing exceeding the bounds of probability, has a right to demand that they should believe him who cannot contradict him.
>
> He appears, by his modest and unaffected narration, to have described things as he saw them, to have copied nature from the life, and to have consulted his senses, not his imagination. He meets with no basilisks that destroy with their eyes, his crocodiles devour their prey without tears, and his cataracts fall from the rocks without deafening the neighboring inhabitants.

Here are some of the same literary devices and mannerisms he later used with such skill. Witness the great rolling passage which follows, with its ponderous weight, its antitheses and formal generalizations.

> The reader will here find no regions cursed with irremediable barrenness, or blessed with spontaneous fecundity; no perpetual gloom, or unceasing sunshine; nor are the nations here described either devoid of all sense of humanity, or consummate in all private and social virtues. Here are no Hottentots without religion, polity, or articulate language; no Chinese perfectly polite, and completely skilled in all sciences; he will discover, what will always be discovered by a diligent and impartial inquirer, that wherever human na-

ture is to be found, there is a mixture of vice and virtue, a contest of passion and reason; and that the Creator doth not appear partial in his distributions, but has balanced, in most countries, their particular inconveniences by particular favors.

If the authorship were not already well known, if one stumbled on these sentences merely by chance, there would be an irresistible impulse to cry out "Samuel Johnson." Already the style is the man. Moreover, he had developed it carefully. He once told Boswell "that he had formed his style upon that of Sir William Temple and upon Chambers's Proposal for his Dictionary." [47] While it may be difficult to see specific resemblances to these models, the important point is that Johnson made a conscious effort to shape his powers of expression to fit his ideas.

It might be added that the volume about Abyssinia brought Johnson his earliest extensive review. In the *Literary Magazine: or Select British Library* for March, 1735, over fifteen pages were devoted to an analysis and excerpts from the work. Johnson's own confessions as to the liberties he had taken with the original are repeated, but there is no harsh criticism at which the translator might take offense. Also, the amount of space given to the discussion was undoubtedly flattering.

One way of getting a start in the literary world was to publish by subscription. At one time or another almost every author of the day attempted it, and Johnson was no exception. There were the Latin poems of Politian, a late Renaissance writer, which he now considered editing with notes, a life of the author, and a history of Latin poetry from the age of Petrarch to that of Politian. As with the translation of Le Grand, it was first necessary to obtain an authentic text. Hearing that an old Pembroke man, the minister of the church at Smethwick on the outskirts of Birmingham, was going back to Oxford on a visit, Johnson asked him to pick up the volume. The register of books borrowed from Pembroke College Library shows that he did so. The volume was not returned, and fifty years later, after Johnson's death, it was found among his books.[48]

On August 5, printed proposals were sent out, soliciting subscriptions for the edition, which was to contain thirty sheets. The advertised price was 2/6 at the time of subscribing and a similar amount payable on the delivery of the book unbound. Subscriptions were to be taken by the editor or by Nathaniel Johnson, "bookseller, of Lichfield." Johnson actively solicited purchasers in the neighborhood and wrote to one man: "I hope you will excuse the liberty I have taken of troubling you with my proposals. I doubt not of your willingness to encourage any undertaking in the way of letters, and am satisfied that my success may be much promoted by your recommendation." [49] Unfortunately the inhabitants of provincial towns were not eager to have a copy of the Latin poems of Politian even at such a low price. Although a few of Johnson's personal friends subscribed, there were not enough to make the printing worth while, and the project was finally dropped.

In this unsettled period, Johnson seriously tried keeping a diary. Part of the compulsion, no doubt, came from his tendency to morbid introspection. But the strict self-discipline imposed by a diary was part of a recognized evangelical, methodistic pattern. There was always a strong Calvinistic strain in his religious convictions. According to Hawkins, "To enable him at times to review his progress in life, and to estimate his improvement in religion, he, in the year 1734, began to note down the transactions of each day, recollecting, as well as he was able, those of his youth, and interspersing such reflections and resolutions as, under particular circumstances, he was induced to make." [50] Hawkins added, "This register, which he intitled 'Annales,' does not form an entire volume, but is contained in a variety of little books folded and stitched together by himself."

The existing fragments, however, scarcely correspond to any such description. There are a few sheets, dated November 10, 1734, and boldly labeled "Annales," in which he set down in Latin the chief events of his life up to that year. But it is not clear whether this title also referred to the other scattered entries. Perhaps a part of what Hawkins saw was lost in the fire which destroyed his house in 1785. Or it is possible that in that last holocaust just before Johnson's death, when he burned so many of his family papers, some complete diaries may have been consumed. On the other hand, considering his temperament, the chances are strong that he was never a very voluminous or regular diarist. He did not have the irresistible "itch to record" or the energy of a Pepys or a Boswell.

Sam Johnson, now twenty-five years old, was still wholly unsuccessful in finding a profession, no more certain of how he could make a living than he had been at fifteen. There was ample reason for his general dejection.

CHAPTER IX

"Tetty" and the
Edial Experiment

J UST at this low point in Johnson's life an event occurred in
Birmingham which was to bring about a momentous change.
At the early age of forty-three, his good friend Harry Porter the
mercer died and was buried at Edgbaston on September 5. The
surviving records are tantalizingly vague as to what caused his
death or whether he had long been ill. The only pertinent comment is the improbable tale of Anna Seward that Johnson attended Porter's sickbed conscientiously during his last days.[1] If
so, he was making frequent trips back and forth from Lichfield.

What is certain is that Johnson was assiduous in comforting the
widow, especially when it became apparent that she was not
averse to remarrying. At the death of her husband "the Widow
Porter" was forty-five years old, the mother of three children —
Lucy, aged eighteen; Jervis Henry, sixteen; and Joseph, ten. Although Harry Porter had been unsuccessful as a merchant and
left his affairs in a tangled condition, a large part of his wife's
dowry of over six hundred pounds was legally still hers through
the marriage settlement.[2] To the impecunious Sam Johnson it
would have appeared a large sum indeed. Yet no one with any
knowledge of Johnson has ever suggested that he married Mrs.
Porter for her money. While it did not make her any less attractive, there were other reasons more compelling.

For two centuries people have wondered about the attraction
of this mature woman for the man twenty years her junior. Why
should he who had written glowing verses to various young ladies
in their teens suddenly succumb to someone approaching middle
age? Yet Johnson's behavior seems to fall into a characteristic

151

pattern. An emotionally unstable young man with physical disabilities often finds himself more at home with older women than with girls of his own age. With the latter there is the dread of rejection because of real or imagined faults, or the fear of embarrassing difficulties as the result of fumbling approaches. A widow, on the other hand, might be expected to have passed through the sentimental vapors of romantic illusion. She would be more likely to see real worth beneath a rough exterior. And she could be a ready teacher in the mysterious realm of sex.

That sexual attraction played a large part in the matter is certain. "Sir, it was a love marriage upon both sides," Johnson later told Beauclerk. There is no reason to doubt the assertion.[3] He was not the type to be satisfied with merely an intellectual relationship. In Boswell's words, "unless a woman has amorous heat she is a dull companion." [4] He desperately needed physical love, as well as affection and mothering. Up to this time all he had done was to dream, exerting rigid self-control and refusing to indulge in any philandering. He needed a wife. Nevertheless, it is doubtful that he would ever have worked himself up to active courtship without open partiality from the buxom widow herself.

It is customary to think of Tetty as unattractive. Most of the unflattering descriptions, however, stem from her later years. Garrick described her as "very fat, with a bosom of more than ordinary protuberance, with swelled cheeks, of a florid red, produced by thick painting, and increased by the liberal use of cordials; flaring and fantastic in her dress, and affected both in her speech and her general behavior." [5] On another occasion he called her "a little painted poppet; full of affectation and rural airs of elegance." Anna Seward, quoting secondhand from her mother, who represented the point of view of the Porter family, wrote: "She had a very red face, and very indifferent features; and her manners in advanced life, for her children were all grown up when Johnson first saw her, had an unbecoming excess of girlish levity, and disgusting affectation."

Some have scornfully tried to explain the choice as a result of his nearsightedness, but such an explanation slanders both parties.[6] Johnson always saw well enough to recognize feminine beauty.

Besides, how certain is it that the widow when she remarried lacked physical charms? The only surviving portrait shows her as an attractive young woman, and Shaw insists that when Johnson first knew her she was "still young and handsome" — so good-looking that Sam's friends marveled at the difference between them. Moreover, she had a strong and original mind — she was "a lady of great sensibility and worth; so shrewd and cultivated, that in the earlier part of their connection, he was very fond of consulting her in all his literary pursuits." Johnson himself insisted that she read comedy better than anyone he had ever heard, though in tragedy "she always mouthed too much." He so respected her abilities that he used to get her daughter Lucy on his side before beginning a dispute.

If the nature of the lady's charms has caused some wonder, equally puzzling must be what she found attractive in the lank young man with the nervous, convulsive starts and the depressed state of mind. As a tolerably good-looking widow with money, why should she have set her cap for such a husband? It could scarcely have been, as Mrs. Desmoulins later claimed, that she wanted someone to take care of her.[7] Nor could it have been that she suspected he would one day be famous. It is more reasonable to suppose, as did Johnson, that she was genuinely in love with him. There were strong physical and mental attractions on both sides. Later evidence shows clearly that other ladies found Johnson appealing. For her part, Tetty appears to have been quite carried away by her infatuation.

Her family and friends were horrified at such an unsuitable match. Her older son, then in training for the navy, refused ever to see his mother again. The younger, who became a merchant at Leghorn, apparently never lived with his new stepfather and was for many years unreconciled. Only her daughter Lucy bowed to the inevitable. It is said that Harry Porter's brother was so shocked by the prospect of the marriage that he offered his sister-in-law a handsome annuity if she would give up "the literary cub." [8] Yet she obstinately withstood all pressures. Like another widow in her forties, Johnson's later friend Mrs. Thrale, with her Italian musician, Piozzi, she was quite willing, where her heart was concerned, to ignore the prudent voice of society and tradition. Besides, she knew that her two sons would be well provided for by their wealthy bachelor uncle, though their continuing resentment was a source of deep sorrow to her.

During the autumn and winter of 1734–1735 Johnson was back and forth between Lichfield and Birmingham. Although she had vacated her house in the High Street, Mrs. Porter and her daughter probably remained in lodgings nearby.

With thoughts of marriage uppermost in his mind, Sam began to consider other schemes for making a living. The best-known monthly periodical of the day, and one that was ultimately to play an important part in Johnson's career, was the *Gentleman's Magazine*. Begun in London in 1731 by Edward Cave, it speedily gained popularity, and Johnson had undoubtedly followed its rise with interest, naturally longing to be connected with such an undertaking. On November 25, 1734, he wrote from Birmingham to Cave, offering his services "on reasonable terms sometimes to fill a column" of the poetry section. With some lack of tact he suggested numerous improvements by which the literary part of the magazine might "be better recommended to the public, than by low jests, awkward buffoonery, or the dull scurrilities of either party." He agreed to supply unpublished poems, inscriptions, short dissertations in Latin and English, and critical remarks. Cave's recent offer of a prize of fifty pounds for the best original poem on "life, death, judgment, heaven, and hell," he remarked, had led him to expect generous payment. As a further lure, he added, "If you engage in any literary projects beside this paper, I have other designs to impart if I could be secure from having others reap the advantage of what I should hint." Hoping for a reply "in two posts," he asked that the letter be "directed to S. Smith," at the Castle Inn in Birmingham.[9]

It is not clear why Johnson should have written under an assumed name. Cave was a complete stranger to whom Smith and Johnson would have been equally unknown. Could it have been that Johnson had written earlier from Lichfield under his own name, with no success, and now wished to try again from another place? Or did he think the obvious pseudonym might lead Cave to suspect a noble author wishing to hide his identity? On the original letter Cave methodically noted "Answered Dec. 2," and there is a tradition that he accepted "S. Smith's" offer.[10] If so, nothing definite came of it at this time.

Meanwhile the pursuit of the widow continued, and by May, at least, everything was settled. "Tetty" — Sam used the then common contraction of Elizabeth — had consented to marry him.[11] Naturally, before taking the step he consulted his mother. Boswell claimed that Mrs. Johnson, knowing the ardor of her son's temper, was too sensible to oppose his choice, whatever she might have thought. Anna Seward tells a different story. From her lively imagination, fortified by how much genuine evidence it is impossible to tell, she later provided a colorful account of just what happened when Sam came to ask his mother's consent.[12] After expressing her surprise at so extraordinary an alliance, his mother said:

> No, Sam, my willing consent you will never have to so preposterous a union. You are not twenty-five, and she is turned fifty. If she had any prudence, this request had never been made to me. Where are your means of subsistence? Porter has died poor, in consequence of his wife's expensive habits. You have great talents, but, as yet, have turned them into no profitable channel.

To this Sam is supposed to have replied:

> Mother, I have not deceived Mrs. Porter: I have told her the worst of me; that I am of mean extraction; that I have no money; and that I have had an uncle hanged. She replied, that she valued no one more or less for his descent; that she had no more money than myself; and that, though she had not had a relation hanged, she had fifty who deserved hanging.

Though decided upon by late spring, the marriage did not take place until summer, perhaps to make it appear less precipitous. To fill the intervening time, Johnson became a private tutor in the household of Thomas Whitby of Great Haywood, not far from Lichfield.[13] It was Theophilus Levett, the town clerk, always a good friend, and John Addenbrooke, then perpetual curate of

St. Chad's and later Dean of Lichfield, who helped him to the post. At first Whitby wanted to hire someone for six months, to prepare his eldest boy for the university, but when Adden-brooke wrote on May 10 that Johnson's plans "won't give him leave to be with your son so long," a shorter period was agreed upon. In the end he was there for less than two months.

Addenbrooke's qualified recommendation suggests Sam's local reputation. Everyone was aware of the young man's tremendous capabilities, but there could never be any certainty as to how he would apply them. "I can only say, that if Mr. Johnson will do what he is capable of doing in that time he will be of more service to your son than a year spent in the usual way at the university."

There were five children in the Whitby family, and while John, who was nineteen, was ostensibly Johnson's charge, the tutor was expected also to give some care to the others. Long afterward, Jane, the youngest, who was thirteen at the time, remembered vividly her frequent instruction "in the English language." [14] On Sundays the family went the mile and a half to Colwich Church, where the vicar was a young Oxford man. Upon their return home Johnson frequently astonished them all by "repeating the greatest part of the sermon, with criticisms, additions, and improvements." But the short interlude at Great Haywood left little impression on Johnson, a man about to plunge into marriage and busy making plans for the future.

With Tetty's personal fortune, he could now do something he had long contemplated — set up a school of his own. The first practical step was to get back his extensive library, which had been left at Oxford more than five years before. When a chance meeting with one of the Repingtons of Tamworth brought an offer of help, Johnson wrote from Lichfield to Gilbert Repington, then in his first year at Christ Church, asking that the boxes be sent to him at the Castle Inn in Birmingham.

> The books (of which I have written a catalogue on the other side) were left with Mr. Taylor, from whom I had some reason to expect a regard to my affairs. There were in the same box, which I left locked, some papers of a very private nature, which I hope fell into

good hands. The books are now, I hear, with Mr. Spicer of Christ Church.[15]

Evidently he got the books, for some of them were still in his possession at the time of his death.

The letter to Repington provided an opportunity to send regards to another old Lichfield schoolmate, Richard Congreve, who stiffly acknowledged the message a few weeks later. To this Johnson wrote back from Great Haywood on June 25, complaining of the "excess of ceremony" which his younger friend had used.[16] Their previous familiarity had not led him to expect such formality. Yet Johnson himself indulged in some uncharacteristic flights in the high style, with prating about rural retreats "unpolluted by flattery and falsehood," and "thickets where interest and artifice never lay concealed!" Obviously it was all written with tongue in cheek. For once he could safely let himself go in the popular high-flown vein, since this was the taste of his correspondent.

It is usual, Johnson continued, for friends long separated to tell each other what has happened since last they met, "but as little has happened to me that you can receive any pleasure from the relation of, I will not trouble you with an account of time not always very agreeably spent, but instead of past disappointments shall acquaint you with my present scheme of life." He then continued:

I am now going to furnish a house in the country, and keep a private boarding school for young gentlemen whom I shall endeavor to instruct in a method somewhat more rational than those commonly practiced which you know there is no great vanity in presuming to attempt. Before I draw up my plan of education, I shall attempt to procure an account of the different ways of teaching in use at the most celebrated schools, and shall therefore hope you will favor me with the method of the Charterhouse, and procure me that of Westminster.

It may be written in a few lines by only mentioning under each class their exercise and authors.

You see I ask new favors before I have thanked you for those I have received. . . .

Not a word about the widow Porter or his approaching marriage! While appealing to Congreve for a frank exchange of ideas, Johnson failed to mention his own most important piece of news. He must have foreseen what would be the reactions of the young Christ Church undergraduates to his choice of a wife. Better to let his marriage become known later, after the step was taken.

Soon after this letter was written, Johnson left Great Haywood. On July 8, 1735, a license was issued at Derby for the marriage of Samuel Johnson, of the parish of St. Mary in Lichfield, bachelor, aged twenty-five years, to Elizabeth Porter, of the parish of St. Philip in Birmingham, widow, aged "forty." [17] The license was issued by the Rev. William Lockett, Vicar of St. Werburgh's; and Sam's boyhood friend, Charles Howard, now proctor of the ecclesiastical court in Lichfield, stood surety to the customary bond. The next day, a little over ten months after the death of Harry Porter, the couple were married in St. Werburgh's Church.

There need be no mystery about the choice of Derby for the wedding. The strong opposition to the match by Tetty's family and friends eliminated Birmingham. Besides, Johnson had never been popular there, except in his own small circle. Lucy Porter told Boswell that "the Birmingham people could not bear Mr. Johnson." [18] Lichfield may have been passed by for a similar reason, to avoid the sneers and jokes of his old companions. A penniless young man marrying a much older woman with money would obviously prefer a place where they were not well known. Derby must have appeared a suitable spot.

The couple rode to the wedding, presumably from Lichfield, where Tetty may have been quietly staying for a few days in the Cathedral Close. On the way occurred the well-known episode when Johnson thought best to discipline his coquettish bride. He told Boswell what happened.

Sir, she had read the old romances, and had got into her head the fantastical notion that a woman of spirit should use her lover like a

dog. So, Sir, at first she told me that I rode too fast, and she could
not keep up with me; and, when I rode a little slower, she passed
me, and complained that I lagged behind. I was not to be made the
slave of caprice; and I resolved to begin as I meant to end. I therefore pushed on briskly, till I was fairly out of her sight. The road lay
between two hedges, so I was sure she could not miss it; and I
contrived that she should soon come up with me. When she did, I
observed her to be in tears.[19]

His reaction was characteristic. Johnson could never give himself up wholeheartedly to romance, whether in life or in literature. There was in him a continual struggle between sentiment
and common sense, between emotion and reason. Thus, while he
always insisted that his had been a love match, he once remarked
to Boswell that it was "commonly a weak man who marries for
love." [20]

There is no record of where they spent their honeymoon or
where they lived for the next few months. The furnished house
mentioned in the letter to Congreve had not progressed beyond
the planning stage. Johnson seemed quite willing to give up the
whole scheme of the school if something better developed. When
news came about the middle of July that the headmaster of the
school at Solihull, a small village some seven miles southeast of
Birmingham, was leaving to take over the post at Market Bosworth, Johnson made every effort to be his successor.

Gilbert Walmesley immediately wrote on his behalf to Henry
Greswold at Solihull. But when the latter replied on the thirtieth,
it was the same old story. Greswold had delayed writing, he explained, since the feoffees, the governing body of the school, "desired some time to make inquiry of the character of Mr. Johnson,
who all agree that he is an excellent scholar, and upon that account deserves much better than to be schoolmaster of Solihull.
But then he has the character of being a very haughty, ill-natured
gent., and that he has such a way of distorting his face (which
though he can't help) the gent. think it may affect some young
lads; for these two reasons he is not approved on, the late master
Mr. Crompton's huffing the feoffees being still in their memory." [21]

Johnson could not have been greatly disappointed, since Solihull was not a very attractive post. Now that this possibility had
proved abortive, he could actively start to set up his own academy.
Walmesley, his kind patron, took the lead in every detail. He
suggested as suitable a big house at Edial (pronounced, and sometimes written, Edjal), about two and a half miles west of Lichfield. It was a square brick house, enclosed by a court and garden
walls, which had been built shortly after the Restoration. Archi-
tecturally something of a monstrosity, it had a steep pyramidal
roof, interrupted about two-thirds of the way up by a flat roof,
which was surrounded by an ornamental balustrade. In the center
rose a tall timber cupola, with a pointed top, used as an ob-
servatory. There were small dormer windows near the top of
the roof slopes.[22]

Perhaps the large structure was already a white elephant in
1735, and Johnson could secure it as a subtenant at a low rental.
In many ways it must have been ideal for a boarding school, although it took time to make the necessary alterations — to fit up
the back room on the ground floor as a schoolroom and to furnish
the rest of the house. Not until late autumn or early winter did
the project actually get under way.

While he was waiting, Johnson gave more thought to his plan of
instruction. But the "somewhat more rational" method promised in his letter to Congreve turned out to be not very different
from what he himself had followed under Hawkins and Hunter.
The authors to be studied were much the same, and there were
to be similar examination periods on Thursdays and Saturdays.
Moreover, when his younger cousin Samuel Ford asked his advice, late in 1735, about a course of reading to prepare him to
enter Oxford the next spring, Johnson's suggestions were purely
conventional.[23] "Apply yourself wholly to the languages," he
wrote. The Greek authors should be studied chronologically —
from Cebes to Euripides — in order that the student be "tolerably skilled in all the dialects, beginning with the Attic, to which
the rest must be referred." Accepting without question the traditional mimetic theory and the desire for correctness, he gave as his
final piece of advice: "The greatest and most necessary task still

remains, to attain a habit of expression, without which knowledge is of little use. This is necessary in Latin, and more necessary in English; and can only be acquired by a daily imitation of the best and correctest authors."

When all was ready it was Walmesley again who secured at least three of the pupils — David Garrick, his younger brother George, and Lawrence Offley, a relative of the Astons. Boswell refers to the three as "the only pupils that were put under his care," and Tom Davies speaks of "three or four." Hawkins, however, thought there were more. Conditions were so adverse that neither Johnson's abilities, "nor the patronage of Mr. Walmesley, nor the exertions of Mrs. Johnson and her relations, succeeded farther than to produce an accession of about five or six pupils; so that his number, at no time, exceeded eight, and of those not all were boarders." [24]

Realizing that he must have more students if the project were to be self-supporting, Johnson inserted an advertisement in the *Gentleman's Magazine* for June and July, 1736. "At Edial, near Lichfield, in Staffordshire, young gentlemen are boarded and taught the Latin and Greek languages, by Samuel Johnson." There was no response. Nor was there likely to be. The Lichfield Grammar School was much better known and was more accessible. Johnson had no reputation outside his own circle. He was only twenty-six and had no university degree; he had published nothing under his own name. His physical infirmities and eccentricities were only too well known to his acquaintances. Not many parents were anxious to place their sons under a master of such doubtful qualifications.

The truth is, Johnson was not fitted temperamentally to be a good teacher, even when running his own school. For one whose own knowledge had been acquired in such an irregular manner, so Boswell remarked, "it could not be expected that his impatience would be subdued, and his impetuosity restrained, so as to fit him for a quiet guide to novices." [25] Though later critics can see how unsuited Johnson was for such a post, he himself was not so easily convinced. He struggled on at Edial as best he could, always hoping for some change of fortune.

The Edial experiment would be memorable if only for one of the pupils, and he possibly the least cooperative. In 1736 David Garrick was a high-spirited youth of nineteen, somewhat behind in his classical studies, because, as he always insisted, of time spent visiting his merchant uncle in Lisbon. But that was only an excuse. He had not done well under Hunter at the Grammar School, all his interests being concentrated on acting and the drama. Nor did the move to Edial alter his attitude. As his first biographer put it, his new master, "however rich in the stores of Greece and Rome, was not better disposed to teach the precepts of learning with that exactness which is necessary to form the classical scholar, than young Garrick was willing to learn them." [26] The dull minutiae of Latin grammar held no charms. "When his master expected from him some exercise or composition upon a theme, he showed him several scenes of a new comedy, which had engrossed his time; and these, he told him, were the produce of his third attempt in dramatic poetry."

The boy was too volatile ever to make a sober, steady student, even if he had wanted to. He preferred to live dramatically, in extremes. There is a story, perhaps apocryphal, that Mrs. Garrick once asked Johnson his opinion of her son. "Why, Madam," was his reply, "David will either be hanged, or become a great man." [27]

As might have been expected, Johnson's odd manners and strange gesticulations caused much merriment among the pupils. They mimicked him behind his back, and even listened at the door of his bedroom and peeped through the keyhole, in order to turn into ridicule his tumultuous and awkward lovemaking to Tetty. Years afterward, when Garrick had become the greatest actor of his time, he used to entertain his intimates at stag parties with a graphic description of what he had seen. With deplorable taste, but ludicrous effect, he took off the endearments of the eccentric pair. In particular there was a dialogue between Mrs. Johnson in bed and Johnson in his shirt, "the lady thinking he delayed too long to come to bed." With outrageous mimicry Garrick would act the lumbering Johnson, running round the bed after she had retired, crying, "I'm coming, my Tetsie. I'm coming, my Tetsie," blowing and puffing all the time in his peculiar manner.[28]

Specific details of this skit must have varied from time to time depending on the nature of the audience. In the version seen by Joseph Cradock, Johnson was portrayed as seated by the side of the bed, hard at work composing a tragedy.[29] Rather than join his wife as she wished, he regaled her with ponderous verses, the choicest bits from his play, and in absent-minded concentration he seized the bedclothes instead of his own shirttails and tried to tuck them into his breeches. Garrick's burlesque of this scene must have been sidesplitting. While his spectators were convulsed with laughter, he played first Johnson grabbing at the imaginary sheets and stuffing them down, and then poor Tetty, exposed to the cold air, frantically trying to cling to some of the covering. It became one of Garrick's most popular off-stage performances — one, it is certain, never seen by his former master.

There are few authentic descriptions of the life in the Edial household. Lucy Porter was staying with her mother and stepfather, but she was not the kind to gladden the heart of a biographer with intimate details. Charles Bird, one of the servants, then only a lad of about sixteen, could remember in later life only "that Johnson was not much of a scholar to look at, but that Master Garrick was a strange one for leaping over a stile."[30] Two pieces of furniture — a chair and a desk — purporting to come from the Edial house still survive. Likewise there is a miniature of Johnson, said to have been painted in 1736 at the express desire of Tetty. There is also an entry in Johnson's diary which may belong in 1736: "Friday, August 27   10 at night. This day I have trifled away, except that I have attended the school in the morning. I read tonight in Rogers's sermons. Tonight I began the breakfast law anew."[31] But aside from the puzzling reference to the "breakfast law," the notation adds little.

It may have been during the Edial period that a group of traveling players came to Lichfield, to perform in the Guildhall, with its hammer-beam roof, minstrel gallery, and oak-paneled walls. The play was Colley Cibber's farce, *Hob: Or the Country Wake*.

Forty years later Johnson jokingly confessed to Boswell that he had fallen in love with the principal actress, who played the part of Flora, a simulated passion possibly put on to tease Tetty. At this performance, or a similar one, occurred Johnson's feat of strength which Garrick was later to describe so vividly. Johnson had taken a seat on the stage between the side scenes, but left it for a few minutes. While he was gone a Scottish officer, who disliked him, persuaded a local innkeeper to take the chair. Johnson returned and civilly told the intruder that it was his. When the innkeeper, encouraged by the officer, refused to budge, Johnson picked up both man and chair and threw them "at one jerk into the pit." Horrified, the Scotsman cried out, "Damn him, he has broke his limbs." But with Walmesley's intervention peace was restored, and Johnson resumed his place and "with great composure sat out the play." [32]

With performances by strolling players in the neighborhood and a pupil scribbling comedies, Johnson's thoughts naturally turned to the stage. Not that he needed an extra stimulus to think of writing a classic tragedy. It was a choice conventional enough. To be the author of a successful play, like Addison's *Cato* or even Ambrose Philips's *The Distressed Mother,* was the surest way to make money and establish one's literary reputation.

As no more pupils came to the school, and the failure of the project became increasingly apparent, Johnson set to work on a tragedy to be called *Mahomet and Irene.* Borrowing from David Garrick's elder brother Peter a copy of Richard Knolles's *General History of the Turks,* he found the dramatic story of Sultan Mahomet II, who, in order to prove to his soldiers that he had not lost all manhood in the delights of love, savagely slew his favorite, a beautiful Greek slave. Johnson saw in the tale something more than mere lust and cruelty. It might be used as a dramatic framework for a moral struggle, stressing virtue and the corruption resulting from absolute power. He set to work, jotting down what was to occur in each scene, with descriptions of the various characters and drafts of some of the speeches.[33] To supply the details of a proper background, he even noted page numbers in the authorities he was consulting, taking more pains than usual with his composition. But he had started something which he could not speedily finish; it was to be thirteen years before he saw his play produced. During all that time *Irene* would work its way in and out of the narrative of his life, now appearing as a major interest, now unwillingly pushed aside — a constantly recurring theme.

During the late summer he was in a sober mood, and on his birthday, September 7, set down a prayer: "I have this day entered upon my twenty-eighth year. Mayest thou, O God, enable me for Jesus Christ's sake, to spend this in such a manner that I may receive comfort from it at the hour of death and in the day of judgment. Amen. I intend tomorrow to review the rules I have at any time laid down, in order to practice them." [34] It was always the next day that he was to mend his ways.

Meanwhile he had family worries, this time connected with his younger brother. Nathaniel Johnson is, at best, a shadowy figure. Doubtless he went to the Lichfield Grammar School for a while, and then became his father's helper in the shop. As a bookbinder, he may well have become more skillful than his elder brother. By 1734 he had taken charge of the shop for his mother.

In all of Johnson's later recollections there is scarcely a mention of him. Only one trait drew a specific comment. Nathaniel, like his father, spent much of his time visiting neighboring towns. Once when somebody was complaining of the terrible conditions of the highways, Nathaniel "inquired where they could be, as he traveled the country more than most people, and had never seen a bad road in his life." [35] When telling this story to Mrs. Thrale, Johnson used it as an example of his brother's "manly spirit" in disregarding the inconveniences of travel, but it might have been mere bravado or a lack of sensitivity.

Another possible allusion to the same quality has only recently come to light. In a copy of the *Miscellanies* of John Norris, used by Johnson for quotations in the *Dictionary*, there is a significant annotation. Opposite an observation that because of his sensitivity Christ suffered more than would another, less complex

man, Johnson wrote in the margin "my brother." [36] Nathaniel was
not the kind of man who allowed little things to affect his mood.

About the year 1736 he moved to Burton-on-Trent in order
to take charge of a branch of the bookshop. There in the late
summer of that year he was apparently involved in something dis-
creditable, perhaps dishonest, which shocked his mother and elder
brother and led to some kind of family quarrel. Nothing of all
this would ever have been known, except for a long letter from
Nathaniel to his mother which has survived. From it comes one
authentic glimpse of tensions in the Johnson family.

Although undated, the letter was postmarked September 30
and was apparently dispatched from London.[37] From internal
evidence the year must have been 1736. "Honored Mother,"
Nathaniel began, "I did not receive your letter soon enough yesterday to send the Burton shop book by the carrier but I will send
it next week and with it all the bills that I can recollect to be due
either on Burton side or anywhere else." Then came a long list of
customers and what they owed. Pathetically he went on to review
his own desperate condition.

> I have neither money nor credit to buy one quire of paper. It is
> true I did make a positive bargain for a shop at Stourbridge in which
> I believe I might have lived happily and had I gone when I first de-
> sired it none of these crimes had been committed which have given
> both you and me so much trouble. I don't know that you ever denied
> me part of the working tools but you never told me you would give
> or lend them me. As to my brother's assisting me I had but little
> reason to expect it when he would scarce ever use me with common
> civility and to whose advice was owing that unwillingness you
> showed to my going to Stourbridge. If I should ever be able I would
> make my Stourbridge friends amends for the trouble and charge I
> have put them to. I know not nor do I much care in what way of life
> I shall hereafter live, but this I know that it shall be an honest one
> and that it cant be more unpleasant than some part of my life past,
> I believe I shall go to Georgia in about a fortnight, cottons things I
> will send.
>
> I thank you heartily for your generous forgiveness and your prayers

which pray continue. Have courage my dear Mother God will bear you through all your troubles. If my brother did design doing anything for me I am much obliged to him and thank him, give my service to him and my sister I wish them both well, I am dear Mother your affectionate and obedient son   Nath Johnson

It was a letter calculated to move any mother to tears and a hardhearted brother to some soul searching. Yet it is easy to understand Sam's reluctance to have his brother settle at Stourbridge, where his own associations had been so happy. There was still a chance that the socially prominent Hickmans and Fords might be of more service. He did not want that chance jeopardized by the not too creditable Nathaniel, whom he must have suspected of wishing to sponge off their rich relatives.

Despite his announced intention, Nathaniel did not emigrate to Georgia, to join General Oglethorpe's newly founded colony. Yet he may have gone as far as Bristol and prepared to embark, for apparently later in the year he was working at Frome in Somerset. Perhaps at the last minute he lost his nerve and took the first job that he could find in a neighboring town.

Evidence supporting this conjecture comes in a strange way. In 1780 Dr. Johnson, as an old man, thinking back over his early life and curious to know more about what had happened to his ill-fated brother, wrote two letters to a Miss Prowse near Frome.[38] In the first he asked that her servants "collect any little tradition that may yet remain, of one Johnson, who more than forty years ago was for a short time, a bookbinder or stationer in that town." When nothing could be found, he wrote again.

It was beside my intention that you should make so much enquiry after Johnson. What can be known of him must start up by accident. He was not a native of your town or country, but an adventurer who came from a distant part in quest of a livelihood, and did not stay a year. He came in 36. and went away in 37. He was likely enough to attract notice while he stayed, as a lively noisy man, that loved company. His memory might probably continue for some time in some favorite alehouse. But after so many years perhaps there is no man left that remembers him. He was my near relation.

This description also provides an explanation of why the two brothers had so little in common. The noisy man who loved company in an alehouse and the omnivorous scholar planning a classic tragedy might well have got on each other's nerves. Even if Sam later found a tavern seat a place of utmost felicity, his and Nathaniel's conversations were of a different order.

During the late autumn of 1736 the Edial venture was gradually coming to an end. Yet Johnson was still not convinced of the futility of trying to be a teacher. He made overtures to the Rev. William Budworth, the very able headmaster of the Grammar School at Brewood, about fifteen miles west of Lichfield, in an attempt to secure a place as his assistant. But Budworth, like Henry Greswold of Solihull and the others, had heard of Johnson's physical infirmities and was afraid that they "might become the object of imitation or of ridicule, among his pupils." [39] Again Johnson was prejudged because of something he could not help.

Gradually the few students he had at Edial began to leave. Lawrence Offley was admitted to Clare College, Cambridge, in November, 1736, and matriculated early the next year. The Garrick brothers, too, were seeking other places. Early in February, 1737, Walmesley wrote to his old friend the Rev. John Colson, master of the Free School at Rochester, about David, with a view of having him instructed in "mathematics, and philosophy, and humane learning," to prepare him to study for the bar. [40] On February 16 George Garrick was admitted to the Appleby Latin School. By this time the school at Edial was closed, though the Johnsons continued to live on in the big house. Tetty's money, which had made the experiment possible, was irretrievably lost.

It may have been during these last months that Johnson solaced himself with Burton's *Anatomy of Melancholy*, seeking in that fascinating volume new ways to divert his own returning depression. [41] It was the only book, he later admitted, "that ever took him out of bed two hours sooner than he wished to rise."

Meanwhile, he devoted many hours to his tragedy. The rambling first draft of the earlier acts of *Irene* had now to be revised and shaped into dramatic form. Material had to be regrouped, speeches transferred from one section to another, whole scenes rewritten. As he worked, he showed what was completed to his chief adviser, Gilbert Walmesley. The story is told that Walmesley praised highly what he had seen, but added that he was afraid the first part was so tragic that there was no possibility left "of heightening the catastrophe in the concluding part of the play." "Sir," replied Johnson, "I have enough in reserve for my purpose; for, in the last act, I intend to put my heroine into the ecclesiastical court of Lichfield, which will fill up the utmost measure of human calamity." [42]

Sam's shrewd dig referred to well-known abuses. Only a few years earlier resentment at the highhanded and arbitrary manner in which affairs were handled in the Lichfield court had reached such a point that a petition for redress was sent to Parliament by the grand jury, justices of the peace, and other gentlemen of Derby. Included were specific complaints of substitution of surrogates who were not duly qualified, illegal processes, illegal visitations, unusual payments and fees, expensive and vexatious delays, and other oppressive practices. The fact that Walmesley, who was personally involved, took no offense at Sam's remark is a tribute to their close friendship.

Gilbert Walmesley was now a married man. The spring before, the bachelor of fifty-six, tired, as he himself admitted, of living alone, finally found a wife in Magdalen Aston, a young lady from Cheshire nearly thirty years younger. If the entries of his later account books may be believed, the union was a very happy one. Whenever payments were made to his wife, and that was often, there was always the sentimental notation "To my love." [43] The explosive, opinionated autocrat apparently became a docile lamb in her hands.

The marriage strengthened Johnson's friendship with the Aston family, with the result that he saw more of her sisters, especially "Molly," Elizabeth, and "Kitty," the wife of Henry Hervey. On the other hand, it was a blow to young David Garrick, who for years had been such a favorite of the aging bachelor that many people had hoped he might be one of Walmesley's heirs. Now those expectations were at an end. Nevertheless, Walmesley's devoted interest in his two protégés had in no way lessened. Although bringing the two together as master and pupil at Edial had not proved much of a success, he continued his friendly help.

Sam was now faced with another major decision as to his future. The school had failed. He was determined not to return to the bookshop. He was unprepared for any technical position or trade. All that was left was to try his fortune in the literary profession in London. For years he had vaguely dreamed that he might one day be a part of that fabulous fraternity of wit and genius which he had heard so much about. Despite the failure of his halfhearted attempts by mail to interest a magazine editor, something might turn up if he were actually on the ground. The thing to do was to make the great plunge.

David Garrick was going through London on his way to a new school. Why not go that far with him? Perhaps it was Walmesley who first made the suggestion. Certainly Walmesley was active in final arrangements for the erstwhile master and pupil to go up to the capital together — the elder with three acts of a tragedy in his pocket, and the younger to continue his education. The plan must have appeared admirable in many ways. The Garrick family would have felt happier about "Davy," accompanied by a sober chaperon, and for Johnson there would have been agreeable company along the way. Meanwhile Tetty, with her daughter Lucy, would remain in the country while her husband investigated conditions in the capital.

So on the morning of March 2, 1737, the two oddly matched companions set out on their great adventure. Later the same day Walmesley wrote to Colson at Rochester, thanking him for accepting David as his pupil, and adding, "He and another neighbor of mine, one Mr. Johnson, set out this morning for London together: Davy Garrick to be with you early the next week, and Mr. Johnson to try his fate with a tragedy, and to see to get himself employed in some translation either from the Latin or the French. Johnson is a very good scholar and poet, and I have great hopes will turn out a fine tragedy writer. If it should any way lie in your way I doubt not but you would be ready to recommend and assist your countryman." [44]

It was about a hundred and twenty miles to London, and the two travelers made the trip on horseback. Garrick once laughingly claimed that they "rode and tied," that is, had only one horse between them.[45] By this method one rode ahead, tethered the horse by the side of the road, and walked on, while his companion, coming up on foot, would then have a turn. It was an efficient, if not very sociable, way of traveling.

These two, who were to become so eminent in London, had the happiest of memories of their trip and used to joke pleasantly about it. The Bishop of Killaloe told Boswell that on one occasion when the two were dining together in a large company, Johnson humorously ascertained the chronology of some event thus: "That was the year when I came to London with twopence halfpenny in my pocket." Garrick, overhearing him, exclaimed, "Eh? What do you say? With twopence halfpenny in your pocket?" JOHNSON. "Why yes; when I came with twopence halfpenny in *my* pocket, and thou, Davy, with three halfpence in thine."

Having left Lichfield on Wednesday morning, they were in London by the end of the week. Yet even before they were well settled there came tragic news from home — first of the sudden death of Johnson's younger brother, Nathaniel, who was buried at St. Michael's Church on Saturday, March 5; and then a few days later of the death of Garrick's father.[46]

The death of Nathaniel is one of the most puzzling episodes in Johnson's life. The young man of twenty-four must have passed away very shortly — a few hours, or at most a day or two — after Sam's departure. Yet if his only brother were dying would Johnson have gaily set off on the trip? And when had Nathaniel returned home from Frome in Somerset?

It has been suggested that Nathaniel, brooding over his own failure, and seeing his elder brother set off to make his way in the capital, took his own life. The tone of his letter to his mother the previous September certainly showed him to be in a low state of mind. Yet the fact that he was buried in consecrated ground would appear to rule out suicide, and years later Johnson could refer in an epitaph to his pious death.[47] Another possibility, that he was carried off in an epidemic, also appears doubtful, since the registers of St. Michael's Church show fewer funerals during this period than usual. It may be, of course, that the explanation is very simple — that Nathaniel returned home in February a sick man, that he appeared somewhat better when his brother departed, but suffered a sudden relapse almost immediately afterward.

Whatever the cause, the news of his death must have come to Sam as a terrific shock. This was the companion of his youth whom he had scarcely treated with Christian forbearance. This was his only brother, whose possibly happy establishment at Stourbridge he had selfishly blocked. Now there was no chance ever to make amends to his brother for the harsh treatment. It is likely that a deep sense of regret and guilt remained with Johnson always. His conscience would never let him forget, even if on the surface he showed no sign. He might dream about Nathaniel, but he avoided mentioning him even to his most intimate friends.[48]

LONDON

London

"THE HAPPINESS of London," Johnson once remarked to Boswell, "is not to be conceived but by those who have been in it. I will venture to say, there is more learning and science within the circumference of ten miles from where we now sit, than in all the rest of the kingdom." "When a man is tired of London," he added on a later occasion, "he is tired of life." Charing Cross was for him "the full tide of human existence." [1]

So well known is Johnson's preference for the city that it is difficult to think of him anywhere else. In later years he loved London with a steady devotion. But it was scarcely love at first sight. As his poem *London* was to show, he had to overcome an initial repugnance to the sordid side of city life. The young man from the country was shocked as well as excited by the raw brutality of much he saw about him.

London in 1737 was a noisy, brawling, sprawling, dirty place with over half a million inhabitants. [2] Few of the streets were well paved, and pedestrians had to pick their way through mud and garbage, being careful to avoid worse things pitched from the windows above. The stench from the filth and offal, sluggishly flowing down the channel in the middle of the roadway, must have been overpowering. Keeping the streets clean was supposed to be the duty of each householder; the officials had nothing to do with it. But there were more serious threats to unescorted travelers than splashing mud and slime. At night in the ill-lighted streets it was risking one's life to go alone into certain sections. Footpads, pickpockets, streetwalkers were everywhere. One had always to be on guard against stray animals, quarrelsome citizens, and speeding vehicles. Day after day there were gory reports in the newspapers of people run over by careless drivers. When one cart overturned — so it was recorded — a woman passenger fell under the wheels, "which running over her head her brains were pressed out, and she died on the spot." Another poor lady, stooping to look after her dog, fell out of a wagon, "and one of the wheels running over her neck, in a manner separated her head from her body."

Animals were constantly getting loose and spreading terror in the streets. "Monday in the afternoon a woman very well dressed was gored in a terrible manner by a cow near Bow Church." Another time "a mad ox ran through the city, and did considerable damage to several people, then ran at a child of about three years of age, and dashed out its brains."

Gangs of thieves and pickpockets infested the Piazza in Covent Garden, Cornhill, Spital-Fields, openly robbing people and enforcing their silence by threats of murder. Anyone who resisted might be beaten to death. Sometimes even acquiescence did not bring safety, as when a man was stopped near Ludgate Hill by three street robbers, "one of whom, without speaking a word, drew out a hanger, and cut him on the face in a most shocking manner, so that his teeth and jawbone could be seen." On the outskirts highwaymen robbed coaches and riders in daylight. During the spring of 1737 everyone was talking of the exploits of Turpin, one of the most celebrated of the profession.

If the streets were dangerous, the Thames was not much safer. In an age when few knew how to swim there were many drownings when boats overturned through the carelessness of drunken boatmen or playful passengers. Once within the short space of four days three boats capsized, causing fatalities. On another occasion there was a report of a young gentlewoman being ravished by a waterman in his boat.

As always, the papers were filled with accounts of fires, murders, babies found dead in the streets, robberies, suicides. There was a sensation when the well-known Eustace Budgell, Addison's cousin and contributor to the *Spectator,* drowned himself in the Thames.[3] There were all sorts of tragic accidents — houses falling down and burying children in the debris — a barber and periwig maker from Soho "squeezed to death" while attempting to view a great boxing match — a boy shot dead by two soldiers shooting for a wager at a mark fixed on a gate in Tottenham Court Road. Yet the brutality of city life was apparently accepted as so normal that the reporters rarely showed any excitement. With calm detachment the account is given of "Mr. Johnson, a blacksmith in the Old Change," who, "being under some discontent of mind, cut his throat from ear to ear. He was so resolute in his purpose that he cut through the pipe to the top of the spine." And there is the laconic description of the birth of an illegitimate child to an unnamed girl, and how the woman who assisted her in her delivery casually beat the baby to death "against the church, and flung it among some nettles." The reporters seldom missed a detail, as when a toll collector on the turnpike was savagely beaten down by a coachman, "so that his head fell under the coach, and the wheel run over him, part of his brains came out, and he expired on the spot, and one of his eyes was found in his leather pocket that was tied before him, wherein he puts his tickets."

The London mob was always ready to rise, particularly against informers. Since the excise tax on liquor was universally unpopular, convictions could only be secured through large cash rewards, both to those giving evidence and to the excise officers. A report in the papers that one vigilant officer instrumental in convicting ninety-six persons had received £480 as his generous official share of the rewards did nothing to increase the popularity of the enforcement proceedings. It took little to rouse the populace to attack a bailiff and his followers, or to start the cry of "informer." One poor woman having given evidence against "a person at Chelsea for retailing spirituous liquors contrary to act of Parliament, the populace used her with such severity, by beating, kicking, and cramming dirt into her mouth, that we hear she is since dead of her wounds; even her own sex exposed her to great indecencies." Another informer was dragged through the horse pond in Cotton's stable yard in Dean Street, Soho, and used so barbarously that he expired soon after the mob left him. An aroused citizenry found it easy to take matters into its own hands. So a woman detected selling rotten eggs was simply tossed into the Thames.

Legal punishments of the day were no less brutal. For the murder of her husband a woman was "drawn on a hurdle to the place of execution and there burned." For lesser offenses ears might be cut off, nostrils slit, hands burned. And merely standing in the pillory might entail some danger if the crowd felt minded to pelt the offender with stones as well as rotten oranges and eggs.

But the London streets provided humor along with the savagery. The citizens were much given to wagers, and once a man undertook "to walk blindfold from the Monument to Tottenham High Cross in six hours, and performed it in little more than five." For fifty guineas "a reputable tradesman in the borough rode a pony from the Three Tun Tavern door in Southwark to Kingston and back again, in two hours and ten minutes; he was allowed two hours and a half to perform it." There was always a risk from pranksters and drunken roisterers. The boys from the famous school, the Blue Coat Hospital, were not above cutting off the tails of ladies' gowns, or even venturing to slash off the skirt of a gentleman's coat. And there was always something laughable to watch, whether it was the distresses of pompous citizens doused in the mud, or a drunken "night walker," "having lost the use of her limbs by too great a use of gin," trundled to Bridewell in a wheelbarrow.

This was only one aspect of the London about which Johnson wandered in the spring of 1737. The other side — the beautiful buildings and shops, the streams of fine ladies and gentlemen in coaches and sedan chairs, hinting at a society of which he could only guess, the tremendous surge of commerce — he had naturally expected to see. It impressed but did not startle him. The sharpest first reaction came to the harshness of the place, something he may not quite have expected. But the distaste did not last long. Not particularly squeamish himself, he gradually came to overlook the filth and the suffering, though he could never condone cruelty or depravity. He learned to ignore the unlovely side of the city because of the exhilaration of being at the center of the nation's intellectual life. As one critic has pointed out, Johnson saw London as the greatest of man's achievements in attempting to "lift himself above the animal level, to create a world of thoughts and aims and institutions human rather than natural." [4] London was the center of learning, the spawning place of ideas and of books.

During those early days in March, however, he was chiefly a sightseer. As he strode down the muddy streets or lounged about the coffeehouses, watched the milling crowds and charging traffic, and kept a wary eye open for sharpers and pickpockets, he must have felt both insecure and detached. For all his consciousness of mental superiority, he knew he was a newcomer. He was aware that anyone giving him more than a casual glance would think him a typical country visitor, with awkward rural manners and a pronounced Midland accent.

Not surprisingly, he found his first lodgings with someone who had Lichfield connections — "Mr. Norris, a staymaker, in Exeter Street, adjoining Catharine Street, in the Strand." [5] Very likely it was through his traveling companion that Johnson came to that little cul-de-sac which was blocked off from the Strand by Exeter Change, for Richard Norris was related in some way to the Staffordshire Bailyes, and therefore to the Garricks.[6] For a time David may also have occupied an upstairs room in the stay-maker's house. This was Johnson's headquarters during his early months in London.

One would like to know more about Johnson's first London landlord. What was he like, this Richard Norris? How much did he help the Lichfield visitor to fit into city life? Among Boswell's archives there is a scrap of paper which appears to be an epitome of all Johnson could later remember about the family. But the notes are so terse that it is difficult to tell what they mean. "Norris the staymaker — fair Esther — w. the cat — children — inspection of the hand — stays returned — lodging — guinea at the stairs — Esther died — ordered to want nothing — house broken up — advertisement — eldest son — quarrel." [7] One thing has been discovered: "Fair Esther," Norris's first wife, died in October, 1743. But what of "w. the cat"? Whose hand was inspected? Did Johnson pay a guinea at the stairs for his lodging? Each cryptic phrase remains a separate mystery.

Shortly after reaching the capital Johnson and Garrick may

have parted, though seeing each other on occasion. On March 9
Garrick was entered at Lincoln's Inn — his only gesture toward
the law — but the death of his father necessarily changed all his
plans.⁸ Depending on advances from the thousand-pound legacy
from his uncle, which he could not receive in full until he came
of age, David was left for the time being with nothing more than
the meager funds carried with him from Lichfield. Thus the
scheme of going to Rochester to study under Colson had to be
temporarily abandoned.

For his part Johnson had a little money saved from the fiasco
of the Edial adventure, and he knew how to live in the cheapest
manner. One of his acquaintances in Birmingham, an Irish painter
named Ford, had supplied valuable hints. More than once Johnson talked about this advice to Boswell. Thirty pounds a year, the
painter had said, was enough to enable a man to live in London
"without being contemptible."

> He allowed ten pounds for clothes and linen. He said a man might
> live in a garret at eighteenpence a week; few people would inquire
> where he lodged; and if they did, it was easy to say, "Sir, I am to be
> found at such a place." By spending threepence in a coffeehouse, he
> might be for some hours every day in very good company; he might
> dine for sixpence, breakfast on bread and milk for a penny, and do
> without supper. On *clean-shirt day* he went abroad, and paid visits.⁹

Always recollecting his frugal friend with great esteem, Johnson
did not like to have anyone smile at his suggestions. "This man
(said he, gravely) was a very sensible man, who perfectly understood common affairs: a man of a great deal of knowledge of
the world, fresh from life, not strained through books."

Moreover, the advice was evidently put to good use. Johnson
described his own practice on this first trip to the city.

> I dined very well for eightpence, with very good company, at the
> Pine Apple in New Street, just by. Several of them had traveled. They
> expected to meet every day; but did not know one another's names.
> It used to cost the rest a shilling, for they drank wine; but I had
> a cut of meat for sixpence, and bread for a penny, and gave the

waiter a penny; so that I was quite well served, nay, better than the rest, for they gave the waiter nothing.

Before long, however, both Johnson and Garrick were in financial straits, having used up what money they had brought and not having received more. "In this extremity," says Hawkins, "Garrick suggested the thought of obtaining credit from a tradesman, whom he had a slight knowledge of, Mr. Wilcox, a bookseller, in the Strand: to him they applied, and representing themselves to him, as they really were, two young men, friends, and travelers from the same place, and just arrived with a view to settle here, he was so moved with their artless tale, that, on their joint note, he advanced them all that their modesty would permit them to ask (five pounds), which was, soon after, punctually repaid." [10]

Wilcox is reported to have asked Johnson how he meant to earn his livelihood in London, to which the latter answered: "By my literary labors." With a significant look at Johnson's huge muscular frame, Wilcox replied, "Young man, you had better buy a porter's knot." [11] More amused than offended, Johnson afterward spoke of Wilcox as one of his best friends.

It may be that Johnson sought work from other booksellers, but very doubtful is Lucy Porter's story that Walmesley had provided a letter of introduction to Lintot, his bookseller, and that Johnson wrote some things for him.[12] On this first trip to London he was apparently more interested in becoming acclimated to city life, and this proved so fascinating that he could not force himself to any serious composition. Without his wife at hand to urge him to work on any particular job, he wandered about the streets, watching the people and dreaming of what he would accomplish someday.

He saw more than the jostling crowds and the company in cheap taverns. In one home, at least, he mixed with fashionable society. The improvident Harry Hervey, now a captain in Lord Robert Montagu's regiment, had taken a house in London — against his father's advice — where, characteristically, he was living beyond his means. Here, drowned in port, he hospitably welcomed the two travelers from Lichfield and entertained them frequently. They regaled Mrs. Hervey with the latest news of her sister Mrs. Walmesley; they met numbers of genteel Londoners, among them Harry's polished brother Tom, who was at this time engaged in luring away Sir Thomas Hanmer's wife; they discussed their host's verses and argued about literary news of the day. The generosity of the Herveys made a permanent impression. Nothing would ever shake Johnson's gratitude for help and friendship at a time when it counted most. Long afterward he remarked of Harry Hervey to Boswell: "He was a vicious man, but very kind to me. If you call a dog Hervey, I shall love him." [13]

Ostensibly Johnson had come to London to complete his tragedy and then to find a producer, but the city's diversions proved so attractive that he could not settle down to solid work on the last two acts. Not until the city emptied early in the summer could he get anything done. In July he retired to Greenwich, to lodgings next door to the Golden Heart in Church Street, hoping to be able to concentrate.[14] Composition still proved tediously slow, for *Irene* was giving him more trouble than would any of his later works. Perhaps there was a growing realization of his lack of dramatic skill. Or possibly he encountered increasing difficulty in fashioning the noble character of Aspasia into an idealized portrait of Tetty.[15] Whatever the reason, his progress was slow indeed.

His mind wandered to new projects which might help to keep him alive in London. In Walmesley's letter to Colson, translation had been mentioned as something Johnson meant to try in the city, and during the spring months he may have vainly sought employment of this kind. All that is certain is that by July 12 he had evolved a specific proposition. On that day, from Greenwich, he wrote once again to Edward Cave, the proprietor of the *Gentleman's Magazine*, this time using his own name instead of a pseudonym: "Having observed in your papers very uncommon offers of encouragement to men of letters, I have chosen, being a stranger in London, to communicate to you the following design, which, I hope, if you join in it, will be of advantage to both of us." [16] The proposal was for a new English translation of Father

Paul Sarpi's *History of the Council of Trent,* only the year before rendered into French with valuable notes by Pierre François Le Courayer. The earlier seventeenth-century English translation, Johnson suggested, might easily be improved, both in style and in annotation, particularly with the help of Le Courayer's notes. The letter closed with the request: "Be pleased to favor me with a speedy answer, if you are not willing to engage in this scheme, and appoint me a day to wait upon you, if you are." Although there is no record of what Cave replied, it is reasonable to suppose that the two men did meet for the first time in July, 1737, and that when Johnson returned to Lichfield later in the summer he had a vague promise of work if he should come back to London.

Only one curious anecdote survives of this return home. When his mother had been in London as a young woman, there had been, she said, two sets of people, those who hugged the walls as they walked down the streets, in order to keep out of the mud of the central gutters, forcing others into the slime; and those who were willing to give way — the quarrelsome and the peaceable.[17] She asked her son whether he had been "one of those who gave the wall, or those who took it." Sarah well knew her son's temperament. She also sensed that a person's safety in a big city might well depend on how much he insisted on his rights. Telling the story to Boswell in the Hebrides, Johnson used it to suggest the progress in human relations: "Now it is fixed that every man keeps to the right; or, if one is taking the wall, another yields it, and it is never a dispute."

For once he was not in a dismal, depressed mood. He had a definite plan for the future. Nevertheless, he was in no great haste, and took three months to settle his affairs. During this time he put the finishing touches on his tragedy, and possibly dismantled the establishment at Edial.[18] The final winding up of that venture would have left him with a small sum of ready money from Tetty's fortune, enough, at least, to begin life together in London. Lucy Porter agreed to stay on with Sarah Johnson, helping with the bookshop, doing what she could to make up for the loss of Nathaniel. Finally, late in the autumn, Johnson and Tetty set off for London, there to make their home.

In the beginning the two took lodgings in Woodstock Street, near Hanover Square; then they moved to the house of a Mrs. Crow at No. 6, Castle Street, near Cavendish Square.[19] Having completed his play, Johnson sought out Peter Garrick, who had been interested in the work from the start, and they retired to the Fountain Tavern in the Strand, where Johnson read through the five acts. In Lichfield in 1776, when Boswell heard the story, Joseph Porter, Tetty's youngest son, chanced to be in the company and objected that the Fountain was a "notorious bawdy-house." [20] Evidently he wondered at the incongruity of reading *Irene* in such surroundings. But actually, as Peter Garrick retorted, "people might be decently there as well as anywhere else." It was a regular meeting place for the masters of the Inner Temple Bench, and for various clubs and societies. The line between types of pleasures in the eighteenth century was not sharply drawn.

Peter Garrick, who was on friendly terms with Charles Fleetwood, the patentee of the Drury Lane Theatre, did all he could to push the tragedy, but the manager was more interested in pantomimes than in classic drama and would not even read the manuscript.[21] Without some support from prominent patrons, he felt that the play had little chance of success. Despite all that Johnson's loyal friends could do, there was no immediate prospect of production. Consequently he tried the other string to his bow. He went to work for the editor of the *Gentleman's Magazine,* and became one of the strange group of writers who haunted St. John's Gate in Clerkenwell. There in the historic sixteenth-century gate, with its two towers flanking a wide arch, he found out what it was like to be a hack writer.

Edward Cave was an example of a man eminently successful, not so much by reason of superior ability as by stubborn determination. Early in life he had tried various professions, none with much success — clerk to a collector of excise, assistant to a timber merchant, printer, clerk in the post office, and miscellaneous writer.[22] Then he hit upon an idea — scoffed at by the other printers — which made him famous. In 1731 he established the first real monthly magazine, which by 1737 was so popular that when Johnson saw the building where it was produced, he "beheld it with reverence." At one time the circulation may have reached ten thousand copies a month, and the demand for earlier issues was so great that edition after edition had to be reprinted. Although there were active rivals such as the *London Magazine,* Cave's *Gentleman's Magazine* was easily the foremost periodical of the day.

Physically Cave was a large bulky man; mentally he was a strange combination of shrewdness and obtuseness. By temperament he was cold, even phlegmatic; his mind was not quick. As Johnson put it, "He saw little at a time, but that little he saw with great exactness. He was long in finding the right, but seldom failed to find it at last." Always cool and deliberate, he was hesitant in making advances. "Upon the first approach of a stranger, his practice was to continue sitting, a posture in which he was ever to be found, and, for a few minutes, to continue silent: if at any time he was inclined to begin the discourse, it was generally by putting a leaf of the magazine, then in the press, into the hand of his visitor, and asking his opinion of it."

Although he often gave the impression of inattention, beneath his sluggish manner he was carefully digesting what was being said, and his visitor might be "surprised when he came a second time, by preparations to execute the scheme which he supposed never to have been heard." Tenacious, resolute, and hard-working, he refused to allow expense or fatigue to stand in his way. Once his mind was made up, "he always went forward, though he moved slowly."

He had, says Hawkins, few of the qualities of urbanity suggested by his magazine pseudonym, "Sylvanus Urban." He could say tactlessly to an author: "I hear you have just published a pamphlet, and am told there is a very good paragraph in it, upon the subject of music: did you write that yourself?" And once when he had offended a friend by omitting the "Mr." from his name on an illustration, he thought he had made ample amends when he had an engraver insert the missing title, with a caret under the line.

Although lacking in tact and critical sense, Cave was an able

journalist and a gifted organizer. He lived for his magazine, and
at times drove his staff to superhuman labors. One of his assistants
complained that Cave kept him working "from twenty-four to
fifty hours at a stretch, and even on Sundays, to get copy ready."
He was tireless in thinking up new schemes. He never looked out
of the window, Johnson commented, except with a thought to
the improvement of his periodical. He was constantly devising
poetry contests and other means of stimulating circulation. For
the scientifically inclined there were accounts of new discoveries,
mathematical and astronomical problems, methods for curing
worms or the bites of mad dogs. Moreover, as a shrewd businessman, he kept his eye always on the total sales. So anxious was he
not to lose a single customer that if he chanced to hear anyone
talk of giving up his subscription, Cave would say to his sub-
ordinates, "Let us have something good next month."

Scrupulous in his business dealings, he was generally a penuri-
ous paymaster. As Johnson later put it, he would contract for
lines by the hundred "and expect the long hundred." He would
deal out his payments in driblets, being certain to extract full
copy in return. Yet if he appeared on the surface a casual rather
than zealous friend, he was always ready to help in times of desperate need. Despite his failings — and those who worked for
him saw many — he retained Johnson's respect and affection to
the end.

Around him at St. John's Gate, Cave had assembled a remarkable assortment of helpers who contributed to the magazine and
to his other projects. As chief adviser there was the Rev. Thomas
Birch, who lived nearby in St. John's Street. Fellow and later
secretary of the Royal Society, indefatigable author and editor,
contributor to the *General Dictionary,* "brisk" Tom Birch had a
finger in every pie. He knew all that was going on in literary
London. Everyone admitted that he was a most amusing companion, that he "knew more small particulars than anybody." [23]
His stream of anecdotes, said Johnson, flowed on like the river
Thames. Horace Walpole described him as "running about like
a young setting dog in quest of anything, new or old," yet saw
also, as did Johnson, Birch's lack of taste and the numbing dull-

ness of his prose style. That anyone in the twentieth century would want to read Tom Birch's letters would have astounded Walpole. But what Birch wrote and saved is invaluable for historians today. Among other things, his correspondence provides some of the most interesting glimpses of Johnson during the least-known period of his life in London.

Birch was a friendly adviser, not one of the active staff. As co-adjutor Cave had his brother-in-law, David Henry; as contributors, a rapidly shifting group of ladies and gentlemen, hard-working scholars, and Grub Street hacks.[24] There was William Guthrie, a Scot, who Johnson admitted was "a man of parts," though with "no great regular fund of knowledge." [25] There were two cousins, Presbyterians, pen cutters by trade, Moses Browne and John Duick.[26] Though having little formal education, both were ardent versifiers and kept the magazine well supplied in that category, Browne winning most of Cave's prizes for poetry. Duick, who lived in Clerkenwell with a large family in squalid poverty, with no books in the house but a Bible and a copy of Watts's hymns, was the proverbial needy journalist.

Cave also enlisted the help of others better known: Elizabeth Carter, the future bluestocking; Mark Akenside, physician and philosophic poet; and Richard Savage, notorious claimant of illegitimate noble birth, fluent poet and dramatist. Many of these people came to St. John's Gate to chat and smoke a pipe with Cave and to bring their contributions for the magazine. In this way the old gate of the Knights Hospitalers became a gathering place of aspiring authors.

Johnson's first contribution appeared in the issue of March, 1738 — a Latin poem *Ad Urbanum,* defending Cave against the current attacks of his competitors.[27] Although lacking the spontaneity of some of his other Latin poems, it was dignified and elegant. As Boswell put it, "Cave must have been destitute both of taste and sensibility had he not felt himself highly gratified." Perhaps the best proof that he did is that Johnson soon became one of the editor's most trusted assistants [28] — but not before Johnson gained some local reputation by a separate publication of his own.

London was his subject — undoubtedly what he was thinking most about — and he chose to write in a form very popular in the 1730s, a loose imitation of a famous classical poem. Johnson was not the first or the last to see the possibility of Juvenal's third satire on the follies and rottenness of Roman life as a model for a modern work. Boileau had adapted this same satire to describe Paris; Oldham had turned its pointed shafts against the English capital.[29] Following in a great tradition, Johnson merely provided new and modern contexts.

Every educated reader of the day would have known Juvenal backward and forward, for the works of the Roman satirist were part of the common heritage of cultivated persons. A poet could presume on such general knowledge and use it. He might depend upon it for the same kinds of effects achieved by T. S. Eliot with his buried allusions, or by James Joyce with the Homeric framework of *Ulysses*. Moreover, the Augustan imitator need feel no obligation to follow his original slavishly. He could pick what he liked and discard the rest. Sometimes he might please by close imitation, showing how universal were the themes employed; or the process could be reversed, and the comparison provide a suggestion of progress or decay. Often the merest hint of resemblance would create moving overtones, subtle levels of meaning, apparent to the readers of his day though almost completely lost in our own.

Johnson was well aware of the possibilities of the genre. Where he followed Juvenal most closely, he insisted, as had Pope in his imitations, on having the relevant Latin passages put at the bottom of the page, so that the adaptation might be better enjoyed. He expected readers to notice when the thoughts were happily applicable and the parallels lucky.[30] But he was also ready to shift the whole tone of the poem, to use Juvenal merely as a basis for his own special pleading. What had been in Juvenal preeminently an exposure of city life and an exaltation by contrast of supposedly better conditions in the country developed in Johnson's hand into a political attack on Walpole's administration. The mood was changed, as was the direction of attack. The poem became Johnson's.

In the noble music of the verse, too, he was able to impose his own strong personality. Though the heroic couplets at times lack the sparkle, the ironic wit, of Pope, they have a majestic quality all their own. The slow-moving, sometimes ponderous lines produce the effect of the deep booming notes of a great organ.

His style is Augustan — there is no doubt of that — with its balance and antithesis, its compressions, its emphasis on moral values, and its use of personified abstractions. But with Johnson the abstractions, which for others are so often a mere pictorial device, have the force of true metaphor.[31] In them is concentrated the weight of personal experience, so that the powerful emotion which is submerged beneath the decorous surface supercharges the total effect. With controlled passion, Johnson admirably generalizes the particular.

Garrick once remarked that "when Johnson lived much with the Herveys, and saw a good deal of what was passing in life, he wrote his *London*." [32] It may well be that the dinner-table conversations of Harry Hervey and his friends provided the political tone of the piece. For Hervey, never on very good terms with his father and elder brother, who were stanch supporters of the court, felt hurt over his own failure to secure patronage plums. For the time, at least, he was sympathetic with the Opposition, the so-called "Patriots." Furthermore, during the winter of 1738 Hervey was more than ever at cross-purposes with his family, having shocked them late in the autumn by issuing subscriptions for an edition of his own poems. Such a beggarly way of raising money had roused the Earl of Bristol to frenzy. While he grudgingly lent his son a little more money, he vehemently urged him to leave London with his wife and children and go where they could live more economically. Stubbornly Harry refused, even when his affairs grew so desperate that some of his possessions were seized and he was arrested for debt. Resentful and obdurate, he would have applauded in private Johnson's digs at the faction then in power, or even an open sneer at Lord Hervey, his elder brother.

It may be, also, that about the same time that Johnson was

working on *London* he was helping Hervey with some of his compositions. As a means of getting back into the King's good graces, Harry turned Lord Hervey's Latin epitaph on the late Queen Caroline into heroic couplets. The translation was made sometime between December, 1737, and June, 1738, just the period of his closest association with Johnson.[33] Quite possibly the latter took an active hand in fashioning his host's verses. Many of the couplets in the surviving manuscript have an undeniably Johnsonian ring. The somber, measured style is scarcely what might have been expected from Harry Hervey.

Johnson's own poem was completed about the end of March, when a copy was shown to Cave.[34] Once it was done, the author naturally desired immediate publication. The assertion by one early biographer that *London* was turned down by a succession of publishers appears unlikely.[35] Cave would have been his obvious first choice, unless Johnson suspected that the political bias of the piece might be offensive. Indeed such a suspicion may have been the reason for the devious scheme by which Johnson did approach Cave — at first implying that the poem was the work of another poor author, for whom he was acting. Showing unusual diffidence, he even offered to alter "any stroke of satire" which Cave disliked. He may have imagined the work more dangerous than it really was.

Fortunately Cave was inclined to print the poem, though he suggested that Dodsley's name, as a better-known publisher, should be on the title page. After some negotiations, hinted at in Johnson's letters to Cave, Dodsley agreed to give ten guineas for the copyright. "I might, perhaps, have accepted of less," Johnson later confided, "but that Paul Whitehead had a little before got ten guineas for a poem; and I would not take less than Paul Whitehead."[36] He would not be outdone by a notorious freethinker.

Cave rushed the poem into print in order to allow publication before the city emptied at the rise of Parliament. With no author's name on the title page, it is reputed to have appeared on May 13, the very same day as the first part of Pope's *One Thousand Seven Hundred and Thirty-Eight*.[37] This accidental juxtaposition of the work of an anonymous poet with that of the acknowledged master of the day naturally set tongues wagging. Those who hated or were jealous of the author of the *Dunciad* — and there were many — excitedly passed the word around: "Here is an unknown poet, greater even than Pope." As a result, a second edition, both in folio and octavo, was called for within a week, and a third appeared the same year. Though not advertised widely in the newspapers, *London* was an undoubted success.

Pope, with his characteristic generosity toward real merit, showed no jealousy. According to Hawkins, George Lyttelton, "the instant it was published, carried it in rapture to Mr. Pope, who, having read it, commended it highly, and was very importunate with Dodsley to know the author's name." [38] At first Lyttelton was certain Pope himself must be the hidden author, and refused to be convinced. How astonished he would have been to know that the poem was the production of his old antagonist at Pedmore!

Since Dodsley kept the secret well, Pope was forced to get the younger Jonathan Richardson to find out about the new author. All Richardson was able to report was that it was someone named Johnson and that he was an obscure man. To which Pope replied, "He will soon be *déterré*." [39]

The high praise of Lyttelton and Pope, and the popularity of the poem in certain circles, were not entirely motivated by its artistic excellence. It was welcomed as another broadside of the political Opposition, as an anti-administration pamphlet, rather than as a beautiful set of verses. In the late 1730s the tide of opposition to Sir Robert Walpole, the prime minister, was rising to its height. He and his policies were subject to constant attack; at court, corruption and bribery were said to be rampant. Yet all the while the chief minister remained unperturbed. Although an able and efficient administrator, Walpole appeared on the surface to be a cynical politician who made no bones about his practical use of power. Solidly entrenched as he was, he could afford to be scornful of vague talk of reform, or of high-flown generalities spouted by his enemies.

The Opposition was made up of all those out of power who

yearned to get in — old Tories, Jacobites, various splinter groups of Whigs, the Prince of Wales's circle, disgruntled London merchants who were calling for war with Spain.[40] This ill-assorted band, though united in their outcries against corruption and their equally loud professions of patriotic devotion to The Whole, were increasingly suspicious of their fellows. The Tory followers of Bolingbroke, the disaffected Whigs who followed Pulteney and Carteret, the "Young Patriots" under the guidance of Lord Cobham could never wholly agree on a leader. Only the objection to the strong-arm tactics of Walpole gave them some semblance of unity. Liberty, patriotism, independence, honesty in government, abhorrence of narrow party control were popular themes of opposition. It was easy to attribute to the national government injustices of every sort: the increase in crime, censorship, the low state of general morals.[41]

Almost two weeks after the appearance of *London* the loyal administration paper, the *Daily Gazetteer,* ironically commented that the nation had already begun "to feel the happy effects of that gentle correction and chastisement which have been administered to them in those excellent satires and essays that prescribe such admirable rules for our deportment and behavior, both in public and private life, and at the same time that give such just and reasonable reproof to those that deviate from them." It was undoubtedly high time, the editor continued, "for these great masters of satire to enter upon their province, and to begin this laudable work of reformation, for if their representation of things is true, there never was a people so degenerated and sunk so low in vileness and infamy as we; for I think, according to their account of the matter, there are not above ten or a dozen wise and honest men in the nation, and those all within the circle of their own friends and acquaintance. . . ." [42]

It is not difficult to see why Johnson was drawn into the Opposition camp. Having led a sheltered, bookish life, with little experience in practical politics, he was easily impressed by high ideals. The noble sentiments of the Patriots struck a responsive chord. He was quite willing to believe that Walpole and his minions were conspiring to destroy the liberties and moral stamina of valiant Englishmen.

Long ago Sam had shown that he was a natural rebel. He was still a moody, unhappy, ambitious young man, full of confidence in himself yet bitterly resenting past failure. Perhaps he was a little homesick for the country; certainly he was unsettled and insecure. His attacks on entrenched authority and his descriptions of the wickedness he saw all about him were in part projections of his own irritation with the world.[43]

Besides, he had been brought up as an outsider. He was fresh from long arguments with Walmesley and full of Tory sentiments. The ideals of a king who would be above and outside party politics and of a government not influenced by the financial interests appealed deeply to his conception of justice and to his common sense. He had as obvious models the two most effective writers of his day, Pope and Swift. He was quite ready to add his own voice to those of the other Jeremiahs lamenting the sad state of his beloved country.

London became a sonorous call to reform, as well as a vivid description of the dangers and degradation of city life. He did not mince words as to the latter.

> Here malice, rapine, accident, conspire,
> And now a rabble rages, now a fire;
> Their ambush here relentless ruffians lay,
> And here the fell attorney prowls for prey;
> Here falling houses thunder on your head,
> And here a female atheist talks you dead.[44]

This is the London so vividly portrayed in the contemporary newspapers. "Prepare for death, if here at night you roam,/ And sign your will before you sup from home." "All crimes are safe," he laments, "but hated poverty./ This, only this, the rigid law pursues."

Closely following the line of the Opposition papers — *The Craftsman* and *Common Sense* — he alluded pointedly to the degenerate state of his country: "Ere masquerades debauch'd, excise oppress'd,/Or English honour grew a standing jest"; to the tyranny of the licensing laws; to the widespread use of bribery: "Here let those reign, whom pensions can incite/To vote a patriot black, a courtier white." The poem is filled with expressions such as "a thoughtless age," "the cheated nation," "the sinking land."

From a conservative Tory point of view it was plain that the old national vigor and simple honesty were fast disappearing. With no immediate hope for a change, the future of England was black indeed. Thus it was natural for Johnson to follow Juvenal in having his disappointed hero long for some better place "where honesty and sense are no disgrace" — some distant spot in purer air where the follies and crimes of London could be forgotten.

> Has heaven reserv'd, in pity to the poor,
> No pathless waste, or undiscover'd shore;
> No secret island in the boundless main?
> No peaceful desart yet unclaim'd by Spain?
> Quick let us rise, the happy seats explore,
> And bear oppression's insolence no more.
> This mournful truth is ev'ry where confess'd,
> SLOW RISES WORTH, BY POVERTY DEPRESS'D:
> But here more slow, where all are slaves to gold,
> Where looks are merchandise, and smiles are sold;
> Where won by bribes, by flatteries implor'd,
> The groom retails the favours of his lord.

Such longing for peaceful desert isles, for "happy seats" where merit is rewarded, merely followed an ancient literary tradition. It hardly implied that Johnson himself was ready to give up the city struggle so speedily. He might harbor an occasional doubt, but London was too exhilarating to be abandoned.

London is a young man's poem. It breathes the ardor, the vehemence, the keen sense of right and wrong of youth. It is the work of a man newly come to the city, shocked by much of what he sees and still clinging to his early ideals, still hoping that a change of leadership may bring improvement. It has the impetuous zest of someone ready to throw himself into the political arena. A decade later, when next he imitated Juvenal, in *The Vanity of Human Wishes,* much of this youthful impetuosity would be gone. Ten years of poverty and struggle in London would complete his education.

CHAPTER XI

"Slow Rises Worth, by Poverty Depress'd"

URING the next year Johnson was to have concrete evidence
of the difficulty of getting ahead in the literary world. Mere
merit was not enough. At the end of the period he would be
worse off than at the start, his small capital gone, and his hopes
for the future dimmed. Yet the time was not wasted. He was experimenting, trying out his critical faculties. Before he could be
sure of his powers, he needed to see what he could do as a writer
for the periodicals, as a translator, and as a political pamphleteer.

In the late spring of 1738, however, most of his thoughts were
still on his tragedy. He began one of his letters to Cave with the
comment: "I am extremely obliged by your kind letter, and will
not fail to attend you tomorrow with Irene, who looks upon you
as one of her best friends." [1] But while waiting for the managers
of the theater to recognize the play's beauties, he was forced to
make a living somehow.

By a strange set of circumstances, an action of the House of
Commons on April 13, 1738, apparently brought him his first
specific assignment as an active member of Cave's journalistic staff.
On that day the House unanimously resolved that it was a notorious breach of privilege to publish accounts of the debates in
Parliament, during term or when in recess. [2] For years such reports had been one of the chief attractions of the *Gentleman's
Magazine* and its foremost rival, the *London Magazine*. The reports had never been official, being merely journalistic versions
made up from meager notes taken by reporters in the gallery, or
sometimes from recollections of the members themselves. In the
early thirties both magazines had depended almost exclusively

on the printed accounts in another journal, *The Political State of Great Britain.* When these became irregular, the *London Magazine* took the lead in expanding the service, and Cave casually helped himself to what he wanted from his rival's pages, though trying to inject as much fresh material as possible. Such high-handed methods drew repeated attacks from the *London Magazine,* with newspaper advertisements denouncing the thievery.

This was the situation when a flagrant breach of privilege by one of the newspapers precipitated the stringent parliamentary action. The resourceful rival editors soon found a way to evade the law — dangerous, but financially worth the risk. First to think of a solution was the *London Magazine.* In its May number began a new section entitled "Proceedings of the Political Club," in which were recounted the meetings of a club of noblemen and gentlemen, who dined together three times a week and discussed public questions. The members were referred to under the names of ancient Greek and Roman celebrities — Walpole as Cicero, Pulteney as Cato, and so forth. Under this thin disguise the sessions of Parliament were described.

Cave followed suit the next month with another ingenious scheme. In the June issue of the *Gentleman's* there was a humorous account of the voyage of Captain Lemuel Gulliver's grandson to the lands described in *Gulliver's Travels,* which set the stage for a series of reports of the "Debates in the Senate of Lilliput." The speakers' names were fairly obvious anagrams — "Walelop" for Walpole, "Pulnub" for Pulteney, "Ptit" for Pitt — though some were less recognizable, as, for example, "Castroflet" for Chesterfield. The Lords were "Hurgoes," Knights, "Hurgolets." The High Heels or Tories were "Tramecsan," and the Low Heels or Whigs, "Slamecsan." Although there was a certain amount of Swiftian framework — just enough for legal protection — the actual reports were not much different from those published before the new law was passed.

How much Johnson had to do with the use of Gulliver and Lilliput is uncertain. Those who would like to believe that it was originally his suggestion may be right, for some of the main themes, as well as the style of the fictional introduction to the debates, are unmistakably Johnsonian.[3] If not responsible for creating this ingenious account, he must have been the member of the staff who shaped the final version.

Once the series was started, the speeches were written by William Guthrie, who assembled the detailed accounts largely from notes and hints dug up by Cave or borrowed from the *London Magazine.* Then they were revised stylistically by Johnson. It was not until some time later that he took over the sole responsibility for composition as well.

In the beginning there must have been constant fear of parliamentary action against this open violation of the intent of the recent ruling. Undoubtedly some risk was involved. It was not uncommon in those days for editors and newspaper printers to languish in Newgate as a result of too much enterprise. Happily for Cave and his helpers, there was no immediate prosecution, perhaps because the debates were never published during the actual session of Parliament described, and because they were brought out in a rather haphazard fashion. Moreover, as one critic has suggested, dread of ridicule always stood in the way. Sir John Barnard, late Lord Mayor of London, might well have hesitated before identifying himself as the "Hurgolet Branard, who in the former session was Pretor of Mildendo." [4] There was never any real attempt at disguise. The early debates carried extensive footnotes giving clues to the meaning of the terms, and at the end of the year the magazine went so far as to publish a list of "Anagrammata Rediviva," together with their interpretations.

As might have been expected, the new plan did nothing to decrease the hostility of the two principal magazines, and there were continued blasts from the *London Magazine,* with accusations of stealing, mangling, and defacing by its rival.[5] Guthrie was obviously following Cave's old tactics of helping himself to what he wanted.

By midsummer, 1738, the twenty-eight-year-old Johnson had become one of Cave's active assistants. He made selections from important new books, decided which verses should be printed, was supposed to act as judge in awarding the prizes, and answered the queries of correspondents. He corrected the style of various contributions and probably did other routine work. But that did not mean he spent most of his time at St. John's Gate. A large part of the writing and editing was done by the hack writers in their own garrets. When necessary, Johnson went from his lodgings in Castle Street for conferences, but he was not anxious to waste his energy on casual errands. He once excused himself to Cave by saying that it was "a long way to walk." [6]

Although glad to have Johnson on his staff, Cave may not have immediately recognized the scope of his talents. The story is told that, meaning to impress his new helper, Cave suggested that if Johnson would meet him at a certain alehouse in the Clerkenwell neighborhood one evening he might see the poet Moses Browne and other luminaries connected with the magazine. Accordingly, Johnson appeared, "dressed in a loose horseman's coat" and "a great bushy uncombed wig," and was presented to Browne, "whom he found sitting at the upper end of a long table, in a cloud of tobacco smoke." Thus, as Hawkins ironically concluded the account, Johnson "had his curiosity gratified." [7] To be fair to Cave, the invitation must have been prompted more by a friendly wish to introduce the unprepossessing young man from the country to some congenial literary company, than by any intent to make invidious comparisons.

Wʜᴀᴛ had brought Johnson and Cave together the year before had been a proposed translation of Father Paul Sarpi's *History of the Council of Trent*. Despite the enthusiastic encouragement of Walmesley, Birch, and William Caslon, Johnson had been slow to begin. Finally, however, on August 2 Cave made the first of a series of advance payments for the work. In "sums of one, two, three, and sometimes four guineas at a time, most frequently two," for approximately the next eight months payment was made for this and other work as copy was produced.[8] Boswell, who saw the actual sheet on which the account was kept, later commented, "It is curious to observe the minute and scrupulous accuracy with which Johnson has pasted upon it a slip of paper, which he has entitled 'Small Account,' and which contains one article, 'Sept. 9th, Mr. Cave laid down 2s. 6d.' "

As usual, Johnson had difficulty keeping up with his commitments. Possibly late in September he answered a prodding note from the impatient editor:

> I did not care to detain your servant while I wrote an answer to your letter, in which you seem to insinuate that I had promised more than I am ready to perform. If I have raised your expectations by anything that may have escaped my memory I am sorry, and if you remind me of it shall thank you for the favor. If I made fewer alterations than usual in the debates it is only because there appeared, and still appears to me to be less need of alteration. The verses on Lady Firebrace may be had when you please, for you know that such a subject neither deserves much thought nor requires it. The Chinese stories may be had folded down when you please to send, in which I do not recollect that you desired any alterations to be made.[9]

He expressed willingness to answer a recent query sent in by a subscriber, tried to explain his inability to come to any decision in the poetry contest, and was properly apologetic over other failures.

> As to Father Paul, I have not yet been just to my proposal, but have met with impediments which I hope, are now at an end, and if you find the progress hereafter not such as you have a right to expect, you can easily stimulate a negligent translator.
>
> If any or all these have contributed to your discontent, I will endeavor to remove it.

It was a straightforward letter, which offered no mealymouthed excuses. He would not confess to others his deep-seated inability to do sustained work. But there was little complacence or rationalization in his own mind. He was convinced that he was a deficient, sinful man. He knew that indolence was his worst enemy. In this sorrowful spirit he set down a solemn prayer on his first birthday spent in London:

O God, the Creator and Preserver of all mankind, Father of all mercies, I thine unworthy servant do give thee most humble thanks, for all thy goodness and lovingkindness to me. . . . In the days of childhood and youth, in the midst of weakness, blindness, and danger, thou hast protected me; amidst afflictions of mind, body, and estate, thou hast supported me; and amidst vanity and wickedness thou hast spared me. Grant, O merciful Father, that I may have a lively sense of thy mercies. Create in me a contrite heart, that I may worthily lament my sins and acknowledge my wickedness, and obtain remission and forgiveness, through the satisfaction of Jesus Christ. And, O Lord, enable me, by thy grace, to redeem the time which I have spent in sloth, vanity, and wickedness; to make use of thy gifts to the honour of thy name; to lead a new life in thy faith, fear, and love; and finally to obtain everlasting life. . . .[10]

As plans for the Sarpi translation went slowly forward, an advertisement was placed in the *Daily Advertiser* of October 11, announcing "proposals" for subscribers. The work, to be in two quarto volumes, was described as "now in the press, and will be diligently prosecuted." [11] In the advertisement the words "By S. Johnson" stood out in large type. There was to be no anonymity about this great project.

But all was not to run smoothly. On October 20 the same newspaper carried an indignant letter from one John Johnson, keeper of Archbishop Tenison's library near St. Martin's in the Fields, insisting that for some time he had been engaged in a translation of the *History of the Council of Trent*, that he had the approbation of Le Courayer, the French editor, together with promises of help, and that he was under the patronage of a number of prominent clergymen.[12] He claimed to have a more extensive design than was evident from S. Johnson's proposals, and even went so far as to hint that the appearance of a rival with the same surname must be a trick to lure away his unsuspecting adherents.

The next day Cave defended his project in a vigorous reply. With his own translator evidently standing at his side providing pungent phrases, Cave pointed out that the Rev. Mr. John Johnson had no reason to think himself injured. Nothing was underhanded. So far as public announcement was concerned, the St. John's Gate enterprise was first in the field.

> To obviate any suspicion that we are indebted for our scheme to some private account of Mr. John Johnson's, I am ready to produce the proposals made to me above a year ago, and communicated by me to several of the clergy at that time, which will not only show the date of our design, *but prove (since that* is likely to be controverted) that Mr. Johnson's surname is no new acquisition.
>
> As to the greater extent of Mr. J. Johnson's design, we know not by what means he is so well acquainted with the limits of ours. We shall endeavor to comprise everything necessary for clearing obscurity, detecting errors, and establishing truth, and if his design extends farther, shall neither envy nor adopt it.

Sam Johnson was not to be frightened away, at least not by a single claim.

Gradually subscriptions dribbled in. Among Cave's papers is a letter from a gentleman in Suffolk, dated November 12, asking to be put on the list, and volunteering information about a mistake in identity in the French version. On the back of the letter Cave scrawled "John [that is, Johnson] send word whether you be come to Michael Newton it is put in page xii, and worked off." [13] By such casual messages back and forth Cave and his helper kept constantly in touch.

In order to stir up more interest Johnson contributed a short life of Sarpi to the November *Gentleman's Magazine,* where further mention was made of the proposals. Yet after all this flourish everything came to nought. The opposition was too formidable. As Boswell commented, in the end the rival translators "destroyed each other, for neither of them went on with the work." [14] Although at least half a dozen sheets were already in print, the decision was made to go no further, and Cave was out of pocket all that he had paid in small advances.

Meanwhile Johnson had become better acquainted with the other contributors to the magazine, especially with Miss Elizabeth Carter, the erudite twenty-year-old daughter of a clergyman from Deal in Kent. She was often a guest in the Cave home, where

Johnson may first have met her — the beginning of a close friendship which would continue for almost half a century.

Apparently Miss Carter won the respect and admiration of men by her intelligence and attractive manner and her knowledge of classical and modern languages. Cave considered her his special favorite. The young widower Thomas Birch was extravagant with compliments and pursued her with invitations to dinner. He may even have hoped for a romantic conclusion to their close relationship.

Not to be outdone by the others, Johnson contributed eulogistic verses to the April, 1738, *Gentleman's*. In sending copy to the editor, he commented: "I have composed a Greek epigram to Eliza, and think she ought to be celebrated in as many different languages as Louis le Grand." [15] During the summer and autumn their friendship ripened. On several occasions Johnson dined with Birch and Miss Carter, perhaps as a kind of chaperon in their incipient romance. Then during the early winter there were more meetings *à trois*. According to Birch's list of engagements, characteristically kept in Latin, they dined together at least seven times between November 17 and February 10.[16] They became so intimate that Birch in a Latin letter to the lady referred to "Johnsonus noster," at the same time jokingly suggesting an affinity between Johnson and Aristarchus, a proverbially strict grammarian and pedant.

For a while they worked together on one of Cave's publishing projects. Always with an eye to immediate public interest, Cave was anxious to rush into print English versions of two works by the Swiss theologian Jean Pierre de Crousaz, who had attacked the religious orthodoxy of Pope's immensely popular *Essay on Man*. Miss Carter was chosen to translate the *Examen de l'Essay de M. Pope sur l'Homme,* and Johnson agreed to do the later *Commentaire.*

Although undertaken merely as another piece of journalistic work, the translation turned out to be much more than that: it was the first published volume containing any of Johnson's literary criticism. In this instance he served both as translator and editor. In the footnotes appear the earliest of his trenchant remarks about other authors and their ideas. Moreover, the work deserves explanation because Boswell in the *Life* was confused about it. He knew that Johnson had been involved in an English rendering of one of Crousaz' works, but was baffled by Miss Carter's known connection with the *Examen,* the only one he knew.[17] Only recently has the individual responsibility of Cave's two assistants been straightened out.

Late in November, 1738, when Miss Carter had completed her task and Johnson was characteristically lagging behind, a rival production suddenly appeared. On the twenty-first the notorious publisher and long-time antagonist of Pope, Edmund Curll, announced publication of an English version by Charles Forman of the first part of the *Commentary.*[18] Thoroughly dismayed, Cave called upon his helpers for advice. What was to be done? Johnson at once agreed that his *Commentary* should be temporarily put aside, but insisted that Miss Carter's translation of the *Examination* "should be pushed forward with the utmost expedition." [19] In order to forestall further competition he advised putting an announcement in the newspapers, "this day is published," even though the book may not have been quite ready. "It will above all be necessary to take notice that it is a thing distinct from the Commentary."

Accordingly, an advertisement was inserted in the *Daily Advertiser* of November 23 largely embodying these suggestions. But while pushing the *Examination* Cave had no intention of giving up the companion volume of the *Commentary,* and made this clear in his newspaper announcements.[20] Curll replied at once that his would be pursued regularly but not precipitately, and the war was on. As it turned out, Curll might bluster, but nothing more was heard of his proposed continuation and only the first part of Forman's translation appeared.

One reason that Cave and Johnson decided to take the risk and go on with their version was that Forman's treatment of the text was far from satisfactory. Crousaz had relied throughout on a faulty translation of the *Essay on Man* made by the Abbé du Resnel, so that Pope's meaning was often completely misinterpreted. Forman had merely inserted Pope's own lines into the text, thus rendering many of the remarks of the Swiss theologian unintelligible. Johnson, much more sensibly, planned to include du Resnel's French version of the couplets, together with a literal English translation in a kind of rhythmic prose. Moreover, Johnson planned to treat all four parts of the *Commentary*.

As was his way, it was completed by fits and starts, sometimes at breakneck speed. He later told Boswell that he had "once written six sheets in one day: 48 quarto pages of a translation of Crousaz on Pope." [21] For the first epistle he had Forman's version for comparison, and there are some verbal similarities. For the other three he had to work independently.

The *Commentary*, although promised in various newspaper advertisements, in the November *Gentleman's Magazine*, and in a note at the back of the *Examination*, did not appear promptly. One copy, at least, survives with 1739 on the title page, yet no publication date has ever been discovered. In all probability, Johnson's volume was shelved while Miss Carter's was being highly publicized. Then, almost three years later, in November, 1741, the old sheets were bound up with a new title page, dated 1742. Even then the work made little stir, and today it is a rarity.[22] Financially the *Commentary* must have been almost as great a loss for Cave as the unfinished version of Father Sarpi. He was not finding the help of his new aide very profitable, at least as a translator.

If not a practical success, the editing of Crousaz was a valuable experience for Johnson. His rendering of the French text may have been pedestrian, but in the annotation he could set down in writing the same kind of pithy independent observations that he was accustomed to make in conversation with his friends.

For one thing, he was eager to point out the many mistakes of Crousaz in imputing to Pope statements which were only in the faulty French translation which he used. "Of these lines I need not say how distant they are from Mr. Pope's sense, and how much inferior to it"; "the two lines that give occasion to these questions, are entirely inserted by the translator." Again and again he takes Crousaz to task for mistaken interpretations. "Mr. Crousaz, in this reflection, seems to have forgotten either the candor of a

moralist, or the sagacity of a commentator." And later, referring
to the line "Which of pure seraphim consumes and nourishes the
soul," he adds the stinging rebuke: "Mr. Crousaz is so watchful
against impiety, that he lets nonsense pass without censure: Can
anything consume and nourish at the same time?"

Far from being a blind idolater of Pope, Johnson could not resist having his say on some of the major questions raised by the
poet himself. The germ of many of his subsequent settled opinions
appears first in these notes. Witness his remarks on the "ruling
passion," a concept about which he was always dubious.

> There seem to me to be many reasonable objections against this
> system, of a *ruling passion* interwoven with the original constitution,
> and perpetually presiding over its motions, invariable, incessant, and
> insuperable. I have at present no design of entering into an accurate
> discussion of the question, which is perhaps rather a question of
> fact and experience than of reason. The author may, perhaps be
> conscious of a *ruling passion* that has influenced all his actions and
> designs. I am conscious of none but the general desire of happiness,
> which is not here intended, so that there appears equal evidence
> on both sides.

Here and in the elaboration that follows he adopts much the
same kind of skeptical position that he took over forty years
later in the *Life of Pope*.

Throughout the commentary there is one example after another of Johnson's dogged common sense and intellectual honesty. "Mr. Pope's assertion, in plain prose, seems to be this . . ."
or "The last line of this passage I cannot understand; how can
kings be degraded by the supposition that whole nations were
made for them?" Before he was thirty years old, Johnson had developed the straightforward and outspoken approach to life and
literature which was to make him the foremost critic of his age.

All the while, Johnson was increasingly active on the *Gentleman's Magazine*. He wrote the preface to the collected 1738 volume and to others in succeeding years; put together a life of the
celebrated Dutch physician Boerhaave, which appeared serially in

four successive numbers; and contributed various poems and short pieces. On occasion he also defended his editor in print from sniping rivals.

From the start Cave had tried to keep his magazine out of controversial politics, and although quoting from articles in Opposition papers, he was careful to see that nothing very objectionable to either side was used. Nevertheless, the ardent Patriots thought he was on the government side and let loose a barrage of invective against him. *Common Sense* in February, 1739, asserted that the *Gentleman's* had been ordered by the government party "to deface and mangle what they could not answer." [23] Mr. Urban (Cave's pseudonym), it continued, had performed his part "without the least mercy." "He hath diligently cut out all those parts where the strength of our argument lay." The howls were loud and long. *"Urban robs like a ruffian: — He lives by what he steals from us, and yet abuses us."* The *Gentleman's* was called in one newspaper blast a *"farrago of nonsense and stupidity."*

Little urging would have been needed to stir Johnson up to answer such diatribes. Early in 1739 he threw himself wholeheartedly into the battle of the rival periodicals, with spirited support of Cave and the magazine. He wrote a formal "Appeal to the Public" in the March number and an address "To the Reader" in May, and may have been the author of a dignified defense of his employer's policies which appeared in a letter to the *Daily Advertiser* of April 13.[24]

It is likely that he was involved in other, lighthearted skirmishes with the enemy, this time over matters of style. Johnson's hand seems evident in a number of places. In February the *Gentleman's* quoted a passage from one of the protesting papers in order to show how diffuse the style was. The next month there was an ironic attack on the *London Magazine* for a statement in its pages that the letter *d* is not sounded in the words "bold" and "cold." As one recent investigator has commented, "All Cave's enemies had to live in terror of their own solecisms and turgidity from the time when Johnson was added to the staff of the *Gentleman's Magazine.*" [25] With a future dictionary maker as his right-hand man, Cave was well armed.

Above, left: Miniature of Samuel Johnson, painted about the year 1736. Artist unknown. See note 2, Illustrations. *Above, right:* "Tetty"— Mrs. Harry Porter, later Mrs. Samuel Johnson. Artist unknown. Now in the possession of Mr. Arthur Pennant, Nantlys, St. Asaph. *Below:* Edial Hall. From a drawing by C. Pye. Published by Cadell and Davis in 1805.

Molly Aston. Artist unknown. Formerly in the library at Stowe Hill.

Reputed to be Samuel Johnson as a young man. This portrait hangs in the Birthplace Museum, Lichfield. See note 3, Illustrations.

Although ready to defend in print Cave's neutral political position, Johnson was himself growing even more violent in his opposition to the government. A possible spur to his discontent came from his increasing intimacy with a man who at one time had been an active Jacobite and who was now close to the circle of the Prince of Wales. This was the forty-two-year-old Richard Savage, one of the most exciting and controversial figures of the period.

The first suggestion of any connection between the two came when Johnson contributed a Latin epigram addressed to Savage — "in whose breast burns zeal for humankind" — to the April, 1738, *Gentleman's Magazine*. This is not proof that they were personally acquainted at that time, for Johnson may merely have heard about him from his good friends Birch and Cave. The sensational history of the gifted but erratic poet must have been common gossip at St. John's Gate. Long afterward Johnson insisted to at least one acquaintance that he had not met Savage when *London* was written.[26] The poem was not published until May, 1738.

Despite Johnson's disclaimer, generations of critics have found a striking resemblance between Savage and the protagonist of the poem. Both were thwarted patriots, who finally left the corrupt city for exile in Wales. Both were full of moral indignation and fierce in denunciation of conditions as they found them. There is even a possible allusion in one couplet to Savage's adopted title of "Volunteer Laureate." [27] Yet standing in the way of this identification is the inescapable fact that Savage did not leave London until July, 1739, over a year after the publication of the poem.

One may hazard a guess at what happened. Closely following his Juvenalian model, Johnson began his satire with a disillusioned idealist leaving the city for the purer air of the country. Wales was chosen as an obvious distant point, rustic, but not so wild as would have been the Highlands of Scotland. Then, as he wrote, Johnson either consciously or unconsciously identified the hero of his poem with another romantic but unhappy patriot, whose story he had often heard. Savage may even this early have been talking to his friends about leaving London. Johnson could afterward honestly say that Savage had not been the model for Thales, but it could also be true that there was much of him in the portrait.

If not the hero of Johnson's poem, Savage soon became his constant companion. By the winter and spring of the next year they were intimate. These were the last months of Savage's fantastic career in London. Most of his life had been spent in a struggle to gain recognition for his claim to be the illegitimate son of Earl Rivers and the Countess of Macclesfield. When his supposed mother refused to recognize him, he followed her about, dramatizing her rejection, and even went so far as to publicize his plight in a sensational poem with the title *The Bastard*. With superior talents as a dramatist and poet, he had a succession of beneficent patrons, one of them being Lady Macclesfield's own nephew, Lord Tyrconnel. Someone always appeared ready to support Savage. For a time he received a pension from the popular actress Anne Oldfield, and later a similar one from Queen Caroline. Yet as the years passed, he alienated one would-be helper after another and was at last in desperate straits.

Was he, or was he not, a complete fraud? Under the spell of Savage's convincing tale, Johnson was certain of his honesty; Boswell, later, was skeptical. Most subsequent commentators have assumed that he was not what he claimed to be, though some have generously believed him to have been self-deceived. Yet his latest biographer, after an exhaustive examination of the evidence, is confident the man was not an impostor.[28] Although his claim to noble parentage may never be proved, there is a possibility that it was genuine. In the face of all the facts, the case against him is more difficult to believe than his own. Johnson may have been less gullible than has been suspected.

Johnson was undeniably impressed by this brilliant and eccentric man of the world. Even when in greatest distress Savage remained courteous, genteel in manner, and captivating in approach. He was charming and generous. It is said that "in the taking off his hat and disposing it under his arm, and in his bow, he displayed as much grace as those actions were capable of." [29] The airs of a fine gentleman were complemented by intellectual gifts of a high order. No wonder the Lichfield bookseller's son was dazzled!

Besides, the two had much in common, and it could well have been a deep-seated feeling of emotional kinship that drew Johnson to the wayward Savage. Both were intensely proud, even in their poverty. Their political sympathies were similar; they entertained rebellious thoughts and passions but were never overt rebels. As turbulent idealists, they were disgusted with life as they found it but were unable to focus their energies on constructive reform. They were temperamentally unstable, men of moods and strong prejudices. Yet their violence was only on the surface. Beneath, both were deeply sensitive. The fact that Savage once killed a man in a tavern brawl and was saved from the gallows only by the Queen's pardon is not to be taken as a sign that he was callous or brutal.

There may have been a more specific psychological similarity. One scholar — using startling evidence from Johnson's later life — has recently suggested a masochistic strain as one of the roots of Johnson's torturing melancholy.[30] Though most of the manifestations of this came late in his life, the basic maladjustment must have been formed early. In Savage the pattern is much more obvious. As one psychiatrist has pointed out, he is a perfect paradigm of the type. It would be hard to find anyone more emotionally dependent upon pain and disappointment, often self-inflicted.

Yet if there was some unconscious understanding of each other's problems, the social pattern of their lives differed strikingly. Savage had a peculiar capacity for destroying his own chances of success. Though he had an enduring self-confidence and eagerly sought prosperity, he affronted his benefactors and drove away one after another of his friends. He constantly made his own troubles and obviously took pleasure in the experience. Though Johnson, too, was notoriously blunt and forthright, there was something about his manner, something about his patent honesty, which attracted rather than alienated sensible people. He may have been the cause of many of his own difficulties, but it was not through insulting those who would help him.

Chiefly what bound the two men together was a common love of talk. Like Parson Ford and Walmesley, Savage had been intimate with well-known literary figures — Steele, Aaron Hill, Thomson, Pope — and was full of anecdotes about them. He was reputed to have supplied Pope with coffeehouse gossip useful for his satires. Steele had tried to persuade him to marry his illegitimate daughter. The tales of high and low life, of lords and wastrels, flowed from Savage's lips, and the younger Johnson listened with wide-eyed admiration.

Usually without obvious means of support, Savage lived from hand to mouth. He was continually borrowing small sums from friends and acquaintances, making no pretense of repayment. He never had the slightest idea of thrift. Money received was instantly spent. The story is told that once shortly after he had received a sum of money Johnson met him wearing what was then the current fashion, a sumptuous scarlet cloak trimmed with gold lace, while his naked toes were peeping through his shoes.[31]

He was able to exist through standing invitations to dine at the homes of various long-suffering friends. By rotating his visits he managed to avoid wearing out his welcome, and he could usually be sure of one substantial meal a day. In the evenings he could prevail upon a tavern acquaintance to buy him a bottle of wine in exchange for hours of fascinating talk. There were occasions, however, when all hospitality failed and he was forced to spend the night in shabby one-night lodging houses or in cellars with the "meanest and most profligate of the rabble." [32] When unable to pay for even such poor accommodations, he walked the streets, finding a hard bed on some projecting part of a building, or in winter creeping close to the walls of a glass factory and lying on the warm ashes.

At times Johnson joined him on his nocturnal rambles, neither having enough money to go to a tavern. According to Arthur Murphy, "Johnson has been often heard to relate, that he and Savage walked round Grosvenor Square till four in the morning; in the course of their conversation reforming the world, dethroning princes, establishing new forms of government, and giving laws to the several states of Europe, till, fatigued at length with their legislative office, they began to feel the want of refreshment; but could not muster up more than fourpence halfpenny." [33]

The long discussions with Savage kept Johnson's political fervor at fever pitch. He later told Sir Joshua Reynolds that "one night in particular, when Savage and he walked round St. James's Square for want of a lodging, they were not at all depressed by their situation; but in high spirits and brimful of patriotism, traversed the square for several hours, inveighed against the minister, and 'resolved they would *stand by their country.*'"

Alone, or with Savage, Johnson apparently wandered unperturbed through the ill-lighted streets and back alleys. With his shabby clothes and huge muscular frame, he was no mark for pickpockets and street robbers. On one occasion, however, he was attacked in the street by four men; refusing to yield, he was able to keep them all at bay until the watch came up. [34]

Boswell suspected that association with Savage, "who was habituated to the dissipation and licentiousness of the town," led Johnson into "indulgencies" which he regretted for the rest of his life. Hawkins did not go quite so far, merely suggesting cautiously that Johnson "reflected with as little approbation on the hours he spent with Savage as on any period of his life." But Boswell was perhaps judging from his own thorough knowledge of the temptations of the London stews, and Hawkins, always dubious about other people's behavior, may have been giving his imagination free rein. There is no surviving credible evidence to support such suspicions. During these years Johnson had given up the use of alcohol, and there is no proof anywhere of sexual laxity. [35] Though in his wanderings through the seamy parts of London he met the most degraded kinds of women, he apparently remained chaste.

In later life Johnson was ever ready to admit that "he used to take women of the town to taverns, and hear them relate their history." One day when talking with a handsome prostitute in the street, he asked her what she thought she was made for. To which she answered, "She supposed to please the gentlemen." With his deep-seated interest in human nature, he was intensely curious about their life; yet mixed in also was a genuine desire to dissuade them from their evil courses. At least so Bishop Percy thought, and so Johnson expected his hearers to believe. When a friend had the temerity to imply a more sensual reason, "Johnson expressed the highest indignation that any other motive could ever be suspected." [36]

There is little evidence, either, that Savage was openly licentious in word or deed. His weaknesses were of other sorts. He was intemperate, insolent, improvident. He was selfish, rude, and bitter in his hatreds. But he was not grossly indecent. In one letter to Birch he expressed himself as much upset over certain "downright obscene" pieces published in the magazines. One set of verses, he added, was "so very nasty" that it made his "stomach quite squeamish." [37] Though he often mistook the theory for the practice of virtue, he was not the type who would have shocked the moral Johnson. With his deep sense of tolerance, Johnson could accept all who sincerely meant well, and no matter what others might think, Savage had convinced him of his integrity.

But where was Tetty all this time? Why was Johnson wandering about the dark squares of London with no place to lay his head? Why was he not safely at home with his wife? There are few contemporary references to her, and even in later recollections there is nothing very specific. Once she went to the rather unsavory Hummums bagnio to investigate a story about the ghost of Parson Ford, which had appeared to a waiter.[38] Another time she picked up a useful bit of literary gossip from a publisher. But there is nothing to date these incidents early in their London stay.

Hawkins thought that the friendship with Savage, which confirmed Johnson in indolence and other bad habits, actually caused a temporary separation. While the husband lived precariously in lodgings in Fleet Street, the wife was "harbored by a friend near the Tower." [39] It appears probable that the Johnsons did have some misunderstanding which led to their parting for a while (it is certainly hinted at in a letter the next year), though there is no indication of a major rupture. The separation might well have resulted from poverty following the dissipation of the small capital brought from Lichfield. This may have been the period when they were in such straits that they were forced to sell many of their belongings. Long afterward, when Johnson was writing about the little silver cup which his mother had bought for him as a child, he added that it "was one of the last pieces of plate which dear Tetty sold in our distress." [40] Whatever the cause, it is possible that Johnson was not living with Tetty at the time of his greatest intimacy with Savage.

On those nocturnal ramblings, while debating the sad state of the nation, the two friends may have planned the inflammable political pamphlets which Johnson produced in the spring of 1739 — *Marmor Norfolciense* and *A Complete Vindication of the Licensers of the Stage*. Even if Savage had no hand in the composition, he undoubtedly provided a large part of the inspiration. The style of the pieces is not typically Johnsonian, and while Johnson was not exactly ashamed of them, they were never among his favorites. He may have been remembering his own early Opposition blasts when he later described one of George Lyttelton's pieces as having "something of that indistinct and headstrong ardor for liberty which a man of genius always catches when he enters the world, and always suffers to cool as he passes forward." [41] Johnson's own period of rebellion was short, but it was violent.

The plan and the style of *Marmor Norfolciense* were modeled on Swift.[42] The savage Dean in Dublin was the most brilliant of all the Opposition prose writers, the one any young author would have most liked to follow. In his work on the "Debates in the Senate of Lilliput" for the *Gentleman's Magazine,* Johnson had been carefully studying *Gulliver's Travels,* and his mind was impregnated by the Swiftian irony.

Swift once employed the well-worn device of a rediscovered inscription to flay the Duchess of Somerset, whom he suspected of insidious influence on Queen Anne. His *Windsor Prophecy* was crude and violent, but immensely effective, and earned him the lady's undying hatred. Johnson, adopting a similar scheme, imagined the discovery in Walpole's county of Norfolk of a large square stone having on it an ancient Latin inscription. He supplied the usual circumstantial details about the finding of the stone by a farmer, and of various attempts to decipher the monkish rhyme.

Once translated, it turned out to be a remarkable prophecy of contemporary conditions.

> Whene'er this stone, now hid beneath the lake,
> The horse shall trample, or the plough shall break,
> Then, O my country! shalt thou groan distrest,
> Grief swell thine eyes, and terrour chill thy breast.

The meaning was all pretty obvious. There were the usual Opposition complaints about violence, the dangers of a standing army ("Then through thy fields shall scarlet reptiles stray,/And rapine and pollution mark their way"), industrious peasants robbed of the fruits of their labors, and the British lion, now a passive coward, a shadow of its former greatness. Since one purpose of this kind of propaganda was to incite a war with Spain, he included savage allusions to atrocities committed on British sailors. Hidden behind the general satire were some covert gibes at the King's mistress ("His tortur'd sons shall die before his face,/While he lies melting in a lewd embrace").

The most dangerous prediction came in the couplet: "Then o'er the world shall discord stretch her wings;/Kings change their laws, and kingdoms change their kings." For twentieth-century readers the allusion may appear innocuous enough, but Johnson's contemporaries saw it as an open attack on the Hanoverian succession. With the ever-present possibility of another Stuart rebellion, any such reference was enough to show where a man's loyalties lay. A later Whig critic, ironically using a phrase from *Marmor,* called it a "bloody Jacobitical pamphlet." [43]

Since the careful Cave would obviously have nothing to do with such a violently partisan satire, it was necessary to find a more venturesome publisher. This proved easy, for John Brett, printer of a rabid Opposition newspaper and seller of anti-Walpole pamphlets at his shop "over against St. Clement's Church in the Strand," was quite willing to take a chance. But he was not anxious to waste much time over such an ephemeral piece. Carelessly printed, it was published before the middle of May. [44]

Marmor was immediately hailed by the Opposition. The editor of *Old Common Sense* wrote on May 19, "I make no apology to the author of a pamphlet just published, entitled *Marmor Norfolciense,* for inserting the introduction to his most ingenious essay, together with the inscription, which is the subject of it; since it is meant only to recommend it to the public to be read with the attention, and receive the applause it deserves." The *London Magazine* in its May issue repeated the same selections, as did the *Political State of Great Britain* for August. Alexander Pope found "the whole very humorous," and shortly afterward tried to help the author.[45] There can be no question as to its warm reception in some circles. What the Walpolians thought of it can easily be imagined.

Hawkins later reported that the government, which could scarcely condone "a publication so inflammatory," filled with principles "such as the Jacobites of the time openly avowed," decided to move against the anonymous author. By assiduous investigation his name was discovered and warrants were issued for his arrest. "To elude the search after him," Johnson, "together with his wife, took an obscure lodging in a house in Lambeth marsh, and lay there concealed till the scent after him was grown cold." [46] Boswell, on the other hand, was convinced that Hawkins's story was without foundation. Long search of the official records by one of the secretaries of the treasury had turned up no trace whatsoever of any such warrant. And so the matter still stands. Lovers of romance would like to imagine the stanch conservative of later life hiding in his youth, as Boswell put it in his first version of the *Life*, "as if he had been a great duck," to avoid political arrest.[47] Unfortunately there is only Hawkins's word against a complete lack of confirming evidence.

It may be that Johnson heard a rumor that action was going to be taken, and chose discretion as the wiser role. Or perhaps he felt a warrant ought to have been taken out against him. There can be no doubt that he was in some danger. In 1738 the printer of the *Craftsman* had been sentenced to a large fine and imprisonment for an alleged libel in his paper; and Opposition publishers were constantly annoyed by having their "papers and utensils seized, themselves bound over, prosecuted, declaimed against by all *people in office*." [48] Less than two months after the appearance of *Marmor,* its printer, John Brett, was taken into custody because of a passage in an issue of *Common Sense.*

On the title page of *Marmor* Johnson called himself "Probus Britanicus"; his second blast, *A Complete Vindication,* which followed shortly after, was signed "An Impartial Hand." The theatrical licensing act of 1737 had been under constant attack from the Patriots, and when in March, 1739, the Lord Chamberlain forbade the production of Henry Brooke's tragedy *Gustavus Vasa,* the protests increased. Here was concrete evidence of tyranny. Because of the ban, Brooke printed his play instead, obtaining nearly a thousand subscribers, including Johnson.

It was at the height of the furor that Johnson stepped in with his ironic pamphlet, *A Complete Vindication of the Licensers of the Stage, from the Malicious and Scandalous Aspersions of Mr. Brooke, Author of Gustavus Vasa: with a Proposal for Making the Office of Licenser More Extensive and Effectual.* Published by the well-known bookseller Charles Corbett in Fleet Street, it appeared late in May.[49]

This time another favorite device of Swift was used — the "dead-pan" advocacy of a position just the reverse of his own. By slight exaggeration the errors of the other side might be shown up in their true colors. Unfortunately, Johnson's irony lacks the superb control, the mock aloofness, of his model, and in places is heavy-handed and obvious. He could not lose himself, as could Swift, in the character of his imaginary speaker. Nonetheless the piece is vigorous political invective, with its torrent of caustic innuendoes.

In Johnson's pamphlet the imaginary spokesman of the government is properly disdainful of all the ideas of his fanatic opponents. He ridicules their constant thought of future generations. He sneers at their vague theories of the "high prerogatives of human nature, of a sacred unalienable birthright, which no man has conferred upon us, and which neither kings can take, nor senates give away."

> The natural consequence of these chimeras is contempt of authority, and an irreverence for any superiority but what is founded upon

merit; and their notions of merit are very peculiar, for it is among them no great proof of merit to be wealthy and powerful, to wear a garter or a star, to command a regiment or a senate, to have the ear of the minister or of the king, or to possess any of those virtues and excellencies, which, among us, entitle a man to little less than worship and prostration.

He is scornful of Brooke's complaints and his appeal for sympathy. "Is a man without title, pension, or place, to suspect the impartiality of the judgment of those who are entrusted with the administration of public affairs?"

Throughout, the piece was sharply anti-Walpole and anti-administration, but it was not basically Tory at all. As has recently been pointed out, its tone was "Opposition Whig, and 'left-wing' Opposition Whig at that." [50] Just as in *Marmor*, there was considerable startling republicanism. Under the spell of his friend Savage, Johnson was here allying himself with the "young Patriots," not with the real country Tories. Brooke's play, which by implication he was defending, was filled with vague revolutionary sentiments. Indeed, Johnson was apparently adopting the kind of ideas that led inevitably to Tom Paine. The only difference was that he never espoused anticlericalism. While caught for the moment in the tide of propaganda for the "outs," he had not lost his feeling for the Church or his skepticism about simple panaceas.

The *Complete Vindication* caused no stir. The newspapers failed to comment upon it, and no excerpts were included in the magazines. Of all of Johnson's pamphlets it is today one of the rarest, and there is a possibility that it was actually suppressed. [51] It added little to his purse or to his reputation.

The two pamphlets, along with the poem *London,* may be taken as signs of Johnson's "growing pains," spasms in the slow maturing of his political convictions. He knew that he heartily disliked the party in power, but was uncertain what to do about it. He was ready to accept the Opposition on its own terms, too naïve still to differentiate between fundamental ideals and campaign slogans. By temporarily joining such a diverse group, Johnson in his own contributions to the struggle sounds sometimes like a Jacobite, sometimes like an old Tory, and sometimes like a revolutionary Whig.

He was a young man of twenty-nine, still torn between conflicting pressures. Tradition, orthodoxy, strict legitimacy of succession, had powerful appeals. The Stuart cause roused in him deep responses. But by temperament he was also rational and realistic, placing common sense high in the scale of human values. Like his father before him, he was faced with a hard decision. He must choose between tradition and practicality, between sentiment and sober judgment. Would he, like the others, have to accept the great Hanoverian compromise?

By 1739 the answer was evidently not yet clear. He was still wondering whether allegiance to the House of Hanover was absolutely necessary for the preservation of a stable society. He was still feeding emotionally on his resentment at the loss of royal prerogative and the gradual triumph of secular over sacramental and spiritual forces. But the final decision was inevitable. For one who held that "the peace and happiness of society" was a paramount concern, almost anything was preferable to civil war, bloodshed, and anarchy. Thus, as the years went by, he grudgingly came to conform with the growing majority. Yet because he hated the necessity of making the choice, he continued to relieve his injured feelings by occasional petulant gestures. The story is told that once, during the reign of George II, Johnson refused to walk in the Royal Gardens because they were in the possession of a usurper.[52] That was as far as sentiment would carry him.

Marmor Norfolciense and the *Complete Vindication* came at the high point of Johnson's rebellion. The tide soon began to recede, more speedily perhaps than most people realize. In further work on the parliamentary debates for the magazine, he began to see that politics was complex, that the clear-cut rights and wrongs existed only in his youthful mind.[53] It was not quite so simple as he had supposed.

Furthermore, his increasingly serious study of the law gave him a clearer conception of the problems of sovereignty and authority. From college days he had been fascinated with matters pertaining to the law. In the summer of 1739, to help his employer, he

investigated a knotty legal puzzle. The June *Gentleman's Magazine* had included the first installment of an abridgment of the
popular sermons of Joseph Trapp. When there was a threat of
legal action on the part of Trapp's publishers, Cave turned to
Johnson for advice. Up to this time the question of abridgments
had never been raised in the courts, and there were no specifically
applicable laws. Johnson, accordingly, drew up a list of thirty-one
"considerations," proving to his own satisfaction that abridgment was no violation of the rights of the proprietor, a position
later upheld by the courts.[54] All this required a detailed, sober
search through the older authorities, and the more he read, the
more respectful he became toward the constitutional authority in
England. The investigation for Cave contributed its bit to the
gradual diminution of his anti-Hanoverian bias.

In the early summer of 1739 Johnson was discontented and
restless. He was unhappy about the state of the nation, about his
own domestic situation, and about his future as a writer. His
tragedy was unproduced; his translations, failures; his journalistic
work, unremunerative. He was miserably poor. Even if the term
"impransus" (without a dinner), with which he ended one of his
letters to Cave, may have meant only that he had been too busy to
think of eating, it is a certainty that on occasion he was desperately
in need of money.[55] He later told Richard Cumberland that there
was one period in his life when he had to subsist on fourpence
halfpenny a day. There were times when he was forced to be idle
for want of a light. Nothing had turned out as he had so bravely
hoped when he came to the city in 1737.

Savage was preparing to leave London, to live in Wales on an
allowance collected by his friends, and was romantically lyrical
over the imagined delights of rural life. A thoroughgoing city
man, he knew nothing of the country except what he had read in
pastorals and songs, and, as Johnson later reported, "imagined
that he should be transported to scenes of flowery felicity, like
those which one poet has reflected to another; and had projected
a perpetual round of innocent pleasures, of which he suspected
no interruption from pride, or ignorance, or brutality."[56] He
thought a nightingale "was to be heard from every bramble." The

country-born Johnson was amused by such foolish imaginings. He urged his friend to stay in the city instead and try manfully to support himself by his own labors. Nevertheless, their long discussions may have stirred up some twinges of homesickness for Lichfield. He, too, might find somewhere at least a rational, if not an idyllic, life in a cottage.

In July Savage bade Johnson farewell "with tears in his eyes." They were never to see each other again. With his friend gone, Johnson himself grasped at the first opportunity to get away. Word had come of a vacancy at the Appleby Grammar School in Leicestershire, not far from Lichfield.[57] Someone had suggested Johnson for the post. In fact, there was considerable activity on his behalf, and Pope on his own accord sent a recommendation to the prominent Midland landowner, Lord Gower. It was disinterested generosity, for Pope knew nothing about Johnson except his authorship of *London* and the political pieces, and the fact that he had "an infirmity of the convulsive kind, that attacks him sometimes, so as to make him a sad spectacle." [58]

Again the lack of a degree proved an insuperable bar. If he were ever to be a successful schoolmaster he must somehow acquire the all-important M.A. Obviously he had not enough reputation to manage one from Oxford. Someone hit upon the idea that through the interposition of Dean Swift in Dublin a degree might be secured from Trinity College there. On just what pretense is not entirely clear, unless his imitations of the Dean were thought to be sufficient. Very dubious, and fearing it was "an impracticable thing" (as it turned out to be!), Lord Gower, nevertheless, was prevailed on to write to a friend of Swift:

> Mr. Samuel Johnson (author of London, a satire, and some other poetical pieces) is a native of this county, and much respected by some worthy gentlemen in his neighborhood, who are trustees of a charity school now vacant, the certain salary of which is sixty pounds per year, of which they are desirous to make him master; but unfortunately he is not capable of receiving their bounty, which would make him happy for life, by not being a *master of arts,* which by the statutes of this school the master of it must be.[59]

After suggesting the possibility of a degree from Trinity College, Gower added:

> They say he is not afraid of the strictest examination, though he is of so long a journey, and will venture it, if the Dean thinks it necessary, choosing rather to die upon the road, *than be starved to death in translating for booksellers,* which has been his only subsistence for some time past.

The last phrases have an authentic ring. Johnson may well have spoken them. He was undoubtedly discouraged by his lack of success at earning a living as a writer. Though he still found the city fascinating, he was quite ready to go elsewhere. Sometime in August, 1739, leaving Tetty in London, he set off for the Midlands to try to find another profession.

A Country Interlude

WHEN Johnson journeyed to Leicestershire, late in the summer of 1739, it was his last attempt to become a schoolmaster. Thereafter, until honored by a royal pension, there was never a time when he was not entirely dependent on his own pen for a livelihood.

Anyone might have guessed that he would fail.[1] Without an Oxford or Cambridge degree, he had no chance. Even if Swift in far-off Ireland had bestirred himself at Lord Gower's request, as obviously he did not, Johnson would not have qualified. The Appleby School statutes make that very clear. But because the governors of the school were having difficulty in agreeing on a candidate, Johnson's friends urged him to make application anyway. It was a place he must have known well. Among the students there was always a sprinkling of Lichfield boys, and it is likely that young George Garrick, who had been at Edial, was there at the time. Most of the governors were gentlemen of the neighborhood, many of them, perhaps, former customers of Michael Johnson. Only some dozen miles from Lichfield, Appleby was near Ashby-de-la-Zouch, where the bookseller had kept a stall.

Johnson's candidacy made no real headway. Despite his personal application and the reputed activities of his supporters the records do not show him as a serious contender. Near the end of the year, when no decision had been reached, the Bishop stepped in and appointed Thomas Mould as master — a man who had his M.A. from Oxford, and in addition was "a founder's near kinsman." He was to hold the post for forty years.

Johnson must have been disappointed, even though from the start he considered his chances slim. What justification for hope could he have had? He had been unsuccessful as a teacher at Stourbridge, at Market Bosworth, and at Edial. Largely because of his physical disabilities he had been rejected by one school after another — at Ashbourne, Solihull, Brewood. He can scarcely have had many illusions left about his future in the teaching profession. But he was deeply hurt, just the same, and in later years never liked to be reminded of these unhappy experiences. On at least one occasion his anger was aroused when someone incautiously addressed him as "Domine." [2]

Despite his failure to get the Appleby position Johnson was in no haste to return to the steady toil in London. Instead he enjoyed a long vacation in the country, and for over six months idled his time away, leaving Tetty alone in the city. Their marriage ties were certainly being strained to the limit.

During the autumn and early winter he apparently rambled about, making at least one lengthy visit to his old schoolmate John Taylor at Ashbourne, who was now married and living in the large and comfortable "Mansion," close by the church and directly on one of the main thoroughfares entering the town.[3] Taylor had succeeded to his father's legal practice but was too indolent to be very happy in the profession. He was instead toying with the idea of taking holy orders, although he had no apparent spiritual call. He was no mystic, no self-sacrificing Christian devotee. One can only guess at his motives, and such speculations may be unfair. But from what is known of his character the chances are that the easy life of a church pluralist appealed more than the active business of the law. With his money and political connections there was no reason why he should not aspire to some deanery or even to a bishopric. The first step was to acquire a lucrative benefice, one that could be handled by a resident curate; and the very next summer, in August, 1740, he was presented to the rectory of Market Bosworth by Johnson's old aversion Sir Wolstan Dixie. Taylor secured the "living" only after certain cash payments to the donor, testified to by actual documents which still survive.[4]

As Johnson lingered on at Ashbourne, he and his host settled down to an agreeable round of social activity. Taylor was intimate with most of the local gentry, who also accepted his guest gladly. For a while, Johnson moved in the best society of Derby-shire. Once again he could enjoy that well-to-do Whig society which had so attracted and disturbed him in the past. He could slip back into the kind of life he had first tasted at Pedmore and Hagley Park with Cornelius Ford.

It was a pleasant contrast to his insecure and unhappy exist-ence in London. Instead of living in cheap, dreary lodgings, or sometimes tramping the streets all night with no place to lay his head, he was provided with every comfort. No wonder he could not bear to drag himself away. At the neighboring great houses, which he visited with his friend, he could forget his vexing prob-lems and relax in the Castle of Indolence. He could get up when he pleased. There were long hours with nothing to do but read and talk, and no dreary assignments to do for Cave. There were servants everywhere — butlers, housekeepers, maids, cooks, gar-deners, stableboys — ready to fulfill every wish. At mealtimes there was a profusion of food — perhaps a dinner of "hashed calf's head," or a cold collation of ham and fowls, venison pasty, cold tongue, and orange cheese cakes.

From contemporary accounts it is possible to recreate a typical day at one of those Derbyshire country houses.[5] After breakfast the company would separate, the men for fishing in the river Dove (Izaak Walton's old favorite) or perhaps riding or playing with the dogs. Meanwhile the ladies walked about the park or busied themselves with domestic concerns. After the large midday din-ner the ladies would retire while the gentlemen indulged in drink-ing and often bawdy conversation. Later there might be games: bowls outside, or cards or backgammon inside. There was almost sure to be music in the drawing room, with one of the ladies sing-ing, accompanied by gentlemen on German flutes. Needlework, gossip, and talk of local philanthropies provided further enter-tainment. There was shooting, hunting, every sort of game for the sportsmen. Traditionally a late cold supper and family prayers ended the day.

The people Johnson saw most during this visit were the Meynells of Bradley, some three miles from Ashbourne, the Fitzherberts of Tissington, and the Boothbys of Ashbourne Hall. There was the

Chauncy family, as well as the learned but eccentric John Kennedy and his wife. Sam remembered them all vividly, and in later years was not loath to talk about them.

Littleton Poyntz Meynell, the head of the family at Bradley, was a bluff country squire, who has come down to us as the epitome of British insularity by his priceless remark, "For anything I see, foreigners are fools." [6] Johnson must have been amused when he first heard the outburst, although he quoted it with apparent approval long afterward at Old Slaughter's Coffeehouse in London. "Old Meynell" was a sportsman and a rake, a violent man of variable moods. Once his irascible temper was aroused, he was "absolutely malignant." As Johnson later remarked, "He really wished evil to others, and rejoiced at it." [7] According to one account he was something of a freethinker, who forbade his children to be taught anything about formal religion.[8] In his softer moods, however, he liked to think of himself as a Shaftesburian benevolist; and after his wife's death, which affected him deeply, he made the vain and foolish resolve to cherish his grief permanently "with a kind of sacred fondness." His predominant passion, and his son's after him, was his horses and hounds.

But the chief attraction of Bradley for Johnson was not the kennels. We have the word of one witness that his visits were "much desired by the ladies of the family, who were, perhaps, in point of elegance and accomplishments, inferior to few of those with whom he was afterward acquainted." [9] While he could hold his own in the rough give-and-take of masculine company, Johnson relished most the softer blandishments of the drawing room. It should not be forgotten that he always considered himself a ladies' man, and that he was, in fact, a great favorite with women. After the first shocking impression they ceased to be offended by his fearsome exterior and occasional harsh manners, and sensed the qualities of courtesy and deep tenderness beneath.

The center of the household was Mrs. Meynell, daughter of a Barbados planter. Though probably in bad health (she died the following spring) she was still an inspiration to all who knew her. She was a deeply religious woman who, secretly circumventing her husband, saw to it that her children were well instructed in the Scriptures. A Horatian verse epitaph written by a neighbor praises her wit, her native sweetness, her unspotted honor. Proof that the formalized verses were not too far from the truth may be seen in the fact that they were at once inserted in the *Gentleman's Magazine,* apparently at the instigation of Johnson, who must have thought them just.[10]

It was her seventeen-year-old daughter Mary, however, who was the brightest star. Johnson's admiration for her became unbounded, and he later commented that "she had the best understanding he ever met with in any human being." [11] To be sure, Johnson was given to such fits of exuberant hyperbole in nostalgic recollection, especially about someone whose merits were moral as well as social. When out of curiosity Mrs. Thrale asked him if Mary Meynell had been handsome, he replied: "She would have been handsome for a queen; her beauty had more in it of majesty than of attraction, more of the dignity of virtue than the vivacity of wit." [12]

A few years later Mary Meynell married a neighbor, William Fitzherbert of Tissington, another agreeable member of the group, whom Johnson characterized as "a gay good-humored fellow, generous of his money and of his meat, and desirous of nothing but cheerful society among people distinguished in *some* way, in *any way,* I think." [13] Rousseau and St. Augustine, he continued, would have been equally welcome to this man's table and to his kindness. There was "no sparkle, no brilliancy" in Fitzherbert, Johnson told Boswell, but he never knew a man "so generally acceptable. He made everybody quite easy, overpowered nobody by superiority of talents, made no man think worse of himself by being his rival, seemed to listen, did not oblige you to hear much from him, and did not oppose what you said."

After Fitzherbert and Mary Meynell were married, however, it is evident the lady took charge. "Her first care was to preserve her husband's soul from corruption; her second, to keep his estate entire for their children." Johnson always suspected he owed his own warm reception in the family to her idea that he was a good influence on Fitzherbert. "They dare not (said she) swear, and take other conversation-liberties before *you.*" When Mrs. Thrale pressed Johnson to know whether the husband appreciated such attentions from his wife, Johnson added, "He felt her influence too powerfully: no man will be fond of what forces him daily to feel himself inferior. She stood at the door of her Paradise in Derbyshire, like the angel with the flaming sword, to keep the devil at a distance. But she was not immortal, poor dear! She died, and her husband felt at once afflicted and released."

She had as an intimate friend a spinster some fourteen years older, Miss Hill Boothby, the granddaughter of Michael Johnson's assiduous customer of the 1680s. This lady was even more noted for piety. "The sublimated, Methodistic Hill Boothby, who read her Bible in Hebrew" — so the acid Anna Seward later described her.[14] As "Miss Sainthill" she appears in Graves's novel *The Spiritual Quixote* — pleasantly argumentative and strictly virtuous. For Hill Boothby, Johnson also developed an enduring admiration, but it was not until the mid-fifties that their intimacy really developed and their correspondence became regular. This was after the death of Tetty, when, some people have supposed, he may have considered marrying the spinster one year his elder.[15] Perhaps it was then, too, that his reported jealousy developed over her preference for Lord Lyttelton of Hagley Park. In 1739, however, Hill Boothby was merely one of the group of attractive, pious ladies whose conversation rendered the environs of Ashbourne so pleasant to the disappointed schoolmaster.

WHEN not visiting Taylor, Johnson presumably spent the rest of the autumn of 1739 and early winter of 1740 in Lichfield with his mother and stepdaughter. Sarah Johnson was trying to keep the bookshop going with the help of her faithful maid, Catherine Chambers, and Tetty's daughter, Lucy Porter, who took her turn in standing behind the counter. Through her father, Lucy was well connected in Lichfield, and moved in the best circles, but, according to Anna Seward's later recollections, "would make no engagement on market days lest Granny, as she called Mrs. Johnson, should catch cold by serving in the shop." Lucy thought it no "disgrace to thank a poor person who purchased

from her a penny battledore." [16] Unfortunately, despite the ladies' efforts, the business was slowly going to pieces. In Gilbert
Walmesley's surviving account book, kept somewhat later, there
is only one listing of a bill paid to Mrs. Johnson, as compared to
frequent large payments to "Mr. Bayley bookseller," to "Robt.
Shaw bookbinder," to Thomas Williams, and even to Thomas
Warren of Birmingham.[17] The two ladies were no match for their
more aggressive rivals.

While idling away his days in the house by the market place,
Johnson undoubtedly dropped back into his old social pattern,
seeing the accustomed friends of his boyhood, spending long
hours at the palace, arguing with Walmesley about political and
literary matters, and enjoying the delights of his drawing room.
Chief among these delights was his host's sister-in-law, "Molly"
Aston.

Molly always held a special place in Johnson's heart. It is to
be suspected that as a gauche, insecure young man he had long
admired her from afar. For her he had developed that hopeless,
admiring worship of a country boy for a bright luminary from
another sphere. She remained a symbol for Johnson of something
rare and beautiful outside his reach. The few letters he had from
her, he confided later to Mrs. Thrale, would be the last papers
he would destroy. The one time in his life, he said, that he had
experienced "measureless delight" was the first evening wholly
spent talking to Molly Aston. The memory of that rapture colored
his recollections of the entire year.[18] This meeting probably occurred at the palace during the autumn of 1739.

Molly was no recent addition to Lichfield society. Her grand-
mother had been an Offley, great-aunt to the Offley boys who went
to Lichfield School and to Johnson's Edial Academy and who were
bosom friends of David Garrick. It is not difficult to imagine that
the Aston sisters, as they grew up, often visited their cousins at
Wichnor, only a mile or two away. It may even be that it was here
that Gilbert Walmesley first met Magdalen Aston, who later became his wife. The story is told that one day when Walmesley and
young David rode over to Wichnor, the older man slyly slipped
two half-crowns to the boy so that he might grandly tip the butler

and groom at "Mr. Offley's." [19] Through the Offleys, as well as
through the Herveys and later through Walmesley himself, Johnson must for some time have been acquainted with the eight Aston
sisters. For them all he had high regard, but it was Molly who became his idol.

If Molly's surviving portrait shows a nose too long for pure
beauty, if her features do not have classic proportions, her eyes
look out at one with sparkle and animation.[20] This is no languid
beauty of the card table. There is a hint of a coming epigram in
the set of her lips. It was her animation, the challenge of her
active mind that attracted Johnson. To be sure, she had auburn
hair, a smooth complexion, a fine figure, and elegant manners.
Anna Seward thought her handsome but haughty. The ladies,
Johnson confessed to Mrs. Thrale (who was another of the same
type), never liked Molly. There was too much cutting wit in her
tongue, too much intellectual vigor.

Her one flaw from Johnson's point of view was that she was as
arrant a Whig as Walmesley himself. When on that celebrated
evening she talked all in praise of liberty, immediately on parting
Johnson could not resist dashing off a Latin epigram:

> Liber ut esse velim, suasisti, pulchra *Maria:*
> Ut maneam liber, pulchra *Maria,* vale.

It was later translated, impromptu, by Mrs. Thrale as:

> Persuasions to freedom fall oddly from you,
> If freedom we seek, fair Maria Adieu! [21]

Molly's interests were varied. On a later occasion she explained a question in economics which had puzzled both Johnson
and Lord Kames.[22] Her criticism of one of Pope's epitaphs, as well
as her relegation of the poet Gay to a lower rank, Johnson never
forgot, and he quoted her in the *Lives of the Poets.* She wrote
verses herself. Once when she had refused to give a copy to a
cousin, Johnson sat down and dashed off the entire twelve lines,
though he had heard them only once. The manuscript is still preserved in the Bodleian Library.

It may be that the chance of seeing more of Molly at the palace was one reason that Johnson lingered on in the Midlands. Then late in January two pieces of startling news from London jolted him out of his lethargy. Things were stirring again about his play *Irene,* and Tetty had hurt her leg badly. On the thirty-first he wrote to her at Mrs. Crow's in Castle Street, near Cavendish Square in London:

> After hearing that you are in so much danger, as I apprehend from a hurt on the tendon, I shall be very uneasy till I know that you are recovered, and beg that you will omit nothing that can contribute to it, nor deny yourself anything that may make confinement less melancholy. You have already suffered more than I can bear to reflect upon, and I hope more than either of us shall suffer again. One part at least I have often flattered myself we shall avoid for the future, our troubles will surely never separate us more.[23]

He urged her to get the best medical advice, to spare no expense, and promised to send more money for that purpose the first of the week.

> I beg therefore that you will more regard my happiness, than to expose yourself to any hazards. I still promise myself many happy years from your tenderness and affection, which I sometimes hope our misfortunes have not yet deprived me of.

The wording is a bit equivocal. He "sometimes" hopes that their troubles have not cut him off from her tenderness and affection. He promises himself many happy years ahead. There is enough uncertainty of tone to suggest a bad conscience. Can he have been unsure just how much of his wife's love he has retained? Is he having twinges of regret over his own long absence in the country? The letter, as well as the long separation itself, indicates some basis for Hawkins's claim of a temporary estrangement.

Even though Tetty may not have been writing fretful letters of complaint, Johnson felt that some explanation was required, and added:

> Of the time which I have spent from thee, and of my dear Lucy and other affairs, my heart will be at ease on Monday to give thee a

particular account, especially if a letter should inform me that thy leg is better, for I hope you do not think so unkindly of me as to imagine that I can be at rest while I believe my dear Tetty in pain.

There is almost a hint that this is the first letter written to his wife since he parted from her the previous summer. Perhaps Tetty's unhappiness stemmed not only from a hurt leg but also from lacerated feelings, for news of her husband's mild flirtations with the handsome ladies in Ashbourne and Walmesley's house may well have reached her in far-off London. She certainly had much to complain about. His final words may have been intended as an answer to her possible suspicions.

Be assured, my dear girl, that I have seen nobody in these rambles upon which I have been forced, that has not contribute to confirm my esteem and affection for thee, though that esteem and affection only contributed to increase my unhappiness when I reflected that the most amiable woman in the world was exposed by my means to miseries which I could not relieve.

In later years Tetty showed open jealousy, as well she might. No wife likes to have another woman continually held up as a model of beauty and intelligence, particularly when, like Molly Aston, she is much younger and wealthier. The tactless Johnson evidently could not refrain from some invidious comparisons. Possibly he had no idea of the depths of his wife's resentment and considered the imagined rivalry a huge joke. When Mrs. Thrale long afterward asked what Tetty had thought of his open admiration of the lovely Miss Aston, Johnson replied: "She was jealous to be sure, and teased me sometimes when I would let her; and one day, as a fortune-telling gypsy passed us when we were walking out in company with two or three friends in the country, she made the wench look at my hand, but soon repented her curiosity; for (says the gypsy) your heart is divided, Sir, between a Betty and a Molly: Betty loves you best, but you take most delight in Molly's company: when I turned about to laugh, I saw my wife was crying. Pretty charmer! she had no reason!" [24]

Knowing his own faithfulness, Johnson might laugh, but the gypsy's chance remark cut too close for Tetty's equanimity. She must always have been aware that the twenty years' difference in their ages rendered her continually vulnerable.

Characteristically, if somewhat unfeelingly, Johnson made no mention in his long letter of the bitter cold which had settled over England in January, 1740. Yet he must have wondered about his wife's situation. Especially in London was suffering widespread, and the newspapers carried accounts of people frozen in the streets, one right in Drury Lane. The Thames was solidly frozen over, and a sheep was roasted whole on the ice off Pepper Alley stairs. Booths were erected, and "Frost Fair" drew hundreds of venturesome spectators. The plight of the watermen, deprived of their livelihood, became so desperate that they carried a boat to the Exchange to dramatize their sad condition. Everywhere collections were being made for charity, and Ralph Thrale, one of the candidates for Parliament in the forthcoming election at Southwark, gave £125 to be distributed among the poor of the various parishes.[25]

In the Midlands the unusual cold was long remembered. Snow that fell on New Year's Day remained until March. People's breath froze immediately on their bedclothes. It was the most severe winter in living memory. Yet Johnson — sturdy philosopher that he was — remained completely unmoved. Although he would remember it as "the dreadful winter of Forty," he did not see fit to mention such matters in his letter.[26]

One legitimate excuse for his lingering in the country was the necessity of raising money. Having failed in the attempt to get a dependable income as a schoolmaster, he was faced with the immediate need for ready cash, not only to send to his wife in London, but to pay his own current expenses. His mother's bookshop could furnish no extra income. The only thing left was to mortgage the big house in the market place, the one valuable family asset that remained. Accordingly, on January 31, Theophilus Levett, coroner and town clerk, advanced to Sarah Johnson and to Samuel Johnson, "son and heir," the sum of eighty pounds, at 4½ per cent interest, with the house as collateral security.[27]

For the moment, then, Johnson was in an expansive mood — able and willing out of his share of the money to send Tetty twenty pounds the following Monday. He could afford to urge her to consult a fashionable surgeon about her injured leg. Besides, he had hopes of more income in the near future from another source, for a letter from Garrick had revived the whole matter of *Irene*. So he commented to Tetty:

> David wrote to me this day on the affair of Irene, who is at last become a kind of favorite among the players. Mr. Fleetwood promises to give a promise in writing that it shall be the first next season, if it cannot be introduced now, and Chetwood the prompter is desirous of bargaining for the copy, and offers fifty guineas for the right of printing after it shall be played. I hope it will at length reward me for my perplexities.[28]

But there is nothing to suggest that once the mortgage on his birthplace was settled Johnson hurried to London to comfort Tetty and see about his play. It may not have been until late March or early April that he finally reached the capital, to throw himself into what proved to be fruitless negotiations with the manager at Drury Lane. In these his former pupil played a prominent part.

Although David Garrick was now ostensibly engaged in the wine business with his brother Peter, his heart lay elsewhere. He haunted the theaters, became intimate with the principal players, talked theater in the coffeehouses, and dreamed of a career for himself on the stage. Also, his nimble pen still scratched away. Early in the spring of 1740 he had thrown together a short comic sketch, designed as an afterpiece, which he called *Lethe: or Aesop in the Shades*. In the original version it was a slight piece, scarcely more than a fraction of what it later became after numerous reworkings, but it was effective theater. He had taken two popular characters from one of Fielding's farces and given them opportunities for some entertaining songs and for witty dialogue embodying the favorite jokes of the day. Already with an unerring sense of what would act well, Garrick had written what was essentially a clever vaudeville skit.

Lethe was played for the first time at Drury Lane on April 15, 1740, as part of a special benefit for the actor Henry Giffard. With an excellent cast, including Macklin, Woodward, John Beard, and Kitty Clive, the piece was an immediate success. What is important to us is Johnson's connection with the production. If he had failed young Davy years before when the boy acted in the bishop's palace at Lichfield, this time he came stanchly to his aid with a special prologue for his earliest produced piece.[29]

Johnson must have been back in London for the performance. It is hard to believe that he would not have been present at Drury Lane to share in the excitement of his pupil, and to hear his own verses declaimed on the public stage. Since he was a would-be dramatist himself, the chance to ingratiate himself with Fleetwood, the manager, would have been irresistible.

The prologue, which has only recently come to light, is in Johnson's characteristic vein:

> Prodigious Madness of the writing Race!
> Ardent of Fame, yet fearless of Disgrace.
> Without a boding Fear, or anxious Sigh,
> The Bard obdurate sees his Brother die.
> Deaf to the Critick, Sullen to the Friend,
> Not One takes Warning, by Another's End.
> Oft has our Bard in this disastrous Year,
> Beheld the Tragic Heroes taught to fear.
> Oft has he seen the Poignant Orange fly,
> And heard th' ill Omen'd Catcall's direful Cry.
> Yet dares to venture on the dangerous Stage,
> And weakly hopes to 'scape the Critick's Rage.
> This Night he hopes to shew that Farce may charm,
> Tho' no lewd Hint the mantling Virgin warm.
> That useful Truth with Humour may unite,
> That Mirth may mend, and Innocence delight.

In spite of Johnson's evident willingness to please, Fleetwood still proved difficult to pin down. Profuse in promises, he refused either to commit himself in writing or to make definite plans for an early production of *Irene*. There can be no doubt that he seriously considered production. He considered but delayed. Consequently Johnson was kept on tenterhooks, hopeful and discouraged by turns.

The failure was partly his own fault. A year and a half later, when he grew desperate and tried to sell the copyright of the play, Cave wrote to Birch:

> I have put Mr. Johnson's play into Mr. Gray's hands, in order to sell it to him, if he is inclined to buy it, but I doubt whether he will or not. He would dispose of copy and whatever advantage may be made by acting it. Would your society, or any gentleman or body of men, that you know, take such a bargain? Both he and I are very unfit to deal with the theatrical persons. Fleetwood was to have acted it last season, but Johnson's diffidence or   prevented it.[30]

The blank space showed Cave's own bewilderment. Something, he knew, had gone wrong, but he did not know what. Doubtless the answer lay merely in what Cave suggested. The plain-speaking, downright Johnson was "very unfit" to deal with a slippery theatrical manager.

Although he had no inkling at the time, the long trip to the Midlands in the autumn and winter of 1739–1740 was the end of an epoch in Johnson's life. It was over twenty years before he returned to his birthplace. He never again saw his mother. There were to be no more friendly arguments with Gilbert Walmesley at the bishop's palace. Fate had not intended Sam Johnson to be a countryman or a schoolmaster. From now on he was irrevocably committed to London and to literature.

His immediate problem, however, was to earn a living for himself and Tetty, for the money from the mortgage of the Lichfield house was fast running out. Doggedly, he returned to his old post with Cave at St. John's Gate.

London Cronies

Speedily he slipped back into the old routine — the uneasy domesticity with Tetty, the walks to St. John's Gate to discuss plans for the magazine, the bursts of writing to meet deadlines, and the long hours of talk in the coffeehouses and taverns. If a man wanted to waste time, a coffeehouse was a perfect spot. Here he could find almost everything for his comfort and well-being — a crackling fire on cold days, any kind of drink to meet his taste (chocolate, tea, coffee, hot liquors, or punch), paper and pens if he wanted to write a letter, and, even more important, newspapers and periodicals. All this at a cost of only a few pence! Chiefly the coffeehouse was the place for news. Some establishments had available ten or a dozen copies of the most recent papers. In a leisurely fashion a man could read and talk and drink for as long as he wanted. There was no hurrying, no trying to push him out. A favorite coffeehouse became one's second home, where appointments might be made, letters received, business transacted.

At first the Johnsons had lodgings somewhere in the Strand, but during the next few years they apparently moved about considerably — to Boswell Court, at or near the Black Boy "over against Durham Yard, Strand," to Bow Street, to Fetter Lane, and to Holborn.[1] It was a precarious hand-to-mouth existence which depended on the meager payments from Cave. But since most of Johnson's friends and acquaintances were just as poor, there was a camaraderie in want and privation.

They were a strange group, those cronies of Johnson's in the early 1740s — bohemian poets, impractical idealists, reformed impostors, eager inventors, drunken rakes, and serious clergymen, many of them with only one tie in common, a compulsion to write. From the most dissolute vagabond to the most exquisite gentleman, they were in one way or another drawn into Cave's net. Some sent in elegant contributions; some slaved away over specific assignments at so much a line; some came to Clerkenwell merely to talk. A few were brought into the circle because they were involved in other publishing ventures carried on in the neighborhood.

The most colorful were Samuel Boyse and George Psalmanazar. Boyse was the typical improvident poet, often in trouble, always in debt.[2] Gifted but erratic, with a taste for the arts, he could translate expertly from the French or spin verses "as fast as most men write prose," but he only worked when he could not sponge off forgiving patrons and friends. He made use of the most disgraceful expedients to excite charity, sometimes raising subscriptions for nonexistent poems, and sometimes having his wife report that he was dying. Nor was he much embarrassed when friends met him on the street the next day.

The greater part of what is known of the eccentric Boyse — his ability, his waywardness, his dissolute behavior — comes from Johnson, who loved to tell stories about him. Apparently Johnson had something of the same feeling for Boyse that he had for the more gifted but exiled Savage — he enjoyed his conversation, laughed at his follies, and was moved by his continual distress. The fact that a man's troubles were self-inflicted made no difference, for misery, however caused, was enough to enlist Johnson's sympathy.

What impressed others most vividly was Boyse's complete irresponsibility about his own and other people's possessions. In order to keep alive, he had continual recourse to the pawnbrokers. If he was engaged to do a translation from the French, by the time the first sheet was done he would pawn the original volume. "If the employer redeemed it, a second sheet would be completed, and the book again be pawned, and this perpetually." His own clothes went the same way. When he lacked a shirt, he cut white paper into slips, which he tied around his wrists for cuffs, and used the same material for a collar. Though the loss of other garments was more hampering, even then he was not completely immobilized.

On one occasion he was sent for by a printer, presumably Cave, who had commissioned a poem for his magazine. At the time Boyse had neither breeches nor waistcoat. He did still possess a coat, and he bundled himself up in it and hurried to the printer's house. When he came into the room several women were present "whom his extraordinary appearance obliged immediately to retire."

Sometimes everything was fed to the same devouring monster. Once in 1740 Boyse pawned all his clothes, even the sheets from his bed, but "sat up in bed with the blanket wrapt about him, through which he had cut a hole large enough to admit his arm, and placing the paper upon his knee, scribbled in the best manner he could the verses he was obliged to make."

On another occasion he wrote emotionally to Cave from a coffeehouse:

> I am every moment threatened to be turned out here because, I have not money to pay for my bed two nights past, which is usually paid beforehand. . . . I hope therefore you will have the humanity to send me half a guinea for support, till I finish your papers in my hands. The ode on the British Nation I hope to have done today and want proof copy of that part of Stowe you'd choose for the present magazine, that it may be compressed as far as possible. . . . I humbly entreat your answer, having not tasted anything since Tuesday evening I came in here, and my coat will be taken off my back, for the charge of the bed. So that I must go into prison naked, which is too shocking for me to think of.

At the bottom of the letter Cave methodically wrote "sent" and at the top added "Mr. S. Boyse poetical writer. A singular character." [3]

No contribution ever gave more than temporary relief. When Johnson collected a sum of money to redeem his friend's clothes, in two days they were pawned again. "The sum," Johnson commented sadly, "was collected by sixpences, at a time when to me sixpence was a serious consideration." Like Savage, Boyse had the utmost scorn of economy. Even when he was almost perishing with hunger "and some money was produced to purchase him a

Above: St. John's Gate, home of the *Gentleman's Magazine. Below, left:* Edward Cave. From portrait by F. Kyte, 1740. *Below, right:* Thomas Birch. An oil painting by an unknown artist, perhaps J. Wills. Courtesy of the National Portrait Gallery, London.

A portion of the original manuscript of the poem *London*, never before reproduced. From the collection of Mr. and Mrs. Donald F. Hyde.

dinner, he got a bit of roast beef, but could not eat it without ketchup, and laid out the last half-guinea he possessed in truffles and mushrooms, eating them in bed too, for want of clothes, or even a shirt to sit up in." According to one account "he was intoxicated whenever he had the means to avoid starving, and was voluptuous, luxurious, and boundlessly expensive." Yet for all his faults, Johnson pitied and loved him in the way he did the other sad strays who had a permanent claim on his heart.

The aging George Psalmanazar was a very different sort. Perpetrator of one of the most celebrated of hoaxes, he had as a young man pretended to be a native of Formosa and actually had gone so far as to invent an elaborate alphabet and grammar of the language and even to publish a historical and geographical description of the island.[4] So little was known at that time about Formosa that he was invited to spend some months at Christ Church in Oxford teaching his pretended language to a set of gentlemen who planned to go out to convert the natives to Christianity. Gradually he was disbelieved, and ultimately fell into obscurity. When he experienced a genuine religious conversion and made a complete confession of his deceptions, his repentance was so sincere that in late life he was revered for piety and exemplary behavior.

A suggestion of how Psalmanazar was drawn into the Clerkenwell circle is contained in a letter of August 18, 1741, from Birch to his patron Philip Yorke. "Who do you imagine has offered himself for one of my index makers to Thurloe? No less a person than the renowned Psalmanazar, the pretended Prince of Formosa, now, by a fate not unlike that of Dionysius, condemned to a punishment severe enough for an impostor or a tyrant."[5]

Later letters show that he was hired straight away and for several months did compile the indexes to *A Collection of the State Papers of John Thurloe*. Quite possibly it was at this time that Johnson made his acquaintance. One thing is certain: the wide learning, the purity of thought, and the pious life of the reformed impostor made an immediate and indelible impression. Mrs. Thrale once asked Johnson who was the best man he had ever known, and the reply came at once: "Psalmanazar." The man's virtues, Johnson insisted, exceeded what would be considered wonderful even in the lives of the saints.

Psalmanazar spent his evenings at a public house in Old Street, where he was the center of an admiring group who came to hear him talk. There Johnson sought him out, for once making the opening advances and yielding first place to another. From his speech Johnson assumed the old man had been born a Gascon. He spoke English coarsely with a London city accent. Although the talk touched many topics, chiefly religion and learning, one subject was never mentioned. When someone asked Johnson later whether they had ever referred to Formosa, he replied that he himself had been afraid to mention even China. He revered the older man too much. When asked whether he had ever contradicted Psalmanazar, Johnson added: "I should as soon have thought of contradicting a bishop."

One other member of that Old Street group left a vivid mark in Johnson's memory. Long afterward he chanced to ask John Hoole, the translator of Ariosto, about his education and who had been his earliest instructor. To which Hoole replied, " 'My uncle, Sir, who was a tailor'; Johnson, recollecting himself, said, 'Sir, I knew him; we called him the *metaphysical tailor*. He was of a club in Old Street, with me and George Psalmanazar, and some others: but pray, Sir, was he a good tailor?' Mr. Hoole having answered that he believed he was too mathematical, and used to draw squares and triangles on his shop board, so that he did not excel in the cut of a coat; — 'I am sorry for it (said Johnson,) for I would have every man to be master of his own business.' " [6]

Only one interchange between the two has come down to us. When Johnson "took occasion to remark on the human mind, that it had a necessary tendency to improvement, and that it would frequently anticipate instruction," the other retorted, "Sir, that I deny; I am a tailor, and have had many apprentices, but never one that could make a coat till I had taken great pains in teaching him." [7] If only there had been a Boswell lurking in the shadows of that alehouse in Ironmonger's Row, to preserve more of the spirited conversations of the reformed charlatan, the metaphysical tailor, and the serious-minded young periodical writer!

Doubtless this informal association of Old Street cronies helped to confirm Johnson in the conviction that a tavern chair was the throne of human felicity. "As soon as I enter the door of a tavern," he once confessed, "I experience an oblivion of care, and a freedom from solicitude: when I am seated, I find the master courteous, and the servants obsequious to my call; anxious to know and ready to supply my wants: wine there exhilarates my spirits, and prompts me to free conversation and an interchange of discourse with those whom I most love: I dogmatize and am contradicted, and in this conflict of opinions and sentiments I find delight." [8]

Another of Johnson's early friends was Tom Cumming, the so-called "fighting" Quaker. During the '45, when patriotic fervor was at its height, Cumming said he would not actually fight, but would drive an ammunition cart.[9] Years later, so it was reported, Cumming on one occasion fairly thrashed Johnson "with a forcible natural eloquence when fully provoked by him; and that Johnson cried mercy." The truth of the matter was, so the latter confided to Boswell, that "Cumming was drunk and attacked him with rudeness; and that he did not answer him because he was in such a situation; and that he walked home with him." Under any circumstances Johnson had a high regard for the pugnacious Quaker's friendship.

Then there was the inventor and promoter Lewis Paul, who, together with John Wyatt, produced the first roller-spinning machine, the basis of modern cotton manufacture. Wyatt was the practical mechanic, Paul the man of ideas and salesman.[10] Paul was once described as "having the spirit of a projector (though no stock of the mechanics)." "He is a man as talks a great deal to set forth himself and will be buying anything of anybody that he can impose upon," added an early acquaintance. Paul was enthusiastic and visionary, an entertaining companion and a convincing talker. He appears to have hoodwinked many people, including Johnson. The truth is that the invention was basically sound and the exciting sample machines showed what could be done. As one prospective investor commented, "The sight of the thing is demonstration enough. I am certain that if Paul could begin with ten thousand pounds he must, or at least might, get more money in twenty years than the City of London is worth." [11] Unfortunately Paul's bound-less enthusiasm in the early stages led his backers to expect too much, too soon.

Undoubtedly it was through Birmingham connections that Johnson became involved in Paul's frenzied schemes, his grandiose promises, and his devious tactics. Thomas Warren, Dr. Robert James, and finally even the careful Cave himself, poured money into the project, thinking that they were going to make fabulous fortunes. "In consideration of a large sum" Cave was given a license to set up 250 spindles. But Paul was shifty; there were difficulties, quarrels, and disappointments. The affair was further complicated by other disagreements between Warren and James and by Warren's increasing financial troubles.

When an impasse developed, Johnson vainly tried to act as intermediary. In January, 1741, he wrote from St. John's Gate to Paul hoping for a speedy conclusion, pleading the personal reason that "Mr. Cave was in some degree diverted from attending to the arbitration by my assiduity in expediting the agreement between you." Two months later, when nothing had happened, he wrote again suggesting a compromise settlement.[12] "I hope to write soon on some more agreeable subject, for though perhaps a man cannot easily find more pleasing employment than that of reconciling variances, he may certainly amuse himself better, by any other business, than that of interposing in controversies which grow every [day] more distant from accommodation." Despite the excitement of the venture, Johnson found the position of referee in the affairs of an impractical inventor-promoter not a happy one.

Not all of his new acquaintances were so unusual. For instance, there was John Hawkins, Jr., who lived in Sweet Apple Court off Bishopsgate Street. No bohemian, he was industrious and moral, even tending a bit toward stiff-necked formality. He was full of ambition and was planning a legal career, but on the side he wrote lyrics for the musicians and essays and poems for the newspapers and periodicals. As early as 1739 he had begun contributing to the *Gentleman's Magazine,* and the next year Cave wrote to him, agreeing to print whatever Hawkins would send in.[13]

Perhaps through Cave and Birch, Johnson was introduced to a

few important figures. He was never overly impressed by the rich and powerful, but when the "ridiculously polite" Lord Orrery, friend and future biographer of Swift, invited him to his house, Johnson was glad to accept.[14] Though he scornfully thought the nobleman "had no mind of his own," this was hardly a reason for turning down an opportunity for an excellent dinner and some literary gossip. Later he proudly bragged that he had "never sought much after anybody," and when Boswell suggested that Lord Orrery might have been an exception, Johnson sternly replied: "No, Sir; I never went to him but when he sent for me."

Of all of this group of early London friends, only one came close to being a genius — a young man named William Collins, the son of a hatter at Chichester. Only about twenty-three when Johnson met him, he had come from Oxford, "a literary adventurer, with many projects in his head, and very little money in his pocket." [15] Even before going to the university he had sent verses to the *Gentleman's Magazine,* and naturally drifted into the St. John's Gate orbit.

Never had Johnson met anyone so full of plans, so eloquent in talking about them, and so incapable of accomplishment. The instability which later was to send him tragically insane had already begun to show itself. Although he issued proposals for a history of the Revival of Learning, probably not a page was ever written. He planned several tragedies but never could get past the planning stage. All he could do was to write a few imperishable odes.

One day Johnson found him "immured by a bailiff that was prowling in the street." In customary fashion, Johnson at once took charge, and a bookseller was found who, on the strength of a promised translation of Aristotle's *Poetics,* which Collins agreed to make with a large commentary, advanced enough money to enable the poor poet to escape into the country. In recalling the event, Johnson added the circumstantial detail, "He showed me the guineas safe in his hand." When, soon after, the poet came into a small inheritance he paid back the advance and did nothing on the translation. "Poor Collins" was only briefly a member of the fraternity of Grub Street hacks.

In 1740 and 1741 Johnson saw a good deal of the Garrick broth-

ers, and may have been one of their friends who tried to settle
their altercations over the wine business.[16] The arrangement
whereby Peter handled the affairs in Lichfield and David in London was never destined to be a success. It is remarkable that they
continued partners as long as they did.

Once when Johnson and David were sitting together, the latter
repeated a commonplace epitaph by a Doctor Wilkes on the celebrated wandering musician, Claudy Philips, whom both may have
heard play in Lichfield. Johnson shook his head at the dull lines
and said, "I think, Davy, I can make a better." Then stirring his
tea and meditating a moment, he dictated his own version:

> Philips! whose touch harmonious could remove
> The pangs of guilty pow'r, and hapless love,
> Rest here distrest by poverty no more,
> Find here that calm thou gav'st so oft before;
> Sleep undisturb'd within this peaceful shrine,
> Till angels wake thee with a note like thine.

This found its way into the September, 1740, *Gentleman's Magazine*.[17]

Occasionally David accompanied Johnson to St. John's Gate,
where he aroused Cave's curiosity to see him act a comic part. Only
too glad to show his powers, David offered to play the title role of
Fielding's *Mock Doctor,* an adaptation from Molière, if Cave
would supply the supporting cast. The great room over the arch of
the old gate was speedily converted into a temporary theater, some
of the printers and journeymen dragooned into reading other
parts, and the impromptu performance staged. To celebrate the
occasion Garrick wrote a special epilogue, which Cave at once
grabbed for his magazine. It, too, appeared in the September issue,
signed "G." [18]

This was in the summer of 1740, when David was still only a
talented amateur, even before he had slipped out to Ipswich under
the assumed name of Lyddal, blacked his face, and appeared in a
minor role in *Oroonoko.* Not until the autumn of the next year
did his close friendship with Giffard bring about his final decision
to become a professional actor. Unable to obtain a license under

the restrictive act of 1737, Giffard was evading the law by advertising his entertainments in Goodman's Fields as a concert, and then
supplying a play gratis to his customers. There on the nineteenth
of October, 1741, Garrick made his first spectacular appearance
as Richard III, and his future was assured.

More than likely Johnson was in the audience that night for
Garrick's great test. To rally one's friends as a partisan claque was
normal procedure. If he did not witness David's initial triumph,
at other times Johnson did patronize the little unlicensed theater
in the East End, much frequented by City merchants and their
families. On one occasion later in the winter he went out with
his old schoolmate John Taylor, who was visiting in London, and
after the performance passed the rest of the evening at a tavern
with Giffard and Garrick. Taylor, long afterward, told Boswell of
one lively interchange:

> Johnson, who was ever depreciating stage players, after censuring
> some mistakes in emphasis which Garrick had committed in the
> course of that night's acting, said, "The players, Sir, have got a kind
> of rant, with which they run on, without any regard either to accent
> or emphasis." Both Garrick and Giffard were offended at this sar-
> casm, and endeavored to refute it; upon which Johnson rejoined,
> "Well now, I'll give you something to speak, with which you are
> little acquainted, and then we shall see how just my observation is.
> That shall be the criterion. Let me hear you repeat the ninth Com-
> mandment, 'Thou shalt not bear false witness against thy neighbor.' "
> Both tried at it, said Dr. Taylor, and both mistook the emphasis,
> which should be upon *not* and *false witness*. Johnson put them right,
> and enjoyed his victory with great glee.[19]

The anecdote reveals something of the increasing tension between Garrick and Johnson. No doubt the latter's asperity was
sharpened by the fabulous popular success of his former pupil,
whom he meant to keep in his place. But the cutting sneers at
actors and the gibes at his own performance must have been particularly galling to Garrick's pride, especially as these criticisms
were delivered in public. Nevertheless, to his credit, the two men
continued on friendly terms. Next season, when Garrick moved

over to Drury Lane, with the record annual salary of five hundred guineas, Johnson became a familiar visitor to the greenroom there, and was on easy terms with many of the actors and actresses. For Kitty Clive, in particular, he had a high regard.[20] Nor did his basic scorn of the profession and his lack of success with *Irene* keep him from dreaming of future triumphs as a dramatist. In August, 1742, he was apparently thinking of writing a play about Charles XII of Sweden.

Inevitably, however, Johnson and Garrick were moving apart. It was not that they quarreled, only that the literary hack and the most popular performer of the day gradually began to move in different circles and develop diverging interests.[21] The few stories of their relationship in this period which have survived all have a somewhat bitter tinge.

Once, when Garrick was living with Peg Woffington, Johnson dropped in for tea, and was shocked when his host quarreled with his mistress for making the tea too strong.[22] To have a successful public idol resort to such puny savings as not replenishing the tea-pot because the beverage was already "as red as blood" made Johnson angry. Though he realized that Davy's strict habits of economy had been instilled in his youth as a result of necessary caution, he felt that a man who had "money in his purse" ought to be generously hospitable.

Their strained relations were to last as long as they lived, but it is wrong to simplify the matter and say, as did one contemporary, the Dean of Lincoln, that Garrick "was always afraid of Johnson who despised him." [23] It was more complicated than that. They were still drawn together by strong bonds of affection and admiration, even though neither could resist pointed thrusts at minor weaknesses in the other. Johnson was inwardly proud of the achievements of his pupil, and Garrick would never cease to revere his former master. He showed his loyalty by the way he continued to support *Irene,* once he was in a position to wield some influence.

Not many of Johnson's friends ever found their way to his home. He met them at Cave's, or in the taverns and coffeehouses, or oc-

casionally at some well-to-do acquaintance's, but he did not entertain them at his lodgings. Hawkins admitted that he never once
met Tetty, though he heard much about her.[24] It is quite evident
that Johnson kept his two worlds separate. Whether this was the
result of chance or settled policy, of poverty or sensitiveness, there
is no way of telling. Undoubtedly he was not proud of where he
was living, or of the atmosphere of his ménage. Already Tetty
may have been developing the tendency to hypochondria and inclination to strong cordials which characterized her last years. She
would have had neither the stamina nor the desire to play the
hostess to her husband's strange friends.

Only from later stray remarks to Mrs. Thrale, who attempted
to draw him out, is it possible to get any idea of what Johnson's
life with Tetty was like.[25] Apparently there was continual argument over petty details. Though forced to live in cheap lodgings,
she was not content to become slovenly, as her husband was only
too willing to do. "She was extremely neat in her disposition, and
always fretful that I made the house so dirty — a clean floor is *so*
comfortable she would say by way of twitting; till at last I told
her, I thought we had had talk enough about the floor, we would
now have a touch at the *ceiling*." As a man who enjoyed eating,
Johnson often "huffed his wife about his meat." But one day, as
he was about to say grace, she stopped him. "Nay hold says she,
and do not make a farce of thanking God for a dinner which you
will presently protest not eatable."

With a tongue inclined to be satirical, Tetty was too prone to
point out to other people the ugly side of their life or profession.
She would "lament the sorrows of celibacy to an old maid, and
once told a waterman he was no happier than a galley slave — one
was chained to the oar by authority she said, and the other by
want."

Johnson never admitted any major disagreements, only a long
succession of little differences. Perhaps he was remembering Tetty
when he remarked that "women often give great offense by their
spirit of noncompliance: their husband wants them to sit in the
shade, and then they feel earnest desire to walk in the sun." A

man offers to read to his wife, and she insists on doing something else. A faithful wife will indulge in "twenty such tricks" and then wonder at her husband's straying affections.

Not that Johnson wanted supine obedience. He did not like ladies who were soft and "sleepy-souled," or envy any husband with a clinging, "honeysuckle" wife. He admired Tetty's forceful intelligence and her ready wit, and he learned how to adjust to her whims. Hawkins, reporting from the accounts of others, described their "crazy" behavior, with "profound respect on his part, and the airs of an antiquated beauty on hers."

Most of what is known about Johnson's home life comes from his own recollections and those of his friends. No one saw fit to record Tetty's version. Yet living with an untidy, impecunious journalist, particularly one subject to such erratic moods, cannot have been easy. She, too, had cause for valid complaint. Not the least must have been her husband's predilection for wasting long hours in the coffeehouses with a bizarre set of poets and dreamers.

The *"Gentleman's Magazine"*

URING the early 1740s Johnson gave most of his creative time and energy to the *Gentleman's Magazine,* and soon became responsible for a large part of each issue. In some months over half the material came directly from his pen. While Cave was his own chief editor, supervising the selection of quotations from other papers and journals, directing general policy, and pulling the strings, it was Johnson who was the most active staff writer.

For the most part, he supplied the sort of fare the public was demanding. Catering to an increased interest in public affairs occasioned by the steadily rising attacks on Walpole, his impeachment, and ultimate fall, Johnson gave more time to the writing of the parliamentary debates. He reviewed at least one controversial book and had more to say about the Crousaz controversy. He translated a "Dissertation on the Amazons" from the French of Abbé de Guyon. He wrote publicity for some of Cave's other publishing ventures and continued to defend his editor from the bitter attacks of his rivals. Apparently he made an abridgment of a seventeenth-century report concerning a proposal by Parliament to Cromwell that he should assume the title of king.[1] Most important, he wrote a series of short lives of famous men.[2]

"The proper study of mankind," Pope had written, "is man." For a skeptical age the minutiae of everyday life were more important than the possible vague delights of the next world. It was the human, not the sub- or superhuman level, that fascinated the person of common sense. Hence a growing interest in biography. Accounts of celebrated historical characters, as well as of highwaymen, shoplifters, housebreakers, and notorious criminals of all kinds, appeared in pamphlets, newspapers, and periodicals. The "unspeakable" Curll himself had published as many as fifty scurrilous biographies of eminent or disreputable persons. There was an insatiable demand for anything which mirrored the lives of actual men and women.

With the public taste so apparent, there is no need to seek any special reason for Cave's decision to include a series of accounts of famous men in his magazine. Yet it is reasonable to believe that Johnson made the suggestion. Not only did he love the genre, but he was one of the first to think deeply about its techniques, and he was destined to become, partly because of his disciple Boswell, the father of modern biography.

His initial efforts in the *Gentleman's Magazine* — the lives of Sarpi and the Dutch physician Boerhaave — had been largely condensations, made from French and Latin sources. When he came back to his old post in St. John's Gate in the spring of 1740, his first contribution was another digest of the same sort. In tune with the current patriotic fervor, the subject was a famous English admiral of the commonwealth, Robert Blake. Without giving any indication of his source, Johnson took most of his information from an anonymous biography of the admiral, published in 1704, to which he added details culled from such authors as Anthony à Wood, Clarendon, and Whitlock.

One can picture him sitting at his desk with a single main source before him, reading a long passage, turning it over in his mind, and then summarizing it all in a few forceful paragraphs. Occasionally he might reach for a standard historical authority, in order to check or amplify the account, and at times pause to interpolate a moral comment of his own. The few reference works he needed could have been borrowed from Birch or some other friend.[3] There was never any attempt at original research; he was a journalist, reworking well-known material to make it palatable for the readers of the magazine.

The choice of Blake as a subject was topical. England was embroiled with Spain in the farcical war of Jenkins' Ear, and the early exploits of Admiral Vernon in the West Indies had roused public excitement to fever pitch. The papers and magazines were filled with firsthand accounts from the scene of action. Moreover, the political Opposition, which had been largely responsible for forcing hostilities on a reluctant Walpole, was quick to make use of every triumph of its hero. It took no great cleverness for an enterprising journalist to see the usefulness of recalling the days of Britain's naval greatness as a means of inspiring further support for the war. Apparently this is what Johnson intended, and there is no reason to search for hidden ironies in his introductory note:

> At a time when a nation is engaged in a war with an enemy, whose insults, ravages and barbarities have long called for vengeance, an account of such English commanders as have merited the acknowledgments of posterity, by extending the powers, and raising the honor of their country, seems to be no improper entertainment for our readers. We shall, therefore, attempt a succinct narration of the life and actions of Admiral Blake, in which we have nothing further in view, than to do justice to his bravery and conduct, without intending any parallel between his achievements, and those of our present admirals.

This experiment having proved successful, Cave announced in the next number a series of articles on the Elizabethan hero, Sir Francis Drake, and to whet the readers' appetites a short excerpt was given in advance, together with comments pointing out the contemporary parallel. The first installment appeared in the August number, and it was continued in those of September, October, December, and January. Again Johnson summarized from a single volume, a seventeenth-century reprint of four pamphlets describing Drake's principal voyages; he added an introduction from another volume, and supplementary information from other authorities. Although relying more on primary materials, he still had no intention of doing original research.

After recounting the exploits of two admirals, Johnson turned to heroes of another sort, and during the next two years provided accounts of famous scholars and physicians — of Dr. Lewis Morin, the French botanist; Peter Burman, professor of history and poetry at the University of Leyden; and Dr. Thomas Sydenham. None of the pieces show any significant change of technique.

The fact that Johnson made no attempt at laborious historical search does not mean that he was careless or scornful of factual accuracy. Though he saw no reason to exert himself for casual magazine articles, he still took special care in the selection of details, and when errors or omissions came to his attention he was quick to note them. It is not true, as some have supposed, that Johnson lost all interest in this journalistic work once it was accepted by Cave. When a few of the lives were later printed separately, he was careful to revise them.[4]

A case in point is his life of Barretier, which originally appeared in the *Gentleman's Magazine* in late 1740 and early 1741. Then in the spring of 1742 he provided an "Additional Account" of four closely packed pages, showing his willingness to make corrections. But he was not yet through. In 1744, when the bookseller James Roberts in Warwick Lane published the life as a separate sixpenny pamphlet, there were more additions and more careful rewriting. As he had steadily collected new evidence, Johnson was eager to pass it on to his readers. Within the narrow limits set by this kind of journalistic work, he exhibited a thoroughgoing scholarly conscience.

Johnson was not, however, making any major discoveries in biographical techniques or creating models to copy. There are no novel experiments in the use of conversation or of personal letters, few outstanding psychological insights. He did not attempt to make use of colorful background material. Yet in places the lives do show something of the gradual maturing of Johnson's skeptical evaluation of evidence, the frank honesty of his mental processes.

He made his attitude quite clear in the beginning of the life of Boerhaave. "We could have made it much larger, by adopting flying reports, and inserting unattested facts; a close adherence to certainty has contracted our narrative, and hindered it from swelling to that bulk, at which modern histories generally arrive." Always suspicious of wild tales or what was apparently fallacious reasoning, he had no hesitation in expressing his doubts. When he came to the descriptions of Barretier's early precocity, on the evidence of the boy's father, Johnson remarked: "Part of this letter I am tempted to suppress, being unwilling to demand the be-

lief of others to that which appears incredible to myself." Then
to be quite fair he hastily added, "As my incredulity may, perhaps, be the product rather of prejudice than reason, as envy may
beget a disinclination to admit so immense a superiority, and as
an account is not to be immediately censured as false, merely
because it is wonderful, I shall proceed to give the rest of his
father's relation." Of similar stories concerning Peter Burman,
so "stupendous" that they "must be allowed far to exceed the
limits of probability," Johnson again expressed open disbelief.

Repeatedly he showed astonishment at the way false rumors
have been accepted as historical fact — how through the "laziness of some, and the pride of others," through the willingness
of those who "would spare themselves the labor of accurate reading and tedious inquiry," the most fallacious stories are circulated. He called continually for facts, and pleaded with those who
knew Boerhaave to set down before it was too late all that could
be remembered about him.

He tried to be just in apportioning praise and blame. If the
men he was describing were heroes — and it is obvious that he
thought them so, each in his own field — they were also human.
Even so great an admiral as Blake could make mistakes. After a
detailed analysis of one unfortunate encounter with the Dutch,
Johnson commented: "We must then admit, amidst our eulogies
and applauses, that the great, the wise, and the valiant Blake, was
once betrayed to an inconsiderate and desperate enterprise, by
the resistless ardor of his own spirit, and a noble jealousy of the
honor of his country."

Johnson's strong personality suffused everything he wrote. He
could never stand completely detached from his material. Though
there might be stretches of routine compression of facts, the temptation to draw sober, moral precepts, whether describing an admiral, a physician, or a scholar, was irresistible. For twentieth-
century readers the chief delight of these early lives lies in the
sudden discovery, again and again, of some quotable aphorism,
some perfectly phrased opinion, that might well have come from
The Rambler or from a conversation with Boswell.

It is not hard to find examples. In recounting the voyages of

Drake, Johnson was brought head on against the doctrine of primitivism. Were the simple savages happier than sophisticated Europeans? Had all the gains of civilization been harmful to natural man, rather than beneficial? Johnson had little patience with such foolish stuff, and stopped the narrative to point out obvious fallacies in the reasoning.[5] In the first place, he insisted, the comparisons were never fair. "The question is not, whether a good Indian or bad Englishman be most happy; but, which state is most desirable, supposing virtue and reason the same in both." Moreover, ignorance of vice should not be confounded with virtue. "He that never saw, or heard, or thought of strong liquors, cannot be proposed as a pattern of sobriety."

The biographies are full of acute observations and aphorisms such as this one in the life of Boerhaave: "It is, I believe, a very just observation, that men's ambition is, generally, proportioned to their capacity. Providence seldom sends any into the world with an inclination to attempt great things, who have not abilities, likewise, to perform them." Or, "Men are generally idle, and ready to satisfy themselves, and intimidate the industry of others, by calling that impossible which is only difficult." In describing the last days of the great physician Sydenham he added the sobering thought: "It is a melancholy reflection, that they who have obtained the highest reputation, by preserving or restoring the health of others, have often been hurried away before the natural decline of life, or have passed many of their years under the torments of those distempers which they profess to relieve." The mood, the somber phrasing, the deep compassion of *Rasselas*, are already fixed.

Not all the lives are equally impregnated with the Johnsonian ether. In some, as with Morin, little was added. In others, where Johnson felt a personal bond with his subject, there was more. Boerhaave, in particular, he found sympathetic, for the two men had much in common. In describing the great Dutch physician, Johnson undoubtedly was often thinking of himself, drawing parallels in his own mind, and finding inspiration in the knowledge of the other's final triumphs.

One might almost piece together a picture of Johnson as he

saw himself, or as he hoped to be, from selected passages in the life of Boerhaave — a man whose fortune had not been "sufficient to bear the expenses of a learned education," but who through sheer determination had broken through "the obstacles of poverty." Always it was Boerhaave's "insatiable curiosity after knowledge" that had driven him on. Though subject to dejection and lowness of spirits, yet "he asserted, on all occasions, the divine authority and sacred efficacy of the holy Scriptures." He had a large, robust physique and was remarkable for physical strength. He was "insensible of any sharpness of air, or inclemency of weather." There was in his whole deportment "something rough and artless, but so majestic and great, at the same time, that no man ever looked upon him without veneration, and a kind of tacit submission to the superiority of his genius." The vigor and activity of his mind "sparkled visibly in his eyes," and "he was always cheerful and desirous of promoting mirth by a facetious and humorous conversation." Never was he "overawed or depressed by the presence, frowns, or insolence of great men." He was naturally "quick of resentment," with an "impetuous and ungovernable passion." Only at the end does this remarkable parallel break down, for of Johnson it could scarcely be said that he "took care never to provoke enemies by severity of censure."

Producing a series of lives of celebrated men was only one of Johnson's tasks for Cave during the early 1740s. When Nathaniel Hooke's *Account of the Conduct of the Duchess of Marlborough* was a popular topic of conversation, Johnson wrote a commentary. Much more than a typical review, which in those days was customarily an extended series of extracts, this was a polished essay in the later manner of *The Rambler*. His theme — basic to his whole philosophy at the time — was the constant need for skepticism in the search for historical truth. "Distrust is a necessary qualification of a student in history." [6] One must be perpetually suspicious of commonly accepted opinions. Included also were comments on the nature of evidence, and praise for the use of letters and colloquial style. It was almost as if Johnson were thinking out loud about the whole subject of memoirs.

How much he had to do with the monthly selection of poetry in the magazine may never be known. The occasional editorial notes scattered between the selections do not have the Johnsonian ring. Although he may often have been consulted by the editor, he was obviously not in charge of that section of the magazine.

Only a very few of his own poems were used, and these chiefly casual *jeux d'esprit* tossed off without much thought. All his life Johnson delighted in extempore composition, both in English and in Latin. Once when he was sitting with his two old schoolfellows Hector and James, the latter suggested the beginning of a Latin epigram and called on Johnson to finish it, which he immediately did. It was included in the magazine of July, 1743. Three months later there was a Latin translation of Pope's verses on his grotto, described as "the casual amusement of half an hour, during several solicitations to proceed." One of his impromptu epigrams, however, was for obvious reasons never used by Cave. Disgusted by one of Colley Cibber's annual laureate odes, Johnson scornfully dashed off the lines:

> Augustus still survives in Maro's strain,
> And Spenser's verse prolongs Eliza's reign;
> Great George's acts let tuneful Cibber sing;
> For Nature form'd the Poet for the King.[7]

Not many of Johnson's verses can be placed in these years. Clearly his mood was not a poetic one.

His thoughts were more centered on public affairs. From his earliest days at St. John's Gate one of his chores had been the revision of the parliamentary debates.[8] Usually he had only to change a few words, or straighten out the syntax of what had been written by Guthrie and others of Cave's assistants. In 1741, however, he took over the whole job. Apparently what brought about the change was the increase in intensity of the proceedings in Parliament and the consequent stepping up of public interest. The great argument in February, 1741, over the motion to remove Walpole aroused tremendous curiosity. Well aware of what was going on, Cave evidently decided that he needed a more effective writer, one with a broader vision and a more forceful style, and proposed to Johnson that he accept full responsibility.

There was no need to set to work immediately. For reasons of prudence the magazines were careful not to print an account of proceedings in Parliament while that particular session was in progress. Sometimes readers had to wait over a year for the reports to appear. Moreover, there had never been any attempt at strict chronology in the reporting. Whatever seemed of current interest was used, and sometimes installments of two different debates ran at the same time. Consequently, although Johnson had probably agreed early in the spring to Cave's new proposal, his first account of the discussions in the House of Lords on February 13, 1741, did not begin until the July number of the magazine. When this was completed in August, he went back to recount the speeches in the House of Commons over the bill for the increase of seamen, which had begun earlier in the session. For almost three years Johnson produced the accounts in this hit-or-miss fashion.[9]

Although the published versions invariably appeared long after the actual debates, Johnson apparently wrote them in great haste, as if to meet an imminent deadline. Still fighting his old enemy procrastination, he probably dashed them off immediately before publication, although some may have been set up in print and put aside until safe to use. According to Nichols, Johnson rarely wrote anything else with such celerity, "three columns of the magazine, in an hour, was no uncommon effort, which was faster than most persons could have transcribed that quantity." Once he wrote ten two-column pages in a day, "and that not a long one, beginning perhaps at noon, and ending early in the evening." [10] Hawkins vividly described his shutting himself up in a room at St. John's Gate, "to which he would not suffer any one to approach, except the compositor or Cave's boy for matter, which, as fast as he composed it, he tumbled out at the door." [11]

This is how the debates were hastily written. But how were they composed? Johnson himself never attended the actual proceedings, nor did he have exhaustive reports from anyone who had. His friend John Nichols is definite in saying that he frequently worked from "very slender materials, and often from none at all"; and Johnson confessed to Boswell that "he had nothing more communicated to him than the names of the several speakers, and the part which they had taken in the debate." The debates were thus usually "the mere coinage of his own imagination." [12]

Because manuscripts of the original speeches have so rarely survived, it has been difficult to estimate the truth of these casual remarks — to tell whether Johnson was claiming more for himself than was actually true or whether he really was the "author" of the debates. Happily, recent exhaustive research does substantiate his statements. [13] There is enough contemporary material for specific comparison — notes kept by Archbishop Secker in the House of Lords, and manuscripts in Sir Robert Walpole's collection. When set against the versions given in the *Gentleman's Magazine* and those in the rival *London Magazine,* these records show clearly what happened.

While it is obvious that Johnson received a fairly accurate list of speakers with their place in the debate, and sometimes hints as to topics, for the most part the elaboration of arguments was left completely to his imagination. For example, there is little resemblance between Pitt's speech in the Commons as reported in the *Gentleman's Magazine* and the summary recorded by Walpole on the spot for his own use. And the Prime Minister's own defense as elaborated in the magazine bears little relation to the account of it given by his biographer, presumably using manuscript sources. Phraseology, examples, even major oratorical maneuvers, had to come from Johnson's own fund of political knowledge. Large sections of the Lilliputian debates, then, must be considered as creative literature.

There is not much variety of tone. Although Johnson evidently tried to suit the style to the well-known character of the speaker — to be temperate and persuasive for Carteret, always quoting Latin, witty and ironic for Chesterfield, stiff and formal for Lyttelton, impetuous and eloquent for Pitt — he was not completely successful. He never quite caught the qualities of the individual members of Parliament. To estimate his failure, one has only to compare Secker's notes of Chesterfield's speech with Johnson's imagined version. Some people — Hawkins among them — have professed to see clearly the characteristic changes of diction and phraseology for different speakers. The story is told that Johnson once had breakfast in Gray's Inn with a man in high office under the Government, who insisted that he could make a differentiation by the style alone; "for that every person spoke in character, and was as certainly and as easily known as a speaker in Homer or in Shakespeare." [14]

Others claimed to find them model speeches, worthy of comparison to those of Demosthenes and Cicero. Yet basically they have little oratorical quality. Despite occasional dramatic touches, with interruptions and quips as if in actual debate, they are more like short essays on a particular theme. They are moral disquisitions, full of abstract reasoning, expressed in Johnson's own characteristic strong and antithetical manner.

Forced to make up a large part of his material, Johnson took the opportunity to stress many of his own dominant interests. In his imagined great arena of Parliament he could discuss what most concerned him — the power of the people, representative government, basic questions of individual liberty and civic morality. He was always intent on a larger design, on universal principles, much more, we may suspect, than were the real parliamentary speakers in their actual orations. Here was a ready-made public forum in which he could discuss at length the major political and ethical problems of the age.

When he was an old man, Johnson obstinately insisted that in writing the debates he always saw to it that "the Whig dogs should not have the best of it," and succeeding generations have assumed that he was systematically slanting his arguments to the Tory side.[15] But it was not so simple as that. The question is — which Whigs did he mean?

The great struggle of the early 1740s was not between two strong political parties, but between rival branches of Whigs. The real Tories stayed on the sidelines. When the final decision had to be made, many of the Tories refused to vote against Walpole, for by this time the true motives of the Opposition leaders were beginning to be apparent. Consequently, in his reporting of the debates Johnson showed scant bias. While he may have allowed himself a few sly digs, his reports were remarkably well balanced, especially in comparison with the openly partisan reports in the *London Magazine,* which was blatantly prejudiced on the Opposition side. If he showed any prejudice at all, it was in giving more space than was necessary for strict accuracy to the supporters of Walpole in the great debate on the motion for removal, and in building up the dramatic quality of the Minister's own speech.[16]

The "Whig dogs," who were not supposed to get the best of it, may conceivably have been the very men he had been openly supporting a few years earlier — Pulteney, Sandys, Pitt, and the other "Patriots" — not Walpole and his minions. As a chronicler of a tense jockeying for power in Parliament, Johnson had been forced to study political realities, and as a result had changed his mind. With facts had come disillusionment, and he could never again let himself go with blind enthusiasm for an active partisan group.

What had started merely as another journalistic assignment for the magazine turned out to be an important milestone in the maturing of Johnson's ideas.[17] The experience strengthened his natural doubt of easy solutions, taught him to be less certain that the right was always on one side, and gave him practice in examining all points of view. Any careful study of the Lilliputian debates shows how effective he was in defending both Whig positions. First for one side and then for the other he fashioned cogent arguments. It was valuable practice for Johnson the later controversialist, who was often ready in the heat of discussion to argue on either side with magnificent abandon.

It is difficult for modern readers to understand why Johnson's fabrications were not instantly exposed. One answer might be that though the published versions did not represent what had actually been said, they were so well done, so eloquent and forceful, that no one wished to complain. But this begs the essential question. Why were there no widespread objections to other, less effective reports?

The members of Parliament knew that the published reports were false. But short of supplying genuine copies of their speeches, they would be unable to convince the public that the reports were fictitious. Traditionally, as in a private club, the events of each session of Parliament were supposed to be kept secret. Moreover, the journalistic profession was jealous to guard its own rights in the matter. Freedom of the press and parliamentary privilege were both involved.

Some insight into the frustrations of the speakers themselves comes from the correspondence of Birch and his patron, Philip Yorke.[18] On one occasion, when one of the latter's speeches had been falsely reported in the *London Magazine,* he and his friends were much upset that "so injurious a forgery" should descend to posterity under his name. When Cave smugly requested a copy of the genuine speech, with the intimation that others had used this means of insuring accurate printed versions, Yorke exploded to Birch:

> Cave's request is an impertinent one — the boast he makes of communications from speakers of the first class, a very inartificial bam to procure the genuine copy of a speech from an orator of the lowest; and the whole intended for nothing else than that he may parade in the magazine with an abuse upon his rivals, and a puff upon his own superior correspondence.

But Yorke's attempt to get some widespread denunciation of the false report of his speech brought him up against a blank wall. As Birch commented:

> Your brother has shown me your letter, wherein you desire my assistance in procuring the publication of your remonstrance against the forgeries of the magazines. I wish I could find out a method of doing this both for your sake and that of the public. But the whole body of the printers and booksellers are so tender of each other's interest, where their own is not concerned, and the publishers of the magazines have so large a share in the daily and weekly papers, that I know it to be absolutely in vain to attempt it. . . .

It was obvious that unless Parliament acted stringently to suppress the whole procedure of fictional rendering, or allowed reporters free access to the galleries, there was little that could be done by individual speakers.

Most subscribers to the *Gentleman's Magazine* must have accepted Johnson's accounts as substantially correct. They were speedily incorporated into separately printed collections of parliamentary debates which were widely distributed. Because these collections had an official look and openly boasted authenticity, they were soon taken as historical fact, and readers tended to forget the doubtful reliability of the sources. As the years wore on, individual speeches as printed in the magazines found their way into the collected works of great historical figures. Even today it is not uncommon to find some of Johnson's fabrications included in collections of famous speeches of Pitt, Walpole, Chesterfield, and Pulteney.

It was not for Johnson to give his professional secret away. He might drop an occasional hint, as he did in 1756 in the *Literary Magazine:* "The speeches inserted in other papers have been long known to be fictitious, and produced sometimes by men who never heard the debate, nor had any authentic information," but it was wiser not to be specific.[19] Not until long afterward did he discuss the matter even with his best friends.

Well known is the story of the dinner party at Foote's when by chance an important debate toward the end of Walpole's administration was mentioned. According to Arthur Murphy, who was present, Dr. Francis, the translator of Horace, observed that Pitt's speech on that occasion "was the best he had ever read," and added that "he had employed eight years of his life in the study of Demosthenes, and finished a translation of that celebrated orator, with all the decorations of style and language within the reach of his capacity; but he had met with nothing equal to the speech above-mentioned." While others of the company spoke of the debate, citing other passages with approbation and applause, Johnson remained silent. Then "as soon as the warmth of praise subsided, he opened with these words: 'That speech I wrote in a garret in Exeter Street.'" Struck with astonishment, Francis eagerly asked for more information. When Johnson told how Cave had secured meager notes about speakers and arguments, and how he himself had been left to make up the long discussions,

Francis answered, "Then, Sir, you have exceeded Demosthenes himself." [20]

There are doubtful aspects to the story, but something of the sort probably did happen. On another occasion, when he was with Boswell at Dilly's, Johnson picked up a splendid edition of Lord Chesterfield's miscellaneous works and laughed to find included some speeches from the *Gentleman's Magazine* and to discover one of them compared with Cicero. [21] By that time a literary celebrity, he could afford to look back and be amused.

For a while popular interest in the Lilliputian proceedings was high. They occupied the most prominent place in each monthly issue. According to Hawkins, while Johnson was writing them the sale of the magazine increased fifty per cent, and Cave "manifested his good fortune by buying an old coach and a pair of older horses." [22] In order to avoid the suspicion of pride in setting up an equipage, Cave "displayed to the world the source of his affluence, by a representation of St. John's Gate, instead of his arms, on the door panel."

Since the debates were so successful, it is not clear why Johnson suddenly gave up writing them in March, 1744. Both Boswell and Hawkins imply that it was a matter of conscience, that Johnson refused to go on because he found that his fictions were thought genuine. He was determined not to "be accessory to the propagation of falsehood." [23] Undoubtedly, this was a contributing factor. But to make it the only one is to assume Johnson more naïve than the evidence warrants. He must have known all along that many readers were being fooled. Separate reprints of some of the debates appeared as early as 1742, and an announcement of a foreign translation was made in March of that year. There must have been other equally valid reasons for his discontinuing the debates.

Actually, by 1744 public interest in the parliamentary proceedings was waning. Once the great argument over the fall of Walpole had died down and it was clearly seen that nothing worldshaking had followed, readers became bored with the same old fare. After the last of Johnson's debates appeared in the March number, there was a short break in the series, and, though started again, they were soon discontinued altogether. Thus his qualms of conscience were powerfully reinforced by the decline in public interest.

An even more important reason was that by the winter of 1743–1744 Johnson had become increasingly involved in editorial work for other booksellers. He no longer wished to be tied to a monthly commitment to Cave and the *Gentleman's Magazine.* The ending of the debates marked Johnson's emergence as an independent writer.

The Bookseller's Hack

THE precise difference between a literary hack and a writer of genius is sometimes difficult to define. The two, as in Goldsmith, may merge in the same man. Often there is no clear point where one begins and the other leaves off. It is true that the traditional Grub Street journalist was weak-willed, improvident, venal, and pathetic, his pen to be bought for any scheme, no matter how dishonest. With a limited capacity, he could never rise above a certain flat level of competence. Yet working along with him were others who had superior ability and needed only a chance in order to produce genuine literature.

Samuel Johnson belonged to the latter group. Though willing to do all kinds of work for meager pay — editing, digesting, reviewing, writing sermons, providing prefaces, dedications, prospectuses, and the like — he always insisted on a high standard of excellence in his writing. He did not pander to popular taste. Though eager to do his assignments with a minimum of effort, with little correction or revision, he never lost his pride or his ambition to excel. In all his desperate struggles to keep alive he clung to a sense of the dignity of literature. It was this conviction of serious calling that ultimately raised him above the other journalists of the day.

Yet for all his later eminence, Johnson in the early 1740s was a hack. He lived from hand to mouth on jobs he could pick up from the booksellers, and he lounged away much of his time in their shops.[1] His pen was for sale for any serious project. From 1740 until 1746, when he began work on the *Dictionary* — the first long-term endeavor on his own — he tried a variety of schemes. Doubtless many will never be identified, but enough

265

have been discovered to give some idea of the multiplicity of his labors.

One of his first jobs away from St. John's Gate came through his old schoolfellow and companion at Walmesley's table, Dr. Robert James. Although not particularly congenial, the two young men from Lichfield had seen something of each other in London and had been thrown together in the negotiations over Lewis Paul's spinning machine. When James thought of producing a huge dictionary which would summarize all the medical learning and controversies of the past, he naturally turned to Johnson.

The first step was to issue a call for subscribers: *Proposals for Printing a Medicinal Dictionary; Designed as a Body of Physic and Surgery Both with Regard to Theory and Practice. Compiled from the Best Writers Ancient and Modern: with Useful Observations.* This appeared as a large four-page sheet, with the date June 24, 1741.[2] The style throughout is unmistakably Johnsonian. "It is doubtless of importance to the happiness of mankind, that whatever is generally useful should be generally known; and he therefore that *diffuses* science, may with justice claim, among the benefactors to the public, the next rank to him that *improves* it." Succinctly and with measured cadence, the writer went on to explain exactly what the proposed work would do and what it did not intend to do. It was a literate advertising blurb calculated to appeal to sober, intelligent readers.

The plan was to issue the dictionary by installments, five sheets every fortnight, interspersed occasionally with pages of copperplate illustrations. Thus subscribers might expect to learn soon about the work of Aesculapius, but would have to restrain their curiosity about matters coming near the end of the alphabet. The first number appeared on February 4, 1742, and the newspaper advertisements show that issues came out every other Thursday through February and March, and then every week.[3] Originally planned to make two volumes, the completed work finally expanded to fill three large folios.

Not only did Johnson assist his friend with the proposals; he wrote a graceful dedication to Dr. Mead, one of the prominent physicians of the day, for which, according to tradition, he received five guineas; and he made some contributions to the main body of the work. Just as he provided Cave with short biographies of celebrated men for the *Gentleman's Magazine,* he wrote accounts of medical men for the installments of James's dictionary. Most of those which have been identified come at the start of the alphabet — Actuarius, Aegineta, Aesculapius, Alexander, Archagathus, Aretaeus, and under "Anatomy" the life of Ruysch. He also included in expanded form his earlier account of Boerhaave.

There is a possibility that Johnson was involved with other sections, in scientific explanations and descriptions of chemical experiments. Long afterward he confided to Boswell that his knowledge of physic had been learned from Dr. James, when he was working with him on the mammoth dictionary. Ever curious, Johnson used such opportunities to increase his information in new fields. All his life he retained a delight in experimenting and in doctoring himself.

By the autumn of 1742 he had become active in another large undertaking managed by the publisher of the *Medicinal Dictionary* — Thomas Osborne. This was the task of cataloguing the great library of Edward Harley, the second Earl of Oxford, who had died the year before. The disposal of the Harleian books had been rumored during the summer, and by the middle of September Thomas Birch could write to his patron, Yorke, that a deal had at last been arranged with "Osborn of Gray's Inn and one Noel, a bookseller, who got a considerable fortune by his lordship, and left off trade many years ago." The price finally paid was thirteen thousand pounds, a sum large enough to cause some stir in the bookselling world.[4]

From Osborne's point of view it was purely a business speculation. He hoped to get as much out of the sale of the books as he possibly could. At first he consulted the classical scholar Michael Maittaire, who suggested the plan of a catalogue. But Osborne was also sensible enough to seek professional advice from others, and on October 4 wrote to Birch, "Having purchased the library of the Earl of Oxford — a more valuable collection than perhaps was ever in the hands of any bookseller, I am desirous of consult-

ing the learned with regard to the disposal of it, and have therefore enclosed the scheme of a catalogue which I intend to publish
in February of which the compiler joins his request that you will
facilitate the composition by your advice, with my entreaty that
you will promote the subscription to it by your recommendation." [5]

Birch was quite ready to oblige, and on October 9 he dined at
Lord Oxford's library in St. Marylebone, along with Martin
Folkes, president of the Royal Society, William Jones, distinguished mathematician, and Sam Johnson.[6] Among these distinguished consultants Johnson was the one who was to be most
involved in practical details, for he was undoubtedly there as a
new employee.

His first assignment was to draft an advertisement of the coming sale to stir up public interest. His proposals, which also contained "A General Account of the Harleian Library," were dated
November 1, but according to the newspapers were not ready for
distribution until about the middle of the month. In December
the "Account" was reprinted in the papers and in the *Gentleman's
Magazine*.[7] Ostensibly the message came from the bookseller —
it is he who explains the reason for the unusual procedure of
charging money for a sale catalogue — but for the most part it
is Johnson who is speaking. Here was his chance to stress the value
of such lists to those engaged in literary and historical research,
to comment on the interests of book collectors, to point out incidentally the shortcomings of the Bodleian collection at Oxford.
In typical fashion he used a specific assignment as an opportunity
to make a few general observations.

> By the means of catalogues only can it be known, what has been writ-
> ten on every part of learning, and the hazard avoided of encounter-
> ing difficulties which have already been cleared, discussing ques-
> tions which have already been decided, and digging in mines of
> literature which former ages have exhausted.
>
> How often this has been the fate of students, every man of letters
> can declare, and, perhaps, there are very few who have not some-
> times valued as new discoveries, made by themselves, those observa-

tions, which have long since been published, and of which the world therefore will refuse them the praise; nor can that refusal be censured as any enormous violation of justice; for, why should they not forfeit by their ignorance, what they might claim by their sagacity?

It may be that the actual copying of titles was done by mere amanuenses, but the selection and annotation were superintended by William Oldys and Johnson, who, as Hawkins commented, "while he was engaged in so servile an employment resembled a lion in harness." [8] What recommended Oldys was that he had been Lord Oxford's literary secretary and thus had intimate knowledge of the books. Oldys was a valuable helper, for he was a "man of eager curiosity and indefatigable diligence," an intelligent antiquary and bibliographer. It has been supposed that at the start he described the English volumes, while Johnson took the Latin, but no one has ever been able to distinguish between the work of the two cataloguers.

Since Osborne wanted his catalogues to be outstanding, as befitted the fame of the library, Johnson was kept busy at the work of annotation through the late autumn and early winter of 1742–43. Early in March, 1743, Volumes I and II of the *Catalogus Bibliothecae Harleianae* were ready for the curious public. For the rest of the month the books were on exhibition in St. Marylebone and Osborne was active in stirring up interest in the actual sale of the first part of the library, which occurred in April. But many collectors objected that the prices of the books were too high and balked at paying five shillings for each volume of the catalogue. Nor did it help for the bookseller to offer to exchange them at the sale for books at the same price. People were not accustomed to paying for book catalogues, even such handsome ones as those of the Harleian Library.

Though the public sale was not a complete success and Osborne was harassed by various attacks and the jealousy of other booksellers, he went ahead with plans for the second part of the library. Throughout the summer and autumn of 1743 Johnson struggled on with the cataloguing. In a letter written December 1 he gave as his address "at Mr. Osborne's, bookseller in Gray's Inn."

Hawkins suggests that Johnson was solely responsible for the annotation of Volumes III and IV, which were published early in January, 1744. The extent of his labors may be inferred from the newspaper advertisement describing the printed lists, "in which are comprised near forty thousand volumes, digested under distinct heads, and very frequently accompanied with curious notes, relating either to the history of the book, the life of the author, the peculiarity of the edition, or the excellence of the particular copy exposed to sale." [9] During the process Johnson must have handled thousands of these rare books, and examined a large number in detail. As a phase of his scholarly development, this task was an invaluable experience.

During December, 1743, Johnson also helped Osborne with plans for another related project — the publication of a series of rare pamphlets from the library of Lord Oxford. It may even be that the suggestion came from Johnson, who had found many of the pieces he was cataloguing particularly interesting. Entitled *The Harleian Miscellany,* it appeared in weekly installments beginning late in March, 1744, and extending into 1746, and ultimately filled eight quarto volumes. Johnson certainly wrote the proposals and the introduction to the first volume, afterward called "An Essay on the Origin and Importance of Small Tracts and Fugitive Pieces," where he again showed his strong historical sense and his feeling about the liberty of the English press. He may have had something to do with the selection of the contents, though more likely it was Oldys who was responsible for the later editing. By this time Johnson and Osborne may have parted company.

In Osborne's ruffled mood, and with the natural differences of temperament, it is not surprising that there should have been a clash between employer and employee. One difference of opinion, according to tradition, resulted in actual physical violence.[10] Though an opulent trader, Osborne was ignorant, mean, and insolent; in general there was an impassive dullness about his deportment. He was rude to customers and scornful of his underlings. As Johnson once put it, he was "entirely destitute of shame, without sense of any disgrace but that of poverty." He expected speedy completion of assignments, and when he found Johnson reading one of the Harleian books instead of providing copy for the printer, Osborne reproached him in coarse language. Johnson's excuse — undoubtedly the necessity of examining books carefully in order to write adequate descriptions for the catalogue — only brought a blunt accusation of lying. In a furious rage Johnson grabbed a nearby folio volume and felled his tormentor with a single blow.

So, in brief, goes the story, one of the best-known incidents in Johnson's life. Like so many fabulous anecdotes, it gathered embellishments as it was repeated, and many of the details are still unclear.

Mrs. Thrale once asked Johnson how much of the popular story was true. "It was true said he that I beat the fellow, and that was all; but the world so hated poor Osborne; that they have never done multiplying the blows, and increasing the weight of them for twenty years together; the blockhead told the story himself too originally, for I am sure I should not, — but says Osborne Johnson beat me this morning in my own house — For what says his friend — why for telling him that he *lied* forsooth." In her later *Anecdotes* she reported Johnson making another pungent comment on the whole affair: "I have beat many a fellow, but the rest had the wit to hold their tongues."

One dramatic version had it that after the blow Johnson put his foot on his prostrate victim and declaimed: "Lie there, thou son of dullness, ignorance, and obscurity"; another, that he forcefully told him "he need not be in a hurry to rise; for if he did, he would have the further trouble of kicking him downstairs." One raconteur described Johnson's foot on Osborne's neck, another on his breast. The variations grew with each retelling, with more and more circumstantial details. A huge sixteenth-century Greek Bible, described as the actual volume used, was listed in an early nineteenth-century catalogue.[11]

Perhaps, after all, one had better go back to Boswell, who tried hard to be accurate: "The simple truth I had from Johnson himself. 'Sir, he was impertinent to me, and I beat him. But it was not in his shop: it was in my own chamber.'"

The story is usually told as a sample of Johnson's irascible temper. But, as Hawkins appreciated, there was another, more distressing side. To see such a man as Johnson subjected to "the insolence of a mean, worthless, ignorant fellow . . . to see such a man, for the supply of food and raiment, submitting to the commands of his inferior, and, as a hireling, looking up to him for the reward of his work, and receiving it accompanied with reproach and contumely, this, I say, is a subject of melancholy reflection."

There is a similar story, not well authenticated, but worth repeating since it probably refers to Osborne.

> He was much with a bookseller of eminence, who frequently consulted him about manuscripts offered for sale, or books newly published; but whenever Johnson's opinion happened to differ from his, he would stare Johnson full in the face, and remark, with much gravity and arrogance, "I wish you could write as well." — This Johnson thought was literally telling a professional man he was an impostor, or that he assumed a character to which he was not equal; he therefore heard the gross imputation once or twice with sullen contempt. One day, however, in the presence of several gentlemen who knew them both, this bookseller very incautiously threw out the same illiberal opinion. Johnson could suppress his indignation no longer. "Sir," said he, "you are not competent to decide a question which you do not understand. If your allegations be true, you have the brutality to insult me with what is not my fault, but my misfortune. If your allegations be not true, your impudent speech only shows how much more detestable a liar is than a brute."
>
> The strong conclusive aspect and ferocity of manner which accompanied the utterance of these words from a poor author to a purse-proud bookseller, made a deep impression in Johnson's favor.[12]

Johnson must often have been close to open rebellion. He must constantly have chafed at servitude to unfeeling employers and at the necessity of giving all his time and energy to routine editing rather than to anything creative. It was frustrating not to be able to enter the literary arena as an acknowledged performer. In many ways the literary period of the early 1740s was an exciting one. There was much to stir up heated argument and critical discussion — Pope's final version of the *Dunciad* and his bitter quarrel with Colley Cibber; Young's somber *Night Thoughts;* Thomson's expanded *Seasons*. There were new poets achieving sudden recognition — like Dr. Akenside with his *Pleasures of Imagination*. There was the rivalry of Richardson and Fielding, suggesting exciting possibilities in prose fiction. Meanwhile, Johnson was forced to slave away for Cave at St. John's Gate and for Osborne at Gray's Inn, as an obscure anonymous journalist. With a mind teeming with projects and conscious of superior powers, he was saddled by hack work, hemmed in by poverty, unable to strike out in new directions.

Only one work during these years was written *con amore* — a biography of his old companion in misery, Richard Savage. Since their pathetic parting in July, 1739, the two men had seen nothing of each other, though they had kept in touch through infrequent letters and messages to common friends. It was to Cave that Savage had sent the manuscript of a violent satire on Bristol society, and it was Cave who had tried to dissuade him from publishing it as it stood.[13] Those at St. John's Gate were well aware of Savage's troubles in Wales and his inability to live quietly on the stipulated remittances from his friends. But the news of his sudden death on August 1, 1743, in a Bristol jail must have come as a tragic shock.

Grief over the loss of their friend, however, did not blind Cave and Johnson to the commercial advantage of getting out immediately an account of his sensational life. Even though Savage's long absence from the capital had resulted in his being largely forgotten by the public, the old colorful scandals were still excellent journalistic copy. The first order of business was to frighten away any possible rival biographer. So, less than two weeks after the first notice in the London papers of Savage's death, the *General Evening Post* carried the announcement:

> In the press, and speedily will be published, an account of the life and writings of Richard Savage, Esq.; in which will be included his satire on the city of Bristol, with remarks. The author of this narrative was informed by Mr. Savage himself of the facts related

in it, to the time of his retirement into Wales; from which time, to that of his death in the prison of Bristol, the particulars are collected from his own letters, and those of his acquaintance.

N.B. Any informations for this work, if left with the printer of this paper, will be communicated to the author.[14]

And in an unsigned letter to the *Gentleman's Magazine,* appearing early in September, Johnson reiterated the claims, adding,

It may be reasonably imagined that others may have the same design, but as it is not credible that they can obtain the same materials, it must be expected that they will supply from invention the want of intelligence, and that under the title of the life of *Savage* they will publish only a novel filled with romantic adventures, and imaginary amours. You may therefore perhaps gratify the lovers of truth and wit by giving me leave to inform them in your magazine, that my account will be published in 8vo by Mr. *Roberts* in *Warwick Lane.*

Once arrangements had been made, Johnson expected Cave to help gather the evidence:

Toward Mr. Savage's life what more have you got? I would willingly have his trial etc. and know whether his defense be at Bristol, and would have his collection of poems on account of the preface — the *Plain Dealer* — all the magazines that have anything of his or relating to him.

Cave willingly complied and even went so far as to purchase for seven guineas the manuscripts of two of Savage's plays from the keeper of Newgate Prison in Bristol.[15]

Realizing that haste was desirable, Johnson promised to send in half a sheet of copy a day. Some of the book was written at even greater speed. When in Scotland, years later, Johnson told Boswell that he had written "forty-eight of the printed octavo pages of the life of Savage at a sitting, but then I sat up all night." Apparently a large section was dashed off in a period of some thirty-six hours. When inspired, Johnson could work with frenzied speed. Nor did he ever feel any undue anxiety about sending what he had written directly to the printer. He always scorned those who worried too much about the possible reception of their work. When Mrs. Thrale once expressed doubt that this had always been so, and added, "The time has been, Sir, when you felt it," Johnson replied, "Why really, Madam, I do not recollect a time when that was the case." [16]

Yet for all his bursts of activity, the work was not quickly completed, for during the autumn of 1743 the life of Savage was only one of a number of projects for which he was responsible. There were the volumes of the Harleian catalogue for Osborne, miscellaneous editing for the *Gentleman's Magazine,* and a mysterious "historical design," perhaps an account of the British Parliament.[17] As Johnson commented to Cave when agreeing to write the life of Savage, "With the debates shall I not have business enough? If I had but good pens." Besides, he was not in good health, and living precariously on what was doled out by his employers, he was at times too poor even to afford lights to work at night. In the same letter he remarked to Cave, "The boy found me writing this almost in the dark, when I could not quite easily read yours. . . ." And pathetically he added, "If you could spare me another guinea for the hist I should take it very kindly to-night, but if you do not shall not think it an injury. — I am almost well again — "

Not until December 14 was the account of Savage in final shape. On that day he received his pay from Cave and gave a receipt for the sum of fifteen guineas, for the writing and compiling, "in full for all materials thereto applied, and not found by the said Edward Cave." [18] As a small octavo of some 180 pages, the life was published by James Roberts, the bookseller in Warwick Lane, on February 11, 1744, with no author's name on the title page. To the public Johnson remained just an anonymous compiler.

Despite the repeated claims of accuracy, Johnson had no intention of doing any thorough research. He might make a show of hunting for evidence, but he was quite willing to accept without verification what was easily obtained. He even failed to consult surviving legal records. He had few doubts of the basic truth of his friend's story or of the despicable character of his reputed mother. His was a labor of love, tossed off at white heat, not a sober historical investigation. As a result, the work is a brilliant character study, but factually unreliable.

For the early years — before Savage's celebrated trial for murder — Johnson had a number of printed authorities. There was some material in issues of the *Plain Dealer,* reprinted in one edition of the poet's *Miscellaneous Poems* in 1726; an anonymous biography in 1727; and various published claims by Savage himself. For the middle years, on the other hand, there were no printed accounts, and Johnson was forced to rely wholly on what he could remember from Savage's conversation and on what separate works he could discover. This section is the least satisfactory of all, with chronology often completely askew. The last period, a time when Johnson had considerable personal knowledge of his subject, is the best.[19]

For us there are other obvious defects in the work. Johnson thought more highly of Savage as a writer than do most twentieth-century critics, who are glad to skip over the lengthy quotations from the poems. There is none of the vivid re-creation of scene which is the strength of Boswell, no reporting of actual conversations. The use of indirect discourse, whenever Savage is quoted, is undramatic. Nothing is brought forward to show why people were willing to sit up all night to listen to him talk. But Johnson did something which had rarely been accomplished in biography before his time. He showed genuine understanding of the essential conflicts of a complex personality.

At the same time he seemed unaware of exactly what was implicit in his stories. He failed to see that for all Savage's ostensible fortitude, his "insurmountable obstinacy" of spirit, he was in reality merely rationalizing a deep-seated neurotic refusal to work. But if unable to make the analysis, Johnson gave all the necessary evidence. He suppressed nothing. Instance after instance was given of Savage's insulting his benefactors, of his unconsciously stimulating dislike and rejection. He showed how Savage constantly invited denial and humiliation, and then reveled in self-pity; how he built up a delusion of continual persecution. Though perhaps unclear about the motives behind Savage's public for-

giveness of the woman of the town who had brought him to the
threshold of execution, Johnson provides what is necessary for a
modern interpretation.[20] That is what makes the life a landmark
in the development of the art of biography.

In later years Johnson thought much about this kind of writing.
In essays in *The Rambler* and *The Idler* and in talks with Boswell
he gradually formulated his theory of what it should be. Though
he himself could never produce a perfect example, he taught his
disciple the proper approach. In writing a life one had to "number the streaks of the tulip," for the mind could not be free from
the rigid rule of fact. One must come to the general from the
specific. But in this early experiment it is doubtful that he considered rules or the needs of different genres. The *Life of Savage*
was not the result of theorizing. It came as a happy accident from
the union of powerful emotion and a deep curiosity about human
nature.

Johnson had loved Savage at the same time that he recognized
all of his weaknesses. Although moved by the apparent tyranny
of a heartless mother over her wayward son, Johnson had seen
only too well that the son had not made the most of his own
abilities. Thus Savage became both a symbol of injustice and an
example of weakness. If his history was a bitter indictment of
the callousness of the world toward native genius, it was also a
warning to those who did not believe in self-discipline. As one
critic has recently pointed out, the life might almost be taken as
an extended study of one of Johnson's favorite themes, the dangerous misuse of the imagination, "for he saw in Savage the embodi-
ment of daydreaming, self-dramatization, self-pity, and all the bad
qualities of mind and heart he so neatly summed up in his word
cant." [21] Throughout, Johnson was an objective moralist as well
as an impassioned partisan. The two often conflicting motivations
gave the work its depth and balance.

Just as in politics, Johnson had learned to think of personality
not always in terms of black and white, but in varying shades of
gray. Rather than picture saints and sinners, a biographer should
fashion real men and women, composed of mixtures of good and

bad. His portrait of Savage, with its subtle insights and shrewd generalizations, was a notable experiment in a new type of writing.

Most readers in 1744 read the book not so much for any brilliant psychological characterization as for the whole sensational story of Savage's career. They accepted it merely as another account of sin and cruelty in high life, in the tradition of Defoe's fictional lives or of the notorious productions of Edmund Curll. Roberts obviously had this in mind in his later newspaper publicity. The next year, in order to stimulate sales, he recommended the book to the lovers of colorful scandal in an advertisement in the *London Evening Post*:

> An account of the life of Mr. Richard Savage, son of the late Earl Rivers. Who was, soon after he came into the world, bastardised by an act of Parliament, and deprived of the title and estate to which he was born; was committed by his mother, the Countess of Macclesfield, to a poor woman, to be bred up as her own son; came to the knowledge of his real mother, now alive, but abandoned by her, persecuted, and condemned for murder, and against all her endeavors, pardoned; made poet laureate to Queen Caroline, became very eminent for his writings, of which many are quoted in this work; particularly the *Bastard*, the *Wanderer, Volunteer Laureate*, and *Author to be Let;* went into Wales, to be supported by a subscription, promoted by Mr. Pope, but at last died in prison.[22]

This remarkable tale has captivated readers from that day to this. Sir Joshua Reynolds confessed to Boswell that he "began to read it while he was standing with his arm leaning against a chimney piece. It seized his attention so strongly, that, not being able to lay down the book till he had finished it, when he attempted to move, he found his arm totally benumbed." [23] Not the least of the book's merits is its smoothness of narration.

Since it was some time before a second edition was printed, the life cannot have had an extensive sale. Nor was it widely reviewed or discussed in print. Apparently at the start it was taken as an excellent piece of sensational journalism and not much more. Yet one enthusiastic review must have gladdened the heart of the anonymous author. The editor of the *Champion* called it "as just and well written a piece as of its kind I ever saw," and went on to add:

> As to the history of the unfortunate person, whose memoirs compose this work, it is carefully penned with equal accuracy and spirit, of which I am so much the better judge, as I know many of the facts mentioned to be strictly true, and very fairly related. Besides, it is not only the story of Mr. Savage, but innumerable incidents relating to other persons, and other affairs, which renders this a very amusing, and, withal, a very instructive and valuable performance. The author's observations are short, significant, and just, as his narrative is remarkably smooth, and well disposed. His reflections open to all the recesses of the human heart; and, in a word, a more just or pleasant, a more engaging or a more improving treatise, on all the excellencies and defects of human nature, is scarce to be found in our own, or, perhaps, any other language.[24]

Such encomiums may have been gratifying, but the book brought Johnson little money or public recognition. He continued to be miserably poor, and he had not yet seen his own name on a title page. To illustrate his sad condition, Boswell tells the story that about this time Walter Harte, tutor to Lord Chesterfield's son, dined with Cave at St. John's Gate, and chanced to praise the newly published *Life of Savage*. "Soon after, meeting him, Cave said, 'You made a man very happy t'other day.' — 'How could that be,' says Harte; 'nobody was there but ourselves.' Cave answered, by reminding him that a plate of victuals was sent behind a screen, which was to Johnson, dressed so shabbily, that he did not choose to appear." [25]

Poverty and obscurity were to be recurring themes for the next few years. Johnson and Tetty were finding it difficult enough to keep alive, let alone to put anything aside for other purposes, such as the interest on the mortgage of the Lichfield house. For three years nothing had been paid, and by December, 1743, the arrears had reached twelve pounds. Though Theophilus Levett was a remarkably patient man, he could not be put off forever. But how could the required cash be secured? It was not easy to find even such a small sum, and Johnson wrote to Levett with appreciation for his forbearance, explaining that "a great perplexity of affairs" had hindered him from thinking of the matter, and confessing that he could not speedily come by the money. He begged, if possible, an extension of two months more. There was one more request: "I look upon this and on the future interest of that mortgage as my own debt, and beg that you will be pleased to give me directions how to pay it, and not mention it to my dear mother." [26] In the end Harry Hervey provided the amount, but whether as a gift, a loan, or a payment for some literary help is not certain.

It is hard to say how Johnson managed during the summer and autumn of 1744, unless he was helping with the weekly installments of the *Harleian Miscellany*. In April, to be sure, Roberts issued a revised and expanded version of the *Life of Barretier*, as a separate pamphlet, but this could not have brought Johnson much financial return. In September he wrote proposals for a fortnightly miscellany to be called the *Publisher*. With a special gift for stating clearly and succinctly just what was intended, Johnson in succeeding years was called upon more than once for similar pieces.[27] Like his writing of formal dedications, the outlining of proposals became part of his professional stock in trade.

Although he was no longer so active on the *Gentleman's Magazine,* he was always ready to help with the editing in return for a good dinner and a possible meager pittance. Particularly on the day that copy was made up for the next monthly issue he was apt to be found at St. John's Gate. Thus young Stephen Barrett, fresh from Oxford, dined there with Johnson and Cave when the February, 1745, number was being prepared. As Barrett later recounted:

> After the cloth was removed, and we had drank a glass or two of wine; Cave, opened his budget, "Here is, gentleman, a very indifferent performance [a Latin verse translation of a song by John Byrom], but it is just of an exact length for my purpose; and yet if ye will not brush it up for me, it cannot appear."
>
> Give it to Mr Barrett (says Johnson) he'll correct it for you, in a minute.

Why, no (say I) that I shall not undertake alone, but if Mr. Johnson will take distich for distich with me (as I have half an hour to
stay before I set out for home — I then was curate of Bushey, Herts,
15 miles out of town) we will endeavor to make it just passable. This
was in return for the maneuver of throwing it all upon me; and
as writing Latin verse was my forte I thought I had thereby got my
master upon the hip. But how was I mistaken when I found that he
was as expeditious at it, as myself!

Very well! — then (says he) do you begin.

By no means! (added I) seniores, priores and threw him the paper
cross the table. He returned it, in a moment; and so it passed from
the one to the other, like a shuttlecock; Cave chuckling all the while
to see it pass and repass, so rapidly.[28]

The revised translation of eighty lines evidently met the deadline,
for it appeared, along with Byrom's original verses, in the February magazine.

But one could scarcely make a living by such casual editing or
from short anonymous pamphlets. Johnson needed a major
project of his own, and his thoughts turned to the editing of
Shakespeare. For anyone with his literary and critical interests it
was an inevitable choice. Rowe, Pope, Theobald — none had been
completely satisfactory as editor. There were still fascinating problems of the text to be settled, still much to be said about the plays.
From his youth Johnson had been under the spell of the greatest
of English writers; he had long been pondering over what seemed
to him fresh insights, new readings of disputed passages. Besides,
Shakespeare was always a sure source of profit for the booksellers.

As a sample of what he could do, Johnson set to work to examine *Macbeth,* and during the early winter of 1745 began to jot
down some of his comments. Here was a chance to show the tex-
ture of his mind. A pedantic word-catcher might spend his whole
time trying to emend the faulty text; a scholarly antiquarian, in
explaining obsolete meanings. A superficial commentator might
see only the obvious turns of the plot. Johnson intended to do all
these but go deeper. He would show how a true editor and critic
ought to work.

Just as in the notes to the translation of Crousaz, his approach was a combination of shrewd common sense and skepticism, over-laid with a passionate aesthetic appreciation. He was fully aware of the corruption of the texts — misprints, wrong words, whole passages that appeared incomprehensible in the early printings. And like his predecessors, he was quite ready to guess at what must have been the original meaning. "As the word *very* is here of no other use than to fill up the verse, it is likely that Shakespeare wrote *various*." [29] Or "As the word *owed* affords here no sense, but such as is forced and unnatural, it cannot be doubted that it was originally written, The dearest thing he *owned;* a reading which needs neither defense nor explication."

This was a game which Pope and Lewis Theobald had de-lighted to play in their Shakespearean editions. Johnson was merely following suit. But he was manfully independent of pre-vious authority. He took nothing on trust. "Mr. Theobald has en-deavored unsuccessfully to amend this passage, in which nothing is faulty but the punctuation." To each individual problem John-son brought all the resources of a powerful critical intelligence. When he comes to the lines "thus with his stealthy pace,/ With Tarquin's ravishing *sides* towards his design,/Moves like a ghost," Johnson comments:

> This was the reading of this passage in all the editions before that of Mr. Pope, who for *sides,* inserted in the text *strides,* which Mr. Theobald has tacitly copied from him, though a more proper alter-ation might, perhaps, have been made. A *ravishing stride* is an ac-tion of violence, impetuosity, and tumult, like that of a savage rush-ing on his prey; whereas the poet is here attempting to exhibit an image of secrecy and caution, of anxious circumspection and guilty timidity, the *stealthy pace* of a *ravisher* creeping into the chamber of a virgin, and of an assassin approaching the bed of him whom he proposes to murder, without awaking him; these he describes as *moving like ghosts,* whose progression is so different from *strides,* that it has been in all ages represented to be, as Milton expresses it, smooth sliding without step.

The proper word, Johnson concludes, would be "slides."

In explaining the important use of magic in the play, Johnson combined amused rationalism with an awareness of historical change. Should an eighteenth-century poet make the whole action of the drama depend on enchantment and supernatural agents, "he would be banished from the theater to the nursery, and condemned to write fairy tales instead of tragedies." But in Shakespeare's time such notions were universally accepted. From antiquity the belief in witchcraft had been strong, and King James himself was an expert in demonology. "Thus the doctrine of witchcraft was very powerfully inculcated; and as the greatest part of mankind have no other reason for their opinions than that they are in fashion, it cannot be doubted but this persuasion made rapid progress, since vanity and credulity cooperated in its favor, and it had a tendency to free cowardice from reproach." Shakespeare might be easily justified by the "general infatuation" of his time.

Again and again one sees forming the basic patterns of Johnson's critical approach. He is wary of his own sudden flashes of intuition. He doubts the value of romantic illumination. As he sees it, the function of the critic is to bring together all the evidence. He examines all sides, evaluates, and explains. Where logical analysis is applicable, he is ready to adjudicate. He stands as an interpreter, where explication is necessary, but he makes no claim to unusual powers. Always it is the effect of the work on the reader which is stressed. His most valuable tool is comparison and contrast. If one work is set against another, one idea balanced against its opposite, both may be illumined. So Johnson contrasts Shakespeare's great passage beginning "Now o'er one half the world Nature seems dead" with a similar one in Dryden's *Indian Emperor: or the Conquest of Mexico.*

> Night is described by two great poets, but one describes a night of quiet, the other of perturbation. In the night of Dryden, all the disturbers of the world are laid asleep; in that of Shakespeare, nothing but sorcery, lust, and murder, is awake. He that reads Dryden, finds himself lulled with serenity, and disposed to solitude and contemplation. He that peruses Shakespeare, looks round alarmed, and starts to find himself alone. One is the night of a lover; the other, that of a murderer.

Balance, antithesis, the sharp distinction and the generalized abstraction — these have become an integral part of his mental processes. And the style but mirrors the thought.

Just when his commentary was all in print, another edition appeared — a sumptuous but not very scholarly set of volumes prepared by Sir Thomas Hanmer. In order to take notice of this new rival, Johnson tacked on a few paragraphs at the end and adapted the title page to read: *Miscellaneous Observations on the Tragedy of Macbeth: with Remarks on Sir T. H.'s Edition of Shakespeare.*[30] Mentioned also on the title page, and tucked away among the advertisements at the end of the sixty-four-page pamphlet, was a separate sheet of *Proposals for Printing a New Edition of the Plays of William Shakespeare, with Notes Critical and Explanatory, in Which the Text Will Be Corrected: the Various Readings Remarked: the Conjectures of Former Editors Examined, and Their Omissions Supplied.* Most of the page was given over to a specimen of the text and notes. According to the plan, the whole edition would occupy ten small volumes, to be sold at the low price of one pound five shillings, in sheets. Subscriptions were advertised as taken in by Cave at St. John's Gate and "by the editor."

The *Miscellaneous Observations,* together with the proposal sheet, was published the week end of April 6–8. Everything appeared to be progressing happily when suddenly an unexpected complication put an early end to the undertaking. On the eleventh Jacob Tonson, the famous bookseller, wrote to Cave that he and his associates alone controlled the copyright of Shakespeare. Suggesting that Cave call on him at once to talk the matter over, Tonson made it clear that he would fight to control his valuable property, and ended with a direct threat of a Chancery suit, should anyone invade his rights.[31] Faced with such a determined opponent, Cave had to yield. Johnson was back where he started, vainly seeking something to ensure steady employment.

He talked to friends about several schemes. To Dr. Adams of Pembroke College, who saw him occasionally on visits to London, he confided that his favorite was a life of King Alfred. Adams also remembered that about this time Johnson was thinking of writing a literary journal. He once considered doing a life of Dryden and tried vainly to secure information from a few people who remembered him.[32] It was not a lack of ideas that kept him undecided.

In some early period he began to keep a catalogue of all the various things he would like to do.[33] As the years progressed, his "designs" grew until there were almost fifty titles. There was a history of criticism from Aristotle to the eighteenth century, a history of the Revival of Learning in Europe, an edition of Chaucer from manuscripts and old copies, "with various readings, conjectures, remarks on his language," a translation of Aristotle's *Rhetoric* and his *Ethics,* a translation of Machiavelli's history of Florence, translations of Herodian, Claudian, Cicero, editions of such English writers as Oldham and Roscommon. In a separate category he listed possible works of the imagination: a "Hymn to Ignorance," "The Palace of Sloth — a Vision," "Prejudice — a Poetical Essay," "The Palace of Nonsense — a Vision." Not one was ever completed in the exact form originally planned.

At times, when in a particularly dispirited mood, he still thought of leaving the uncertainty and drudgery of authorship for another profession, and once asked Dr. Adams "to consult Dr. Smalbroke of the Commons, whether a person might be permitted to practice as an advocate there, without a doctor's degree in civil law." [34] With sturdy self-confidence he added, "I am a total stranger to these studies; but whatever is a profession, and maintains numbers, must be within the reach of common abilities, and some degree of industry." Again, just as in teaching, the want of a degree appeared an insuperable obstacle.

Throughout most of 1745 and the first half of the next year there is little evidence of what Johnson was doing. We know he was involved in two small jobs for individuals — a sermon for an old friend and the correction of a long poem for an Irish clergyman — but it is not clear what his assignments from the booksellers were. This is the period of his life about which least is known.

The sermon was for Harry Hervey, who had undergone an amazing metamorphosis. Not only had the improvident, hard-drinking, and gouty soldier exchanged his uniform for a surplice, but he had changed his name as well. He was now the Reverend Henry Hervey Aston, Rector of Shotley in Suffolk. The change of name had come after the death of his wife's brother and her inheritance of part of the Aston fortune. The move into the church is more difficult to explain, but it is perhaps sufficient to say that for a Hervey anything was possible.

In the spring of 1745 the new Rector of Shotley had a great honor bestowed upon him. He was asked to preach at St. Paul's Cathedral on the occasion of the annual feast of the Sons of the Clergy, always a spectacular affair. At once he turned to Johnson, who obligingly produced a sermon on charity suitable for the occasion.[35] It was as easy for the bookseller's assistant to toss off a pulpit oration as to draft proposals or to describe a library. Long afterward he confessed to Boswell that during his career he had composed about forty — "I have begun a sermon after dinner, and sent it off by the post that night." [36] But that was after long practice. With this early one he may well have taken more care.

When the former Harry Hervey, impressive in his handsome gown, delivered the sermon at St. Paul's on May 2, there was a distinguished audience, including the Archbishop of Canterbury and eight other bishops, the Lord Chief Justice, and aldermen of the City. Probably in an obscure back pew a large, shabby man, in a threadbare coat and straggly wig, listened to the words with obvious approval. Although unknown and unrecognized as the author, he would have been pleased to be exhorting all those dignitaries.

After the service the notables went in procession to the Merchant-Taylor's Hall for a sumptuous dinner, but it is unlikely that Johnson was invited. Not that he ever complained. It was a business proposition. When he wrote anything on assignment for a stipulated price, he was quite ready to give up all rights. When the sermon was published late in May it had the Honorable and Reverend Henry Hervey Aston's name on the title page. Nevertheless, it must have delighted Johnson to have his work highly praised in the newspapers, and to know that his appeal had been a practical success, with the collection exceeding by £177 17s. 9d. the largest hitherto made on the occasion.[37]

Ostensibly charity was the main theme of the sermon, but it was

not strictly interpreted. Johnson used the occasion for some salu-
tary remarks on a variety of related topics. There was, for instance,
the danger of narrow patriotism.

> Others have carried their benevolence still farther, and taught, that
> the general duty of life, is the love of our country; these, likewise,
> were mistaken, not in asserting that this was a duty, but that it was
> the only duty; that it was to absorb all other considerations, and
> that consequently nothing was criminal, by which greatness of a
> particular society might be augmented, or its prosperity advanced:
> this principle was the dictate, not of piety, but ambition; we are to
> endeavor, indeed, the happiness of our country; but in subordina-
> tion to the happiness of mankind.

Too great a zeal for charity might lead to other dangers. Johnson could not believe in equality of possessions. He plainly saw a
basic fallacy in the theory of communism.

> Some sects have attempted to recommend themselves by an ardour
> of benevolence, well adapted to dazzle the weak, and to ensnare the
> needy; but which was never commanded by the Author of our
> religion, and is not practicable without confusion. They have in-
> troduced an absolute community of possessions, and asserted, that
> distinction of property, is inconsistent with that love, which we are
> commanded to exercise toward one another. The absurdity of this
> notion, it is not difficult to show. Every man must easily discern that
> difference of property, is necessary to subordination, and subordina-
> tion essential to government; that, where there is no property, there
> can be no motive to industry, but virtue; and that the bad, must
> then always be supported by those, whose generosity inclines them
> to provide for them.

His other known assignment for this period gives evidence of his
growing critical reputation. The Rev. Samuel Madden, an Irish
clergyman, asked him to revise a long poem called *Boulter's Monument,* in memory of the late Primate of Ireland. Recalling the incident years later, Johnson remarked, "I remember I blotted a
great many lines, and might have blotted many more, without
making the poem worse. However, the doctor was very thankful,

and very generous, for he gave me ten guineas, *which was to me at that time a great sum.*" [38]

The poem was printed by Samuel Richardson and published late in October, 1745. In an apologetic postscript Madden confessed that he "had neither leisure or skill to avoid or correct what was censurable" in the poem, and added, "in deference to the reader, some hundred lines have been pruned from it, that were not quite unpardonable, in order to lessen the tediousness of the panegyrical part." The name of the pruner was not mentioned.

THE complete absence of information about Johnson's activities from this time until the spring of 1746, together with his known tenderness for the Stuart cause, has led some people to suspect that he was involved in the celebrated Jacobite uprising of the autumn of 1745. It makes a romantic tale, and more than one writer of fiction has fallen into the trap. [39] Once the assumption is granted, the rest follows naturally.

It is easy to imagine the thirty-six-year-old disappointed author, filled with hatred of the Hanoverian oppressors, excited by the news that the son of the "true King" had landed on British soil, secretly leaving London and hurrying north to join the rebel army; then discovering the unstable character of those in charge of the campaign, becoming convinced of its ultimate failure, and finally slinking disillusioned into hiding until it was safe to reappear in Grub Street. This is the great moralist in a new role. What a pity that there is probably not a word of truth in it!

To be sure, a powerful case can be built up, once the mind is given over to wishful thinking. There are the many slighting references to the House of Hanover, the favorable remarks about the Stuarts. There are numerous little actions, inconclusive when taken alone, but very suspicious when considered all together. [40] For example, why was Johnson in his very last year so anxious to purchase from the sister of Francis Stewart in Edinburgh, whom he may have met in the early 1740s, a particular letter containing personal references? More than once Johnson prodded Boswell, determined to get hold of the mysterious document from an old letter case. Could it have contained some pointed mention of common participation in the rebellion? Then there is William Drummond, Edinburgh bookseller, whom Johnson first met when Drummond was in concealment in London following the defeat of the rebels and before the general act of pardon was announced. And why were visitors in later years never allowed to talk at length with Dr. Levet, the poor practitioner who later lived in Johnson's house? Did he share the secret of the '45? Then there is the episode in 1773 of Goldsmith and the rebels' heads upon Temple Bar. One could go on and on multiplying suspicious circumstances, if only one abandoned one's mind to it.

It has been customary to explain Johnson's Tory leanings as resulting from his upbringing in Lichfield, a place "for a long time tinctured with Jacobitical principles." [41] But apparently in the autumn of 1745 the inhabitants of Lichfield, almost to a man, were loyal to the government in power. Not only the bailiffs and principal citizens, but the bishop, dean, and chapter of the cathedral sent addresses to the King stating their abhorrence of the present rebellion and acknowledging the King's rightful title to the throne. When the Duke of Cumberland arrived at the head of the loyal forces, he was well received and, as one correspondent put it, was looked on as a deliverer. Perhaps one reason was the great stress in all newspaper accounts of the "papist" influence in the Pretender's forces. Even the conservative Tory party in Lichfield was stanchly Protestant, and would support nothing which might threaten the Establishment. Johnson would have found no encouragement to rebel activity in his home town.

Besides, when carefully examined, the evidence of Johnson's loyalty to the Stuarts is not wholly convincing.[42] It is difficult to ignore his later remark to Boswell that if by holding up his right hand he could have secured the victory of Charles at Culloden he was uncertain that he would have held it up. This scarcely sounds like the recollection of an ardent rebel willing to risk his life for a romantic cause. Boswell is very clear in saying, "Mr. Johnson is not properly a *Jacobite*. He does not hold the *jus divinum* of kings. He founds their right on long possession, which ought not to be disturbed upon slight grounds." A firm member of the

established church, he had never once been in a nonjuring meetinghouse. As for the bits of circumstantial evidence, none are con-
clusive. Each can be explained just as well in some other way.

.Throughout all the excitement Johnson probably remained in
London, emotionally pulled apart by conflicting pressures, avidly
reading the newspapers for accounts from the Midlands, following with feverish excitement the reported progress of the Prince's
army as far as Derby, but doing nothing to aid or to oppose the
Stuart cause. In heated arguments he may at times have uttered
treasonable remarks, enough to give him the reputation of being
a violent Jacobite. The blatant Whig propaganda in the papers
must often have made him angry. But at the moment of decision
a deep conviction of the supreme importance of civil peace kept
him from rash acts.

The winter of 1745–46 was another low point in Johnson's
career. As a practicing journalist he had had some successes. In
"the trade" he was highly regarded as an able craftsman who,
though cranky and independent, could be relied upon to do superior work on any kind of assignment. But he had done nothing
since *London* in 1738 to spread his reputation outside the small
inner circle of active booksellers.[43] After eight years of slavery in
London he was still just a poorly paid hack. The future must
have seemed grim indeed.

The spring of 1746, however, brought a change. Johnson finally
found his great project. In the autumn of that same year Gilbert
Walmesley, writing from Bath to his protégé David Garrick, now
the toast of theatrical London, added; "When you see Mr. Johnson, pray my compliments, and tell him I esteem him as a great
genius — quite lost both to himself and the world." [44] Judging
by appearances, Walmesley was quite right. He could not know
that Sam Johnson was then hard at work on something which
would ensure him a place among the world's great literary men.

CHAPTER XVI

"*A Harmless Drudge*"

J AMES DODSLEY told Boswell that one day several years before this period he had heard his brother the celebrated bookseller suggest to Johnson, who was sitting in the shop, "that a dictionary of the English language would be a work that would be well received by the public; that Johnson seemed at first to catch at the proposition, but, after a pause, said, in his abrupt decisive manner, 'I believe I shall not undertake it.' " [1] Later, while admitting that the initial suggestion had come from Robert Dodsley, Johnson insisted that he "had long thought of it."

Everyone who seriously considered the subject realized the need for something in English comparable to the great works of the French and Italian academies. Though there were numbers of English dictionaries, there was nothing definitive, nothing made on historical principles, or on the scale of those on the Continent. For well over a century writers had been calling for an adequate dictionary of the language. One after another considered the scheme, made plans, and gave them up. It was rumored that Tonson had offered Addison three thousand pounds "to make an English dictionary and put it out under his name." [2] According to one account he went so far as to choose his authorities and collect some quotations. Pope toyed with the idea and similarly drew up a list of authors to be used. Ambrose Philips actually issued proposals for such a work, to be in two volumes, folio. [3] Johnson was familiar with all this. He knew about Pope's notes; he used Philips's proposals. The need, the ideal form, the exact nature of the contents, were well established before he entered the field. There was nothing novel, nothing astonishing in the idea.

Of the reference works already available, the most important was Nathan Bailey's *Universal Etymological English Dictionary*, first published in 1721, and later expanded into a great folio *Dictionarium Britannicum,* which actually contained more words than would Johnson's. But Bailey and the rest left much to be desired. Readers eager for exact definitions might well be dissatisfied with Bailey's description of a mouse as "an animal well known," or of a net as "a device for catching fish, birds, etc."

After many plans, many false starts, the time had come when someone had to satisfy the general demand. In Johnson the booksellers finally found a man with all the necessary qualifications — a wide knowledge of literature, a tenacious memory, a keen logical mind, and a genius for the succinct definition. All he required was the financial security to keep him alive through the long tedious period of compilation.

It appears likely that some sort of oral agreement was reached between Robert Dodsley and Johnson early in the spring of 1746. In order to make clear exactly what he intended, Johnson wrote an explanation of his scheme. The manuscript is dated April 30.[4] As soon as the plan was agreed upon, the next step was to arrange the financial details. Since no single bookseller wished to be solely responsible for such a large project, a group was finally organized including Robert Dodsley, Andrew Millar, Charles Hitch, John and Paul Knapton, and Thomas Longman and his nephew. By June full agreement had been reached. For the stipulated sum of £1,575 Johnson contracted to produce the dictionary, hoping to have it finished in three years.

For a task in many ways more difficult than those of the Continental scholars, this was a remarkable example of unrealistic optimism. At least so Boswell thought, and he once suggested that Johnson had not known what he was undertaking; to which the older man characteristically replied: "Yes, Sir, I knew very well what I was undertaking, — and very well how to do it, — and have done it very well." When Dr. Adams expostulated with him, "But Sir, how can you do this in three years?" Johnson answered simply, "Sir, I have no doubt that I can do it in three years." When Adams persisted, "But the French Academy, which consists of forty members, took forty years to compile their dictionary," Johnson remained adamant. "Sir, thus it is. This is the proportion. Let me see; forty times forty is sixteen hundred. As three to sixteen hundred, so is the proportion of an Englishman to a Frenchman." [5]

As the great day for signing approached, Johnson wrote from the Golden Anchor near Holborn Bar to Dodsley and to Thomas Longman. The message to Longman read:

> The contract fairly engrossed was sent to me yesterday, I suppose by Mr. Knapton's direction who is out of town. I should think it a favor if you and the rest of the gentlemen would breakfast with me that we may sign. If you will appoint a day and write a note to the rest, the bearer will take it to each of them, or if any other place be more convenient, the writings shall be brought wherever you shall desire.[6]

At last on June 18, 1746, the contract was signed.

One of his first steps was to look for more spacious quarters. As Hawkins remarks, "Johnson, who before this time, together with his wife, had lived in obscurity, lodging at different houses in the courts and alleys in and about the Strand and Fleet Street, had, for the purpose of carrying on this arduous work, and being near the printers employed in it, taken a handsome house in Gough Square, and fitted up a room in it with desks and other accommodations for amanuenses, who, to the number of five or six, he kept constantly under his eye." By the next year, at least, the move was made, for his name appears as the householder in the rate books at the Guildhall.[7]

It was, and still is, a fine substantial building, having three stories and a large garret, where work progressed on the *Dictionary*. Years later visitors vividly described the furnishings of this top floor, including an "old crazy deal table," one solid seat, and an older elbow chair having "only three legs and one arm," on which Johnson balanced "with considerable dexterity and evident practice." [8] He became so accustomed to its defects that when he rose he would "either hold it in his hand, or place it with great composure against some support, taking no notice of its imperfection to his visitor."

The house was the most pretentious home the Johnsons had had since coming to London. A dining room and family sitting

room were on the ground floor. Directly above were a bedroom
and a withdrawing room, the latter partly paneled, with a chair
rail and cornice. These two rooms had double doors which could
be drawn back to the stairway and landing window in order to
form one large room. Above this were two comfortable bed-
rooms. In the basement was the kitchen, with a door leading out
into two large arched cellars which extended under the pavement
of the square. The kitchen had a stone sink and two alcoves for
fireplaces. It is possible that one of the servants — for the establishment was evidently well staffed [9] — slept in the basement,
perhaps under the stairs. At No. 17 Gough Square the Johnsons
lived quite as decently and comfortably as any substantial tradesman.

What the other inhabitants of the square thought of the strange
pair has not come down to us. Sir Harry Gough once told Hector
that he had been obliged to put Johnson out of the house because
the neighbors complained that he kept them awake by walking
about all night talking to himself.[10] But even if true, that would
have been long after Tetty was dead and the *Dictionary* completed, for Johnson lived there until March, 1759.

There is some difference of opinion as to Johnson's procedure
with the new project. From Hawkins and Boswell one might get
the impression that he started by compiling a master list of words
and then searched for authorities to illustrate their use. Bishop
Percy, on the other hand, insists that Johnson first read widely,
picking examples, and then assembled his list. Only near the
end did he depend on the other dictionaries to see what words
had escaped him. Most of the evidence apparently supports this
latter hypothesis.[11]

At some time he probably did use a huge interleaved copy of
Bailey's folio dictionary of 1736. It may have been merely a place
to put miscellaneous notes or a temporary file for the thousands
of slips. It certainly helped to supply words not found in his reading. In the end he failed to use all that he found in Bailey, and
was able to add a good many others, chiefly technical and scientific terms. For these he consulted a variety of special reference
works on the physical sciences, medicine, gardening, and the law.

But finding and listing the words was the least of his tasks. More important was his search for linguistic authority. Intending his work to indicate the best usage by the most correct writers, he prepared to read through a tremendous body of writing in search of examples. Some of the authors he had long known intimately; others were new. Bacon, as he later confessed, was one whom he had not read thoroughly until this time, and one who then became a favorite. As he read, he chose passages for quotation, underlining with a black lead pencil such words as he wished to illustrate. The extent of the quotation was indicated by vertical lines at the beginning and end. Then, for ease in alphabetizing, he wrote in the margin the first letter of the underlined word. Sometimes as many as twenty-four words were marked on a single page.

As soon as he had finished a book, it was passed on to one of his helpers, who methodically copied each marked passage onto a separate slip. Again the word was underlined; and to prevent repetition the capital letter in the margin of the page was crossed through. Then the great stacks of slips were alphabetized, ready for the next step. A number of the volumes actually used survive to this day — stray copies of the works of Shakespeare, Bacon, Izaak Walton, Robert South, Sir Matthew Hale, Isaac Watts, John Norris, and John Fell.[12]

The books were evidently a miscellaneous lot, from his own ragged collection and all he could beg or borrow from friends. The latter, as Hawkins comments, "if ever they came back to those that lent them, were so defaced as to be scarce worth owning, and yet, some of his friends were glad to receive and entertain them as curiosities." [13] If the scrawlings may have irritated some contemporary owners, they delight modern collectors and give priceless evidence of Johnson's regular procedure.

Final copy for the printer was apparently prepared on quarto sheets. According to Boswell, though the story is hard to believe, Johnson at first made a costly mistake. He began with eighty large blank books, using both sides of the leaves. When there was a strenuous objection from the compositors, "it afterward cost him twenty pounds for paper to have them transcribed to be written only on one page." [14] In the final, most practical arrangement, the material was written on the large sheets in two columns, generally only two or three words per column. Johnson in his own hand wrote the words, the etymologies, and the definitions, leaving ample space for the authorities, which were pasted on by the amanuenses. There was constant trouble in providing uniform and tidy copy, and only one of his helpers ever learned to achieve regularity.

In selecting passages for inclusion, Johnson had more than grammatical and stylistic considerations in view. His chief aim was to show how the words were properly used, to illustrate different shades of meaning. But he had also a second requirement, one not always associated with dictionary making.

> When I first collected these authorities, I was desirous that every quotation should be useful to some other end than the illustration of a word; I, therefore, extracted from philosophers principles of science; from historians remarkable facts; from chemists complete processes; from divines striking exhortations; and from poets beautiful descriptions.[15]

His was not to be a mere reference work, but a storehouse of comment on all the important phases of life. His volumes might be read as well as consulted. In choosing his references he was also careful to pick statements consonant with his own convictions. He could inconspicuously teach morals and critical theory at the same time that he helped fix the meaning of the language. He rebelled at the thought of being merely a mechanical drudge.

Though in the end he had to curtail this grandiose plan, forced by limitations of space to leave out many of the collected quotations, enough remained to give the work a strong personal flavor. It did become a compendium of what he considered just criticism. He was able to "relieve the labor of verbal searches, and intersperse with verdure and flowers the dusty deserts of barren philology."

The choice of the word "barren" is revealing. He would never be as interested in the philological part of his task as in the literary and philosophical. When Dr. Adams found him hard at work one day and asked how he was to get all the etymologies,

Johnson casually replied: "Why, Sir, here is a shelf with Junius, and Skinner, and others; and there is a Welsh gentleman who has published a collection of Welsh proverbs, who will help me with the Welsh." [16] He would do what he could easily, but that was all. The classical side he knew well, but he did not have, and never would have, a thorough grounding in Germanic roots.

Boswell proudly pointed out that of Johnson's amanuenses five were Scots — the two Macbeans, Francis Stewart, who died before the *Dictionary* was completed, Robert Shiels, and "Mr. Maitland." Only one, V. J. Peyton, was English. They were a humble lot, improvident and needy; none ever achieved either fame or fortune. But each undoubtedly added something. According to one account, Stewart was useful in explaining "low cant phrases," especially words relating to gambling and card playing. Johnson thought him ingenious and worthy, and spoke well of most of the others. He called Shiels "a man of very acute understanding, though with little scholastic education." He described the unworldly elder Macbean as having great learning and a knowledge of many languages.[17]

For all of them Johnson retained a deep regard long after their intimate connection was over. He loved poor Shiels and helped him in various ways before he died of consumption. When Macbean was starving, Johnson lamented his inability to support him. He did all he could for Peyton, employing him again on later revisions of the *Dictionary*, and was finally "at the expense of burying both him and his wife." If others thought the man "a fool and a drunkard," it was not for Johnson to be censorious. Anyone who had helped him with the great project had a special claim on his affections.

An undated note to the printer, William Strahan, provides some clues as to the financial arrangements:

> I must desire you to add to your other civilities this one, to go to
> Mr Millar and represent to him our manner of going on, and inform
> him that I know not how to manage, I pay three and twenty shillings
> a week to my assistants, in truth without having much assistance from
> them, but they tell me they shall be able to fall better in method,

as indeed I intend they shall. The point is to get two guineas for your humble servant Sam: Johnson.[18]

The bookseller, Andrew Millar, who evidently was the pay-master for the partners, was noted for his generosity to authors, and Johnson once called him the "Maecenas of the age." A very successful businessman, he was "so habitually and equably drunk" that even his closest associate, Strahan, "never perceived that he was more sober at one time than another." It was he who later fervently thanked God when the last sheet of the *Dictionary* was in the printer's hands.

In the early stages it is likely that Johnson was paid a regular sum every Saturday evening, but later the method may have been changed to piece rates of a guinea a printed sheet. Apparently all routine expenses had to be met out of the amount guaranteed him in the contract.

As the group slaved away in the Gough Square garret, copy-ing, pasting, clipping, there must have been amusing interludes. Quite possibly it was a quotation for the *Dictionary* that started Shiels and his employer off on a discussion of the poetry of Thom-son. Although he considered the author of *The Seasons* a true poet, Johnson had some reservations, and described Thomson's chief fault as a cloud of words through which the sense would not always "peep through." In order to prove the point, he took down a copy of the poet's works, read aloud a long passage, and then asked, "Is not this very fine?" The unsuspecting Shiels ex-pressed the highest admiration. "Well," Johnson replied trium-phantly, "I have missed every other line." [19]

Johnson had been at work for almost a year before the public was told about the new undertaking. In March, 1747, however, announcements began to appear in the newspapers: "There is now preparing for the press, and in great forwardness, in two volumes in folio, an English dictionary; etymological, analogical, syntac-tical, explanatory, and critical . . . by Samuel Johnson." [20] Mean-while he was preparing a longer statement of his intentions. The first draft had been drawn up even before signing the contract with the booksellers, but with characteristic procrastination he was slow in getting it ready for the press. Then Dodsley suggested that the plan be dedicated to Lord Chesterfield, one of the most celebrated literary patrons of the day, with the obvious hope of his active support. Not very enthusiastic himself over the idea, Johnson nevertheless agreed. He used this as an excuse for delay: the work must be better done, he claimed, if it were to be presented to Lord Chesterfield. As he remarked to his friend Dr. Bathurst, "Now if any good comes of my addressing to Lord C it will be ascribed to deep policy and address, when in fact it was only a casual excuse for laziness." [21]

While Johnson delayed, however, a copy of the plan reached Chesterfield prematurely by a circuitous and unauthorized route. If anyone was to blame it was John Taylor of Ashbourne, who was visiting in London. He had been given a version for criticism and inadvertently left it lying on his table. There it was seen by a caller, William Whitehead, who was so pleased with the parts he had a chance to read that he begged to take it home with him. When Whitehead failed to return the precious manuscript promptly, Taylor for a week frantically searched everywhere for him. Ruefully he had to confess the state of affairs when Johnson came to see him, but by this time Johnson knew more about what had happened than Taylor. Whitehead had carried the manuscript to Thomas Villiers, later the Earl of Clarendon, who had taken it to Chesterfield. When Taylor tried to argue that it might all have been for the best, Johnson was not convinced. "No Sir it would have come out with more bloom if it had not been seen before by anybody."[22]

Despite any temporary annoyance, Johnson was quite willing to have Chesterfield see and comment on his work. On the final version of his plan, carefully copied by an amanuensis, and later used as printer's copy, Chesterfield wrote eight remarks.[23] For the most part these are merely notes on specific words and phrases and do not contain any general criticism, a fact which may suggest that by the time he saw this last version he had already talked about the project with Dodsley, and possibly had sent messages to Johnson. On the manuscript are other annotations in an unidentified hand, and this second reader, who also discussed specific points, expressed definite approval of one part of the plan.

Johnson refused to adopt all of the suggestions of his readers. While he made some verbal corrections and altered a few passages in deference to the criticisms, there was no servile bowing to his lordship's ideas. But he was glad to quote Chesterfield's opinion, to reinforce his own, about deciding matters of purity and propriety in language.[24]

The Plan of a Dictionary was in print by late July, 1747, and available at Dodsley's shop early in August.[25] In the biweekly periodical *The Museum* of Saturday, August 1, there was an enthusiastic review, with references to "the ingenious author Mr. Samuel Johnson," quotations and summaries of his design, and assurances of his complete fitness for the task. That same day Birch wrote to Yorke, "Johnson has a pamphlet ready for publication at the meeting of the Parliament, upon the scheme of his English dictionary. It is addressed to Ld Chesterfield. I am promised the perusal of it very soon." A week later he added: "Johnson has sent me the *Plan* of his dictionary, of which Dodsley's Museum has given a miserable extract. It is an ingenious performance, but the style too flatulent. Mr. Wray has some objections to his scheme, and even wrote down his remarks upon it." [26]

Others, too, were interested. On the twenty-second Lord Orrery wrote from Ireland of his satisfaction and hopes of seeing the completed work, but not having chanced on the account in the magazine, he was ignorant of many details. In a later letter he asked: "Do you know the author of the Eng. dictionary? I wish the work well done. It is much wanted. I would have a collection of bad phrases, as well as of good, as I would see a bad building to avoid the faults in it." [27]

Although wide distribution of the *Plan* was not scheduled until autumn, one copy at least reached the Continent, to be hailed in the July to September number of the *Bibliothèque raisonnée des ouvrages des savans de l'Europe,* published at Amsterdam. This editor, too, was lavish in praise of the good sense, excellence of view, and subtlety of details shown in the work. "Mr. Johnson" had all the requisites for success, and even those who did not mean to make a special study of English would not find it fruitless to read a letter written "avec une pureté et une élégance peu communes." [28] If the whole work is in the same taste, he concluded, the English will have no cause to complain of having waited for it so long.

Gradually, as the *Plan* reached large numbers of readers, Johnson received more suggestions and comments. Yet the only substantial help came from Zachary Pearce, soon to be Bishop of Bangor, who sent him twenty etymologies.[29] Some of the other suggestions were directly conflicting. In the *Plan* Johnson had pointed out the different pronunciations of the word "great," as a sample of the difficulty of deciding on any one as correct. Many years later he told Boswell, "Lord Chesterfield told me that the word *great* should be pronounced so as to rhyme to *state;* and Sir William Yonge sent me word that it should be pronounced so as to rhyme to *seat,* and that none but an Irishman would pronounce it *grait.* Now here were two men of the highest rank, the one, the best speaker in the House of Lords, the other, the best speaker in the House of Commons, differing entirely." Such conflicting views confirmed him in his decision not to attempt any strict description of proper pronunciation.

In preparing the *Plan*, Johnson apparently waited upon Lord Chesterfield. At first he was graciously received, and once his lordship gave him a present of ten pounds. But the acquaintance never ripened into friendship. Johnson was never invited to dinner.[30] He was kept on the same level as the crowd of sycophants and toadies who clustered about the great man. On occasion he was made to wait or was turned away.

The nineteenth-century painting showing the angry Johnson seated sternly with his hands on his stick in Chesterfield's outer rooms is familiar to everyone. It has even been used to advertise a modern dictionary.[31] Though it is a completely imaginary scene, something like it must have happened in the winter of 1748.

There was a tale, related by Hawkins, and believed by many in Johnson's own time, that the actual split with Chesterfield occurred one day when Johnson made a morning visit and was told that his lordship was engaged with someone else, but would see him as soon as the gentleman left. "It was not till after an hour's waiting that Johnson discovered that this gentleman was Colley Cibber [poet laureate, of course, but second hero of Pope's *Dunciad* and the butt of many Tory jokes], which he had no sooner done, than he rushed out of the house with a resolution never to enter it more." It is a pity to doubt such a dramatic story; yet Johnson told Boswell specifically "that there was not the least foundation for it." As Johnson explained, there never was any particular incident which produced a quarrel between them, "but that his lordship's continued neglect was the reason why he resolved to have no connection with him." [32]

The final break came years later, when the lexicographer's labors were all over. It was then, late in 1754, that Chesterfield was reminded of his responsibilities and highly praised the forthcoming volumes in two unsigned communications to a fashionable periodical. Undoubtedly his motives were excellent. But to Johnson, still smarting from long neglect, it was important that no one should assume that the huge work had been done with the assistance of the nobleman. The record had to be set straight, and so a few months later, when he found out who had written the compliments, Johnson wrote the celebrated letter to his lordship, often called the death knell of patronage.

> Seven years, my Lord, have now passed since I waited in your outward rooms or was repulsed from your door, during which time I have been pushing on my work through difficulties of which it is useless to complain, and have brought it at last to the verge of publication without one act of assistance, one word of encouragement, or one smile of favor. Such treatment I did not expect, for I never had a patron before.

There was a sting in each biting word. The proffered aid now came too late. The little early favors were forgotten, and he remembered only the snubs and the gnawing resentment. He rightly wanted credit for what had been done without support from the great.

The friction was not altogether Chesterfield's fault. He was an important man, in 1748 one of the principal secretaries of state, and was besieged by scores of would-be authors, deluged with dedications, constantly solicited for donations. The great lumbering dictionary maker with the convulsive starts and the rough manners was only one of many. Except for an interest in literature, they had very little in common. Indeed, it would have been hard to find any two men less alike.

The poor scholar and the fashionable courtier, the struggling journalist in his late thirties and the blasé dilettante in his fifties — the contrast has been emphasized over and over again. The passionate and irritable Johnson was always on the verge of an explosion; Chesterfield never allowed anything to ruffle his placid calm, and once boasted that since he had come to maturity he had never once been heard to laugh out loud. The one with sincere piety believed devoutly in God and man; the other, having faith in little besides manners, advised his son for prudential reasons to retain a semblance of morality and religion. Though both were stern realists and each held fast to his own standards, their basic assumptions were worlds apart.

Admittedly such a comparison is unfair to Chesterfield, for the deep humanity of Johnson inevitably makes the other seem hard and brittle. When his lordship is seen by himself, he becomes the symbol of a vanished race, the epitome of an almost forgotten code. He stands for elegance, for the perfect gentleman. Everything considered, he was a remarkable man — brilliant, able, wholly consistent, and kind within his limits. Though he so rigidly repressed all emotions that they became congealed, his intelligence was of a high order, and as a literary stylist he was of the first rank.

In later years Johnson could never quite give the earl his due.[33] In his quoted remarks there was usually some explicit or implied qualification along with the praise. He once said to Boswell that Chesterfield's manner "was exquisitely elegant," and added condescendingly that he "had more knowledge" than he had expected. While admitting the nobleman's dignity, he thought him insolent and the proudest man alive. To another friend he spoke "warmly in commendation of Lord Chesterfield and said that he was the politest man he ever knew — but added, 'indeed he did not think it worth his while to treat me like a gentleman.' " To another he commented that all the celebrated qualities of Chesterfield were "like certain species of fruit which is pleasant enough to the eye, but there is no tasting it without danger."

What did they talk about, this ill-matched pair, on those few occasions when they were together? Language, mostly. When Boswell queried, "Did you find, Sir, his conversation to be of a superior style?" Johnson replied, "Sir, in the conversation which I had with him I had the best right to superiority, for it was upon philology and literature." Yet they also had a few personal ties. They could scarcely have failed to discuss the long-lamented Parson Ford, who had been Chesterfield's friend and chaplain. One topic they undoubtedly did not broach was the fact that they were distantly connected by marriage. It is safe to say that neither had any idea that Chesterfield's younger brother was married to Johnson's cousin's wife's great-niece! [34]

Now that the center of his activity was his own house, there was little need for Johnson to be roaming about the streets. "I am almost always at home," he wrote in one letter.[35] What diversion he had was in literary talk in nearby taverns and coffeehouses, or at the tables of friendly booksellers. He kept making new friends. Two of them were medical men: a strange, grotesque practitioner named Robert Levet, stiff and silent in company, brutal in manners, but "not in his mind"; and the affectionate and agreeable Richard Bathurst, a native of Jamaica.

It was probably at Old Slaughter's Coffee House in St. Martin's Lane — a place much frequented by French emigrés — that he first met Levet. Johnson went there occasionally to learn the language; Levet made the place his headquarters, where he received letters.[36] As a young man he had been a waiter in a Paris coffeehouse and had there attracted the notice of some French surgeons who helped him to a medical education. On returning to London he had picked up a precarious livelihood ministering to the poor. Not much of a reader, he had nevertheless acquired considerable knowledge merely by keeping his ears open. He was diligent and honest. His one failing "was an occasional departure from sobriety." As Johnson later observed, he was the only man he knew who ever became intoxicated "through motives of prudence." When indigent patients, who could pay no fee, offered him a drink instead, he could never resist. No amount of persuasion could break him of the habit of taking his pay "in whatever shape it was exhibited." "He would swallow what he did not like, nay what he knew would injure him, rather than go home with an idea that his skill had been exerted without recompense."

Johnson respected Levet, despite his uncouth manners. For Bathurst, who was also finding it difficult to make a living as a physician, Johnson developed a deep affection, so strong that in later years he could scarcely think of him without tears. He loved him "above all living creatures." [37] Indeed, the two men were completely congenial. In explaining his friend's virtues to Mrs. Thrale, Johnson remarked that Bathurst "was a fine fellow! he hated a fool, and he hated a rogue, and he hated a Whig — he was a very good hater!" With such a companion Johnson could really expand and indulge in the delights of vigorous conversation.

Johnson is best remembered by posterity as a brilliant talker and coiner of phrases. He could express himself in a way that would be easily remembered, and he was proud of this ability. Witty, forceful, succinct — the remarks did not come in a steady stream, but when they did burst forth they were not soon forgotten. There was always some new comparison or colorful example to make an impression. Yet from his early years not many samples have survived. Few of his companions had either the ability or the instincts of a Boswell or a Fanny Burney. Occasionally, however, a saying might be treasured, to be repeated long afterward.

So the painter Francis Hayman remembered a dinner in this period at Tonson's, the bookseller's, when the talk turned to Thomas Edwards's ironical supplement to Warburton's edition of Shakespeare. When most of the guests praised Edwards's book highly, Johnson allowed its merit; but when they went further and appeared to put the author on a level with Warburton, Johnson objected: "Nay, he has given him some smart hits to be sure; but there is no proportion between the two men; they must not be named together. A fly, Sir, may sting a stately horse and make him wince; but one is but an insect, and the other is a horse still." [38]

He had little time for other writing, but he was always ready to help a friend, or to dash off a short piece for a particular assignment. Once there was an emergency at St. John's Gate. John Hawkesworth, who now compiled the poetry section of the *Gentleman's Magazine,* was away, and his substitute, John Ryland, lacked copy for the next issue. When he came begging, Johnson dug out a number of his own early poems and let him have them — "The Winter's Walk," "Stella in Mourning," even some verses written for his friend Harry Hervey to send to an attractive girl in her teens. [39] At times he gave Cave further help, providing a short life of the Earl of Roscommon, and possibly doing some abridgments and notes on foreign history.

When Dodsley planned to rival the publisher Newbery with a work for self-education, he easily secured Johnson's cooperation. To *The Preceptor,* which appeared in April, 1748, the latter made at least two contributions. According to Tyers, both were done in a hurry, the result of early-morning vigils. Johnson sat up a whole night to do the long preface containing a sketch of the entire work; and for the second volume he composed a beautiful allegory of human life called "The Vision of Theodore, the Hermit of Teneriffe," in one night, "after finishing an evening in Holborn." He always wrote his best at top speed. Ideas might mature slowly, but composition came only when the mood was right, and then at white heat. In later years Johnson said that he thought "The Vision of Theodore" the best thing he had ever written. [40]

The preference is understandable, for the tale is a perfect statement of his moral creed. If Reason is "of all subordinate beings the noblest and the greatest," it is only Religion which can lead man through the pitfalls and the mists to the temples of Happiness. Religion alone can bring triumph over Passions and Appetites, and the host of other dangers that lie in wait. For modern readers the piece may be too sententious, too allegorical. Yet the abstract figures do seem to live, and there is a fascination about the troop of Habits, who lie in wait to ensnare travelers on the mountain of Existence, swelling or diminishing as they are welcomed or repelled.

One may perhaps find a clue to what Johnson considered his own worst faults in the convincing description of those lost in the maze of Indolence. Active sinners at least had some pleasures along the way.

> The drunkard for a time laughed over his wine; the ambitious man triumphed in the miscarriage of his rival; but the captives of Indolence had neither superiority nor merriment. Discontent lowered in their looks, and sadness hovered round their shades; yet they crawled on reluctant and gloomy, till they arrived at the depth of the recess, varied only with poppies and nightshade, where the dominion of Indolence terminates, and the hopeless wanderer is delivered up to Melancholy; the chains of Habit are riveted for ever; and Melancholy, having tortured her prisoner for a time, consigns him at last to the cruelty of Despair.

When his former pupil became manager of the Drury Lane Theatre in the autumn of 1747 Johnson provided a special prologue for the opening. Years later he told George Steevens that the entire sixty-two lines were composed before he set down a single couplet, and added, "I did not afterward change more than a word in it, and that was done at the remonstrance of Garrick. I did not think his criticism just; but it was necessary he should be satisfied with what he was to utter." [41]

Possibly Garrick spoke the prologue at the very first performance of the season on September 15, but it was advertised in the papers only for the productions of the 17th and 19th.[42] Then Garrick's illness intervened and it was put aside. As some compensation for the obvious disappointment of the public, the verses, along with an epilogue by someone else, were published on October 8, but with no indication of authorship. Like so many of Johnson's early pieces, it added little to his immediate reputation. His only reward was the enjoyment of hearing his majestic lines reverberating through a major London theater.

If the history of the English stage showed a steady decline from the days of Jonson and Shakespeare; if pantomime, musical extravaganzas, and dancers appeared triumphant, it was the public's fault:

> Ah! let not Censure term our Fate our Choice,
> The Stage but echoes back the publick Voice.
> The Drama's Laws the Drama's Patrons give,
> And we that live to please, must please to live.

The words were Johnson's, but it was Garrick who spoke to the audience. And he ended on a brighter note:

> 'Tis yours this Night to bid the Reign commence
> Of rescu'd Nature, and reviving Sense;
> To chase the Charms of Sound, the Pomp of Show,
> For useful Mirth, and salutary Woe;
> Bid scenic Virtue form the rising Age,
> And Truth diffuse her Radiance from the Stage.

Evidently the young manager, entering on his new responsibilities, had high hopes. Garrick intended to raise the tone of the theater. He would help the serious dramatists of his own day. As part of this brave plan, he had an old commitment, a debt incurred long ago to his own schoolmaster. That much is clear from a comment of Birch to Yorke on September 26, that Garrick "designs Thomson's Coriolanus, Johnson's Irene, and a comedy by Mr. Moore, the author of *Fables in Verse,* for our entertainment this winter." [43]

The inclusion of Johnson's work in the list was more than a mere act of friendship, for Garrick had a genuine, if qualified, respect for the tragedy. The spring before at a private gathering he had repeated lines from *Irene* to an admiring audience.[44] He must have thought it on a par with the dramas of the more famous poets Thomson and Young. Johnson was soon to find, however, that even with a sympathetic manager, getting a new play produced was a slow process.

At first Garrick postponed casting until after Christmas; then other matters occupied his attention, and the season wore on with no action. By the following September there still had been little progress. For almost ten years Johnson had been vainly trying to get *Irene* on the stage. With one disappointment after another, he had seen his hopes raised and then dashed to bits. Now, finally, the end was in sight. On September 3, 1748, Birch wrote, "Johnson tells me, that he is agreed with Garrick for the bringing his *Irene* upon the stage next winter." [45] This time a manager was to live up to his word. In less than six months Johnson would finally take his place as a London playwright.

Meanwhile he had kept steadily at work on the *Dictionary,* and by the late summer of 1748 had made surprising progress. On the face of it, he was keeping to his schedule of completion in three years' time. This much is apparent from a letter of Birch to his patron on August 6:

> Johnson has four amanuenses still employed in his English dictionary; but their business will soon be over; for they have almost transcribed the authorities, which he has marked for them in the writers, whom he considers as the standard of our language. Pope and Spence settled the catalogue of these writers some years ago; and Sir Phil. Sidney and Raleigh are the earliest, who are admitted. When the transcribers have done their task, Johnson will begin to correct their papers, and draw them up into form. He intends to reside several months at Oxford and Cambridge for the benefit of the libraries there, in order to settle the etymological part especially.[46]

To his friends Johnson gave the impression that all was going well. But appearances were deceptive. He was doomed to seven more years of disappointment and frustration before he could bask in universal acclaim as "Dictionary" Johnson.

The Vanity of Human Wishes

DURING the autumn of 1748 Johnson was actually in a somber mood. Despite encouraging progress on the *Dictionary*, despite imminent production of his tragedy, despite better living conditions, there was much to keep him depressed. He was still plagued by financial worries, illness, and his old constitutional lethargy. Moreover, he was soon to find that he had grossly underestimated the difficulties of the latter stages of his great project. What he had done so far was the easiest. It would be two years before even the first three letters of the alphabet were set up by the compositors.[1]

But the chief cause of his low spirits was undoubtedly domestic. At home there was little or nothing to cheer him when he came downstairs after hours of drudgery in the garret. Tetty's health was poor, her temper uncertain, her petty demands increasing.[2] She was no happy wife to calm his jaded nerves or talk him out of his melancholy. Marriage, he was gradually finding out, had many pains.

Depending largely on the fervent references in Johnson's later prayers, Boswell tended to sentimentalize Tetty. He played down or failed to comment on her faults, and allowed readers to imagine manifold virtues. Apparently he considered the unfavorable accounts he heard from Johnson's earlier friends to be biased, and preferred to accept his hero's memories. Succeeding generations have willingly followed suit, seeing no reason to search for shadows when the traditional picture was so appealing. Thus Johnson's tender devotion to "dear Tetty" and his pious cherishing of her memory have become essential parts of the legend of the great man.

Not that the picture is false. The two were held together by

strong ties. He continued to think highly of her intelligence and
critical ability. Until her last years he made a habit of consulting
her about his writings. As Shaw remarked, "Notwithstanding
these petty differences, they regarded each other with true cordiality and affection. Both suffered from oddities, which it was impossible to conquer; but mutually reposed a steadfast confidence,
while it was their happiness to live together." [3]

Johnson did nurse Tetty tenderly during her last illness. He
did keep the anniversary of her death "with prayer and tears." As
he grew older, she was often in his mind: "When I saw the sea
at Brighthelmston, I wished for her to have seen it with me." He
called the saucer on which his roll was placed every morning for
breakfast "Tetty" because it had belonged to her. He desperately
wanted to remember their undoubted mutual devotion: "Poor
Tetty, whatever were our faults and failings, we loved each
other." [4] But this was his later simplification. While they were
living together there had been constant friction. He once confessed that he never knew how dear she was to him until he had
lost her.[5]

Chivalry demands that a lady's imperfections be quickly forgotten. In this instance, however, there is a more important consideration, for one cannot understand Johnson the man without
getting at the whole truth about Tetty. The gradual change of
the buxom, affectionate bride of 1735 into the difficult hypochondriac of 1748 left an indelible mark on the character of her
husband.

Tetty's failings during her last years are described by at least
five people who either knew her intimately or were friendly with
Johnson while she was alive — Garrick, Taylor, Dr. Levet, Mrs.
Desmoulins, and Hawkins. None of the evidence is vague hearsay. Even when it reaches us through a second person, it is the
testimony of those who ought to have known the truth. Each of
the sources alone might reasonably be questioned, but taken col-
lectively they are convincing.

Garrick's unflattering portrait of her as a fat, painted, and affected coquette has already been mentioned.[6] Dr. Robert Levet,
whom Johnson had met as early as 1746, later reported that

Tetty "was always drunk and reading romances in her bed, where she killed herself by taking opium." [7] John Taylor, who knew Johnson as well as anyone, went even further: "She was the plague of Johnson's life, was abominably drunken and despicable. . . . Johnson had frequently complained to him of the wretchedness of his situation with such a wife." [8] It is said that Taylor refused to preach the funeral sermon written by Johnson for his wife because the praise was too excessive. From Mrs. Desmoulins, through both Boswell and Shaw, comes similar evidence.

While discounting obvious exaggeration, one can hardly suspect all these people of conspiring to fabricate a distorted picture of Tetty. Each gave his characterization independently of the others; there was nothing in print which might have suggested a common theme. There was no possible reason why they should all want to present a false image. Moreover, Taylor is corroborated by Shaw, who wrote that "a suspicion of his conjugal infelicity on this account certainly went abroad, and procured him much commiseration among his friends." So persuaded was Hawkins of these domestic tribulations that he even suggested that Johnson's fulsome sentimentalizing "was a lesson that he had learned by rote." [9]

Tetty was too fond of drinking; of that there can be little doubt. The habit may have come late in life, along with the taking of opiates, to assuage sickness and pain. But there is also the possibility that from the start Johnson recognized his wife's weakness, and took steps to help her conquer her craving. The dates of his first giving up wine himself are significant; he appears to have been a total abstainer from about 1736 until the middle or late 1750s — that is, from shortly after his marriage until a few years after Tetty's death. [10] He might have given up drinking himself as an example to her.

Of even more importance to Johnson emotionally was the waning of her amorous inclinations. At Tetty's request, they did not sleep together for many years. Using the excuse of constant illness, she said that she could not bear to have a bedfellow. This startling piece of information comes from Mrs. Desmoulins, who spoke with authority, since as a young woman she had lived with Tetty on a number of occasions. To illustrate her point, Mrs. Desmoulins described for Boswell one particular incident which occurred out at Hampstead.[11] (He wrote the conversation down, though obviously he could never put it into print.) At the time Mrs. Desmoulins was sleeping on a small bed in the same room with Tetty. When another woman came for a visit, it was evident that the small bed would not hold two, and so Tetty allowed Mrs. Desmoulins to come in with her. But it was only after a strict promise not to tell her husband. If he heard that she allowed anyone at all as a bedfellow, he would be more persistent himself.

What had begun as a love match, with strong attraction on both sides, had turned into something very different. Still young and vigorous, Johnson had strong passions. He craved love and tenderness. Yet now he found himself yoked to an ailing old woman whose chief desire was to be let alone. And moralist that he was, he could not easily look elsewhere for satisfaction, as others would have done.

Not that Tetty would have objected strenuously. As he once told Boswell, in an exchange canceled from the *Life* only at the last minute, "My wife told me I might lie with as many women as I pleased, provided I *loved* her alone." Boswell, much shocked, expostulated, "She was not in earnest." "But she was," Johnson went on; "consider, Sir, how gross it is in a wife to complain of her husband's going to other women, merely as women; it is that she has not enough of what she would be ashamed to avow." [12] When Boswell characteristically probed further, the colloquy continued: BOSWELL. "Suppose, Sir, a woman to be of a very cold constitution, has she any right to complain of her husband's infidelity?" JOHNSON. "Sir, if she refuses, she has no right to complain." BOSWELL. "Then, Sir, according to your doctrine, upon every such occasion a man may make a note in his pocket-book, and do as he pleases." Johnson's reply to this sally is not recorded. Though he might talk thus in the heat of conversation, he was arguing theoretically about a woman's right to feel hurt. He might well have taken an opposite position on moral grounds. At the beginning he had carefully made the qualification, "Between a man and his Maker it is a different question."

As much of the time as possible Tetty remained away from the dirt and fogs of the city. "She indulged herself in country air and nice living, at an unsuitable expense, while her husband was drudging in the smoke of London." This was Boswell's way of putting it.[13] Her favorite refuge was Hampstead, then a popular resort, whose fine air and chalybeate springs were thought to have great health-giving properties. Here Tetty had lodgings in a small house beyond the church, known as Priory Lodge, and her husband joined her whenever he could. According to one account they had visited the place as early as 1746; they were certainly there in the autumn of 1748.

It must have been about this time that an incident occurred which Mrs. Desmoulins later described so vividly to Boswell to illustrate how Johnson restrained his strong passions.[14] When his wife was at Hampstead he came out two or three days every week, and sometimes when Dr. Bathurst was in the neighborhood would spend the evening with his friend, staying up until two or three in the morning. Since Tetty went to bed early and the maid could not be expected to wait up that late, it devolved upon Mrs. Desmoulins to sit up to let him in and to warm his bed with a pan of coals. Thus it happened that the thirty-two-year-old daughter of his godfather, Dr. Swinfen, assumed some of the duties of his wife. Hating to go to sleep, desperately needing affection, Johnson would quickly undress and then call her back to sit on his bed and talk. While Tetty slept soundly in another room, he would discuss the affairs of the day and would kiss and fondle the younger woman, who sometimes even lay with her head on his pillow. Not that the endearments ever went too far. Mrs. Desmoulins was very clear on that point. She always respected him as a father. There had never been anything beyond the bounds of decency. For her it was the humoring of an honored friend. For him it was something more — a pathetic longing for tenderness and sympathy, combined with a dangerous playing with smoldering passions he was determined to repress. As she once confessed to another lady, such was the awe and respect she had for him she

could never have resisted if matters had come to extremities. It was
Johnson who drew back. When the desire became almost more
than he could bear he would push her away and cry out in an-
guish for her to leave him. She could plainly see the struggle and
the conquest.

The same struggle was to go on for the rest of his life. In his
later prayers come frequent pleas to the Almighty to "purify my
thoughts from pollutions," "grant me chaste in thoughts, words
and actions," "reject or expel sensual images." He asks that "all
corrupt desires may be extinguished." There are repeated sad comments: "I have lived totally useless, more sensual in thought . . ."
"My thoughts have been clouded with sensuality." [15]

Was he always able to suppress his craving? Many have wondered, and there have been dark hints that sometime during his
youth he had been led into immorality, the remembrance of
which haunted him until his death. Peter Garrick told Boswell the
rather improbable tale that "a lady, a very fine woman, said to
him that Mr. Johnson was a very seducing man among the
women when he chose it; and he added that it was suspected he
had seduced her." There was even a report that the popular and
promiscuous actress Peg Woffington had made advances to him.[16]
Boswell recorded that in May, 1785, he and Sir John Hawkins had
a pleasant meeting, "stood in a corner and talked grave and
earnest." Then followed a remarkable exchange. "He accounted
for Johnson's fear of death. 'I have read his diary. I wish I had
not read so much. He had strong amorous passions.' BOSWELL. 'But
he did not indulge them?' HAWKINS. 'I have said enough.' " [17]

The obvious suggestion is that Hawkins had seen definite
confessions, and it may be that there was something explicit in
the diaries supposedly burned by Johnson just before his death.
But there is not a shred of authentic evidence of immorality in
any of the surviving records. It would not have taken much to stir
up the suspicions of the strait-laced Hawkins. The constant references in Johnson's *Prayers and Meditations* to "sensuality" and
"corrupt desires," together with the continual harping on guilt
and mortification, might well have led him to a false conclusion.

Johnson's repeated admissions of guilt could refer to something else. The sins which he constantly lamented may have been selfish demands on a reluctant wife. It is quite possible that, looking back, he felt his emphasis on his conjugal rights had contributed to Tetty's drinking and to her other ills.

A little over a year after her death he asked forgiveness for "all the sins committed," and for "all duties neglected, in my union with the wife whom thou hast taken from me," and added, "grant that the loss of my wife may so mortify all inordinate affections in me, that I may henceforth please thee by holiness of life." And on another day, "Let the remembrance of thy judgments by which my wife is taken away awaken me to repentance." [18]

Johnson was the kind of man who magnified his sins and instead of forgetting them brooded over and stressed past offenses. Because of his overscrupulosity he would have blamed himself for anything which resembled excessive lust, even in his marriage. Thus the reiterated expressions of remorse in later years, reflecting so clearly a deep-seated sense of guilt, might well have been caused by his aggressive attitude toward Tetty. [19]

With such strong passions, why did he never take a second wife? He had no settled aversion to remarriage. The truth is he did consider such a step. He went even further and actually planned to fill Tetty's place. The evidence, long hidden, was known to Boswell, who presumably censored it out of respect for Johnson and for Tetty's memory. But it is clear and to the point. [20] In his diary entry of April 22, 1753, about a year and a month after his wife's death, Johnson wrote, "As I purpose to try on Monday to seek a new wife without any derogation from dear Tetty's memory I purpose at Sacrament in the morning to take my leave of Tetty in a solemn commendation of her soul to God."

The next day he added, "Yesterday as I purposed I went to Bromley where dear Tetty lies buried and received the Sacrament first praying before I went to the altar, according to the prayer precomposed for Tetty and a prayer which I made against unchastity idleness and neglect of public worship. I made it during sermon which I could not perfectly hear." Over and over he repeated his commendation of her, in church, in the garden later, and at home at night. The entry ended with the comment, "During the whole service I was never once distracted by any thoughts of any other woman or with my design of a new wife which freedom of mind I remembered with gladness in the garden. God guide me."

What he intended specifically to do on Monday, whether he had anyone definitely in mind, or why nothing ever came of his determination — these questions remain unanswered. There were a number of ladies whom he greatly admired, among them the pious Hill Boothby and the attractive Charlotte Cotterell. But he may not have planned an immediate proposal. Doubtless all he meant was that, having grieved for a decent interval, he now felt at liberty to consider his own future. The episode is important here chiefly as it shows Johnson's common-sense willingness, after the death of Tetty, to find another, perhaps more compliant, helpmate.

But in 1748 Tetty was still very much alive and Johnson was involved in many vexing problems. Everything seemed to increase the "gloomy irritability of his existence." [21] Unhappily he looked about him, only to find much to be endured and little to be enjoyed. In this sober, depressed mood he wrote his finest poem, *The Vanity of Human Wishes*.

Part of his dejection, no doubt, came from the temper of the times, for the 1740s in England were largely years of dissatisfaction and unrest. Instead of improvement, the long-awaited fall of Walpole had brought only political stagnation. Frustrating foreign wars and miserable internal corruption contributed to the general distress. By 1748 one newspaper could comment on the "wretched condition of the English people" — a condition "nobody denies: It is severely felt in every family." [22] The poets, too, mirrored this dejection. This was the period of the so-called "Graveyard School," when Young, Blair, Gray, and the others showed the uncertainties of creative artists in that shadow land where doubt of Augustan critical standards had not yet been replaced by any positive romantic creed.

The papers were full of advertisements for patent medicines designed to cure the "hypochondriac melancholy *in men* and the hysteric disease or vapors *in women*" — most noble elixirs guaranteed to bring "a new train of cheerful and pleasant ideas, instead of those deep and black thoughts, those direful apprehensions." [23]

But no "true cordial quintessence of vipers" would chase away Johnson's depressed, melancholy musings. Nor could he attain purgation through the "congenial glooms" of graveyard poetry. Skulls, coffins, epitaphs, and worms were not to his taste. When he read Blair's *The Grave,* he was not enthusiastic,[24] and he remained unmoved by the new literary trends. For him the noblest expression of the old theme of Ecclesiastes — "Vanity of vanities; all is vanity" — could be found elsewhere.

According to Boswell, Johnson once admitted that he had all of Juvenal's satires "in his head." [25] The one that haunted him most in the autumn of 1748 was the tenth. How easy it would be to fit its theme to life as he saw it! Over sixteen centuries earlier Juvenal had weighed each human desire and found it wanting. He set up one ambition after another, only to see it toppled by its own weight. Johnson, brooding over the eternal problems, found nothing changed. Wealth, power, glory, scholarship, heroism, old age, beauty — none would bring perfect happiness. For every worldly pleasure there was a corresponding pain. Gold inevitably brought more troubles than delights; greatness brought dangers; beauty, suspicion and rivalry; old age, sickness and regrets.

> Year chases year, decay pursues decay,
> Still drops some joy from with'ring life away.

As he strode ponderously up and down the gardens at Hampstead, faced the bracing breezes on the upper heath, or sat in his room in the "small house beyond the church," Johnson fashioned modern counterparts to the examples of the bitter Roman. Couplet after couplet fell quickly into place. It is impossible to be sure that all of the poem was composed in the autumn of 1748; perhaps for years passages had been vaguely in his mind. But the first

seventy lines, he admitted, were written down in the course of a
morning at Hampstead.[26] There he found the leisure as well as
the emotional compulsion.

The whole poem was well worked out before he put anything
on paper. Bishop Percy thought the reason was his poor eyesight,
the fact that writing was inconvenient for him, since he was
obliged to hold the paper close to his face.[27] But there was also
his temperamental dislike of physical work. Once Johnson explained to Boswell how he made verses. "I have generally had
them in my mind, perhaps fifty at a time, walking up and down
in my room; and then I have written them down, and often, from
laziness, have written only half lines. . . . I remember I wrote a
hundred lines of 'The Vanity of Human Wishes' in a day." [28]

It was completed by late November, and on the twenty-fifth he
sold the copyright to Dodsley for fifteen guineas. Early the following January it appeared as a thin quarto of twenty-eight pages.

Though fashioned in the classic mode, *The Vanity of Human
Wishes* was not a mere imitation. Even more than in *London,*
Johnson allowed himself every liberty. He took what he wanted
from Juvenal and infused it with his own personality. The tone
was changed and there were constant shifts of emphasis. As one
recent critic has commented, Juvenal's "mordant mockery" was
transmuted into "abstract gloom." [29] In many ways the resulting
poem was just as much Johnson's as if he had had no model.

Many of the details came directly out of Johnson's own experience. He had been a sensitive observer; he had seen only too well
the struggles of those about him for happiness. He was not fooled
by the mirth and jollity of the merrymakers. Underneath, he suspected, there was universal disappointment. The pleasures of this
world were only drugs to keep the mind occupied. Such were his
thoughts when he visited the pleasure gardens at Ranelagh. The
first view "gave an expansion and gay sensation to his mind that
nothing else had done." Then came the sobering reflection: "But
as Xerxes wept to think that not one of his great army would be
alive [a hundred] years after, he thought that there was not one
in the brilliant crowd at Ranelagh that was not afraid to go home

and think. The thoughts of each individual there would be distressing when alone." [30] When Boswell objected that "being in love or having some fine project for next day might preserve felicity," Johnson admitted "there might be such instances," but he would not alter his general conclusion.

As he composed his sonorous lines, Johnson must have been haunted by the inevitable question of what all this meant to him. Had he found anything the philosophers of the past had missed? Had he, Sam Johnson, anything of consequence to look forward to? Great wealth, power, beauty — these were obviously beyond him. Love and passion, domestic bliss? He thought of what had happened to his own marriage. He remembered the quarrels of his own parents. A tranquil old age? The years would bring only more physical infirmity. Fame as a scholar and author?

> Yet hope not life from grief or danger free,
> Nor think the doom of man revers'd for thee:
> Deign on the passing world to turn thine eyes,
> And pause awhile from learning to be wise;
> There mark what ills the scholar's life assail;
> Toil, envy, want, the garret, and the jail.
> See nations slowly wise, and meanly just,
> To buried merit raise the tardy bust.
> If dreams yet flatter, once again attend,
> Hear Lydiat's life, and Galileo's end.[31]

A munificent patron? Not Lord Chesterfield. The line would soon be changed to read "Toil, envy, want, the patron, and the jail."

Again, as in *London,* the abstract truths were charged with deep emotion. This was no casual playing with words. This was life as he himself had known it, and the personifications and general terms were transfused with the weight of human experience.

Was there nothing for man to do?

> Where then shall Hope and Fear their objects find?
> Must dull Suspense corrupt the stagnant mind?
> Must helpless man, in ignorance sedate,
> Roll darkling down the torrent of his fate?

> Must no dislike alarm, no wishes rise,
> No cries attempt the mercies of the skies?
> Enquirer, cease, petitions yet remain,
> Which heav'n may hear, nor deem religion vain.
> Still raise for good the supplicating voice,
> But leave to heav'n the measure and the choice,
> Safe in his pow'r, whose eyes discern afar
> The secret ambush of a specious pray'r.
> Implore his aid, in his decisions rest,
> Secure whate'er he gives, he gives the best.

Yet faith alone was not enough.

> Pour forth thy fervours for a healthful mind,
> Obedient passions, and a will resign'd;
> For love, which scarce collective man can fill;
> For patience sov'reign o'er transmuted ill;
> For faith, that panting for a happier seat,
> Counts death kind Nature's signal of retreat:
> These goods for man the laws of heav'n ordain,
> These goods he grants, who grants the pow'r to gain;
> With these celestial wisdom calms the mind,
> And makes the happiness she does not find.

Thus the poem ended on the note of Christian stoicism. But it was a resignation brightened by hope for the next world. He would never give up his firm hold on orthodox Christian faith. Though skeptical of almost everything else, Johnson clung to the one authority he would not allow himself to doubt.

In one way the poem was a milestone; in another, an epitome. As the first of his works to bear his name boldly on the title page, it symbolized his emergence as an author. His days as an unknown, anonymous hack were over. It was also a summation of his ripened philosophy of life. By the beginning of his fortieth year his character was fully formed, his convictions settled. He knew exactly where he stood, and he would change little in the years to come. Ten years later *Rasselas* would largely repeat in prose the conclusions of *The Vanity of Human Wishes*.

He had something significant to say to his own age, which was alien to the nineteenth-century point of view but has more and more relevance to the mid-twentieth. The important thing, he stresses over and over again, is to be realistic, never to fool oneself. One should see clearly the inevitable tragedy of mankind as well as its nobility. A sensible person must realize the hopelessness of most human aspirations — man cannot by himself create a brave new world — and yet keep them as goals. Though the best that can be done is to palliate suffering, not remove it altogether, men must not sink back into supine inaction. Retirement from society is not the answer, nor is a blind refusal to recognize evil. It is necessary, he felt, to accept the improbability of major improvement and yet try continually to better the conditions of individual men and women.

Johnson could never be a bitter cynic. There is an exhilaration, almost a feeling of triumph, in his despair. Like the classic dramatists, he sensed the grandeur of man's struggle, at the same time that he was sure there could be no victory except in heaven.

Courage is his theme, just as it was the dominant driving force of his life. He was always ready to face with obstinate tenacity whatever was to come. He had endured one trouble and disappointment after another — the physical ills of childhood, the insecurity at home, the business decline of his father, the break in his own university education, the long series of failures as a schoolmaster, the harrowing struggles as a translator and journalist, the disappointments of his marriage. He well knew his own weaknesses, that he was lazy, indolent, irritable, subject to fits of deep melancholy. Yet despite all, he had absolute confidence in his own superior ability. The "brave boy" who had had such trouble breathing in his first moments of life had developed powerful resources sufficient to surmount most obstacles.

Besides, there was still much to enjoy. Though life was basically tragic, one could accept what was pleasant without becoming either a naïve optimist or a hedonist. In his own personality Johnson epitomized this fundamental compromise. Having little hope, he enjoyed to the utmost those pleasures available to him. In theory despondent, he could find many things to relish. No one has more succinctly summed up the basic paradox of his character than Joseph Wood Krutch: "Samuel Johnson was a pessimist with an enormous zest for living." [32]

Even as his statement of the vanity of all human wishes was coming from the press, Johnson characteristically found time for frivolity. *Irene* was at last to be produced at Drury Lane. To be ready for the occasion, he ordered a scarlet waistcoat, with rich gold lace, and a gold-laced hat.[33]

One of the best antidotes for melancholy, he had found, was conversation. He might form a club with Bathurst, Hawkesworth, John Hawkins, and others. They could meet every Tuesday at the King's Head, the famous beefsteak house in Ivy Lane near St. Paul's. While the others had their punch and wine, he could drink gallons of lemonade and still be the wittiest and gayest of the party.[34] He would talk far into the morning, as long as anyone would sit up with him.

Young Sam Johnson, the Lichfield bookseller's son, was now Samuel Johnson, soon to be well known as the author of two widely admired poems and of a tragedy which had moderate success, and as compiler of the best dictionary of the English language.[35] He would be Mr. Samuel Johnson, author of that much-respected but meagerly supported periodical *The Rambler*. Moralist, editor, literary critic, he would eventually become Dr. Johnson, center of a fabulous group of the most gifted men and women in the realm. He would be more written about and better described than any other literary man of his age. Though his greatest works still lay ahead, he had become, to all intents and purposes, the man Boswell was to describe. The curtain was just going up on the spectacle of his life which has become so well known.

In 1749, however, Johnson could scarcely have guessed what was in store for him. He could have had no premonition of the brilliant social life at Streatham or in the London bluestocking assemblies. Only in his fondest dreams would he have imagined a personal meeting with the King, or an honorary doctor's degree from the university he had attended only thirteen months and left because his toes were sticking out from his shoes. But most astonishing of all would have been the knowledge that a Scottish boy of eight in far-off Edinburgh was preparing to assist him toward immortality. Jamie Boswell, conning his lessons in his father's house in Parliament Close, was also on his way toward lasting fame. Two life lines were slowly converging toward that historic meeting in Tom Davies's back parlor.

Notes

CUE TITLES

Account — An Account of the Life of Dr. Samuel Johnson, from His Birth to His Eleventh Year, Written by Himself, ed. Richard Wright (London, 1805); reprinted in G. B. Hill's *Johnsonian Miscellanies* (Oxford, 1897), Vol. I, where it is misnamed "Annals." Page references are to the latter, more accessible, source; quotations are from the first printing.

BP — The Private Papers of James Boswell from Malahide Castle in the Collection of Lieut.-Col. Ralph H. Isham, ed. Geoffrey Scott and Frederick A. Pottle, 18 vols. (privately printed, 1928–1934).

Bibliography — William P. Courtney and David Nichol Smith, *A Bibliography of Samuel Johnson,* revised edition (Oxford, 1925).

Boswell, *Tour to the Hebrides — Boswell's Journal of A Tour to the Hebrides with Samuel Johnson, LL.D. Now First Published from the Original Manuscript,* ed. Frederick A. Pottle and Charles H. Bennett (New York and London, 1936).

Boswell's Note Book — Boswell's Note Book 1776–1777, ed. R. W. Chapman (London, 1925).

Gleanings — Aleyn Lyell Reade, *Johnsonian Gleanings,* 11 volumes (privately printed, 1909–1952).

Greene — Donald J. Greene, *The Politics of Samuel Johnson: an Introductory Study of His Political Milieu, Activities, Attitudes, and Ideas,* dissertation, Columbia University (Ann Arbor, Mich.: University Microfilms, 1954).

Hawkins — Sir John Hawkins, *The Life of Samuel Johnson, LL.D.* (London, 1787).

Johns. Misc. — Johnsonian Miscellanies, ed. G. B. Hill, 2 vols. (Oxford, 1897).

Johnson's *Letters* — *The Letters of Samuel Johnson,* ed. R. W. Chapman, 3 vols. (Oxford, 1952).

Krutch — Joseph Wood Krutch, *Samuel Johnson* (New York, 1944).

Life — *Boswell's Life of Johnson,* ed. G. B. Hill, revised and enlarged by L. F. Powell, 6 vols. (Oxford, 1934, 1950).

Lives of the Poets — *Lives of the English Poets by Samuel Johnson, LL.D.,* ed. G. B. Hill, 3 vols. (Oxford, 1905).

Piozzi, *Anecdotes* — Hester Lynch Piozzi, *Anecdotes of the Late Samuel Johnson, LL.D.,* ed. G. B. Hill in *Johnsonian Miscellanies,* Vol. I (Oxford, 1897). All references are made to this edition.

Poems — *The Poems of Samuel Johnson,* ed. David Nichol Smith and Edward L. McAdam, Jr. (Oxford, 1941).

Prayers and Meditations — *Prayers and Meditations, Composed by Samuel Johnson, LL.D.,* ed. G. B. Hill in *Johnsonian Miscellanies,* Vol. I (Oxford, 1897).

Shaw — William Shaw, *Memoirs of the Life and Writings of the Late Dr. Samuel Johnson* (published anonymously, London, 1785).

Thraliana — *Thraliana: The Diary of Mrs. Hester Lynch Thrale (Later Mrs. Piozzi) 1776–1809,* ed. Katharine C. Balderston, 2 vols. (Oxford, 1942; reprinted 1951).

Tyers — Thomas Tyers, *A Biographical Sketch of Dr. Samuel Johnson.* The original version appeared in *Gentleman's Magazine* for December, 1784. A revised and expanded separate printing has been reproduced in facsimile by the Augustan Reprint Society (1952), and references are to this edition.

Works — *The Works of Samuel Johnson, LL.D.,* 11 vols. (Oxford, 1825). The edition most generally available.

Yale Boswell Papers — Unprinted manuscripts from the collection of James Boswell now in the Library of Yale University, New Haven, Conn.

PREFACE

1. Piozzi, *Anecdotes,* p. 148. On occasion Johnson readily answered Boswell's questions about his early life (*BP,* VI, 105; *Tour to the Hebrides,* p. 300), but the younger man was apparently afraid to probe very deeply into family matters.

ILLUSTRATIONS

1. Supposed to be Michael Johnson, engraved in 1835 by E. Finden from a drawing then in the possession of the publisher John Murray. It was published the same year in Murray's *Graphic Illustrations of the Life and Times of Samuel Johnson,* and in 1836 in his *Johnsoniana.* I have been unable to find the original or check its authenticity in any way.

2. First described in *Gent. Mag.* LXXXVIII (March, 1818), 194. According to this account, the miniature was given by Dr. Johnson, shortly before his death, to Mrs. Barber, wife of his servant. It was first reproduced as a frontispiece to Vol. 1 of the Croker edition of the *Life* (1831), where it was described as "a miniature worn in a bracelet by Mrs. Johnson." For further details see *Life,* IV, 458; *Gleanings,* II, 85. I have been unable to find the original.

3. Original oil painting now at Johnson's Birthplace, Lichfield. There are no contemporary references to it. In the mid-nineteenth century it was in the collection of the Bishop of Ely, who thought it a genuine portrait of Johnson by Sir Joshua Reynolds. If so, it could not have been done from life since the two men did not meet until early in the 1750s. It may, of course, have been an imaginary re-creation of what Reynolds thought Johnson looked like in his youth, but more likely it was painted earlier by an unknown artist. In 1854 the picture was engraved in mezzotint by George Zobel, who made Johnson lean on a thick copy of *Irene,* not in the original version. Dr. L. F. Powell (*Life,* IV. 453) accepts it as meant to represent Johnson, and Mr. Herman W. Liebert, the foremost American expert on Johnson iconography, concurs. The features and expression, however, have obviously been romanticized.

CHAPTER I

1. The *Account* was not available to Boswell, for it was first printed in 1805 by Richard Wright, who had secured it from the widow of Francis Barber, Johnson's old servant. See list of cue titles. I have been unable to discover the present whereabouts of the original manuscript. The date of composition is derived from a note by Wright, on what authority it is not clear. In this chapter, unless otherwise noted, all remarks specifically by Johnson himself are from this source.

2. The description of Johnson and his mood about the time of writing the *Account* comes from *Life,* I, 483–486, and *Prayers and Meditations,* pp. 32–33. For his place of residence see *Life,* III, 535.

3. This refers to the Gregorian calendar, not adopted in England until 1752. For the most detailed analysis of

all the evidence concerning Johnson's early years and his family see *Gleanings,* particularly Vols. III and X.

4. Percy Laithwaite, *History of the Lichfield Conduit Lands Trust* (1947), 70–71. The street was variously called "Sadler" or "Market," the latter being the present name.

5. *The Rambler,* No. 60.

6. *Johns. Misc.,* I, 360; Sophie v. la Roche, *Sophie in London, 1786,* ed. Clare Williams (1933), 186; Peter Pineo Chase, "The Ailments and Physicians of Dr. Johnson," *Yale Journal of Biology and Medicine,* XXIII (April, 1951), 370–379.

7. For details of the trip see *Gleanings,* III, 61–66; *Account,* pp. 133–135; *Life,* I, 41–43; *Thraliana,* p. 160. Descriptions of the ceremony come from Raymond Crawfurd, *The King's Evil* (1911), 144–149; M. R. Hopkinson, *Anne of England* (1935), 179–180. See also W. T. Jackman, *The Development of Transportation in Modern England* (1916).

8. See Percy Laithwaite, "Lynam Memorial Prize Essay," *Transactions of the North Staffs Field Club,* LXVI (1932), 63–90.

9. *Gleanings,* IV, 2–32.

10. *Gleanings,* III, 14–17; *Life,* I, 37, 525. The story came from Anna Seward.

11. *Gleanings,* III, 9–10; X, 6.

12. *Thraliana,* p. 159; *Gleanings,* III, 100–101. It is likely that his widowed mother lived with Michael from 1683 until her death in 1692, and that his brother Andrew was there until late in 1696.

13. *Boswell's Note Book,* p. 4. Hector's characterization, however, may well have been colored by his memory

of her independence after Michael's death. The same would apply to another story related in *Thraliana,* pp. 159–160.

14. Piozzi, *Anecdotes,* p. 154; *Account,* p. 133; Shaw, p. 8. For Michael see also *Lives of the Poets,* II, 37.

15. There was, to be sure, the prominent Dr. Gerard Skrymsher, who had apparently married one of Michael's sisters. But Skrymsher died in 1700, long before Michael's marriage. See *Gleanings,* III, 16, 20–24; X, 10–11.

16. *Life,* II, 261. William Johnson is usually spoken of as a native of Derbyshire, but local records show that there had been Johnsons in Lichfield since the early seventeenth century. There was a William Johnson in the parish of St. Mary's in the early 1640s, the recipient of stockings and a coat from a church charity. But there is nothing to connect him with the man of the same name who was living in Cubley when his eldest son Michael was born in 1657. Nevertheless, there is a possibility that Samuel Johnson's grandfather was actually a native of Lichfield, who had moved some twenty-five miles up in the country during the disturbances of the Civil War.

17. See note 4 and *Gleanings,* III, 6–8, 12.

18. *Gleanings,* III, 37, 49–50.

19. Piozzi, *Anecdotes,* p. 154.

20. Material for this and the two following paragraphs comes from Piozzi, *Anecdotes,* pp. 150, 159–163; *Thraliana,* p. 181.

21. Shaw, p. 8.

22. *Boswell's London Journal,* ed. F. A. Pottle (1950), 284, 301.

23. *Life*, I, 40–41; Hawkins, p. 6; Piozzi, *Anecdotes*, p. 153. Boswell's original notation may be found in the *Note Book*, p. 3. See also *Gleanings*, III, 72–74.

24. Piozzi, *Anecdotes*, p. 152; *Thraliana*, p. 181.

25. *Thraliana*, pp. 1, 181; Piozzi, *Anecdotes*, p. 154.

26. *Life*, I, 38–39; *Gleanings*, III, 67–71.

27. *Account*, p. 135; *Life*, I, 38; *Thraliana*, p. 160.

28. *Life*, IV, 299; A. L. Reade, *Reades of Blackwood Hill* (1906), 133–134.

29. *Boswell's Note Book*, p. 3.

30. *Thraliana*, p. 160; Piozzi, *Anecdotes*, p. 156. The maid could not have been Catherine Chambers, but perhaps another with the same first name.

31. *Life*, I, 43.

32. *Boswell's Note Book*, p. 12; *Life*, I, 39. Bishop Percy was responsible for the details of Sam's getting down on all fours and of his kicking Dame Oliver.

33. Yale Boswell Papers. The complete documents containing the information given by Hector to Boswell are being edited by Dr. Marshall Waingrow for the Yale Editions of the Private Papers of James Boswell.

34. Charles Norman, *Mr. Oddity* (1951), 41–42.

35. For the various interpretations see W. Russell Brain, "Some Reflections on Genius," *Lancet* (1948), 661–665; and "Authors and Psychopaths," *British Medical Journal*, II (Dec. 24, 1949), 1433–1439; Edward Hitschmann, "Samuel Johnson's Character: a Psychoanalytic Interpretation," *Psychoanalytic Review*, XXXII (April, 1945), 207–218; Frederic M. Hanes, "The Particularities of Dr. Johnson," *South Atlantic Quarterly*, XXXIX (April, 1940), 203–212; R. M. Ladell, "The Neurosis of Dr. Samuel Johnson," *British Journal of Medical Psychology*, IX (1929), 314–323; Herman W. Liebert, "Reflections on Samuel Johnson: Two Recent Books and where They Lead," *Journal of English and Germanic Philology*, XLVII (January, 1948), 80–88. I am also indebted to Dr. Harry Bone for valuable suggestions.

36. See Liebert, *op. cit.*, p. 84.

CHAPTER II

1. Michael was elected to the same office again in 1721. Much of the information from local records has very kindly been supplied to me by Mr. Percy Laithwaite. See also his *History of the Lichfield Conduit Lands Trust* (1947).

2. *Gleanings*, III, 95–96; advertisements in the London *Post Boy*, July 25, 1696; *London Gazette*, Feb. 28, 1706; *Post Man*, April 18, 1706, etc. See also note 21, Chapter IV.

3. Thomas Newte, *Prospects and Observations* (1791), 15; Marcia Rice, *Abbots Bromley* (1939), 195–196.

4. Johnson's *Letters*, No. 616.

5. *Account*, p. 130; Johnson's *Letters*, No. 220; *Lives of the Poets*, III, 4.

6. Boswell, *Tour to the Hebrides*, p. 208. For details concerning the

parchment factory see Percy Laithwaite, "Lynam Memorial Prize Essay," *Transactions of the North Staffs
Field Club*, LXVI (1932), 12, 15, 18;
Gleanings, III, 89–95.

7. Latin version in *Poems*, pp. 227–
228; English version largely by Mr.
Eugene V. Mohr.

8. Piozzi, *Anecdotes*, p. 224; also
Life, II, 299.

9. *Life*, II, 463–464; *Johns. Misc.*, II,
410, 418–419.

10. Boswell, *Tour to the Hebrides*,
pp. 39, 350.

11. *Works of Thomas Newton*
(1782), I, 22–23; Daniel Defoe, *A Tour
Through the Whole Island of Great
Britain* (4th ed. 1748), II, 405.

12. The original term was "de-
cinner," a man chosen to represent
ten households.

13. Thomas Harwood, *History and
Antiquities of Lichfield* (1806), 20–49.

14. *Weekly Entertainer*, March 13,
1786, pp. 251–252 (letter from Richard
Greene).

15. Josiah C. Wedgwood, *Staffordshire Parliamentary History* (1922),
II, xxx–xxxi, 212; Greene, pp. 66–82.

16. Greene, Chapter III. Tyers (p.

4) called Michael "a Whig in principle," and Anna Seward remarked on
his "very loyal principles" [*Poetical
Works of Anna Seward* (1810), I, lxx].

17. This summary of the political
background is derived largely from
Robert Walcott, Jr., "English Party
Politics (1688–1714)," *Essays in Modern English History in Honor of Wil-
bur Cortez Abbott* (1941); William
Thomas Morgan, "Some Sidelights
upon the General Election of 1715"
in the same volume; Lewis B. Namier,
*England in the Age of the American
Revolution* (1930), *Structure of Politics at the Accession of George III*
(1929), *Monarchy and the Party System* (1952); Greene, Chapter 1.

18. *Life*, I, 37; II, 322; *Gleanings*, IV,
201–203. Transcriptions of oaths from
documents at Lichfield.

19. Corroboration of one of the details of the story comes in an entry
from the parish books: "Paid for
mending the church windows,
broken on Easter Sunday, 13s. 10d."
(Harwood, *op. cit.*, p. 460); *Gleanings*,
III, 80–81.

20. *Boswell's Note Book*, p. 20;
Gleanings, III, 81.

CHAPTER III

1. *Lives of the Poets*, II, 79. The
quotation used as the title of the chapter comes from *Life*, I, 46.

2. *Gleanings*, III, 79–80, 84.

3. John Campbell, *Lives of the
Chief Justices*, II, 279. See Percy Laithwaite, *A Short History of Lichfield
Grammar School* (1925) for the best
general account of the school. There
were other schools in Lichfield where

poor children could be taught to read
and write in English.

4. Document now in the Johnson
Birthplace in Lichfield. Other details
concerning Hawkins come from *Gleanings*, III, 87–89, and from Mr. Laithwaite.

5. *Life*, I, 43–44; *Account*, p. 138.

6. *Gleanings*, III, 84–88; Laithwaite,
op. cit. The so-called "Lily's Latin

Grammar" was actually the work of a number of scholars.

7. Book VII, Chapter 12.

8. Krutch, p. 6.

9. In "Of Education." See Columbia edition of Milton, IV, 277; Donald L. Clark, *John Milton at St. Paul's School* (1948), 138.

10. Slightly different versions may be found in Hawkins, pp. 7–8; *Life*, I, 47–48; *Boswell's Note Book*, p. 4; Yale Boswell Papers.

11. *Life*, I, 48.

12. Piozzi, *Anecdotes*, p. 149.

13. *Thraliana*, p. 380.

14. *Johnsoniana* (London, John Murray, 1836), 435. From Isaac Reed.

15. *Johns. Misc.*, II, 278.

16. Hawkins, p. 7; *Boswell's Note Book*, p. 4; Yale Boswell Papers.

17. *Gleanings*, III, 110, 134; *Account*, p. 138.

18. *Account*, p. 139; *Gleanings*, III, 105–109.

19. *Gleanings*, III, 109.

20. *Life*, I, 44; Yale Boswell Papers; *Account*, p. 138.

21. *BP*, IX, 21; *Life*, I, 44–46; *Gleanings*, III, 110–114; Laithwaite, *op. cit.*, pp. 46–48.

22. From manuscript in the Hyde collection. Another version is given in *Life*, I, 46. For the following anecdotes see Henry Francis Cary, *Lives of English Poets* (1846), 3 (reported from Thomas Price, headmaster of the school, 1764–1776); Piozzi, *Anecdotes*, p. 159; *Life*, I, 45–47; Yale Boswell Papers.

23. Campbell, *op. cit.*, II, 280. The recollection came from John Eardley Wilmot. See also *Gleanings*, III, 122; Hawkins, pp. 7–8; *Life*, I, 47; Yale Boswell Papers.

24. Thomas Davies, *Memoirs of the Life of David Garrick* (1781), I, 4; Yale Boswell Papers; *Life*, I, 44.

25. *Johns. Misc.*, II, 414 (anecdotes of the Rev. Mr. Parker).

26. From H. F. Cary. See note 22.

27. Yale Boswell Papers (anecdotes from John Taylor, c. May, 1785; the original documents are being edited by Dr. Marshall Waingrow. See note 33, Chapter I); Hawkins, p. 7.

28. *Gleanings*, III, Chapter VI.

29. *Life*, II, 463. Two others, of whom we know nothing, not even their first names, were Sedgwick and Brodhurst.

30. See note 27.

31. Hawkins, p. 38.

32. *Life*, I, 48.

33. Hawkins, p. 7.

34. Piozzi, *Anecdotes*, p. 161.

35. *Prayers and Meditations*, p. 31; Boswell, *Tour to the Hebrides*, p. 192.

36. *Prayers and Meditations*, p. 72.

37. *Life*, I, 64. For one modern psychological interpretation of "Neurotic Disturbances in Work" see Chapter XIII in Karen Horney's *Neurosis and Human Growth* (1950).

38. Stressed throughout the *Gleanings*. For Johnson's own opinion see Boswell, *Tour to the Hebrides*, p. 174.

39. T. G. Lomax, *A Short Account of Lichfield* (1819), 118.

40. Hawkins, pp. 6–7.

CHAPTER IV

1. Boswell, *Tour to the Hebrides*, p. 39.

2. *Life*, I, 49.

3. *Life*, I, 70; *Thraliana*, p. 161. The kitchen would have been some six steps below the street level (*Gleanings*, III, 89). See also general observations on *King Lear* in Johnson's edition of Shakespeare.

4. *Boswell's Note Book*, p. 19.

5. The manuscript notebook is in the Birthplace Museum, Lichfield. The exact date when Johnson made the annotations is not certain.

6. *Boswell's Note Book*, p. 19; *Johns. Misc.*, I, 363; Krutch, p. 12.

7. *Thraliana*, pp. 163–164; Piozzi, *Anecdotes*, p. 332.

8. *Life*, I, 71; *Johns. Misc.*, II, 254.

9. Shaw, p. 14; Laetitia Matilda Hawkins, *Memoirs* (1824), I, 216.

10. *Life*, V, 13.

11. At the Birthplace Museum, Lichfield.

12. *Lives of the Poets*, I, 373.

13. A. L. Reade, "Michael Johnson and Lord Derby's Library," *TLS*, July 27, 1940, pp. 363, 365.

14. Sir John Floyer's *The Touchstone of Medicines* (1687) (*Gleanings*, III, 10). For claims that Michael sold books at other places see William Talbot, "Birmingham's First Bookseller," *Publisher's Circular and Bookseller's Record*, Dec. 17, 1932, p. 719; Marcia Rice, *Abbots Bromley* (1939), p. 195; etc.

15. Copies of letters covering only ten months (Oct., 1684, to Aug., 1685) are now in the William Salt Library in Stafford. They are described by A. L. Reade in *TLS*, June 17, 1949, p. 404. Another letter book for the period just preceding (April, 1683, to Sept., 1684) is now in the possession of Sir Hugo Brooke Boothby of Fonman Castle. It will shortly be described by Mr. Geoffrey Beard. What is available is obviously only a small part of Sir William's voluminous correspondence with Michael Johnson.

16. First printed in *Gent. Mag.*, LXI (Oct., 1791), 893. Reprinted in *Life*, I, 36. See also *Gleanings*, I, 25–26. In *BP*, VI, 106, Boswell records that Michael "knew Latin pretty well, but no Greek; that he did not read so much as he might have done. . . ."

17. *Gleanings*, X, 6, 9.

18. Francis Redfern, *History of Uttoxeter* (2d ed. 1886), 174. Proof that he stored books at Uttoxeter comes in a letter from Sir William Boothby of Nov. 20, 1683. See note 15.

19. A. L. Reade, *Reades of Blackwood Hill* (1906), 216; *Thraliana*, p. 159; Johnson's *Letters*, No. 492.

20. Piozzi, *Anecdotes*, pp. 287–288; *Life*, V, 253; Hawkins, p. 458.

21. I have not been able to trace the actual copy of the sale catalogue. The first two pages were reprinted in the early nineteenth century, as a single sheet, and I quote from this.

22. In the possession of Mr. H. E. Palfrey, Stourbridge; the Birthplace Museum, Lichfield; and Pembroke College, Oxford.

23. Percival Stockdale, *Memoirs* (1809), II, 102.

24. *Gleanings*, III, 89–90; *Reades of Blackwood Hill*, pp. 211–216.

25. *Life*, I, 37; *Gleanings*, III, 119–120; Greene, p. 87.

26. All details of official Lichfield procedures have been secured from Mr. Percy Laithwaite.

27. *Boswell's Note Book*, p. 20. The discussion in this and the two paragraphs that follow is derived from *Thraliana*, pp. 160–161; *Life*, I, 67–69; II, 14; *BP*, VII, 74; *Gleanings*, III, 119.

28. *Prayers and Meditations*, p. 61; *Boswell's Note Book*, pp. 19–20.

29. Piozzi, *Anecdotes*, p. 159.

30. *Life*, I, 51; II, 55; *Poems*, pp. 65–67, 403.

31. *Boswell's Note Book*, p. 19.

32. Yale Boswell Papers. Boswell had two copies in different handwritings, one sent by Hector Feb. 5, 1785, together with anecdotes; the other sent Oct. 31, 1791, after the appearance of the *Life*. Hector described the poem as "the first production of his pen I ever saw." For Herrick's poems see Oxford edition, pp. 125, 205.

33. *Life*, I, 377.

34. Yale Boswell Papers. For later printings see *Poems*, pp. 97–100. Hector's chronology for the early verses is not clear.

CHAPTER V

1. *Gleanings*, III, 41–42, 48–49, 149; IV, 5–8.

2. Hawkins, p. 8; manuscript "Annales" in the Hyde collection.

3. The description of Johnson comes from a number of authorities, chiefly *Thraliana*, p. 189. There is no surviving portrait of Ford, but I accept the identification of him as the clergyman in Hogarth's print (see note 15), where, though it may possibly be a caricature, a certain likeness may be presumed.

4. For the most complete account of Ford see *Gleanings*, III, 138–153; IX, 1–15, X, 54–58.

5. Hawkins, p. 8.

6. *Thraliana*, pp. 232–234; *Poems*, pp. 184–186. Concerning Martial, see M. Pennington, *Memoirs of Mrs. Elizabeth Carter* (1808), I, 39.

7. This and the following quotations are taken from an account of Ford in *The Hyp-Doctor* for August 24–31, 1731, probably written by his close friend John Henley. See *Gleanings*, IX, 1–15.

8. *Lives of the Poets*, III, 75.

9. *Thraliana*, p. 171.

10. Piozzi, *Ancedotes*, p. 155. For an excellent analysis of the anecdote see A. L. Reade, *Reades of Blackwood Hill*, p. 160, and *Gleanings*, III, 151.

11. Compare *Life*, II, 100; III, 23.

12. *Johns. Misc.*, II, 208. For analysis see *Gleanings*, III, 161.

13. *Gleanings*, III, 148.

14. James M. Osborn, "Lord Hailes and Dr. Johnson," *TLS*, April 16, 1938, p. 262. Lord Hailes quoted "a person who knew *Parson Ford*."

15. See opposite p. 78. The identification with Ford is not absolutely certain, since some critics have suggested "Orator" Henley as the model. But I agree with A. L. Reade that Ford is more likely. See *Gleanings*, IX, 11–12; also *Thraliana*, p. 159; *Life*, III, 348–349, 528.

16. For various versions of this anec-

dote see *Reades of Blackwood Hill*, pp. 160–161.

17. Manuscript in the Hyde collection, entitled "Annales."

18. The "Annales" entry is "S.J. ad se vocavit C.F. a quo, anno proxime insequente, Pentecostes feriis Lichfieldiam rediit." See also *Life*, I, 50; *Gleanings*, III, 153–154.

19. Letter of Bishop Percy to Edmond Malone, Oct. 17, 1786 [*The Percy Letters* (1944), 43]. In the *Life* (I, 50) Boswell softened the anecdote, substituting "little" for "nothing." For details about the school see G. H. C. Burley, *The History of King Edward's School, Stourbridge* (privately printed, 1948); George Griffith, *The Free Schools of Worcestershire* (1852), 392ff. For everything concerned with Stourbridge I rely on Mr. Burley and Mr. Geoffrey Beard.

20. *BP*, IX, 257; *Life*, I, 50. Just what he "stole" is not clear — perhaps material for exercises. For Wentworth see *Gleanings*, III, 155–156. In 1732 he was dismissed as headmaster by the school governors "for too long absence and giving too long an holiday at Whitsuntide," but he refused to go and there was a long dispute (Burley, *op. cit.*). Boswell secured Johnson's school exercises from what he thought was Wentworth's son, actually his nephew, through William Bowles of Heale in Wiltshire (Yale Boswell Papers). The originals have been largely scattered, but a number of transcripts are in the Yale collection.

21. Shepperd was usher from May 17, 1715, to the appointment of John Roe of Merton College, Oxford, Feb. 20, 1726/27 (list of ushers in school archives).

22. J. Nichols, *Literary Illustrations*, VII, 306; *Life*, I, 50; *Gleanings*, III, 156.

23. See Burley, *op. cit.*, p. 8.

24. Robert Anderson, *Life of Samuel Johnson* (3d ed. 1815), p. 20.

25. Mr. Burley has examined all of the surviving volumes, and finds no evidence of Johnsonian annotation. The Hickman Library is now in a special case at the school. Information about the furnishings comes from the Governor's Accounts.

26. The original anecdote appeared in the *St. James's Chronicle*, Jan. 13, 1785, sent in by George Steevens. See also *Life*, I, 50–56; *Poems*, pp. 63–77; Yale Boswell Papers. It may have been under Wentworth that Johnson wrote a Latin theme on the assigned topic "To Harbor Malefactors is Hardly Safe." This exercise, now in the possession of Mr. Herman W. Liebert, is impossible to date, though the simplicity of style suggests that it was not a college paper.

27. *Poems*, pp. 65–73. One epode is still unpublished; a transcript is in the Yale Boswell Papers. For the following analysis I am indebted to Professor Gilbert Highet, who has made a careful comparison of some of the translations with the Horatian originals.

28. *Poems*, p. 403.

29. *Poems*, p. 77; *Life*, I, 92; *Gleanings*, III, 159; *Reades of Blackwood Hill*, p. 151. Original in Hyde collection.

30. *Poems*, pp. 78–80. Original in Hyde collection.

31. Yale Boswell Papers (see note 33, Chapter I); *Gleanings*, III, 162; and note 18.

CHAPTER VI

1. *Gleanings*, III, 180, note 1; *Johns. Misc.*, I, 361; Hawkins, p. 9.

2. Stebbing Shaw, *Staffordshire*, I, 324.

3. W. Shaw, pp. 14–15.

4. See note 37, Chapter III.

5. *Life*, I, 57, 445; *Diary of William Windham* (1866), 17. Some of Johnson's early books are now at the Birthplace Museum, Lichfield, and at Pembroke College, Oxford. See *Gleanings*, V, 219; VIII, 108, etc.

6. *Life*, II, 459–461; *BP*, XI, 183; A. L. Reade, *Reades of Blackwood Hill*, pp. 152–153. The proper spelling of her married name is Carless.

7. Piozzi, *Anecdotes*, p. 318. The people who were kind to Johnson are described in *Gleanings*, III, 171–179.

8. Piozzi, *Anecdotes*, pp. 268–269, 287.

9. *Lives of the Poets*, II, 20; *Life*, I, 81.

10. For the principal facts about Walmesley see *Gleanings*, III, 171–174; VI, 150–153; VIII, 4–6. A certificate of Walmesley's appointment to the lottery position is in the possession of the law firm, Hinckley, Birch, and Crarer in Lichfield.

11. *Poetical Works of Anna Seward* (1810), I, lxix.

12. Walmesley's letters are in the Bodleian Library, Oxford. The letters of Duckett and Burnet have been edited by Professor D. Nichol Smith in a limited edition (Roxburghe Club, 1914). Most of Walmesley's are still unprinted.

13. At Pembroke College, Oxford.

They were first printed by G. B. Hill in his edition of Johnson's *Letters*, but he misinterpreted some of the accompanying letters. See *Gleanings*, III, 171–172.

14. *Life*, III, 389, VI, 448; *Boswelliana*, p. 323 (given in *Life*, IV, 33).

15. Thomas Davies, *Memoirs of the Life of David Garrick* (1781), 3. Some corroboration comes in one of Walmesley's receipted bills, dated Feb. 7, 1732, which was witnessed by David Garrick (now in the Birthplace Museum, Lichfield).

16. *Poems*, pp. 83–84.

17. For details of the performance see Davies, *op. cit.*, pp. 4–6. It has not, I believe, been previously suggested that this particular room in the palace was the one used. Davies in his "Author's Advertisement" states that he is indebted to Johnson "for the early part of Mr. Garrick's life," and since this was in print while Johnson was alive, we may assume the correctness of the account. Since no reason was given, Johnson had perhaps himself forgotten why he did not provide the prologue.

18. *Life*, II, 404; Krutch, pp. 268–269.

19. E. L. McAdam, Jr., *Dr. Johnson and the English Law* (1951), 7.

20. Boswell, *Tour to the Hebrides*, p. 378.

21. *The Post Boy*, June 4, 1713.

22. *Pineapples of Finest Flavour*, ed. D. M. Little (1930), 7–8.

23. *Boswell's London Journal*, p. 315; *Life*, I, 441; Krutch, p. 369.

24. *Life*, II, 299; V, 329.

25. *D'Arblay Diary*, ed. Austin Dobson (1904), I, 115.

26. Bertrand H. Bronson, *Johnson Agonistes* (1946), 2, 6, 43–44; H. W. Liebert (see note 35, Chapter 1).

27. Sermon, No. 24 [*Sermons on Different Subjects*, published by Samuel Hayes (3d ed. 1795), II, 209].

28. *Life*, II, 212.

29. *Life*, III, 326. For other deroga-tory references to Whigs see index to the Hill-Powell edition of the *Life*.

30. According to Anna Seward, Johnson so characterized Walmesley to her. See J. Nichols, *Illustrations*, VII, 323, 343.

31. His rough copies of these letters are now in the Birthplace Museum, Lichfield. They have hitherto not been known to scholars.

CHAPTER VII

1. *Gleanings*, III, 180–181; V, 1; A. L. Reade, *Reades of Blackwood Hill*, p. 194.

2. Yale Boswell Papers (See note 27, Chapter III); Hawkins, p. 9; *Gleanings*, V, 3–4.

3. Even more connections are listed in *Gleanings*, V, 4–5.

4. *Life*, I, 43; *Gleanings*, III, 78.

5. The probable route is discussed in F. D. MacKinnon, "Samuel Johnson, Undergraduate," *Cornhill Magazine*, n.s. LXI (Oct., 1926), 444–458, an interesting older summary of Johnson's experiences at Oxford. For details concerning his Pembroke charges, see *Gleanings*, V, 5–6, 9.

6. Yale Boswell Papers. For the color of Johnson's eyes see H. F. Cary, *Lives of English Poets* (1846), 71.

7. *Boswell's Note Book*, p. 7; *Life*, I, 59–61, 272. Other accounts may be found in *Thraliana*, p. 466; Piozzi, *Anecdotes*, pp. 164, 170, etc. For an analysis of the various versions see *Gleanings*, V, 8–9. I have preferred to give a composite story, believing that the Adams and Warton versions are both correct, but represent two different occasions.

8. *Gleanings*, V, 8.

9. *Life*, I, 60. Elsewhere (I, 71) Boswell says that Johnson wrote his first exercise twice over.

10. *Thraliana*, p. 466; Piozzi, *Anecdotes*, p. 165; *Diary of William Windham* (1866), 17; *Johns. Misc.*, II, 312. Two of Johnson's prose exercises are still treasured at Pembroke.

11. See Douglas Macleane, *A History of Pembroke College* (Oxford, 1897).

12. I am indebted to Mr. G. R. F. Bredin, the present bursar of Pembroke, and to Mr. W. C. Costin of St. John's College for what information I have been able to secure. The old system of notation was discontinued in 1793, and for many years no one at the college has been able to explain the former charges. For a full examination of the buttery books and the general charges, see *Gleanings*, V, Appendix H.

13. For descriptions of college life at this time see A. D. Godley, *Oxford in the Eighteenth Century* (1908), Chapter V. For Johnson's early rising see *Prayers and Meditations*, p. 16.

14. *Life*, II, 52; I, 75.

15. Yale Boswell Papers. See note 27, Chapter III.

16. Boswell, *Tour to the Hebrides*, p. 20; Hawkins, pp. 14–15.

17. This and the following occurrences were recorded by Thomas Hearne (*Collections*, X, 114, 150, 155, 164).

18. Excerpts from the diary of Erasmus Philipps included in Macleane, *op. cit.*, pp. 323–329.

19. *Gleanings*, III, 127.

20. *Boswell's Note Book*, p. 8; *Life*, II, 444. For detailed accounts of these men see *Gleanings*, V, 129–139. One of the caricatures from the buttery books is reproduced there, as well as some of the scribblings.

21. *Life*, I, 271–274.

22. Hawkins, p. 18.

23. *Gleanings*, V, 175–213.

24. For the cricket see *Johns. Misc.*, II, 199; for the verses, *Poems*, p. 85; *Life*, I, 271. Suggestions for the translation come from Mr. Eugene V. Mohr.

25. *Life*, III, 304; *Gleanings*, V, 146.

26. *Life*, I, 73–74. Professor F. W. Hilles tells me that Boswell in his original note, made while in Oxford in June, 1784, wrote "rude" rather than "mad" as printed in the *Life*, but presumably could not read his own handwriting and thus inadvertently changed the meaning. The "Ah, Sir," at the beginning, is not in the note.

27. *Life*, I, 74.

28. Hawkins, pp. 12–13.

29. Tyers, p. 4. Other details in this paragraph come from Piozzi, *Anecdotes*, pp. 164–165; Hawkins, p. 9; *Life*, I, 74; Yale Boswell Papers (letter from Adams to Boswell, July 12, 1786).

30. *Life*, III, 303.

31. *Life*, IV, 94; *BP*, XIV, 200.

32. *Boswell's Note Book*, pp. 7–8; *Life*, I, 72–73.

33. Yale Boswell Papers (see note 27, Chapter III). Other information in the paragraph comes from *Boswell's Note Book*, p. 9; *Johns. Misc.*, II, 312. Hawkins (p. 13) states that it was a punishment, and Murphy (*Johns. Misc.*, I, 362) says that it was an imposed exercise.

34. Hawkins, p. 13.

35. Boswell, *Tour to the Hebrides*, p. 60.

36. According to a note on a copy of the poem in the Yale Boswell Papers the verses were written in Johnson's twentieth year, almost all of which he spent at Oxford. For the complete text see *Poems*, pp. 81–82.

37. *Life*, I, 70. An old gentleman at the university said to him: "Young man, ply your book diligently now, and acquire a stock of knowledge; for when years come upon you, you will find that poring upon books will be but an irksome task" (*Life*, I, 446). See also Hawkins, pp. 12, 14; *Johns. Misc.*, I, 362.

38. For details in this paragraph see Hawkins, p. 12; *Diary of William Windham* (1866), 17; *Memoirs of Richard Cumberland* (1806), 263; *Life*, I, 70–71; *Boswell's Note Book*, p. 21.

39. The original fragmentary diary is now in the Hyde collection. See *Life*, I, 72, for Boswell's analysis.

40. On the other side of his letter of May 18, 1735, to Gilbert Repington (Johnson's *Letters*, No. 3.1). The list contains no book that Johnson could not have brought with him to Oxford in 1728. For an examination of the books see *Gleanings*, V, 27–29, 213–229.

41. *Life*, I, 128 (from Northcote's *Reynolds*, I, 236).

42. *Thraliana*, p. 184; *Life*, I, 86; III, 292.

43. *Life*, I, 68; Hawkins, p. 18; Edward Gibbon, *Autobiography* (Everyman's Library), 18; S. G. Brown, "Dr. Johnson and the Religious Problem," *English Studies*, XX (Feb., 1938), 1–17.

44. Original manuscript in the Hyde collection; *Life*, I, 74. There is some evidence that he may have been keeping a diary in September.

45. *Life*, I, 63–66; *Gleanings*, V, 43–44.

46. Yale Boswell Papers; Hawkins, pp. 10–11. The donor of the shoes had already been identified by A. L. Reade (*Gleanings*, V, 21).

47. *Gleanings*, V, 27, 56–57.

48. Yale Boswell Papers (see note 27, Chapter III).

CHAPTER VIII

1. *Life*, I, 63; IV, 147–148; Hawkins, p. 8; *Gleanings*, V, 26. For the problem of the exact dating of the onset of melancholia, see *Gleanings*, VIII, 108–109; *Life*, IV, 147, 215; *Johns. Misc.*, II, 322. In the original manuscript of the *Life* (now at Yale University), p. 883, Boswell reported Johnson as saying: "I once walked a good deal. I left it off at two-and-twenty when I grew melancholy."

2. A. L. Reade, "A New Admirer for Dr. Johnson," *London Mercury*, XXI (Jan., 1930), 247. The remark, to be sure, comes third-hand.

3. *Life*, I, 64; *Gleanings*, V, 26. The apparent discrepancy of this account and the reference to giving up walking quoted in note 1 may possibly be explained by chronology. Perhaps he gave up long walks when he found them ineffective in warding off his depression.

4. *Life*, I, 66; *Thraliana*, pp. 384–385; K. C. Balderston, "Johnson's Vile Melancholy," *The Age of Johnson: Essays Presented to C. B. Tinker* (1949), pp. 3–14. According to R. M. Ladell, Johnson was suffering from an anxiety hysteria, which is produced when the developing libido receives some serious check. The incident of crisis is not repressed or forgotten, as in some forms of neurosis, but the effect attached to it is displaced and projected into the outer world in the form of morbid fears, obsessive acts, and tics [*British Journal of Medical Psychology*, IX (1929), 314–323].

5. Shaw, p. 9. Michael was careful to attend all meetings of the Corporation when his lease was under consideration. The reference to his innate cheerfulness is startling in the light of other accounts.

6. Piozzi, *Anecdotes*, p. 148. Johnson thought this a sign of madness.

7. Hawkins, p. 581; *Gleanings*, III, 98–100.

8. Percy Laithwaite, *History of the Lichfield Conduit Lands Trust* (1947), 69. From the position of the entry it would appear that the payment was made in August or September, 1731.

9. For details about Hervey see S. H. A. Hervey, *Suffolk Green Books*,

XIV (1906), xlix–liii; XVI (1912), 329–333; *Letter-Books of John Hervey* (3 vols., 1894); D. A. Ponsonby, *Call a Dog Hervey* (1949), Chapter IX. For the opportunity to consult Hervey's manuscript verses, now at Ickworth, I am indebted to the Marchioness of Bristol and to the Hon. David Erskine.

10. Yale Boswell Papers.

11. *Poems*, pp. 92–95. My version ignores Anna Seward, and is a composite made up from the accounts of Mrs. Piozzi, John Nichols, and Hector.

12. Information secured from Mr. G. H. C. Burley of the Stourbridge School.

13. Mr. Geoffrey Beard tells me that the account books of Sir Thomas Lyttelton at Hagley Park show that George was home from his travels by June, 1730. See also note 12, Chapter V. For the verses to Miss Hickman see *Poems*, pp. 95–97; A. L. Reade, *Reades of Blackwood Hill*, pp. 149–150. Manuscript in Hyde collection.

14. *The Grub Street Journal*, Sept. 9, 1731. See *Gleanings*, IX, 2–14.

15. Document at the Stourbridge School.

16. Johnson's *Letters*, No. 1. The original is in the Hyde collection. *Gleanings*, V, 64–66.

17. *Life*, IV, 372–373. Another account is found in Richard Warner, *Tour Through the Northern Counties* (1802), I, 105. See also Francis Redfern, *History of Uttoxeter* (2nd ed. 1886), 162–175. Most commentators heretofore have dated the original disobedience in 1727, but the autumn of 1731 appears more probable. As an Oxford student Johnson would have been less

willing to sell wares in a market place. Moreover, his mood when in Lichfield in the autumn of 1781 was more conducive to penance than in 1777. See Johnson's *Letters*, Nos. 745–746.

18. Piozzi, *Anecdotes*, p. 151; *Life*, II, 43; *Gleanings*, V, 68–69.

19. *Gleanings*, V, 73–74; III, 48–49.

20. In the Hyde collection.

21. For information about Dixie see *Gleanings*, V, 82–85; *Boswell's Note Book*, p. 10.

22. *Life*, I, 84.

23. For two differing versions of the story see S. Hopewell, *The Book of Bosworth School* (1950), 52; and Abraham Hayward, *Autobiography of Mrs. Piozzi* (2nd ed. 1861), II, 103–104.

24. Hopewell, *op. cit.*, p. 53. In April, 1730, the headmaster Blackwall died; his real successor, John Kilby, was appointed in September (*Gleanings*, V, 77–78). During this time, Mr. Hopewell tells me, there was a butler in Sir Wolstan's employ named Williams. In June some bills were signed at the school by a headmaster named Williams.

25. Yale Boswell Papers. For the statutes see S.A. Grundy-Newman writing in the *Lichfield Mercury*, May 23, 1924.

26. *Life*, I, 84; Shaw, p. 19.

27. Original manuscript in the Hyde collection. Entry for "July [June] 17." English translation by Professor E. L. McAdam, Jr.

28. The translation is that by Hawkins (p. 21), with minor corrections by Professor McAdam. Boswell's version is a little more florid (*Life*, I, 80). As Professor McAdam points out, both Boswell and Hawkins missed the fact that Johnson had crossed out "viginti"

and inserted "19," and ignored a note explaining about the one pound. Boswell also missed Johnson's note, which Hawkins silently used, pointing out a mistake in dating: "On this page I have put July for June." As a result, most commentators have erred in putting the event in the wrong month. The entries were doubtless written in July but referred to June. The probable route taken is suggested in A. Gissing, "On Foot to Market Bosworth," *Cornhill Magazine*, n.s. LVII (July, 1924), 7–16.

29. In the collection of Lord Rothschild. The date of leaving Dixie's house comes from "Annales."

30. Johnson's *Letters*, No. 2; *Gleanings*, v, 80–81.

31. *Gleanings*, v, 88–90.

32. *The Daily Courant*, Sept. **23**, Nov. 13, 1732. *Gleanings*, v, 92–93.

33. *Life of William Hutton* (1816), 41; *Life*, II, 464; Johnson's *Letters*, No. 560.

34. Yale Boswell Papers. See also Joseph Hill, *The Book Makers of Old Birmingham* (1907), 40–41.

35. For Anna Seward's incredible story that Sam had earlier been in love with Lucy Porter, the daughter, see *Gleanings*, I, 19; v, 103.

36. *Life*, I, 94.

37. Piozzi, *Anecdotes*, p. 248. For an early portrait see opposite p. 206. See also pp. 152, 311–312.

38. *Life*, III, 389; Yale Boswell Papers.

39. Yale Boswell Papers (see note 33, Chapter I). The Ford of the story could not have been Parson Ford, who died before Johnson came to live with Hector, but must have been another member of the family at Stour-

bridge. Most of the information concerning Johnson's stay in Birmingham comes from this source, secured by Boswell in 1785. See also *Life*, I, 85–86, 94; Johnson's *Letters*, No. 69; J. Hill and R. K. Dent, *Memorials of the Old Square* (1897).

40. See note 39; also *Life*, I, 93.

41. *Life*, I, 85. The only known copy is for May 21, 1733 (now in the office of the *Birmingham Post*), after Johnson had ceased writing for the paper. There is nothing sounding remotely like Johnson in this issue.

42. "Annales" (Hyde collection): "Junii lmo apud F. Jervis Birminghamia habitare incepi." See also Hawkins, p. 21.

43. Although Hector specifically told Boswell (Yale Boswell Papers) that he had borrowed the book from Oxford, the *Life* indicates that Johnson himself did so. No copy is listed as ever having been in the Pembroke College Library (*Life*, I, 528), and it is probable that the work was secured from a private source. The time of year in which the work was done is determined from an entry in "Annales." For other details concerning the translation see *Life*, I, 86–87; John Hennig, "Young Johnson and the Jesuits," *The Month*, CLXXXII (Nov.–Dec., 1946), 440–449.

44. "Annales." Johnson had been left £5 in the will of his godfather, Richard Wakefield, proved Sept. 28, 1733 (*Gleanings*, v, 99).

45. H. W. Liebert, "Dr. Johnson's First Book," *Yale Univ. Library Gazette*, XXV (July, 1950), 23–28.

46. For an important analysis of the ideas in this work, see Greene, pp. 116–132. Also Krutch, pp. 24–26.

47. *Life*, I, 218; *BP*, XVII, 66.

48. *Life*, I, 90; Hawkins, p. 445; *Gleanings*, V, 100.

49. Johnson's *Letters*, No. 2.1 (dated Sept. 18, 1734). "Annales" — "Augusti 5to 1734 conditiones edendi Politiani Poemata emisi"; *Life*, I, 90; Hawkins,

pp. 26–27. Boswell saw a receipt for 2/6 in the hands of "Mr. Levett of Lichfield" (Yale Boswell Papers).

50. Hawkins, p. 163. For an examination of the evidence see Donald and Mary Hyde, "Johnson and Journals," *New Colophon*, III (1950), 165–197.

CHAPTER IX

1. *Letters of Anna Seward* (1811), I, 44–45; *Gleanings*, V, 102–103, X, 99.

2. Shaw, p. 25; *Gleanings*, VI, 34–35.

3. *Life*, I, 96.

4. *BP*, VI, 221. Shaw (p. 25) suggested that the first advances came from the widow.

5. *Life*, I, 99; *Thraliana*, p. 178; *Letters of Anna Seward*, I, 44.

6. For other details in this paragraph see Shaw, pp. 25, 111; *Thraliana*, p. 177; Piozzi, *Anecdotes*, pp. 248, 258.

7. Yale Boswell Papers ("Tacenda" — see note 11, Chapter XVII).

8. Shaw, pp. 25–26; *Letters of Anna Seward*, II, 348; *Gleanings*, VI, 24, 32.

9. Johnson's *Letters*, No. 3; *Adam Catalogue*, I, 13.

10. Hawkins, p. 29.

11. Implied in the letter of Addenbrooke of May 10 (see p. 156).

12. *Letters of Anna Seward*, I, 44–45; A. L. Reade, *Reades of Blackwood Hill*, p. 234; *Life*, I, 95–96. No evidence has ever been discovered about any of Johnson's uncles' having been hanged.

13. *Gleanings*, V, 108–118.

14. S. Shaw, *Staffordshire*, I, 325.

15. Johnson's *Letters*, No. 3.1.

16. Johnson's *Letters*, No. 3.2; *Gleanings*, V, 113–118.

17. *Gleanings*, VI, 129–130.

18. *Boswell's Note Book*, p. 10. Boswell added: "She did not say why. I suppose from envy of his parts; though I do not see how traders could envy such qualities." For the choice of Derby see *Gleanings*, VI, 22–23.

19. *Life*, I, 96; *Thraliana*, p. 178. The incident probably occurred on the day before the wedding. See *Gleanings*, VI, 25, and T. Harwood, *History of Lichfield* (1806), 450.

20. *Life*, III, 3.

21. Original letter at Pembroke College, Oxford (*Gleanings*, VI, 29–30).

22. For an account of the house at Edial see Percy Laithwaite, "Lynam Memorial Prize Essay," *Transactions of the North Staffs Field Club* (1931–1932), 22–28; *Gleanings*, VI, 38–42; Hawkins, p. 35.

23. Johnson's *Letters*, No. 3.3; *Life*, I, 99–100, 531; Hawkins, pp. 37–38; *Gleanings*, VI, 52–53; *TLS*, Sept. 18, 1924, p. 577.

24. *Life*, I, 97; Thomas Davies, *Memoirs of David Garrick*, I, 8; Hawkins, p. 36; *Gleanings*, VI, 44–45.

25. *Life*, I, 97.

26. Davies, *op. cit.*, I, 7–8.

27. Told by George Steevens and later repeated by Reynolds. See *Johns. Misc.*, II, 315; *Portraits by Sir Joshua*

Reynolds, ed. F. W. Hilles (1952), 108–109.

28. A marginal note by Malone in a copy of Mrs. Piozzi's *Anecdotes* (*Life*, I, 531) and Yale Boswell Papers ("Tacenda" — see note 11, Chapter XVII).

29. Joseph Cradock, *Literary and Miscellaneous Memoirs* (1828), IV, 244; *Bicentenary of the Birth of Dr. Samuel Johnson*, ed. J. T. Raby (Stafford, 1909), 132.

30. H. F. Cary, *Lives of English Poets* (1846), 9. For details about Bird see *Gleanings*, VI, 42. For the desk see *Johns. Misc.*, I, 367, note 6. The chair now belongs to Mr. Halstead Van der Poel. For the miniature see p. 327.

31. Hawkins, p. 163, gives the year, in brackets, as 1734, but the entry fits better in 1736, and in this year August 27 came on Friday.

32. For Mrs. Emmet, the actress, see *Life*, II, 464–465; *Gleanings*, VI, 148–149, IX, 220. There are various versions of the story, all stemming from Garrick. Hawkins (p. 439) gives more details. My version is a composite, made from Hawkins and Boswell (*Life*, II, 299) and Mrs. Thrale (*Thraliana*, p. 189). The episode cannot be dated, but it probably occurred about this time. See *Gleanings*, X, 121.

33. *Poems*, pp. 233–239, 336, etc. The first draft is printed on pp. 336–377. See also *Boswell's Note Book*, p. 11. There is a discussion of the themes in Greene, pp. 133–143.

34. Hawkins, pp. 163–164.

35. Piozzi, *Anecdotes*, p. 150. Gilbert Walmesley's receipted bills give further evidence that Nathaniel was active in the bookshop by 1734 (Johnson's *Letters*, ed. G. B. Hill, I, 84).

36. Now in the Yale University Library. The discovery was brought to my attention by Mr. Herman W. Liebert. The position of the annotation indicates that the comparison is not to Christ but to the less sensitive man.

37. The original letter, with a piece torn off, is now in the Birthplace Museum, Lichfield. The entire surviving text was first printed in *Gleanings*, I, 1–2, though the postmark was overlooked. Nathaniel's reference to his sister (Tetty) shows that it was written at least after July, 1735, and his plan to emigrate to Georgia probably led to his going to Frome in 1736.

38. Johnson's *Letters*, Nos. 693 and 710.

39. *Gent. Mag.*, LV (Jan., 1785), 3; Hawkins, p. 32; J. Nichols, *Literary Anecdotes*, III, 333–334; *Gleanings*, VI, 46–48.

40. *Gleanings*, VI, 44, 104; *Garrick Correspondence* (1831), I, 1–2.

41. *Life*, II, 121; *Prayers and Meditations*, p. 16; *Gleanings*, X, 119.

42. John Disney, *Memoirs of the Life and Writings of Arthur Ashley Sykes* (1785), 200. This is a fuller account than that given by Boswell in *Life*, I, 101. For the abuses of the court see *Journal of the House of Commons*, XXII (1732–1733), 37 (March 13, 1733).

43. The original account book is in the possession of the firm of Hinckley, Birch, and Crarer, Lichfield. See also Davies, *op. cit.*, p. 12; *Garrick Correspondence*, (1831), I, 2. Young Mrs. Walmesley was also subject to gout, for in the autumn of 1737 she was very ill with "gout, joined with strong hysterics" (letter of Henry Hastings

to Lord Huntingdon, Nov. 9, 1737, in the Huntington Library).

44. First printed in *The Cambridge Chronicle*, Oct. 19, 1765; reprinted in *Gent. Mag.* the same month. See *Gleanings*, VI, 56, 150–153.

45. *Life*, I, 101.

46. *Gleanings*, VI, 58–63.

47. *Life*, IV, 393.

48. *Prayers and Meditations*, p. 23. "The dream of my brother I shall remember." Once referring to the Burneys' happy family life, Johnson wrote to Mrs. Thrale, "Of this consanguineous unanimity I have had never much experience." (Johnson's *Letters*, No. 749).

CHAPTER X

1. *Life*, II, 75; III, 178; II, 337.

2. Material for the following paragraphs comes from the *London Daily Post* for March 8, 23, 24, April 7, 14, 20, 25, May 6, 23, 27, June 17, 1737, May 20, 1738, Aug. 16, 1743; *London Evening Post* for Jan. 5, 17, Feb. 9, 21, 25, March 2, April 1, 6, May 6, 1738; *London Journal*, Nov. 26, 1737, March 25, April 1, 1738; *Weekly Miscellany*, Dec. 2, 1737; *Common Sense*, Jan. 14, March 11, 1738; *The Craftsman*, Nov. 16, 1728. See also Krutch, pp. 36–41.

3. Budgell's death occurred May 4, almost two months after Johnson's arrival. See *Gleanings*, VI, 64.

4. Krutch, pp. 39–40.

5. *Life*, I, 103.

6. *Gleanings*, VI, 65, 68; X, 127.

7. Yale Boswell Papers. In Johnson's handwriting. Also on the slip is written: "Herne 7. shillings — Haysman — arrested." See also *Gleanings*, VI, 65.

8. Thomas Davies, *Memoirs of the Life of David Garrick*, I, 13–14. For errors in Davies' account see *Gleanings*, VI, 61–62. Garrick's uncle had died two weeks before, so that David had left Lichfield with the knowledge that he would inherit a thousand pounds the next year when he came of age.

9. *Life*, I, 103–105.

10. Hawkins, p. 43.

11. The story is told both by John Nichols (*Literary Anecdotes*, VIII, 416); and by Arthur Murphy (*Johns. Misc.*, I, 380).

12. *Life*, I, 103. Presumably Henry Lintot, whose father, the more famous bookseller, had died in 1736. See also *Gent. Mag.*, n.s. I (Sept., 1856), 271.

13. *Life*, I, 106. See also note 9, Chapter VIII.

14. *Life*, I, 106–107; *Poems*, p. 239; *Gleanings*, VI, 68–69.

15. Bertrand H. Bronson makes the suggestion in *Johnson Agonistes* (1946), 136–137, that Tetty was the model for Aspasia.

16. Johnson's *Letters*, No. 4; *Life*, I, 107.

17. Boswell, *Tour to the Hebrides*, p. 192; *Life*, I, 110.

18. *Life*, I, 107, 110.

19. *Life*, I, 111, 121; *Gleanings*, VI, 118.

20. *Boswell's Note Book*, pp. 11–12.

21. *Boswell's Note Book*, p. 12; *Life*, I, 111.

22. The sketch of Cave has been

drawn from various sources: *Life*, I, 111–113; III, 322; IV, 409; Hawkins, pp. 45–50; *Works*, VI, 434–435. The best short life of Cave may be found in Chapter I of C. Lennart Carlson, *The First Magazine* (1938). For differing estimates of the sale of the magazine see *Life*, III, 322; Hawkins, p. 123; Carlson, p. 62.

23. Boswell, *Tour to the Hebrides*, p. 218; *Life*, I, 159; *Horace Walpole's Correspondence with the Rev. William Cole* (Yale edition, 1937), II, 186.

24. See Carlson, *op. cit.*, pp. 13–18; Hawkins, pp. 45–50, etc.

25. *Life*, II, 52.

26. Bodleian Library, MS. Add. C. 89.

27. *Poems*, pp. 101–102; *Life*, I, 113–115.

28. *Gent. Mag.*, n.s. I (Sept., 1856), 273. The Rev. John Hussey noted that Johnson told him he was employed by Cave as editor from about the middle of 1738 to the middle of 1745 (*Life*, I, 532).

29. *Life*, I, 118.

30. *Poems*, pp. 1–2; *Lives of the Poets*, III, 176.

31. For two critical analyses see Macdonald Emslie, "Johnson's Satires and 'The Proper Wit of Poetry,'" *Cambridge Journal*, VII (March, 1954), 347–360; Chester Chapin, dissertation, Columbia Univ., entitled "Personification in Eighteenth-Century Poetry" (Ann Arbor: University Microfilms, 1954).

32. *Life*, I, 194.

33. The original Latin epitaph was probably done in December or January; it was mentioned in a letter from Lord Hervey to Conyers Middleton of Feb. 2. Harry's imitation "in English verse" was mentioned in a letter from the Earl of Bristol to Lord Hervey on June 12, 1738. A later manuscript of Harry's version in heroic couplets survives in Bodleian MS Add. A. 190. Preceding the verses is a dedication to the King, which from the style appears to have been written by Johnson.

34. See Johnson's *Letters*, Nos. 5–8; *Life*, I, 120–123.

35. Shaw, pp. 31–32, 46.

36. *Life*, I, 124–125. For an incredible story about the printing of the poem see *Universal Magazine*, LXXV (Aug., 1784), 92.

37. *Daily Advertiser*, May 13, 1738; *Life*, I, 126–127; *Poems*, p. 1; *Bibliography*, pp. 7–8; *Gleanings*, VI, 75–76. Parliament rose this year on May 20. Excerpts from the poem appeared in the May *Gent. Mag.* For a portion of the surviving fragment of the manuscript, see opposite p. 239. It gives the date as May 12.

38. Hawkins, p. 60. See also *Life*, I, 128; and Yale Boswell Papers (see note 27, Chapter III).

39. *Life*, I, 128–129. Johnson never met Pope personally (*Johns. Misc.*, I, 373) but he cherished the anecdote, which was later told him (*Life*, II, 85). Manuscript billet by Pope in the Hyde collection.

40. See Greene, Chapters I and V. The *Daily Gazetteer*, July 7, 1739, ironically described the Opposition as "compounded of heterogeneous parties bound together by the wisp of malice: of Jacobites, who make a joke of the Revolution: of old Tories, who make a joke of liberty: of new Tories, who make a joke of the old ones: of discontented Whigs, who make a joke of the true ones: and of discarded

courtiers, who make a joke of all things ever since they became jokes themselves."

41. The *Daily Gazetteer* of May 18, 1738, pointed out that it had been the custom of every age to impute all calamities to the government in power.

42. *Daily Gazetteer,* May 26, 1738.

43. Greene, pp. 160–161.

44. *Poems,* p. 9. See also J. R. Moore, "Johnson's 'Falling Houses,'" *Notes and Queries,* Aug. 5, 1950, p. 342.

CHAPTER XI

1. Johnson's *Letters,* No. 8.

2. For information about the parliamentary debates see Benjamin B. Hoover, *Johnson's Parliamentary Reporting* (1953); Medford Evans, "Johnson's Debates in Parliament," unpublished dissertation, Yale University (1933); and Greene, pp. 184–223. See also C. L. Carlson, *The First Magazine* (1938); and *Life,* I, 501–512. Birch had been helping with details of the speeches (B.M. Add. MS. 4302, ff. 95, 96).

3. G. B. Hill thought so (*Life,* I, 502), and recent authorities agree. Yet see *Gent. Mag.,* n.s. I (Nov., 1856), 671. Though the evidence is all internal, the ascription is very likely. If so, Johnson's first known editing job for Cave was done in June, 1738.

4. *Life,* I, 503.

5. For example, see *London Evening Post,* Sept. 2, 1738.

6. Johnson's *Letters,* No. 7.

7. Hawkins, pp. 49–50.

8. *Life,* I, 135–136; Hawkins, p. 64; Johnson's *Letters,* No. 4; J. Nichols, *Literary Anecdotes,* v, 27.

9. Johnson's *Letters,* No. 9. Though undated, this letter must have been written between late July and late September, 1738. A. L. Reade decided on an early dating (*Gleanings,* VI, 86); a later appears to me more probable.

10. *Prayers and Meditations,* p. 7 (Sept. 7, 1738).

11. Repeated Oct. 12, 19, 20, 25; and in *Weekly Miscellany,* Oct. 21. J. Nichols in the *Rise and Progress of the Gentleman's Magazine* (1821), xx, indicates that 6,000 copies of the proposals were dispersed, but this is doubtful.

12. See Edward Ruhe, "The Two Samuel Johnsons," *Notes and Queries,* n.s. I (Oct., 1954), 432–435. Boswell, following Hawkins, gave the other translator's name as Samuel Johnson (*Life,* I, 135; Hawkins, pp. 64–65). The notice of his death (*Daily Advertiser,* March 2, 1747) suggests that his version may have been almost complete in manuscript.

13. B.M. MS. Stowe 748, f. 165. From D. Wilkins of Hadleigh.

14. *Life,* I, 135. See also Shaw, pp. 44–45; *Gleanings,* VI, 85, 93. Hawkins (p. 65) says that twelve sheets were printed; Nichols (*Literary Anecdotes,* v, 29) says six.

15. Johnson's *Letters,* No. 7; *Poems,* p. 103.

16. Birch's diary, kept for thirty years, is in the British Museum (Add. MS. 4478c). I owe my knowledge of it to Mr. Edward Ruhe. See also B.M. Add. MS. 4302, f. 72. During the spring and early summer of 1739 in

her letters to Cave Miss Carter always ends with compliments to other members of the intimate group, including "Mr. Birch and Mr. Johnson" (B.M. MS. Stowe 748, ff. 169, 171, etc.).

17. L. F. Powell, in *Life*, IV, 494–496. For further information about the Crousaz translations see A. T. Hazen and E. L. McAdam, Jr., "First Editions of Samuel Johnson," *Yale University Library Gazette*, X (Jan., 1936), 45–51; G. A. Bonnard, "Note on the English Translations of Crousaz' Two Books on Pope's 'Essay on Man,'" *Recueil de Travaux*, Univ. of Lausanne, June, 1937, pp. 175–184.

18. *Daily Advertiser*, Nov. 21, 22, 23.

19. Johnson's *Letters*, No. 10. This letter may thus be dated Nov. 21 or 22, 1738.

20. *Daily Advertiser*, Nov. 23, 24, 27, etc.; Curll replied Nov. 25. The *Examination* has 1739 on the title page and may not have been quite ready when the crisis arose.

21. *BP*, XIV, 244.

22. It was announced in *Gent. Mag.* for November, 1741 (p. 614), as a 12mo, price 3s., but the title page has the date 1742. A leaf of errata and eight pages of Cave's advertisements were added. Some extracts later appeared in *Gent. Mag.*, XIII (March, 1743), 152, (Nov.), 587–588. A few of the notes have been printed by Dr. L. F. Powell in *Life*, IV, 495–496, and by Bonnard (see note 17), but otherwise they have been ignored by students of Johnson's criticism. What follows is merely a sample.

23. Feb. 24, 1739; *London Evening Post*, March 6, 1739 (advertisement).

24. This letter has been called to my attention by Professor Arthur Sherbo. For two other identified defenses of Cave see *Bibliography*, p. 11. See also forthcoming study of Johnson as a journalist by Professor Edward A. Bloom.

25. Medford Evans (see note 2). *Gent. Mag.*, IX (Feb., 1739), 54, 79, 80, 82, (March), 148.

26. *Life*, I, 125, 533. Hussey, to be sure, is wrong in saying that *London* was written many years before Johnson met Savage. See also *Lives of the Poets*, II, 414; *Poems*, pp. 8–9, 102; *Johnsonian News Letter*, X, 3:5–6.

27. "Who scarce forbear, tho' Britain's Court he sing, To pluck a titled Poet's borrow'd wing."
The suggestion of the application to Savage was made by a writer in *Gent. Mag.* for Sept., 1856 (pp. 275–276). Actually Savage had considered leaving London as early as 1729 [see C. R. Tracy, *The Artificial Bastard* (1953), 136–137].

28. C. R. Tracy *op. cit.*, pp. vii–viii, 26–27.

29. Hawkins, pp. 52–53.

30. K. C. Balderston (note 4, Chapter VIII). For Savage see Edmund Bergler, "Samuel Johnson's 'Life of the Poet Richard Savage' — a Paradigm for a Type," *American Imago*, IV (Dec., 1947), 42–63.

31. *Johnsoniana* (1836), 415.

32. *Lives of the Poets*, II, 398–399.

33. *Johns. Misc.*, I, 371; *Life*, I, 163–164; Hawkins, p. 53.

34. *Life*, II, 299. There is no way to date the incident.

35. See Chapter XVII; *Life*, I, 164; Hawkins, p. 54. Also *Life*, IV, 396; Hawkins, pp. 320–321; *Johns. Misc.*,

II, 213. For Johnson's drinking see *Life*, I, 103. Murphy, to be sure, dates his leaving off wine after the departure of Savage (*Johns. Misc.*, I, 376).

36. *Johns. Misc.*, II, 213 (from Bishop Percy). Another version of the story may be found in Hawkins, p. 321.

37. B.M. Add. MS. 4318, f. 41. See also *Lives of the Poets*, II, 430.

38. *Life*, III, 349; *BP*, X, 139; *Life*, III, 46.

39. Hawkins, pp. 86, 89. See page 242 for evidence that Hawkins may have met Johnson early in the 1740s. A. L. Reade (*Gleanings*, VI, 121–123) believed that there had been a separation, and that Johnson thought he had been somehow to blame.

40. *Account*, p. 135.

41. *Lives of the Poets*, III, 446.

42. The title may have been suggested by a humorous proposal in *Old Common Sense* of Jan. 6, 1739, for a new Society of Inscriptions to commemorate the deeds of famous men: Marmora Historica, Marmora Honoraria, etc. The text is quoted from *Works*, VI. For an analysis of the satire see Greene, pp. 167–170.

43. *Monthly Review*, LIII (Oct., 1775), 360. See also *St. James's Chronicle*, July 4, 1775.

44. H. W. Liebert, "This Harmless Drudge," *New Colophon*, I (April, 1948), 175–183. The piece was first advertised as "this day is published" in the *Daily Advertiser* of May 11, 1739. Notices continue as late as May 31.

45. *Life*, I, 143. I have found no specific attacks on Johnson's two pamphlets, but they were undoubtedly partly responsible for the active defense of government policy in the

Daily Gazetteer.

46. Hawkins, p. 72; *Life*, I, 141–142.

47. Manuscript of the *Life* (Yale Boswell Papers).

48. *Craftsman*, June 10, 1738; *Common Sense*, May 20, 1738; *London Mag.*, VIII (July, 1739), 359.

49. Advertised as "this day is published" in the *Daily Advertiser* of May 25, 1739. It was a small 4to, price one shilling. Quotations from the *Vindication* are from *Works*, V, 329–344.

50. Greene, p. 177.

51. *Proceedings of the Oxford Bibliographical Society* (1938), 124.

52. From the 1775 reprint of *Marmor* (p. xi). Johnson was always contemptuous of George I and George II (*Life*, II, 342; *Johns. Misc.*, II, 466–467). For his insistence on peace see *Johns. Misc.*, I, 485.

53. Greene, pp. 216–218.

54. Manuscript in the Hyde collection; *Works*, V, 462–467; E. L. McAdam, Jr., *Dr. Johnson and the English Law* (1951), 10–14, 199.

55. Johnson's *Letters*, Nos. 10, 7, 15; *Gleanings*, VI, 91–93; *Life*, I, 123; *Memoirs of Richard Cumberland* (1806), 261.

56. *Lives of the Poets*, II, 410, 413–414.

57. For a complete discussion of the Appleby application see *Gleanings*, VI, Chapter IX; and A. Gissing's article in *Cornhill Magazine*, n.s. LX (April, 1926), 404–414.

58. *Life*, I, 143. A facsimile is in the *Adam Catalogue*, Vol. II.

59. *Life*, I, 133–134, 533. Boswell did not see the original letter. I quote from an earlier appearance in print in *The Beauties of Johnson*, Part I (5th ed. 1782), ix–x.

CHAPTER XII

1. For complete details see *Gleanings*, VI, 96–114; A. Gissing, "Appleby School: an Extra-Illustration to Boswell," *Cornhill Magazine*, n.s. LX (April, 1926), 404–414. Not all of Gissing's theories are acceptable.

2. Hawkins, p. 446; *Gleanings*, VI, 127.

3. *Gleanings*, VI, 123–127. Presumably Taylor's first wife was a member of the household, but there is no mention of her (Letter from Dr. James Gray).

4. Mr. S. Hopewell tells me that in the Bosworth School records there is a letter written on behalf of Dixie which refers to the payment of money for the living. See also E. A. Sadler, "Dr. Johnson's Ashbourne Friends," *Derbyshire Archeological and Natural History Society Journal*, LX (1940), 2.

5. Partly from Richard Graves's *The Spiritual Quixote*, where life at Tissington is described. Graves came to this part of the country about eighteen months after Johnson. See *Gleanings*, VI, 177.

6. *Life*, IV, 15.

7. *Life*, III, 281. He is identified in VI, 444–445. See also III, 136; VI, 440–441.

8. He has been identified as "Lord ———" in Graves's *Spiritual Quixote* (1926 edition, II, 158–159); in *Gleanings*, VI, 176–177. It must be remembered, however, that Graves was writing fiction.

9. *Life*, I, 82–83. A. L. Reade considered the lady an excellent witness.

10. *Gent. Mag.*, X (July, 1740), 353. Introducing the poem is a note, un-doubtedly by Johnson, the only member of the St. John's Gate group who would have known Mrs. Meynell well, thanking the author for the verses and adding, "Our obligation to the ingenious author is the greater, because we were particularly desirous of showing our regard to the memory of this lady." For other details about her see *The Spiritual Quixote* and *Gleanings*, VI, 164; X, 154.

11. *Life*, I, 83; IV, 33.

12. Piozzi, *Anecdotes*, pp. 256–257.

13. The same. For other descriptions of Fitzherbert see *BP*, XIII, 19; *Life*, III, 148, 386; and *The Spiritual Quixote*.

14. *Letters of Anna Seward*, II, 103.

15. See p. 317.

16. *Letters of Anna Seward*, I, 117.

17. See note 43, Chapter IX.

18. *Thraliana*, p. 538; Piozzi, *Anecdotes*, p. 255. The two accounts differ in details, and in the latter there is further information drawn from memory. Concerning Molly Aston's letters see *Letters of Johnson* (1788), II, 383. Anna Seward (*Letters*, II, 347) commented that "Johnson was always fancying himself in love with some princess or other." See also Hawkins, p. 315.

19. *Pineapples of Finest Flavour*, ed. D. M. Little (1930), 5.

20. See opposite p. 207. For descriptions of her see *Letters of Anna Seward*, II, 347; Piozzi, *Anecdotes*, I, 255, 258.

21. *Poems*, pp. 104–105; *Thraliana*, pp. 538–539.

22. *Life*, III, 340–341; Piozzi, *Anec-*

dotes, p. 258; *Lives of the Poets*, III, 262; *Poems*, p. 104.

23. Johnson's *Letters*, No. 12. Facsimile in Hill edition.

24. Piozzi, *Anecdotes*, I, 255.

25. Sample news items may be found in the London *Daily Post* of Dec. 26; *Common Sense*, Dec. 27; London *Evening Post*, Jan. 15, 29.

26. *Gleanings*, VI, 119; *Lives of the Poets*, III, 209; *Life of William Hutton* (1816), 28; *Gent. Mag.*, X (Feb., 1740), 78.

27. Original document in the Birthplace Museum, Lichfield; printed in

Gleanings, IV, 8–9.

28. See note 23.

29. The prologue was identified as by Johnson by Professor Mary E. Knapp in *TLS*, Jan. 4, 1947, p. 9. For further information see her essay "Garrick's Last Command Performance" in *The Age of Johnson* (1949), 61–71. The performance and prologue were advertised in the London newspapers of April 15.

30. Original, dated Sept. 9, 1741, in the British Museum. Printed in *Life*, I, 153.

CHAPTER XIII

1. *Life*, III, 405, 535.

2. The account of Boyse is assembled from: *Life*, IV, 408, 446; Hawkins, pp. 158–160; *Annual Register*, VII (1764), II, 54–58; Piozzi, *Anecdotes*, p. 228; Theophilus Cibber, *Lives of the Poets* (1753), V, 160–176 (Johnson furnished many of the facts); *Johns. Misc.*, II, 411; and a series of begging letters from Boyse to Birch (B.M. Add. MS. 4301, ff. 242–249) and to Cave (B.M. MS. Stowe, 748, ff. 181–183). See also E. A. Bloom in *Notes and Queries*, April, 1954, pp. 163–165.

3. B.M. MS. Stowe, 748, f. 181.

4. For Psalmanazar see *DNB*, *Life*, III, 443–449; Piozzi, *Anecdotes*, p. 266. *Thraliana*, p. 460; Hawkins (2d ed.), 547.

5. B.M. Add. MS. 35,396. See also later letter of Yorke to Birch of May 4, 1742, and letter from Psalmanazar to Birch of Nov. 2, 1741 (B.M. Add. MS. 4317, f. 50).

6. *Life*, IV, 187.

7. Hawkins (2d ed.), 547. See also J. Cradock, *Memoirs* (1828), IV, 297.

8. Hawkins, p. 87.

9. *Life*, IV, 212; *BP*, X, 195; Piozzi, *Anecdotes*, p. 274.

10. There is a difference of opinion as to whether Wyatt or Paul invented this "gimcrack." For a good modern summary see Robert K. Dent, "The Sorrows of an Inventor," *Central Literary Magazine* (Birmingham) XXIII (Oct., 1917), 482–486. My generalizations are made after an examination of a large number of original letters and papers of Wyatt, Paul, Cave, Warren, etc., now in the Reference Library of Birmingham, and descriptions in the *Birmingham Weekly Post* for Sept. 29, 1877, and Aug. 22, 29, 1891, of others which have been destroyed by fire. For a doubtful suggestion of Johnson's earlier connection with the invention see John J. Brown, "Samuel Johnson and the First Roller-Spinning Machine," *Modern*

Language Review, XLI (Jan., 1946), 16–23; and J. de L. Mann, (Oct.), 410–411.

11. Letter of Dr. James to Warren on July 17, 1740 (*Birmingham Weekly Post*, Sept. 29, 1877). James began: "Yesterday we went to see Mr. Paul's machine. . . ." Since the letter was written from London, it is easy to imagine that Johnson and Cave were among the party.

12. Johnson's *Letters*, Nos. 13 and 14.

13. Bodleian MS. Eng. poet, c. 9, f. 249 (letter dated Dec. 16, 1740). See also f. 265. For other information see Percy A. Scholes, *Sir John Hawkins* (1953), pp. 266–267; and C. L. Carlson, *The First Magazine* (1938), 199.

14. *Life*, III, 314; VI, 450–451.

15. *Lives of the Poets*, III, 334; Johnson's *Letters*, No. 96. Apparently the year was 1744.

16. T. Davies, *Memoirs of Garrick*, p. 16.

17. *Poems*, pp. 111–113.

18. Hawkins gives the story, from

Nichols (Hawkins, p. 45). Dating the episode in 1740 is possible only through the identification of the printed epilogue in *Gent. Mag.*

19. *Life*, I, 168. After his first performance in Oct., 1741, Garrick continued to act in Goodman's Fields during the winter.

20. *Life*, IV, 7. For the possible play on Charles XII see Johnson's *Letters*, No. 17.

21. Johnson's *Letters*, No. 17.1 (Jan., 1743). Johnson wrote to a common friend, "I never see Garrick." For the later coolness between the two men see *BP*, IX, 84.

22. *Life*, III, 264; Yale Boswell Papers (1778 Journal).

23. B.M. Add. MS. 18,559–561 — collected anecdotes of Sir Richard Kaye, Dean of Lincoln, pointed out to me by Professor Arthur L. Cooke.

24. Hawkins, p. 314.

25. *Thraliana*, pp. 177–179, 200; Piozzi, *Anecdotes*, pp. 247–249, 264; *Life*, I, 529–530. See also Chapter XVII.

CHAPTER XIV

1. *Life*, I, 150, note 2; Allen T. Hazen, *Samuel Johnson's Prefaces and Dedications* (1937), 248–249.

2. *Bibliography*, pp. 11–14. For information about Johnson's biographical method, see E. L. McAdam, Jr., "Johnson's Lives of Sarpi, Blake, and Drake," *PMLA*, LVIII (June, 1943), 466–476. Quotations are from *Works*, VI, 264–412.

3. In later years Johnson did borrow books from Birch. See Johnson's *Letters*, Nos. 43, 45, etc.

4. Mr. Herman W. Liebert is working on a detailed examination of the changes and corrections in the lives.

5. To be sure, in the *Rambler* and *Adventurer* Johnson occasionally showed that he was attracted to primitivistic theory. See R. B. Sewell in *Philological Quarterly*, XVII (April, 1938), 105–111.

6. *Works*, VI, 5; Greene, pp. 231–233.

7. For the verses mentioned in this paragraph see *Poems*, pp. 114–116.

8. See pp. 195–197.

9. The last to be reported was the debate on the Spirituous Liquors Bill of Feb., 1743; the last to be printed was that on the Hanoverian troops of Dec. 10, 1742. See authorities listed in note 2, Chapter XI; also note 23 following.

10. *Life*, IV, 409; J. Nichols, *Rise and Progress of the Gentleman's Magazine* (1821), xxxi.

11. Hawkins, p. 99.

12. *Life*, I, 118; IV, 408; Shaw, p. 43. To be sure, there is an unsubstantiated claim by William Cooke in his life for Kearsley (1785) that a clergyman named Worthington attended Parliament to get the debates and gave Johnson some difficulty because his memory was so tenacious that he picked up "the very grubs and worms of digression." In the end Johnson made it a rule to receive from him nothing but the main topics.

13. The most recent analysis is in Benjamin B. Hoover, *Johnson's Parliamentary Reporting* (1953), 58–130. For some differing approaches see also Evans and Greene (note 2, Chapter XI).

14. Tyers, p. 5; Hawkins, pp. 125–129; Greene, pp. 191–193, 201–202.

15. Arthur Murphy (*Johns. Misc.*, I, 379).

16. Hoover, *op. cit.*, pp. 55–56, 130; Greene, pp. 208–211, 214.

17. Greene, pp. 212, 216–218.

18. B.M. Add. MS. 35,396. Letters of Birch to P. Yorke of July 7, 21, 1744; Yorke to Birch of July 8.

19. Hazen, *op. cit.*, p. 129.

20. *Johns. Misc.*, I, 378–379. Johnson was probably not living in Exeter Street in the early 1740s. Murphy was writing from memory long after the dinner took place.

21. *Life*, III, 351.

22. Hawkins, p. 123.

23. *Life*, I, 152; Hawkins, p. 129. G. B. Hill (*Life*, I, 505), suggests a connection between the announcement that one debate had been translated into French, German, and Spanish and Johnson's decision, but the translation (if it ever appeared) had been announced long before. See Hoover, pp. 26–27. Possibly of more importance was the appearance in 1743 of the reputable Chandler-Timberland collections of parliamentary speeches, including Johnson's: these volumes had wide circulation.

CHAPTER XV

1. J. Moir, *Gleanings; or Fugitive Pieces* (1785), I, 65; *Life*, III, 310.

2. A copy is in the British Museum. For further details see Allen T. Hazen, *Samuel Johnson's Prefaces and Dedications* (1937), 68–73; and "Samuel Johnson and Dr. Robert James," *Bulletin of the Institute of the History of Medicine*, IV (June, 1936), 455–465. Also *Life*, I, 159; III, 22.

3. *London Evening Post*, Feb. 6, 1742, and succeeding issues. Of the completed work Vol. I is dated 1743; II and III, 1745. See *London Evening Post*, June 1, 1745.

4. B.M. Add. MS. 35,396: letter of Sept. 16, 1742; *Life*, I, 154.

5. B.M. Add. MS. 4316, f. 98.

6. Birch's diary (see note 16, Chapter XI).

7. See *London Evening Post*, Nov. 13; Dec. 9, 1742; Jan. 4, 1743, etc. All of Johnson's "Account" was included in the issue of Dec. 9, and in *Gent. Mag.*, XII (Dec., 1742), 636–639.

8. Hawkins, p. 133; *Life*, I, 175; *Gent. Mag.*, LIV (March, 1784), 161, (April), 260. See also Birch to Yorke (B.M. Add. MS. 35,396), letter of May 28, 1743; *Bibliography*, p. 13; Johnson's *Letters*, No. 19; *London Evening Post*, Feb. 8, March 1, 5, 1743; *Daily Post*, Dec. 2, 1743.

9. *Daily Post*, Dec. 30, 1743; Hawkins, p. 133. It is probable that Johnson had nothing to do with the fifth volume, not published until April, 1745. For details concerning Johnson's help with the *Harleian Miscellany* see *Bibliography*, p. 15; Hazen, *op. cit.*, pp. 50–59.

10. Various versions of this clash may be found in *Life*, I, 154, 534; Hawkins, pp. 149–151; *Thraliana*, p. 195; Piozzi, *Anecdotes*, p. 304; Shaw, pp. 73–75; Tyers, p. 7; William Cooke, *Life of Samuel Johnson* (1785), 24–25; *Westminster Magazine*, V (Nov., 1777), 597.

11. J. Nichols, *Literary Anecdotes*, VIII, 446; *Life*, I, 534.

12. Shaw, pp. 192–194; J. Moir, *op. cit.*, I, 66; *The Weekly Entertainer*, Sept. 10, 1787, p. 243. I quote from this last version.

13. C. L. Carlson, *The First Magazine*, p. 17.

14. Aug. 25, 1743; repeated Aug. 27.

15. *Gent. Mag.*, XIII (Aug., 1743), 416; Johnson's *Letters*, Nos. 15 and 23; C. L. Carlson, *The First Magazine*, p.

17; *Notes and Queries*, Feb. 2, 1952, p. 52.

16. *Life*, III, 33; V, 67; *Gent. Mag.*, LIV (Dec., 1784), 891; Tyers, p. 5.

17. Johnson's *Letters*, No. 15; *Life*, I, 155.

18. J. Nichols, *Literary Anecdotes*, VIII, 416. The book was advertised as published in the *Daily Advertiser* of Feb. 11, 1744.

19. The most complete account of the *Life of Savage* may be found in C. R. Tracy, *The Artificial Bastard* (1953). See also Johnson's *Letters*, No. 15, note 8.

20. For example, see Edmund Bergler, "Samuel Johnson's 'Life of the Poet Richard Savage' — a Paradigm for a Type," *American Imago*, IV (Dec., 1947), 42–63. For Johnson and the art of biography see items 1043, 1332, 1354, 1815, 1822, 1829 listed in J. L. Clifford, *Johnsonian Studies* (1951). See also Krutch, pp. 73–85.

21. C. R. Tracy, "Johnson and the Art of Anecdote," *Univ. of Toronto Quarterly*, XV (Oct., 1945), 92.

22. March 26, 1745; repeated for several numbers. The earlier advertisements were less descriptive.

23. *Life*, I, 165.

24. Feb. 21. Quoted in *Gent. Mag.*, and used by Roberts in later advertisements of the book. I quote from *Life*, I, 169.

25. *Life*, I, 163.

26. Johnson's *Letters*, Nos. 19, 20–22, 32.1, 40, 42.2, etc.

27. The proposals for the *Publisher* were dated Sept. 24, 1744 [R. W. Chapman in *London Mercury*, XXI (March, 1930), 438–444]. Proposals for publishing the debates in the House of Commons from 1667 to 1694, appearing in

Gent. Mag. for March, 1745, were reputedly by Johnson (*Bibliography*, p. 19). In 1747 he aided William Lauder with proposals for a version of Grotius' *Adamus Exsul.* With some changes Johnson's essay was reprinted in *Gent. Mag.* for Aug., 1747. See *Bibliography*, p. 36; Hazen, *op. cit.*, p. 78.

28. From a manuscript volume of Barrett's poems, now in the collection of Mr. James M. Osborn. For an account of this discovery see *TLS*, Oct. 9, 1953, p. 652.

29. Quotation from *Works*, v, 55–94.

30. See *Bibliography*, pp. 17–18; *St. James's Evening Post*, April 6–9, 1745; *Daily Advertiser*, April 8.

31. Samuel Pegge, *Anonymiana* (1809), 33–34.

32. *Life*, I, 177, III, 71. Also letter from Adams to Boswell of Feb. 17, 1785 (Yale Boswell Papers; see note 33, Chapter I).

33. *Life*, IV, 381–384. Croker suspected from the handwriting that the list, which Johnson himself called "designs," was begun early in life, though additions were made in 1752 and 1753. In the actual manuscript, now at Windsor Castle, some of the dates are in a smaller handwriting than that used in other portions.

34. *Life*, I, 134. Boswell puts the application about 1738, but since Smalbroke did not receive his own degrees until 1745, it appears more logical to place the event later. See *Gleanings*, VI, 115–116.

35. For evidence of Johnson's authorship see L. F. Powell, "Dr. Johnson and a Friend," *London Times*, Nov. 25, 1938, pp. 15–16; *Life*, v, 483–484. Printed copies are rare. I have seen only three: in the British Mu-

seum, Cambridge University Library, and the Library at Lambeth Palace. A facsimile is promised by the Augustan Reprint Society for 1955.

36. *Life*, III, 507; v, 67; Hawkins, pp. 84–85, and 2d ed., pp. 391–392. His usual charge was two guineas a sermon.

37. For accounts of the ceremony see *St. James's Evening Post* and *London Evening Post* for May 4, 1745. The publication date is ascertained from the *Daily Advertiser* of May 27.

38. *Life*, I, 318, 545; *Bibliography*, p. 19. The poem was advertised as published in the *London Evening Post* of Oct. 24, 1745. Concerning the poem see G. C. Duggan, "Boulter's Monument: a Poem," *Dublin Magazine*, XXIX (Dec., 1953), 20–27. According to Bishop Percy [Robert Anderson, *Life of Samuel Johnson* (3d ed. 1815), p. 81] it was through Madden, a violent Whig, that Johnson came to dislike Jonathan Swift. More likely the dislike had been fostered by Birch, who delighted to pass on nasty stories about the far-off Dean during his last years. Johnson's mind may well have been poisoned by such insidious lies, not disproved in his lifetime. See, for example, B.M. Add. MS. 35,396, letter to P. Yorke of Sept. 8, 1744. For other explanations see *BP*, x, 164, 195.

39. As samples, see William Everett, "A Possible Glimpse of Samuel Johnson," *Atlantic Monthly*, XC (Nov., 1902), 622–626; and John Buchan, *Midwinter* (1925).

40. Much of the evidence is assembled in J. L. Ward, "Dr. Johnson, the Jacobite," *Chambers's Journal*, 8th Ser. I (May, 1932), 372–374; Sir

Charles Petrie, "Dr. Johnson and the Forty-five," *English Review Magazine*, IV (Feb., 1950), 96–100. For problems referred to, see *Life*, II, 26–27, 224, 238; III, 418, 421; IV, 262, 265.

41. Thomas Newte, *Prospects and Observations* (1791), 16. Yet see Greene, Chapter II; *London Gazette*, Nov. 12, 1745; *St. James's Evening Post*, Dec. 7; *London Evening Post*, Dec. 5, 7; *London Gazette*, Feb. 25, 1744; and Bodley MS. Top. Stafford. Cl. folio 110.

42. See *Life*, I, 430; II, 321; IV, 288; Boswell, *Tour to the Hebrides*, pp. 162–163; *BP*, VI, 91; *Thraliana*, p. 192.

43. Although *London* had originally been published anonymously, as early as 1742 it was advertised as by "S. Johnson" at the back of books brought out by Cave and Roberts. But it was the only early work of Johnson's so designated.

44. *Garrick Correspondence* (1831), I, 44–45.

CHAPTER XVI

1. *Life*, I, 182; III, 405.

2. Manuscript annotation in a copy of David E. Baker's *Companion to the Playhouse* (1764) in the British Museum (11795 t 30).

3. See an important article by Gwin J. Kolb and James H. Sledd, "Johnson's *Dictionary* and Lexicographical Tradition," *Modern Philology*, L (Feb., 1953), 171–194.

4. Manuscript of "A Short Scheme for Compiling a New Dictionary of the English Language" in the Hyde Collection. It is entirely in Johnson's handwriting except for observations on the blank pages, some in pencil, others in ink. The latter were probably made by Taylor. It went through several states, and there is no way of determining exactly when Johnson inserted the reference to Lord Chesterfield. I am indebted to Professors Gwin J. Kolb and James H. Sledd for an analysis of the evidence derived from the manuscripts of the *Plan*. For details of the contract see Hawkins, p. 344; *Life*, I, 183.

5. *Life*, III, 405; I, 186. In his *London Journal* for Aug. 2, 1763, Boswell recorded that Johnson insisted that if he had applied himself properly he might have completed the work in three years.

6. Johnson's *Letters*, No. 23.1.

7. Hawkins, p. 175. He is listed in the rate books in Dec., 1747. I am indebted to Mrs. P. M. Rowell, custodian of the Gough Square Johnson House, for information concerning the plan of the house and the length of Johnson's stay in it.

8. *Life*, I, 328–329.

9. *Life*, I, 530.

10. Yale Boswell Papers (see note 33, Chapter I); *Life*, III, 535.

11. I rely on the advice of Professor W. K. Wimsatt, Jr., who has studied all the evidence. See, however, Hawkins, p. 175; *Life*, I, 188; Robert Anderson, *Life of Samuel Johnson* (3d ed. 1815), 115–116.

12. For an illustration of Johnson's procedure see frontispiece to W. K. Wimsatt Jr.'s *Philosophic Words*

(1948). For a short discussion see Canon J. E. W. Wallis, *Doctor Johnson and His English Dictionary*, Presidential Address of the Lichfield Johnson Society in 1945 (revised edition 1948).

13. Hawkins, p. 175.

14. *Boswell's Note Book*, p. 1. For details concerning the final method see Johnson's *Letters* (ed. Chapman), I, 425; also letter No. 39.

15. "Preface to the English Dictionary" (*Works*, v, 38). For commentary see Wimsatt, *op. cit.*, pp. 24ff.

16. *Life*, I, 186.

17. *Life*, I, 187–188; II, 155, 379; III, 421; *Lives of the Poets*, II, 312.

18. Johnson's *Letters*, No. 38. See also *Gent. Mag.*, LXIX (Supp. 1799), 1171; *Life*, I, 189. For Millar see *Life*, III, 389, 533; I, 287; *BP*, XIII, 235.

19. *Life*, III, 37, *BP*, XI, 246–247. There is no way of dating this incident.

20. *Daily Advertiser*, March 20, July 10; *London Evening Post*, April 16, 1747, etc. I owe this information to Professor Gwin J. Kolb.

21. *Boswell's Note Book*, p. 1; *Life*, I, 183.

22. Yale Boswell Papers (see note 27, Chapter III); *Life*, I, 185.

23. In the Hyde collection. See note 4. For facsimiles of the manuscripts see *Adam Catalogue*, Vol. II. See also discussion by Dr. L. F. Powell, *RES*, VII (April, 1931), 233–234.

24. *Works*, v, 19.

25. In a letter of Aug. 8, 1747, Daniel Wray wrote to P. Yorke that he had bought a copy of the *Plan* at Dodsley's (B.M. Add. MS. 35,401).

26. B.M. Add. MS. 35,397, ff. 63, 67. *The Museum*, III (1747), 385–390 (in-

formation from Professor Kolb). Despite Birch's comment, the extracts are fairly extensive.

27. B.M. Add. MS. 4303, ff. 126, 130. Orrery evidently did not see a copy until late December (f. 133). Yet see also *The Orrery Papers* (1903), II, 8.

28. XXXIX, Part I (1747), 233–234.

29. *Life*, I, 292; II, 161; III, 112. Chesterfield's opinion appears in the fair manuscript copy of the *Plan*. See note 23.

30. *BP*, xv, 181. See also *Life*, I, 261, 267; Hawkins, p. 189; etc.

31. Edward M. Ward's painting was used in advertisements for the *Winston Dictionary*. One original version is now in the Hyde collection.

32. Hawkins, p. 189; *BP*, VI, 94–95; *Life*, I, 256–257. After one unsuccessful attempt to see Chesterfield, Johnson was reputed to have called on Dodsley on his way home. When Dodsley asked him why he was so agitated, Johnson replied "I tell you, I have all this while been only *gilding a rotten post*" [*Gent. Mag.*, LXIV (Jan., 1794), 18]. Possibly apocryphal, it is characteristic of the many stories circulated about Johnson and Chesterfield.

33. See, for example, *Life*, I, 264–266, 541; IV, 174, 332; Shaw, p. 78.

34. The discovery of this relationship was one of the triumphs of the late Mr. A. L. Reade (*Gleanings*, III, 152; *Life*, I, 535).

35. Johnson's *Letters*, No. 26.

36. Hawkins, p. 516; letter to Johnson by John Thompson, Feb. 21, 1782 (Hyde collection); *Life*, I, 243–244; *Prayers and Meditations*, p. 102.

37. *Thraliana*, pp. 161, 184. In T. Harwood, *History and Antiquities of*

Lichfield (1806), pp. 451–452, are printed two affectionate letters from Bathurst to Johnson.

38. *Life,* I, 263.

39. J. Reading, "Poems by Johnson," *TLS,* Sept. 11, 1937, p. 656; *Poems,* pp. 119–127; *Bibliography,* p. 21; *Gent. Mag.,* LXIV (Nov., 1794), 1001.

40. A. T. Hazen, *Samuel Johnson's Prefaces and Dedications* (1937), 171–189; Roger P. McCutcheon, "Johnson and Dodsley's *Preceptor,* 1748," *Tulane Studies in English,* III (1952), 125–132; *Life,* I, 192; Tyers, p. 5. "The Vision" may be found in *Works,* IX, 162–175.

41. *Johns. Misc.,* II, 314.

42. *Poems,* p. 49. See *General Advertiser,* Sept. 16, 17, 18, 19, 1747.

43. B.M. Add. MS. 35,397, f. 83.

44. Described in a letter from Benjamin Martyn to Birch, Sept. 21, 1747 (B.M. Add. MS. 4313, f. 147).

45. B.M. Add. MS. 35,397, ff. 156, 169.

46. B.M. Add. MS. 35,397, f. 140. That he continued to give the impression that progress was satisfactory is shown by a letter from Joseph Ames to Sir Peter Thomson in Sept., 1749. Writing about another dictionary project, Ames commented: "There is one Johnson, who lately made me a visit with Mr. Cave and the chief printer or bookseller in Ireland, has done such a work ready for the press" (listed in Sotheby sale of June 7, 1855). I owe this information to Mrs. Donald Hyde.

CHAPTER XVII

1. Birch to Yorke, Oct. 20, 1750 (B.M. Add. MS. 35,397, f. 307).

2. There are only scattered allusions, but most of Johnson's biographers bear witness to her later continual illness.

3. Shaw, p. 112.

4. *Prayers and Meditations,* March 28, 1753; March 28, 1770; April 20, 1778. The saucer is in the Birthplace Museum, Lichfield, with an explanatory note by the historian, Thomas Harwood.

5. Shaw, p. 112.

6. See p. 152.

7. *Thraliana,* p. 178.

8. The quotation came through Mrs. Nicholas. See A. L. Reade, "A New Admirer for Dr. Johnson," *London Mercury,* XXI (Jan., 1930), 248. See

also *Johns. Misc.,* I, 476; Shaw, pp. 110–111; Yale Boswell Papers; Hawkins (2nd ed.), 314.

9. Shaw, p. 110; Hawkins, p. 313; *Life,* I, 523–524.

10. Johnson's two long periods of total abstinence are discussed in *Life,* I, 103, note 3; V, 214. He once said "I did not leave off wine because I could not bear it." (*Life,* III, 245). Adams wrote Boswell, July 12, 1786 (Yale Boswell Papers; to be edited by Dr. Marshall Waingrow), estimating the first habit of water drinking as extending "15 years or more." Johnson's marriage lasted almost seventeen years.

11. Yale Boswell Papers, April 20, 1783, labeled by Boswell "Tacenda." The whole of this fascinating document will be included by Professor

F. A. Pottle in a later volume of Boswell's journals.

12. From a canceled page in the *Life*. See *Life and Letters*, v (Sept., 1930), 164–166; *Life*, III, 406, 536.

13. *Life*, I, 238; T. J. Barratt, *The Annals of Hampstead* (1912), I, 257–261; III, 299–300.

14. See note 11.

15. *Prayers and Meditations*, March 26, 1758; April 15, 1759; April 21, 1764; Easter, 1761; April 20, 21, 1764, etc.

16. *BP*, x, 142; XIII, 222. Boswell, who had "sat late" with Beauclerk and Langton, noted "stories of Dr. Johnson . . . Mrs. Woffington wanting to play whore with me." Apparently the reference is to Johnson, not to Boswell himself, for Peg Woffington was dead by 1760.

17. *BP*, XVI, 84 (May 7, 1785). See also F. A. Pottle, "The Dark Hints of Sir John Hawkins and Boswell," *Modern Language Notes*, LVI (May, 1941), 325–329. Yet Hawkins (p. 316) specifically states that Johnson "was a man too strict in his morals to give any reasonable cause of jealousy to a wife."

18. *Prayers and Meditations*, pp. 15, 16 (April 22, 1753; March 28, 1754).

19. Laetitia Matilda Hawkins [*Memoirs* (1824), I, 207–208] suspected that he blamed himself chiefly for disregarding his wife's comfort.

20. A separate sheet of excerpts (now in the Hyde collection) copied by Boswell, May 5, 1776, from one of Johnson's diaries. It has been reproduced in facsimile, with an introduction by Donald and Mary Hyde (privately printed 1953). See also *Life*, II, 76–77, where Johnson gives approval to second marriages, though admitting

"that he once had almost asked a promise of Mrs. Johnson that she would not marry again, but had checked himself."

21. *Life*, I, 239–240.

22. *The Remembrancer*, Feb. 20, 1748.

23. *Daily Post*, May 5, Sept. 2, 1743.

24. *BP*, XI, 265; *Life*, III, 47.

25. *Life*, I, 193.

26. *Life*, I, 192; II, 15; *Johns. Misc.*, II, 313–314.

27. *Johns. Misc.*, II, 215; *BP*, IX, 257.

28. *BP*, VII, 83; *Life*, II, 15. *Poems*, p. 25.

29. See Francis G. Schoff, "Johnson on Juvenal," *Notes and Queries*, CXCVIII (July, 1953), 293–296. See also Ian Jack, *Augustan Satire* (1952), 135–145.

30. *Boswell's Note Book*, p. 22; *Life*, III, 199.

31. The text is taken from *Poems*, ed. Nichol Smith and McAdam, using variants from the first edition.

32. Krutch, p. 1.

33. *Life*, I, 200; v, 364; *Johns. Misc.*, I, 386–387.

34. Hawkins (p. 219) puts the founding of the club "in the winter of 1749," and there is no other authentic evidence. Among the members were three physicians (Richard Bathurst, William McGhie, Edmond Barker), one clergyman (Samuel Salter), one intended dissenting minister who was losing his faith (Samuel Dyer), one merchant (John Ryland), one attorney (John Hawkins), one bookseller (John Payne), and one fellow writer (John Hawkesworth).

35. The poem *London* was by this time known to be by Johnson. See note 43, Chapter XV.

GAIA

Deanery

THE CLOSE

The Bishop's Palace

Garrick's House

WEST GATE

Cathedral

Causeway

MOGGS

MINSTER POOL

BIRD STREET

DAM STREET

Brooke House

Swan Inn

Dame Oliver's School

Johnson's Birthplace

The Hectors' House

Market Cross

SANDFORD STREET

St. Mary's Church

The George Inn

SADLER (or Market) ST.

BUTCHER ROW

Three Crowns Inn

BORE STREET

ST. JOHN STREET

Guildhall

BREADMARKET STREET

TAMWORTH STREET

LOMBARD

WADE STREET

FROG LANE

John Hunter's House

CASTLE DITCH

Grammar School

St. John's Hospital

CASTLE DITCH

SCHOOLHOUSE LANE

LEVETT'S FIELD

The "Great Stile"

Theophilus Levett's House

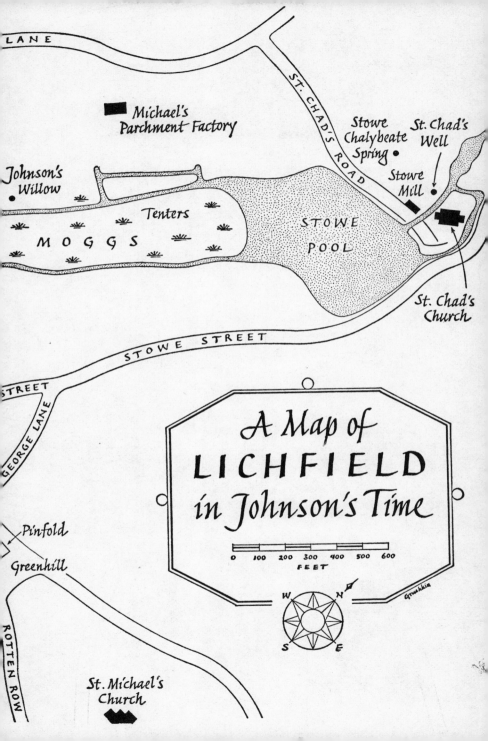

Index

This is a selective index of names, places, and themes. Not all places, streets, classical authors, or authorities cited have been indexed.

future, 323–324; writes his autobiography, 5, 325, 327*n*.1 (Chap. 1)

II. *Character Traits, Habits, Physical Disabilities:* affectation of not letting others see him study, 51, 144; ambition, 60, 145, 322; amorous passions, 313–317; Calvinistic tendencies in religion, 23, 149; Christian stoicism, 321; common sense, 78, 159, 205, 252–253, 282, 317; conflicting attitudes, 20, 105, 145, 159, 218, 277, 323; conversational pugnacity, 85, 104; convulsive movements (tic), 24, 65, 141, 159, 162, 168, 220; courage, 104, 145, 322; critical methods, 78, 204–205, 283; delight in feminine society, 225, 228; domineering personality, 51–52, 122, 159; drinking habits, 142–143, 312, 356*n*.10; emotional tensions, 24–25, 62; eyesight impaired, 8, 78; facility and speed of composition, 55, 122–123, 204, 244, 256, 257, 274; gaiety, love of, 96, 121; guilt, feelings of, 62, 95, 135, 172, 315–316; horsemanship, 69; humanitarian sympathies, 106, 146, 237, 239; idealism, youthful, 193–194; inability to do sustained work, 55, 64, 95, 145, 204; independence of authority, 57, 87, 105, 120–121; insanity, fear of, 5, 62, 129–130, 145; intellectual dexterity, 104, 260; intellectual honesty, 11, 55, 105, 205; law, inclination to study of, 116, 218–219, 285; laziness, 5, 60, 61, 76, 87, 95, 199, 307, 322; lessons, method of getting, 51, 55; masochistic traits, 209; melancholia, 5, 127–130, 168, 209, 310, 322, 338*n*.1; memory, 23, 50, 51, 156; negligent pose, 60; outsider, feeling of being, 104–105, 193; physical descriptions, 5, 50, 62, 81, 111, 141, 164, 181, 211; physical handicaps, 9, 25, 78; portraits of, xv, 327*n*.2, *n*.3 (Illustrations); precocity, 21, 111; pride, 24, 60, 127–128, 243; procrastination, 61, 113, 145, 199, 257; reading, methods of, 51, 63–65, 95; rebellious

nature, 105–106, 121, 193; religion, attitudes toward, 74–75, 92, 127, 143, 146, 321; reticence about early years, vii–viii, 74, 172, 326*n*.1; sex, attitude toward, 75–76, 143, 152, 211–212, 313–316, 357*n*.16, *n*.17; skeptical tendencies, 74–75, 105–107, 147, 205, 255, 260, 283, 321; speech, colloquial Midland, 30–31; strict grammarian, 122, 202, 206; sports, ability in, 45, 50–51, 120; statues of, 4; suicide considered, 129; talk, love of, 84, 103, 210, 305, 323; talking to himself, 61, 294; temper, violence of, 24, 123, 164, 270–271; tolerance, 80, 212, 237; walking, 129, 131, 338*n*.1, *n*.3

III. *Opinions:* actors and acting, 103, 245; ardor for liberty in young men of genius, 213; biography, 8, 277; children, discipline of, 20, 57, 75; children made to show off for strangers, 21–22; children of late marriages, 19–22; children's books, 23–24; church attendance, 43; Civil War and Parliamentarians, 36; communism, 287; domestic discord, 17; education, methods of, 57, 160–161; excise, 72; father-son relationship, 20; flogging at school, 56–57; foreign trade, 106; Hanoverian succession, 41, 218; damnation, 23; Jacobitism, 288; kings, divine right of, 289; London, 175, 178–179; optimism, easy, 105–106, 260; Oxford, 115–116; patriotism, narrow, 287; peace of society, 36–37, 290; poetry, proper subjects for, 78; political affairs, 106–107, 145, 192–194, 211, 214, 217–218, 288–290; poverty, 106; primitivism, 254, 350*n*.5; remembering early events, 9, romantic fictions, 147; "Ruling Passion," doctrine of, 205; scoffers at religion, 80; shopkeeping, 94; skepticism, need for, in biography and history, 252, 255; sudden change, 37, 107; tavern comforts, 241; uniformity of mankind, 147; vanity of human wishes,

HESPERIDES BOOKS
